Wiki

Second edition

Anja Ebersbach · Markus Glaser
Richard Heigl · Alexander Warta

Wiki

Web Collaboration

Second edition

Foreword by Gunter Dueck

Springer

Anja Ebersbach
Ostengasse 10
93047 Regensburg
Germany
anja.ebersbach@sprachlit.uni-regensburg.de

Dr. Richard Heigl
Pfarrergasse 6
93047 Regensburg
Germany
heigl@hallo-welt.biz

Markus Glaser
Ostengasse 18
93047 Regensburg
Germany
glaser@hallo-welt.biz

Alexander Warta
Korntaler Str. 74
70439 Stuttgart
Germany
alexander.warta@de.bosch.com

Translated from the German „Wiki – Kooperation im Web"
(Springer-Verlag, 2. Aufl. 2008, ISBN 978-3-540-35110-8) by Andrea Adelung

ISBN 978-3-540-35150-4 e-ISBN 978-3-540-68173-1

DOI 10.1007/978-3-540

Library of Congress Control Number: 2008922392

Cover design: KünkelLopka, Heidelberg

Printed on acid-free paper

9 8 7 6 5 4 3 2 1

springer.com

Foreword

A book about wikis!
That's what people need.
Because with wiki technology, lots of people can freely work together – they can even generate very large works in the intellectual realm. See for yourself:

Today, we still marvel at our massive church buildings, each constructed over a period of centuries, requiring an immense amount of labor and often bearing the cultural stamp of all of the epochs during which it was created. Someone just has to begin by placing stone upon stone and motivating the people nearby to help out a bit. In places where such enthusiastic fellow men and women lend a hand and donate materials, great things can emerge. And where they are absent? Either scant ruins remain, or the iron will of a pharaoh is required, an army of drivers, the sweat of a people and a mountain of gold. Great things can also be created in that way – take the Pyramids: a clear concept, no blending of styles, pure will.

Those are two very different paths. The one entails passionate people devotedly building something together for the common good; the other: A single will manages a variety of resources to achieve a set goal.

Wikis are tools with which lots of people with a minimum of organization, planning, money and time can create something together and communicate with each other from several scattered computers or over the Internet. Wikis are the technology for that first path of volunteers with a common idea.

This book introduces wikis and provides you with enough tools to create your own wiki; your own work platform. Yet the book will also invite you to join the animated discussion on what one can do with wikis and where it is better not to "abuse" them. It is the intriguing question of those two stimuli: enthusiasm and will.
Allow me to explain by using an anecdote. Some time ago, I received a letter from a reader regarding my books. Someone wrote

that he had inserted my name in the Internet lexicon 'Wikipedia'. He wrote that he initially only added a bit of preliminary data on me and would continue to work on it. I was mighty proud that I was now to be listed in an encyclopedia, and checked on the Internet right away under "Gunter Dueck," but I could'nt find anything. I found strange messages indicating that there had been an article related to my name but that it had been deleted. The reader I mentioned was angry, and he tried posting his article again, but it again was deleted. Days later, another "person" wrote something reasonable. That remained on the Internet for a few days, but disappeared again, ostensibly due to violation of copyright laws. Now wide awake, I then attempted to find the email address of the person deleting everything. I wrote: "Hey, why?" The answer: "The image most likely violates copyright, and the text presumably as well. I am one of the authorized persons assigned to quality and legal issues". I argued: "The picture of me was taken by my daughter Anne in our garden; I give it to everyone. And the text is taken from the cover of one of my books. I grant my permission to use that." Three hours later, "my" entry was back online again. Now I get nervous wondering if the article has been defaced or deleted. Do you understand what I mean? Anybody can do with me what he wants! If that is the case – is everything true that is listed in Wikipedia? Can I treat the information as being just as authentic as what I find in a book? Will anyone award me damages if, through a false entry in Wikipedia, I lose a bet or my reputation as a scientist? Questions abound regarding a variety that grows on its own power! Of course, you could also see it positively. "Wiki lives!" It changes, develops, grows – however, it needs to be weeded, and its garden protected from thieves (lexical vandalism).

Wikipedia is one of the truly colossal wiki projects. Ten thousand contributors are at work on a single intellectual monument. A number of masters run around and find out when someone has cheated. Controllers verify whether the building code is being followed. Anyone can participate whenever and however he or she likes. No time pressures, hardly any regulations, and no pay for the volunteer work – only a profound sense of accomplishment. "One stone of that pyramid is from me!" – That might be something a Wikipedia contributor might exclaim.

Wikis are exceptionally suitable for all such projects of several volunteers. Would you like to connect the parents of students of the Bammental grammar school? All of the members of a sports association? All of the astronomers of the world? All Linux freaks in your company? Do you want to create something in a community with others? To maintain a community? Then you need a wiki! But which one?

The best one! As of today – I just checked – the German Wikipedia homepage reads: “We have just converted the software to MediaWiki 1.4. Please report any problems here ...” This book also presents the wiki technology with the aid of the open source software MediaWiki, which you can download from the Internet. So, if you would like to use MediaWiki for your project, then you are in good hands – several volunteers are working on follow-up versions of “your” software – of that you can be sure! However, if you really want more, or if you perhaps even want it *all*, so to speak, then you’ll enjoy the detailed description of the high-end software TWiki. This program can do much, much more – it can do it all, anything currently technically possible – it offers a cornucopia of supplementary functions, from presentation to drawing to calculating. And as such, up in the technical heights, where anything is possible – you’ll have a bit more difficulty in the installation process, I believe, and will have to be more accomplished in its operation. What is the best wiki? “The standard!” call some, “Extreme wiki!” shout others. And, as usual, both sides are right.

So it’s got to be a wiki? Well, that’s no problem with this book! However, the book will also seriously discuss what a wiki cannot currently accomplish and what it should not even attempt. A wiki should not be “abused” for the “second path” of accomplishing things. The second path would be “finally” turning a community endeavor of spontaneous enthusiasts into “a real project”. We need a plan! We have to organize who is going to do what! We keep lists on how much each person has accomplished! We check progress and define goals! We do everything efficiently and do not waste money! Does it always have to be the newest software? Can’t we save more money?

Imagine if a company were building Wikipedia. Then there would be the equivalent of the pharaoh’s will. A plan of necessary words would be generated. The words would be prioritized according to the importance presented by experts, and to the difficulty in writing new entries. Managers would fervently search for new sources where something could be copied or used more than once. They would set the pay for entries and monitor the rapidity of the work. The once volunteers would make sure they got everything done quickly – without paying attention to details – just quickly, according to plan and the respective remuneration.

That would be the path of the “project” and of efficiency. A pyramid is built according to plan and schedule. It is made to be completely uniform and flawless – nothing about it is spontaneous! Nothing is voluntary. Everything bends to the central will: the project goal.

However, MediaWiki only invites volunteers to work on it! The wiki technology does not assign jobs or assess performance. It does not dole out punishment for insufficient output or errors. It does not organize workflow. So, if you create a wiki for yourself, you should know what a wiki will and will not be able to do. It can take a great deal of spontaneity and create something beautiful, common, or great. Yet it cannot truly be used as a tool to efficiently assert someone's will.

The authors of this book offer a fresh introduction to the topic. They are not afraid to take part in the discussion of the pros and cons of wikis. They discuss the current dialogue using several charming details. The book's style is inviting – it is very factual, but somehow charming nonetheless. While reading it, I imagined the authors as the most passionately motivated of all wiki enthusiasts.
They write: a book about wikis!
And they are confident: That's what people need.

Gunter Dueck

Foreword, Take Two – Into the Blue … almost

A second foreword for the second edition – because I now know a lot more about the subject. This is how it happened:

As a fan of Wikipedia, I repeatedly told people at IBM that we have to have an internal setup something like that. IBM has millions of pages on its intranet, in which, theoretically, we can find anything. But an access page offering a simple encyclopedic entry with a couple of links? That would be perfect. And everyone said, "Yeah, yeah". In late 2006, an IBM executive told me he didn't find the idea so bad. "Would you give me some money to program it?" I replied, and got the answer: "If I only knew whether or not the IBM people really wanted it, perhaps." – "People want it." – "Can you prove it?" So I wrote an article on the IBM intranet with the title *I'd really like a Wikipedia*, and in it, asked for feedback. Wow, it was the first day in my life in which I received so many emails that I could only thank everyone collectively but not answer them individually – that is how much enthusiasm flooded my mailbox.

"So, can I have a little money for a project?" – "And how are you going to achieve it? Can I see a plan?"

At IBM, I am known as *Wild Duck* or *Wild Dueck*, kind of like a strange fellow. My projects are good, but they have no plan because plans bother me. I'd much rather work according to a vision instead of a plan. I already indicated as much indirectly in the first foreword. I want to start! But start with a grand vision! Then others will come along and help. I'm certainly no pharaoh, ordering people to lug around stones for the pyramids. That is not how a Wikipedia is made! Just read my first foreword! … So I received the project financing to get started. But who was going to install MediaWiki for me?

Of course, I hadn't forgotten that I'd written a foreword for this book. So, I thought, I'll just call up the authors of the book. With a little luck, they'd still be working on the finishing touches of their dissertations, and I could "soon hire them at IBM". Or they would launch a company and we would build an IBM Wikipedia together, subsequently supplying Wikipedias professionally to all companies, thus establishing an entire Web 2.0 business in Germany.

So I rang them up … They had already launched a company, Hallo Welt!, which supplies everyone with Web 2.0 as a business. For the first time ever, we sat down together for a project in my living room in Waldhilsbach – bubbling with ideas – and soon began constructing. How? Well, exactly like "you are supposed to".

After sending out an appeal for assistance on the IBM intranet, about thirty volunteers offered to help during their free time. Once a week, we discussed everything via telephone conference. We talked about who wanted to do what, we assigned people tasks. A ruler, manager or pharaoh says when something IS to be done and by whom. In Web 2.0, one is asked when one would like to do something. (At the risk of sounding extremely obtrusive, let me repeat: We are talking here about the other work model 2.0; do you know what I mean? Volunteerism adheres to other laws than does a managed project.) Together, we thought of some nice names for Big Blue IBM's encyclopedia. We ultimately voted to adopt the name *Bluepedia*.

Bluepedia was installed in March and April of 2007. We started out as a small team, entering exemplary articles. In addition, we told any and all IBM colleagues we could reach that we were working on a strictly secret Wikipedia project. We garnered lots of comments: "We already have that sort of thing in 100 different places, and now we've got another one? I made a suggestion for something like that two years ago, and I've also already written a page! What is the meaning of this? Can just anybody contribute, even if it's complete crap? Isn't that dangerous? Where are the controls? What is the plan? Who is doing it? Why in German and not in English? Whaaaat? *Both* languages? Why? That is such a waste! Don't you have to ask IBM USA what they think of the English? Are volunteers allowed to do things on the Intranet? Who gave them permission?" – And my question in return was: "If there are already 100 of them, why can't I do one, too?" If you want to implement an innovation, you are captured by the company's immune system. The white blood cells come along. Pioneers are initially fended off with "You can't do that" and later with "We already have one." However, we also collected enthusiastic emails from co-workers who supported and sometimes even helped us. In fact, we determined that individual IBM employees had already begun working on Web 2.0 projects in various places. The software was okay, their plans nice enough, but none of them had actually conceived the schemes to be a complete IBM community project. Web 2.0 is big and for everybody! "Bluepedia is successful because EVERYONE contributes, not just a few familiar writers or a single department," I repeatedly proclaimed. "We aren't doing something different, we're doing the right thing once and correctly as a community project. Correctly – not differently!"

Every morning, the small Bluepedia team checked the counter on the homepage: "Bluepedia now has 213 entries." We worked out an entire catalogue of topics suggesting everything we wanted Bluepedia to contain. "Everything." Hardware, presentations, site plans, abbreviations, consulting methods, everything. Who wants to serve as the honorary custodian of what topics? ("Wants to!!")

450 entries. At the end of May, we were very satisfied with the way things looked. We began to rouse the interest of our respective nearby co-workers for Bluepedia. They contributed, somewhat hesitantly, and provided us with valuable suggestions for improvement that the *Hallo Welt* Team immediately implemented. Bluepedia matured and grew. 567 entries. In July of 2007, I called on "everyone" on the intranet for their help (which is read by perhaps 2,000 colleagues, of which a few hundred actually take action). Once again, there was another wave of "Are you allowed to do that?" Still, my appeal cranked up the number of entries fairly rapidly, until it had approached 2000 by the beginning of August.

One morning in mid-August, I gave a speech at a conference and demonstrated our Bluepedia online. Shortly before an afternoon discussion, I took a quick look – the counter had in fact increased by 25! One percent growth per day? How would it continue to develop?

I cannot say. The Springer Publishing Company wants my foreword tomorrow. Today, on August 19, 2007, we have 2,768 entries. During the past week, we formed a German-American team to expand the project across the international IBM presence. Enthusiasm is growing everywhere. I first "have to" (as we often say at IBM) take my vacation, and in September, we will then officially announce the project via my General Manager. (Up to that point, it has not officially gone public!) Then it will really take off!

Well – I can't tell you how this will ultimately end, but you can surely feel the excitement that we were able to transfer to IBM with the aid of the authors of this book and the instructions contained in it. You could do the same! But please remember: It has to be a community project, and not one with supervisors and counters. The article counter on the homepage alone is enough to excite us. When we see that number, we want to be happy and not stressed out!

Thus, take this book, a community, and lots of enthusiasm and enter the world of the Web 2.0 … with wikis of all kinds, for a new era in your company or your environment.

Gunter Dueck

The Authors

Anja Ebersbach is an information scientist. She is a university and technical college instructor, and is also active as a freelance IT trainer. Her specialties are cooperative and collaborative work on the Net, as well as collective learning. Furthermore, she is working on her dissertation on the topic of "Wikis as Tools of Scientific Work".

Markus Glaser, also an information scientist, primarily works as a web and application programmer, where he specializes in MediaWiki and TWiki systems. His dissertation focuses on the formation of political opinions in cooperative media.

Dr. Richard Heigl, a historian, works as a freelance instructor, IT trainer and moderator of large group seminars (Open Space, Future Workshop). As the co-owner of the media workshop firm Hallo Welt!-Medienwerkstatt GmbH, he is primarily occupied with the planning and moderation of wiki projects.

Alexander Warta, information scientist, is a doctoral candidate employed at Robert Bosch GmbH in Stuttgart. Warta has been working scientifically and practically in the realm of knowledge management in businesses for several years. He is a specialist for the wiki software Confluence.

The Authors

Content

Appendix

Preface

Why a book about wikis? Some time ago, Anja came back all excited from a conference on technology and social movements in Munich. There, she had taken part in a workshop on working and organizing with wikis. In the meantime, her excitement is also shared by lots of others. The popularity and notoriety of this small bit of software can primarily be attributed to the Internet encyclopedia Wikipedia. Yet a number of organizations have also discovered wikis as a simple and versatile tool for their work. For instance, the hackers of Berlin's Chaos Computer Club used it to organize their conference. We were drawn to wikis chiefly due to the opportunity to utilize wikis as organizational software for small groups. We wanted to find out more.

Yet even the attempt to install a wiki was a puzzle. Information and documentation on the Net were few and far between. There was no manual. The only book on the subject, by Wiki creator Ward Cunningham, was very informative, but not sufficient for our purposes. We sensed that wikis could be used for much more than developing texts in a cooperative manner. However, the wiki world is a jungle rampant with political discussions and racing technological development. What was missing was a survival kit, a practical introduction that recommended paths through the jungle. You are now holding an initial cartography of that jungle. Have a look around the wilderness, and become familiar with its inhabitants. Design your environment by setting up your own camp and blazing new trails.

Who Needs this Book?

While writing this book, we envisioned readers who already have some computer experience and are considering whether to work with a wiki or even install one of their own. Undoubtedly, veteran wiki users will also consult this book, and we are sure that especially the second part of it will be of interest to them.

The Content Concept

Among the multitude of wikis, we have selected three to present to you: the widespread and relatively simple MediaWiki, TWiki, as a piece of ambitioned wiki software, and the successful, commercial Confluence:

- **MediaWiki** is fairly easy to install, and user-friendly in its operation. Yet it also offers a series of features, such as a user administration, and it can be employed as a simple but good communication and organizational tool for groups of the most varied of sizes. In short: It is the ideal introduction to wikis.
- **TWiki** is very challenging to install and, especially for technical applications, assumes a good deal of skill and knowledge. Using TWiki also takes some getting used to. Yet for complex projects, it is worth the effort, because it offers a great deal of design options.
- **Confluence** is the famous system by the Australian company Atlassian that provides this wiki along with an array of attractive extensions at license costs to its customers. It is primarily utilized on the intranet.

The caveman on the cover of the german edition inspired us in putting together our practical examples. Among other projects, he and his clan use a wiki to organize a conference in the Neolithic Age. Admittedly, the combination of 21st-century technology and stone-aged humans is not always consistent, but we hope it is demonstrative and a bit amusing.

In the forefront of the wiki discussion are the social methods of communication that crop up as a result. To this extent, the book also attempts to be something more than a pure software manual. Some will be irritated by the political fifth section. The wiki communities, as the free software culture before them, have provoked extensive socio-political discussions that are conducted at conventions such as the *Wizards of OS* or the *Chaos Communication Congress*. So pour yourself a glass of wine, get comfortable, and enter into a debate of issues discussed there. Don't be shy to spin it out further. We look forward to your reactions, contributions and feedback, and wish to offer a platform for these debates.

How to Use this Book

The book is conceived such that it can be read from front to back. However, it is more realistic to expect readers to jump tō "their" chapters. That is why, next to the section headings, we have also included an indication of how deep into the wiki software a respective chapter delves. Authors need less previous technical knowledge than wiki and web administrators.

- Beginners should start with sections One and Two. **Wiki!?** provides a general introduction to wikis. It treats all questions that crop up with one's first confrontation with wikis. What are wikis? How to they function technically? How do you explain the fascinating phenomenon that open systems do not end in chaos?
- In **Our First Wiki: MediaWiki**, we present MediaWiki, the most well-known wiki clone. Here, we will introduce you to practical work with wikis and invite you to experiment. We'll show you how to install MediaWiki so you can get an idea of how it functions. For instance, you will see how formats or tables are generated, and lots more.
- Don't be discouraged by **TWiki, the Jack-of-all-Trades**. Installing TWiki requires a good deal of experience, and is more aimed at future and current web administrators. Yet this section also contains an introduction to using TWiki, which is also of general interest.
- In **TWiki as a Project Module**, we introduce TWiki as a tool for the management of self-organized projects. Here, we'll show you further useful plugins and add-ons, such as the practical EditTable plugin or a diagram tool. It is difficult to estimate the degree of preliminary knowledge required on a general basis. The installation of the plugin takes some getting used to. However, the function of already installed plugins is easier. On the whole, we wish to demonstrate that you can do a great deal more with wikis than "just" write encyclopedias. They also basically support any other type of project.
- **Go with the Flow: Confluence** provides an overview of the use and administration of this commercial system. Here, you will see what a wiki looks like that has been developed for use in the realm of business.
- **Tools with a Future** intends to expand horizons. On the one hand, it deals with current technical developments and important wiki projects. On the other, we provide a short summary of the social debates taking place within the wiki community.
- A **Glossary** and an **Index** will help you find your way through the book.
- A **CD-ROM** is included in the book where you will find the software discussed.

Our book is for male and female readers. However, for reasons of brevity, the pronouns used will not always expressly address both – but in our examples, both men and women work with wikis.

We Wish to Thank ...

... first and foremost Christine Bühler, who, for years, has consistently been on the scene during critical phases of seminars, master's theses, articles and book projects of the most varied kinds; Radovan Kubani, our hopeful artist, who illustrated our book for us; Gunter Dueck, not only for the foreword, but also for the corresponding stimulating discussion; Andrea Adelung from team interculturale for translating our book into excellent English. Our discussions in December 2004 with Jimmy Wales, the founder of Wikipedia, also provided us with valuable ideas and motivation.

For countless critical notes and concrete suggestions for improvement, we thank our volunteer editorial team: Andreas Schmal, who also supplied us with calories and Bytes; Andreas Legner helped out with corrections and constructive criticism, as did Thomas "Schnaks" Schnakenberg, who weathered out the final phase with us; Carsten Diederichs braved the installation instructions, among other tasks. Richard Hölzl supported us from Göttingen with long-distance diagnoses and the final chapter. Our thanks also to Benjamin Heitmann for his comments, and Dirk Brömmel, who stood by us with technical advice.

Regensburg, June 23, 2005

Anja Ebersbach
Markus Glaser
Richard Heigl

About Two Years Later ...

there is now a second edition of our book, which back then was called Wiki: Web Collaboration. The fact that the title is now shorter does not mean that the book has become thinner with regard to content. At first, we naturally hoped that only a few points would need to be updated. However, we are glad to report that the wiki world has grown quite a bit, and thus we needed to stay abreast of the changes.

On the whole, the structure of the book and its concept regarding content has remained the same. The description of the software MediaWiki and TWiki in Sects. II and III have been brought up to date. They were expanded to include technical improvements to both wiki clones, such as Bots for MediaWiki. Similarly, we have also worked readers' suggestions into the book. Section V has also been expanded and reorganized. In it, we introduce more wiki projects and dedicate special attention to the topics of constructing communities and cooperation in wikis. This task should not be taken lightly, as it involves a very high level of work and time. In fact, the German GründerWiki, offering support for wiki founders, has calculated that an average of two hours a day over a period of two years is needed to establish an active, independent online community.[1]

Thus, we have added more material to provide you with the tools to really take off.

Last but not least, our team of authors has grown by one competent member. For years, Alexander Warta has been working with the wiki clone Confluence as a knowledge management tool in an international company and has included his experience with Confluence in an introductory chapter on that clone.

We hope that the new edition will cater better to the needs of current and future wiki fans. Of course, we are grateful for any measure of criticism and praise. There is sure to be a third edition! ;-)

---

[1] http://www.wikiservice.at/gruender/wiki.cgi?WieGr%fcndetMan EineCommunity, 10.2.2007.

Thanks …

… to our graphic artist Radovan Kubani, who has been delighting us with his sketches for several years, as well as to Michael Rödel, who provided active support in the layout process.

Regensburg, August 20, 2007

Anja Ebersbach
Markus Glaser
Richard Heigl
Alexander Warta

Typography

Various fonts are used in this book.

italics	Paths and URLs
bold	Wiki pages and web titles, names and buttons (and links functioning as such)
`Courier`	Entries and source code
[italics] *`Courier`*	This text is variable and must be customized by you.
MENU1 → MENU2	Steps through a menu tree
<key>	The corresponding key on the keyboard

Source code and entries are generally printed exactly as typed. However, please note the following symbols:

↵	The line is too long and for space reasons must be broken. The actual entry cannot have a break here.
·	A space. Is indicated where the number of spaces is of significance.

So that you won't get confused as to what type of source code is meant, you will find the corresponding symbol in the margin:

Wiki	Code of a wiki page
HTML	Source code in HTML
PHP	Source code in PHP
Perl	Source code in Perl
JS	Source code in JavaScript
CSS	Source code in CSS
CFG	Content of a configuration file

Shell	Entry at the console level
URL	URL
SQL	SQL query
RegEx	Regular print-out

Unless otherwise indicated, directories are written in Unix notation. Under Windows, slashes / must be replaced by backslashes \. If the path begins with a slash, it is an absolute path. Windows users must insert the corresponding drive letter in front.

I. Wiki!?

1 The Wiki Concept

1.1 What is a Wiki?

Imagine you are surfing the Internet, and you stop at a site where you could and would like to add or modify something. For instance, you have a literary reference or link to add. Or you've noticed a typing error. Perhaps you even have a lengthy article that you'd like to display on a separate page. So, you just click on the "edit" button, change everything you wish, add a couple of ideas, confirm it, and the new page is online immediately! In a history, a listing of the saved, older versions of the page, you can view previous changes to the page as well as reverse your entries. If it all was a simple and transparent experience, you were dealing with a wiki. Wiki technology enables virtually anyone to completely edit pages without difficulty. Yet that's not all – anyone can contribute significantly to the structure of the site, simply by creating new links and adding new pages. This openness is the innovative and amazing aspect of wikis. The title of a book on wikis by Bo Leuf and Ward Cunningham puts it in a nutshell: *The Wiki Way. Quick Collaboration on the Web*.

Tools

Wikis are downright fascinating tools. It has never been so easy to become a "correspondent" on the Internet, because the technical hurdles have been reduced to a minimum. People who hear about or use wikis for the first time often experience a bit of culture shock. "Anybody can come along and change my text!" is a popular reaction. The opportunities and consequences of free cooperation in the context of the typical work organization of our society inevitably lead to irritation, because we assume that a contribution from "others" will destroy our own work. We are simply not used to handing over control and responsibility – and to strangers at that. The Swedish data systems specialist Lars Aronsson writes:

"Most people, when they first learn about the wiki concept, assume that a website that can be edited by anybody would soon be rendered useless by destructive input. It sounds like offering free spray cans next to a grey concrete wall. The only likely outcome would be ugly graffiti and simple tagging, and any artistic efforts would not be long lived. Still, it seems to work very well."[1]

Excursion

You can't quite imagine it yet? Then let's take a short excursion, and try out whether or not it is really as easy and free as it sounds. Get on the Internet and go to the site *http://www.wiki-tools.de*. Click on **Sandbox**. In this sandbox, you are free to experiment at will. Click on **edit**. Now, write over the existing text in the middle by typing your name or whatever else comes to mind. Then click on **Save page** below the text field. Congratulations! You have just made your first entry in a wiki.

Definition

A wiki is web-based software that allows all viewers of a page to change the content by editing the page online in a browser. This makes wiki a simple and easy-to-use platform for cooperative work on texts and hypertexts.

Note: Many wikis also correspond to the legal definition of open, free software. Most are subject to the GNU General Public License (GPL), which, among other things, prohibits a program from being converted into "proprietary" software. In this way, copyright laws prevent a program from being claimed as private property by a legal person for commercial purposes. Furthermore, the free use, distribution and editing of the program is ensured.

Origin

The first wiki, with the name WikiWikiWeb, was developed in 1995 by Ward Cunningham.[2] The software developer from Portland, Oregon is considered to be a pioneer in the development of new methods, such as object-oriented programming, design patterns or extreme programming. Because he was dissatisfied with conventional word processing programs, Cunningham searched for a new documentation system that would better suit the needs of programmers. His goal was a relatively simple software that would enable collective work on software codes that could be published immediately. The new program would automatically document all editing steps to make changes easier to trace (document history). Ultimately, the first wiki server went online and has been in operation ever since.[3]

Connotation

"Wikiwiki" is a Hawaiian word that means "quick" or "hurry". The name stands for the programming characteristic of wiki software in which content can be made available in a quick and uncom-

---

[1] Aronsson 2002.
[2] Leuf/Cunningham 2004.
[3] http://c2.com/cgi/wiki

plicated manner. As demonstrated below, there are a number of further developments of Cunningham's first Wiki, which we will subsequently discuss (MediaWiki, TWiki, bitweaver, ProWiki, etc.).

Note: When we refer to "wikis" below, we generally mean the concept, and less so any special implementation.

Functions

The use of wikis is dependent upon the goals of the community, organization or company that utilizes it. Although they were first intended for software development, they are now used in a variety of areas. Due to the further development of the wiki concept via various wiki clones,[4] wikis can integrate an increasing amount of functions.

Areas of Application

Generally, we differentiate between two application options with wikis: They can be used as tools in a closed work group, or they can be directed at potentially everybody over the WWW. Wikis serve as knowledge management tools in planning and documentation. They can also be utilized as an open, web-based content management system (CMS) for the editing and management of a web presence or

Fig. 1.1

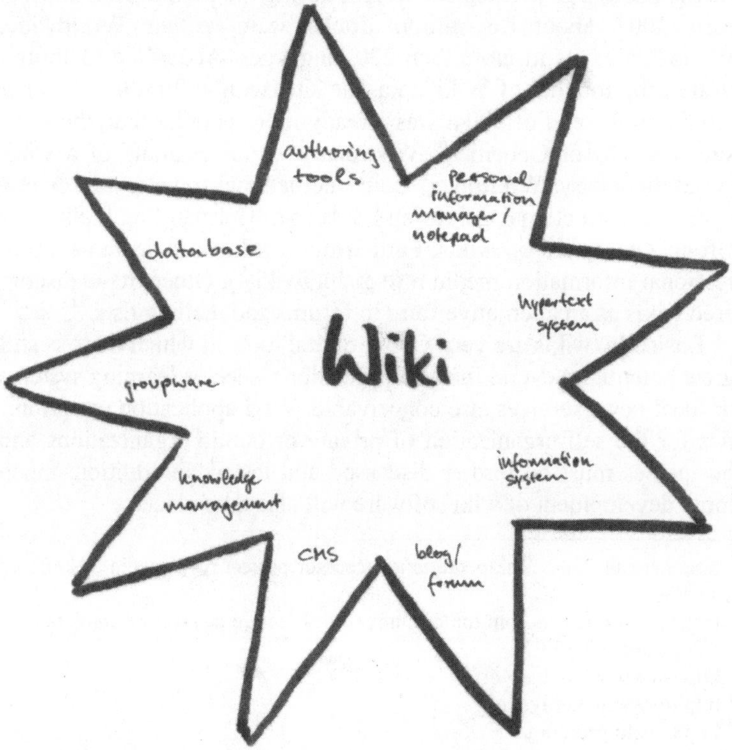

4 See Chap. 4 for wiki clones.

to supplement an existing CMS. You can use wikis as your internationally accessible notepad or as discussion forums for general and specialized discussions.

In the meanwhile, the most varied of institutions have discovered the advantages of wikis. Groups within the so-called civil society, such as the Austria Social Forum or the Chaos Computer Club, use wikis as an organizational aid. Wikis are employed in the classrooms of Swiss schools. Yet even companies such as SAP, Web.de, Motorola or British Telecommunications employ a wiki clone as a decentralized intranet, since, in contrast to conventional groupware, it is considerably more user-friendly.

Growing significance

Wikis are becoming increasingly popular. Primarily due to the success of the free online encyclopedia Wikipedia, wikis have become known to a wide audience.[5] At Wikipedia, the wiki concept is utilized to integrate and display encyclopedic knowledge "from the bottom up". In the German-language edition alone, over 540,000 articles were developed communally from May 2001 to February 2007. To date, however, the flagship of wiki technology remains the English language edition, for which, during the period from 2001 to early 2007, about 1.6 million articles were written. Worldwide, Wikipedia exists in more than 220 languages. According to Jimmy Wales, the founder of Wikipedia, the site, with 400 million hits per month by the end of 2004, was already more popular than the websites of IBM or Geocities[6]. Wiktionary[7] is an example of a wiki-based dictionary; Wikitravel[8] is an international travel guide. A few software instructional guides and aids (e.g. German Smalltalk User Group[9]) are based on wikis. Furthermore, wikis also serve as a professional information medium (e.g. Jurawiki[10]). Others have discovered wikis as an alternative form to forums and mailing lists.[11]

Potential

Basically, wikis are very young digital tools in which there is still great potential. Several further applications, such as learning systems or local news services, are conceivable. Wiki application opportunities for the self-organization of private or public organizations and businesses must be further discussed and tested. In addition, much more development of wiki software will also take place.

---

[5] See Schwall 2003. Wikipedia is a successor project of Nupedia, also based on wikis.

[6] http://www.answers.com/topic/jimmy-wales-lecture-at-stanford-university-on-2-9-2005, 02/10/07.

[7] http://www.wiktionary.org

[8] http://www.wikitravel.org

[9] http://swiki.gsug.org/

[10] http://www.jurawiki.de

[11] See e.g. *WikiUserTypes*, www.twiki.org/cgi-bin/view/Codev/WikiUserTypes, 02/10/07.

Let us briefly summarize:

Non-linear hypertext structure

Firstly, the WikiWikiWeb server technology enables the creation of associative hypertexts with non-linear navigation structures: Typically, each page contains a series of cross-links to other pages. The reader decides which page he or she will view next. In cases where larger wikis employ hierarchical navigation structures, these structures still play a secondary role.

Easy and extensive access

Secondly, using wikis, the technical hurdles and prior knowledge required for communication in and design of the mass medium of the WWW are reduced to a minimum. It is characteristic of wiki technology to allow externally generated texts to be edited "on the fly". The entry and formatting of a text is usually done using a few simple rules. For instance, sequential lines are formatted into lists by placing a star or dash in front of them. Also, pages within a wiki can be linked very easily by writing a sequence of words together without a space and with each word capitalized (called WikiWord or CamelCase, e.g. HomePage) or by placing a text in brackets.

No client software

Thirdly, regular users (clients) require no additional software, but rather can navigate, read, or alter content within wikis using conventional browsers.[12] Similarly, no applets or plug-ins must be loaded by users. Extensive training is not required to participate in a wiki. Cunningham was right when he described the wiki as "the simplest online database that could possibly work".

Social processes in the foreground

Fourthly, the simplicity of the software is the condition under which a number of communities and projects have been able to develop.[13] Not only is the technology of wikis interesting, but also the "wiki philosophy" and the debates on social perspectives linked to its use. For Internet projects based on the wiki concept, the discussion of purely "technical" problems can generally take a back seat to work processes, content-related issues and the social connections of the project. One could say that the wiki concept undoubtedly marks a new level in Internet technology and its usage.

Simple usage and technical hurdles

If wikis are tools that are so easy to use, why would one need a 400-page book? Let us point out a differentiation here. As a normal wiki user, you require hardly any previous knowledge. If you would like to install and maintain a wiki as an administrator, problems may arise for which more detailed explanations are needed.

---

[12] This means that, in contrast to comparable systems, wiki technology does not differentiate between "back end" and "front end".

[13] The relationship between project and community varies. For example, at Wikipedia, a community has developed around a free encyclopedia project. On the other hand, the MeatballWiki is only a community without a central project.

Between these two poles, plug-ins, for instance, offer a series of new possibilities that we would like to present. In addition: As easy as wikis generally are to use, the self-organizational processes that make wikis so fascinating can be very tricky. In such cases, introductory workshops may be necessary.

The fundamental principle of the wiki technology, however, is still simple. Let us have a closer look at the technical side of wikis.

1.2 The Technology of Wikis

Readers

Wiki-Software is installed as a script on a server. The server produces small documents, so-called wiki pages or articles, that can be accessed via a browser. The content of the wiki page itself is written as simple text and then stored in a file or database. When a wiki-based Internet page is accessed, the browser first sends a query to the server that administers the data sets containing the wiki software. This data, which is in the form of simple text, must now be formatted for display in the browser.

Fig. 1.2

To do this, the wiki script translates the file text (wiki code) or data set into HTML and embeds it in the web page (template) to be sent back to the browser. For example, the wiki script can be a PHP script that reads the raw page data from a MySQL database. This raw data is checked line for line, and the specific format commands contained in it are replaced by the corresponding HTML codes.[14]

[14] In this step, all URLs are then clickable, and in place of all URLs that end in gif, .jpg or .png, in other words those displaying images, the corresponding image tags are set (the images themselves are subsequently loaded by the browser).

Subsequently, the page thus created is integrated in the layout template. Every wiki page has its own, distinct name indicating the subject of the page. In addition, there is usually a navigation menu and a few page-specific links of the displayed page. The most important of these links is the "Edit" link.

Authors

If this page is then to be edited, the **edit** button is used. This sends another query to the server. The same page is loaded again, only this time the contents are not converted to HTML format, but rather displayed in "raw form" in a large text field in an HTML form. The user can edit the text in this form and send a new version, which immediately replaces the old version in the database. When the page is accessed again, the new version is displayed.

Fig. 1.3

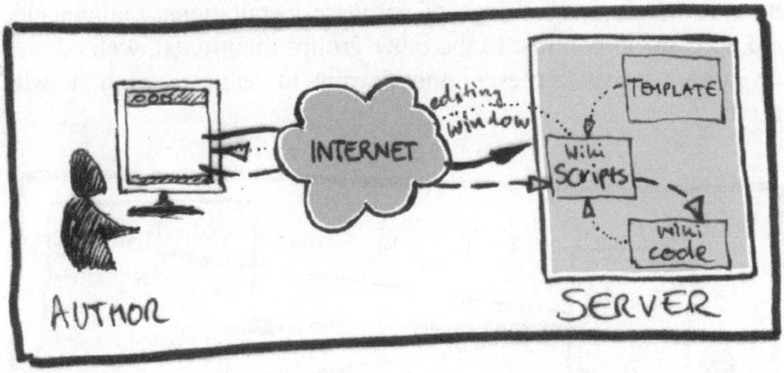

Visitors do not need to know any programming language or HTML in order to use wikis. Wiki pages are written in simple ASCII format, just like emails. There is a series of conventions that you should become familiar with sooner or later, but they are generally easier to learn and more "intuitive" than HTML. For instance, a blank line separates paragraphs. When this page is saved, the system translates the blank line to HTML, that is, it adds a <p> at the respective spot. The wiki link syntax, which we describe in more detail below, is also important.

Wiki Admins

The primary task of wiki administrators is to maintain wiki content and ensure the smooth operation of working in a wiki. They have more extensive rights than regular participants; for example, they can delete pages or block individual user access. To do this, wiki admins usually have their own interface or special pages in the wiki to which only admins have access.

Fig. 1.4

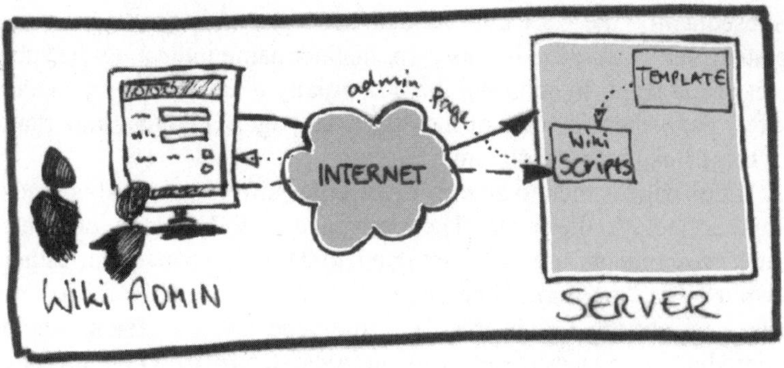

Web admins Yet even a wiki cannot exist without some technology. On this level, the web admin is in charge of software installations, maintenance and updates. In contrast to the other groups mentioned, web admins have direct access to files without needing to detour through the wiki interface.

Fig. 1.5

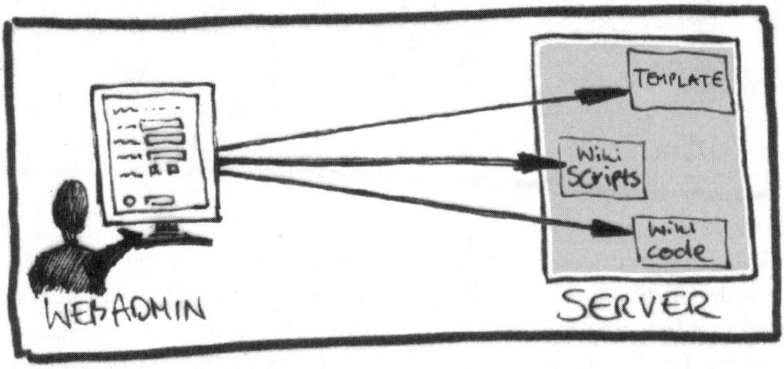

Level model The categories mentioned up to now indicate a model which divides the access of participants into levels that differ technically in type and depth. We add to these the lowest level, which includes the infrastructure, the server and operating system, as well as the necessary software, web server and database. They are maintained by a system administrator.

Thus, while the system and web administrators have direct access to the server and must not necessarily be integrated into the wiki community, wiki administrators, authors and readers navigate the web-based interface of the wiki.

Using the idea of the level model, we can also clearly see that, in contrast to a normal HTML page, the interface with which content can be created is found in the client realm. This means that, from a technical standpoint, conditions have been established in which

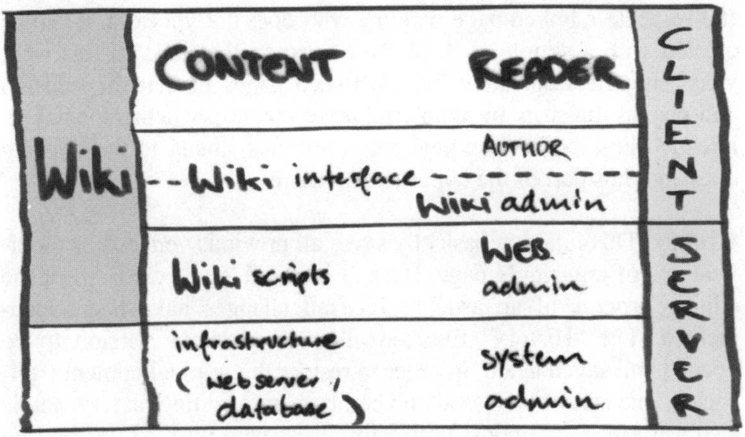

Fig. 1.6

a great number of people can participate extensively in the design of the content without needing to clear any major hurdles (such as access to the server).

1.3 Characteristic Wiki Functions

Regardless of the wiki script used, all wikis offer a few technical core functions, which we will only mention briefly here and later in more detail.

Editing. The **edit** button is the ultimate typical feature of a wiki. Only in extreme cases are specific pages excluded from the editing option. At Wikipedia, for instance, the capability of changing the title page has been made more difficult. A page can also be completely prohibited from editing. Since such blocking goes against the grain of the wiki philosophy, it should be avoided when possible.

Links. Each article can be linked to other articles and thus form a new network structure.

WikiWord/ CamelCase

Note: Links can be created in most wikis using a WikiWord: Words are capitalized and written together without a space (so-called CamelCase, which in itself is an example of such a WikiWord). CamelCase makes linking easy, but can also cause problems in some applications. That is why, in other wikis, links are generated by simply placing the title in square brackets. Regardless of which procedure is chosen, a link is thus generated that appears in the normal view.

If a respective linked page within a wiki does not yet exist, it can be created with a simple click of the mouse on that link. In this way, wikis support associative links between pages in that they design and display links in an almost intuitive manner, whether or not an intended link exists. The new pages are now linked to the existing ones and thus part of the hypertext structure.

History. This function basically saves all previous versions or modifications of any single page. Here, it is possible to exactly track the editing process of an article, since all changes have been documented. The "History" function allows a previous version to be opened and saved again, in order to restore the original content (rollback). This concept is based on Cunningham's editing history, and is also a useful tool against unfriendly users who wish to destroy the page. However, it is being used more and more for regular coordination problems. The history can roll all the way back to the first version, but can also be limited due to space reasons. More complex wiki clones offer a so-called "Diff" function, which displays detailed alterations between two versions, such that authors do not need to compare two texts line for line.

Recent Changes. This page either provides a current overview of a certain number of recent changes to wiki pages or all changes within a predefined time period. It is produced automatically and cannot be changed by users. Some wikis, such as MediaWiki, offer so-called watch lists. Such lists enable selected pages to be monitored over an extended period of time. If you are partial to a particular article, you do not have to continually look through the list of all changes to all pages.

SandBox. Wikis usually offer instructions and introductions on their homepage, which serve to facilitate working with the system. In addition, new users, as well as experienced ones, can use the so-called SandBox or PlayGround to learn how to utilize wikis and try out various solutions without having to use a regular page. You have already been introduced to the sandbox. This test environment is nothing more than a wiki page that is emptied on a regular basis.

Search functions. Most wikis also offer a classic full-text or title search for the wiki pages. Thus, articles in a wiki can be accessed quickly. It has been our experience that if titles are well-thought out, the search can function like an index card system.

1.4 Wiki Clones

With the development and utilization of the WikiWikiWeb, new challenges have emerged, and accordingly, new programs in which the wiki concept has been further developed. Meatball (itself a wiki community) claims that there are currently about 200 different types of wikis.[15] These programs are called clones, since they imitate the original Wiki, but have added a few extra functions. Most of them have the term "wiki" in their name. Here are just a few common examples:

UseModWiki is one of the oldest and most widely-used wiki clones. Written in Perl, they include several small programs that enable a variety of additional functions. UseMod has had a substantial influence on the development of other wikis, such as MediaWiki, whose formatting language (or, more precisely, its syntax) strongly resembles that of UseMod.

MediaWiki was conceived for the needs of the Wikipedia encyclopedia project. It consists of several scripts written in PHP, and contains a few further developments (name spaces, sidebar, and messages regarding processing conflicts).

PmWiki is written in PHP. The focus of its development lies in ease of use, in order to reduce obstacles which might keep people with little IT savvy from using a wiki. Simple installation and configurability are the hallmarks of this clone. With its attractive interface and ability to link namespaces with user rights, it could mean competition for MediaWiki.[16]

MoinMoin is a simple and very widely-used wiki clone written in Python. MoinMoin, whose name reflects a friendly northern German greeting, enables user registration and has a plug-in system for enhancements, among other functions. MoinMoin requires no database connection.

Bitweaver, a descendent of TikiWiki, written in PHP, already offers a whole series of useful features. It can stand up to a comparison with existing content management systems and groupware. However, in this case, the wiki is just one component – albeit a central

[15] Many wikis are listed under: http://c2.com/cgi/wiki?WikiEngines.
[16] An assumption not shared by the authors of this book ☺.

one – in an array of additional groupware features, such as forums, blog functions, newsletters, file and image galleries, and survey, chat or calendar functions.

The Perl-based **TWiki**, with its many plug-ins and features, is, in addition to TikiWiki, the most comprehensive wiki clone. TWiki implements wiki technology more consistently than bitweaver, because additional functions can also be realized with this technology to a large extent. TWiki, which was conceived to be utilized as a company intranet, is being used increasingly for commercial purposes, due to its high level of development.

The target group of **Dokuwiki** is primarily developer teams, work groups, and small companies. This simple wiki clone does not require a database and, due to its practical application, has attracted a number of fans.

ProWiki is written in Perl and primarily conceived for use in so-called wiki farms. Developers place great value in the ability to quickly generate subordinate wikis as copies of existing ones. In doing so, the features of the original wiki are transferred to the subordinated pages. ProWiki aims for high adaptability to a variety of demands within a wiki.

Wetpaint is a special example for a free wiki offering. With it, you can write your own wiki pages on a public domain. However, the wiki software itself is not freely accessible. Several similar commercial wiki clones, such as **Confluence** or **Socialtext**, were developed in the past.

Selection criteria

In the appendix, you will find a small tabular overview of important wiki systems. It cites a few criteria you should look for when selecting a wiki. Section V also contains further tips on selecting the right wiki.

1.5 The Wiki Phenomenon

Brecht's Radio Theory

Bertolt Brecht, in his so-called "Radio Theory", written in 1930, wrote that radio has one side when it should actually have two. "It is purely a distributive apparatus; it just rations out."[17] His now infamous proposal was to convert broadcasting from a distributive appa-

[17] Brecht 1930/1967, 129.

ratus to a communicative apparatus. "Radio could conceivably be the greatest communicative apparatus of public life, an incredible channel system; that is, it would be, if it were capable of not only broadcasting but also receiving, of thus being able to make the listener not only listen but also speak, and not to isolate him but connect him."

Just a few decades later, an innovative mass medium became available in the form of the Internet, which has markedly accommodated Brecht's technical demands of connecting broadcaster and receiver. This was just as much the case with the classic visual and audio media as it is with the "Internet revolution". Yet technology and new inventions alone do not change anything. A complex and difficult reciprocal relationship exists between social progress and technical innovation. We can analyze this relationship with the aid of the following questions: Who uses this technology? What goals and forms are involved? Upon what dependencies does he or she rely? Accordingly, wikis can be used in an emancipated manner – or not.[18]

1.5.1 Creativity Through Group Processes

Wiki effect

Yet beyond the question of the emancipatory potential of wikis is perhaps the question as to why the "wiki effect" even occurs at all. What we mean by "wiki effect" is primarily the self-organization processes that can be observed in well-known and successful wiki projects. It is astounding that people will independently research, organize, write and publish to provide the general public with a free service. For instance, communities have not only formed around the large Internet lexica that largely do without central control models. Their self-organized projects have, in the meanwhile, exhibited considerable successes.

Cathedral and bazaar

In such cases, it is often evident that the communication of large groups is much more effective and thus can react more flexibly to change than when using hierarchical organizational models. Such wiki projects are not the exception to the rule: Similar experiences were previously made with the "subversive" development of open source software (e.g. Linux). Eric Raymond, a well-known author and programmer in the hacker and open source scene, hit the nail on the head when he metaphorically differentiated the various management methods using the principle of the cathedral and the bazaar:[19] While conventional software development assumed that im-

---

[18] See: Ebersbach/Glaser 2004.

[19] Raymond 1999.

portant programs had to be built like cathedrals, "painstakingly chiseled by individual druids or small teams of high priests who worked in complete isolation and were not allowed to issue any unfinished beta releases, [...] the Linux community seemed to be like a large bazaar of wildly intermingled voices having a variety of goals and approaches which could produce a coherent and stable system only through a series of miracles. The fact that the bazaar appeared to work, and work very well at that, was a downright shock."

The appeal of wiki technology lies in the act of rethinking the familiar. Once again, hierarchical control models are at our disposition, and with them, valid ideas of why and how, through the division of labor, complex problems can be solved and products produced and distributed. It is no less than a question of alternative socialization models whose possibility (!) becomes apparent.

Large-group dynamics

People repeatedly ask why wikis work. This question has to be posed more precisely: Why and under what conditions do people cooperate in wiki projects without central control and external pressure? Group processes are a much discussed and investigated topic in the fields of sociology and education; so much so that we cannot present it here in all its theoretical complexity. However, experiences with large group events have revealed a few principles which contribute greatly to the success of large group processes.[20]

Playful creation. "Why Wiki works? It's cool", is the brazen comment at Ward's Wiki. A loose, playful atmosphere and fun at work are important conditions for self-organized processes, because one's creative, social and practical skills can best be unfolded in such an environment. It is motivating when one can make his or her own designs or contribute an article for a large-scale project. Less attractive "obligatory" tasks do not necessarily fall by the wayside if their necessity is recognized.

Flat hierarchies. Flat hierarchies are decisive for creative, self-organized group processes. The responsibility for the entire process, not just for subareas, is transferred completely to those individuals performing that process. These responsibilities are integrated into the planning and workflow control processes as completely as possible. Newer methodological approaches for large-group events transfer workflow and goal definition responsibilities to participants and those concerned. This concept requires of its participants a willingness toward the open nature of the process, as well as an agreement to not only equally distribute the risks, but also the advantages.

[20] Especially at open space conferences. See Petri 2000, Maleh 2000.

Projects based on the wiki philosophy require flat hierarchies. This can be seen, for instance, in the fact that participants contribute considerably to designing the organizational structure of the wiki, e.g. through linking. Yet social structures also develop within a wiki – and they often differ from those the initiators had initially imagined.

Modification pressure and the complex topic. The pressure to modify (as intrinsic motivation) and the will to want to solve a problem represent, according to Raymond, an indispensable motor for the "bazaar". Working on one's own topic creates dedication.[21] Self-organization processes build on a responsibility that stems from interest in the matter. Inevitably, in step with the wiki philosophy, incomplete or faulty wiki pages are bound to remain unedited for a time. Only after someone has deemed it necessary will the page be modified or existing errors corrected.

It is important, as Raymond has explained for the bazaar, to be part of a worthwhile cause and that improvements in which one is involved become apparent. In addition, a complex topic representing an intellectual challenge promotes the dynamics of large-group processes. They develop their full strength through a fascinating and challenging topic which can, by all means, have a high potential for conflict.

Simple system, simple rules. The decision to sit down and join in is the greatest obstacle for self-organization processes. Successful self-organized group processes are often founded on very simple basic systems, because favorable – if complex – decision-making and modification processes depend only on a rough overall concept, access to all relevant information and clear basic conditions. Thus, the conference model *Open Space* functions with just a handful of rules.

Wiki technology, with its low technical access hurdles, is ideal for web-based group processes. Several wiki communities have implemented simple codes of conduct.

Open access. Free will and open access are vital conditions for motivation in self-organization processes. The success of the bazaar principle as well as the wiki philosophy is based on the fact that discussions are removed from alleged expert and specialist circles, right from the start. This creates transparency and incentive.

---

[21] Of course it makes a difference whether a goal is self-set or stipulated, or whether external goals have been taken on as one's own.

A large pool of participants testing the system is also a way to identify errors at an early stage. The system becomes more stable and can be more quickly adapted to the changing needs of its users.

For wikis, this approach is supported by the principle of "open postings". With wikis, users are invited to edit an existing page within their normal browser or add new pages. In contrast to the classic editing principle, articles are not first proofread and only published when completely error-free, but rather as soon as possible, so that users of a page can be integrated in the cooperative process.

Diversity of the participants. For the dynamics of self-organization processes and collaborative work, a climate of openness and mutual trust is necessary – despite inevitable conflicts. A variety of experiences, backgrounds and knowledge is seen as the basis of creative processes and as an enrichment, and thus, every user is initially recognized as an expert.

The wiki philosophy is based on the assumption that those individuals will become involved who also want to contribute to the situation. Their knowledge and motivation are sufficient to contribute to the issue. A certain degree of heterogeneity can also be observed in participants of wiki projects regarding their areas of interest.[22]

Extremely flexible scheduling. A relatively flexible scheduling of one's work time within an overall process is a further motivator. According to the bazaar principle, which knows no deadlines, it is possible to tailor one's work time to suit one's own rhythm and individual daily life. Work begins when the time is ripe, and ends when it is finished. It is less bound to fixed schedules. Time pressures exist only when problems remain untouched.

Self-determined work. People involved in group processes and members of communities have very different strategies and just as varied an understanding of their own function within the overall relationship. In addition, strategies and self-conception are subject to continuous change, such that it is difficult to determine certain roles or types – perhaps it is not even advisable. However, for better understanding, it would be helpful to consider that each individual – once freed from a socio-economic background – enters into relationships with other participants via a wiki in a very multifaceted manner. Cooperation in open wiki projects is attractive because strate-

---

[22] As in the case of many other Internet projects, we must mention the limiting factor that we expect the circle of active wiki users to continue to be limited to certain social groups for the present (keyword: digital divide).

gies, focal points, and work intensity can be self-determined to a large extent.

Reception behavior. We have to distinguish between whether and how often participants visit a wiki system, whether they read the articles fleetingly or closely, and whether they are searching for articles on a particular topic or across several subjects.

Writing behavior. With regard to writing behavior, there are a number of variations. Some visitors of a wiki never write there. Others proofread, edit the style and layout, and make small changes. Others still, the specialists, acquaint themselves in detail with a subject and contribute articles with a great degree of content. In comparison, "generalists" jump from article to article and bring in knowledge from other areas.

Structural behavior. This category refers to the extent to which responsibility for an overall project is assumed. It includes the question as to how intensively one participates in fundamental debates or voices considerations regarding general procedures. Some participants take on functions as mediators or moderators. Others assume regulatory tasks, such as checking orphaned pages. Accordingly, the technical administrators and maintainers also belong to this category. People in self-organized processes ideally receive functions through their authority and the trust they have earned through their work.

Social behavior. This category encompasses atmospheric aspects. It refers to the form in which criticism and encouragement are imparted. Does one enter the discussion with a provocative or cooperative stance? On another level, the organization of the social and cultural periphery is also part of this realm, such as a regulars' table or seminar weekends.

The forms broadly discussed here are naturally not pure, but rather overlap each other and evolve. Due to the interplay between the individual practices and goals, the overall relationship is continually restructured as a process. The members of a community have just as much of an effect on the individual through their actions as the individual does when contributing to the daily design of form and content of the community. All of these behaviors, including those that are passive and, in a broader sense, "destructive", are necessary to a dynamic community. However, the community can also be destroyed by them at any time. Knowledge of specific and general group processes within a wiki community is still in its early stages. At the 21st Chaos Community Congress in 2004 in Berlin, Jimmy Wales presented some initial considerations using the example of Wikipedia. A few of the "types" he outlined serve to illustrate the degree of diversity.

- **Bees.** Wales describes as "bees" those participants who perform very important work and without whom Wikipedia could not achieve or maintain its quality. Nevertheless, they are the least recognized group. They include generalists and specialists. They provide important content articles, proofread texts or negotiate with difficult users.
- **Sock puppets.** This group is comprised of people who publish under more than one account. This is done for a variety of reasons. A few wish to preserve their privacy (such as a professor who also writes as a fan of Britney Spears but fears a loss of authority). For others, such as those using multiple identities to manipulate polls, it represents a despicable attack on the mutual trust upon which open editing is based.
- **Judges.** This is obvious. These are people who focus on conflict resolution and decision-making. They are active in juries and arbitration committees. They organize polls and further develop proposals for regulations.
- **Moths.** This rather strange label becomes clear when considering that "moths are drawn to flames", as Wales explains. Flames in this case refer to flame wars, that is, heated and often insulting verbal duals. While people who start aggressive flame wars generally do not enjoy a good reputation, Wales sees the fact that individual participants seek conflict and do not try to avoid it as not necessarily negative action. On the contrary, these discussions can lead to vital advancements.
- **Vandals** are a common problem in open editing systems. They willfully destroy content, and yet they pose a much smaller threat to the community than is generally assumed.
- **People "outside" of the wiki** are often overlooked in terms of their significance. They continue to develop wiki technology as programmers. Even those individuals who primarily develop wiki content in other communicative media (e.g. chats or mailing lists) also play a role.

1.5.2
Limits of the Wiki Philosophy

Wikis are not automatic "successes", much less a cure-all. Productive group processes are always faced with destructive practices that even the large wiki communities have to combat right from the start. In problem analysis, we need to differentiate between whether the group dynamics have stemmed from a constructive start to the process and then slipped toward the negative, or whether wikis are simply not being accepted as normal tools.

Lack of interest

If wikis are not being accepted as tools and are thus not integrated into the daily work routine, they share the same fate as several knowledge management systems. Usually one person alone does the writing, and the others only read. Or the wiki system is not consulted at all. There are several wiki systems whose possibilities cannot be fully unfurled due to a lack of interest or out of lethargy. The causes are manifold. Generally, social elements are underestimated when dealing with new software. More than a few users already have high expectations when a wiki system is made available, and are quickly disappointed when it is not met with immediate positive response. However: Even if the technical hurdles are few, using wikis must still be "learned;" people still have to be interested in or introduced to the system. This includes the realization that a wiki is never "finished" and that not everything is going to function properly right away. The fact that one is not dealing with a WYSIWYG system can cause apprehensions that need to be taken seriously.

The acceptance of wikis depends on the degree to which I as a person can truly benefit personally from using them. That is why it is still important that the wiki not be empty at the start, but rather provide a certain quantity of content that can be further edited or to which additions can be made. This also means that a small core group that uses wikis for itself and thus feels responsible for it is of great significance.

Social environment and working world

Using wikis, the work environment can be influenced, and at the same time, be dependent upon it. Using open systems in today's working world is met with many types of resistance. The lack of willingness of managerial persons (project managers, area managers, etc.) to permit open systems in private companies is only one example.[23] However, the same thing can occur in authoritarian organizational structures.

[23] Even in companies in which hierarchies are being disassembled, this does not necessarily translate into a higher degree of transparency of company structures.

High workload, family and social responsibilities or social security worries often allow little room for free forms of cooperation which are admittedly also complex.

Vandalism

Let us return to the issue of "vandals" and vandalism. It has generally been observed that in wiki projects, destruction and/or damage remains relatively insignificant. It is assumed that cracking an open system poses no great appeal to "serious" crackers. The WikiWikiWeb server principle provides its own evidently effective antidote in its version control. It enables the previous version to be restored at any time. In systems with a high visitor frequency, disturbances can be detected quickly, as systems with several participants tend to be more "stable". Wikipedia, for instance, places pages that are frequently damaged on a separate list, to which the administrators pay special attention. According to an IBM study, incidences of deliberate destruction at Wikipedia are often eliminated within five minutes: "We were surprised at how often we found vandalism, and then surprised again at how fast it was fixed,"[24] reports Martin Wattenberg, a researcher at IBM TJ Watson Research Center in Cambridge, Mass. The fact that many people can control the process and anyone can take instant action is the most significant element in the quality control of large, public wikis. It only requires a corresponding sense of problem awareness on the part of users, who anticipate such attacks. Yet even willful alterations to small details can greatly inhibit the quality without being immediately noticed. Another – last – method has already been mentioned: blocking a page – which means the end of the wiki philosophy for that page.

Attention-seekers

Greater problems stem from people who use wikis as a platform for attention-seeking or those who do not wish to conduct discussions cooperatively. Provocation and posing general questions can be useful in breaking through a rut in thinking. Various opinions on a topic often develop into "editing wars". So-called trolls knowingly incite flame wars with lengthy, superfluous or provocative articles. Such conflicts, which contribute nothing to the issue, cost a great deal of energy. "Wiki pages represent consensus because it's much easier to delete flames and spam than indulge them."[25] In many wikis, trolls are kept away from the articles through discussion pages, so that, where possible, they only need to vent on this meta-level without "adding noise" to the real content[26]. In addition, at Wikipedia, a few mediation procedures and open instances have been established, such as ad hoc mediation commissions or openly-discussed exclusion petitions.

---

[24] IBM 2003.

[25] Why Wiki Works, http://c2.com/cgi/wiki?WhyWikiWorks, Feb. 10 2007.

[26] Aronsson, 2002.

In very stubborn cases, there is also the opportunity to block certain users for a limited period or forever, using an IP list. In order to promote transparency and exclude arbitrariness, users can access a list of blocked users at any time and find out about the initiator and grounds for exclusion. Such blocking of certain IP addresses, in turn, leads to the problem that non-excluded users may be mistakenly barred from having continued access.[27] A further problem is that the disruptive parties can re-register at any time under a new name.

In his book "Die heimliche Medienrevolution" ("The Secret Media Revolution"), published in 2005, Möller provides a comprehensive look at the problems and possible solutions in dealing with difficult controversies and vandalism in blog and wiki community environments.[28]

Project portal excursion

The best overview of the discussion culture and decision-making processes can be had with a visit to Wikipedia. Let us take a short excursion to the project's Community Portal page.[29] Here, we find guidelines and conventions, discussion pages for admin candidates, moderation information and pages collecting opinion statistics. Completed problem cases are documented on the arbitration committee page. And of course, a visit would not be complete without taking a look at some of the discussion pages of individual articles.

Quality assurance and Wikiquette

As we can see there: For quality assurance and conflict resolution, a few mediating instances, rules and practices have formed at Wikipedia. We find name and formatting conventions; well-made articles are presented as examples, and quality offensives are being performed in certain topic areas. A Wikiquette offers recommendations for cooperative communication with other users:[30] Suggestions such as assuming the good intentions of other users, objectivity, mutual help and encouragement, and kindness are proposed, as is the advice to keep cool in conflicts that will inevitably crop up. After all, there are always the arbitration committees. And yet, the overall character remains true to its democratic fundamental principles. Anything else would cause the project to fail.

Neutral Point of View

One especially touchy subject is the credibility and objectivity problem. At Wikipedia, this is addressed, among other ways, under the heading "Neutral Point of View". Since many people from around the world and having the most varied of political and religious views take part in the project, Wikipedia is obligated to formulate articles as neutrally as possible. The point is not to write them as objectively as possible – this is a common misunderstanding – but to

[27] Since IP addresses are not always issued on a permanent basis.

[28] Möller 2005. To an extent, also in: Möller 2003.

[29] http://de.wikipedia.org/wiki/Wikipedia:Portal, Feb. 10 2007.

[30] http://de.wikipedia.org/wiki/Wikipedia:Wikiquette, Feb. 2 2007.

present all aspects of an issue. Most wiki users have thus learned to express themselves in a conflict-free way, insofar as possible. Instead of writing "Apples taste good", one would instead write "Some people like the taste of apples." We will address the issue of apparent neutrality at the end of this book.

Open editing

Giving up the author principle is an aspect of collaborative work. It leads to a few questions: Is someone who has contributed to collaborative texts legally accountable? Who is the author? It is true that traditional newspapers and encyclopedias also represent a collection of articles by a variety of authors, but in open wikis, there is no traditional relationship between publisher and author. Wiki texts are thus not directly subject to the compulsion of marketability. In such cases, the individual author, on the one hand, receives a much stronger, more independent role, while, on the other hand, he disappears in the open system as an individual author at the same time.

Open text

A further area of interest is the issue of ownership and copyright. Since many individuals contribute to content, the question must be clarified as to whether anyone can claim copyright on individual articles or even the whole collection. Wikipedia, for instance, allows every user the right to protect his or her own contributions. However, when the page is being saved, the user is informed that he or she may only benefit from one type of copyright, namely the GNU Free Documentation License (FDL). In short, this means that anyone may copy and use the text for other purposes as long as he or she makes the original text available to other readers, which is most easily done by linking to the Wikipedia URL.[31]

Another question which arises deals with how materials protected by copyright are used in wikis, and who is responsible for any arising damage. To date, there has not yet been a precedent case. However, the law in most European countries differentiates between newspapers having an editing department for which a publisher is accountable and bulletin board systems or services of an Internet provider, where individual users bear the responsibility. Wikis are more likely to be categorized with the latter.

Careful optimism

Wikis will also have their share of problems and setbacks. The wiki philosophy may see some things too optimistically. Nevertheless, previous experience has given reason to adopt an open and optimistic stance toward these developments. The problems known to date and mentioned here do not negate any grounds for optimism; if one considers human relationships as being permanent collective learning processes, one cannot simply say, "people are the way they are", and stop there. Instead, one must question the causes for obsta-

---

[31] Aronsson, 2002.

cles to "learning" (prejudices, insecurities, lack of complete understanding of group processes). Brecht's comment on "Radio Theory" is good advice for dealing with the "impossibilities" of wikis:

"Not feasible in this social order, feasible in another, the suggestions, which are only a natural consequence of technical development, serve the propagation and form of this other order. [...] If you should consider this utopian, I kindly ask you to consider why it is utopian."

1.6 Wiki Pages

Pictures are worth a thousand words. That is why we would like to present a few sample wiki pages on the following pages. We used no special criteria in selecting these examples; moreover, we wish to convey an impression of the diversity of wiki software.

TeacherWiki *(http://teacherwiki.pbwiki.com):* An open platform for teachers to collaborate and share knowledge on education, curricula, instruction, resources and technology.

Recipes Wiki *(www.recipeswiki.org):* A free collection of cooking and baking recipes to which anyone can contribute easily and without registration. Includes integrated cooking videos.

Wikitravel *(www.wikitravel.org):* Project with the goal of generating a complete, current and reliable international travel guide whose content is freely accessible.

Open Guide to Boston *(boston.openguides.org):* One example from the Open Guide travel guide.

DorfWiki (VillageWiki) *(www.dorfwiki.org):* Virtual wiki-based meeting, learning and workplace to which anyone can and is encouraged to contribute who cares about the topic of "villages" and all things "village-like".

Memory Alpha *(www.memory-alpha.org):* Free, community project for the generation of a comprehensive encyclopedia all about Star Trek.

1.7
Important Resources on the WWW

c2.com/cgi/wiki?WikiEngines WikiEngines on Wards Wiki lists a number of Wiki engines, including categorization according to programmer language.

usemod.com/cgi-bin/mb.pl The English language Meatball Wiki is a platform for practitioners concerned with online communities.

www.wikimatrix.org On WikiMatrix, approximately 70 wiki clones can be compared with one another.

www.opensourcecms.com OpensourceCMS offers the opportunity to test the most popular open source CMS and wikis.

www.wikiservice.at/gruender/wiki.cgi?StartSeite The Gründer-Wiki (Founder Wiki) is a German-language site comparable to Meatball Wiki.

wiki.LIBERAL *(https://my.fdp.de/wiki):* Online dictionary concerning Germany's FDP (Free Democratic Party). A site where information about the FDP, its programs and history can be collected.

Placeopedia *(www.placeopedia.com):* A wiki that links Google Maps and Wikipedia articles.

Semapedia *(semapedia.org):* Its goal is to link the virtual world of Wikipedia with the real world using Semapedia tags, which are physical hyperlinks that can be read by cell phones.

II. Our First Wiki: MediaWiki

2 The Installation

Local installation

In order to become familiar with and test a wiki, it is a good idea to install a system on your own computer, instead of delving straight into the depths of the Internet. Firstly, you have complete control over the software used and its settings. On the Net, this is only the case if you are an administrator on a server on which the wiki is running. Secondly, almost all entries made to an online version can potentially be read by the entire world. You need to ask yourself whether the world would really be interested in every little test; in addition, copyright issues could quickly crop up. In a local testing environment, on the other hand, you can control who has access to your computer, and you can experiment without needing to constantly worry about relevance or legal questions.

Installing wikis

Basically, installing wikis is always done according to a similar pattern. First you need to create and adapt the environment in which the wiki will run, which primarily means setting up the web server and, if necessary, the database. Then you copy the wiki software files to the proper location and adjust one or more configuration files to the system environment, either manually or automatically. Such adjustments mainly include the indication of paths, language and connection to the database. In addition, some wikis offer the possibility of performing some settings directly over the browser. The individual steps for installing and setting up MediaWiki will be detailed below.

Note: The installation described refers to the software version 1.10.1, which you can find on the supplementary CD. If you prefer to download the current packages from the Internet, there may be some deviations.

2.1
A Test Environment with XAMPP

Test environment

Since it is the nature of wikis to be a component of the WWW, you need to create a test environment for the actual software for local operation on your computer. In the case of MediaWiki, such an environment consists of a web server, the script language PHP (Version 5.0 or higher) and the database MySQL (4.0 or higher). The installation and interaction of these components is complex, and descriptions of them fill bookshelves. However, that is not within the scope of our book. Luckily, there is a package that allows us to install all required components with a minimum of configuration effort: XAMPP. This is the abbreviation for "Apache MySQL PHP Perl" (the X is a placeholder for the operating system) and thus for components that together result in possible standard equipment for a web server. If you should already have this software on your computer, you can skip this chapter and go straight to installing the MediaWiki.

Tip: If you already have a web server installed on your computer, it is possible that XAMPP may not work. For instance, this is the case with IIS.

At the time of this printing, XAMPP is available in Version 1.6.3. It can be found on the supplementary CD in the directory */xampp/[operating system]*. The newest version can be downloaded at the URL *http://www.apachefriends.org /de/xampp.html*.

2.1.1
XAMPP for Windows

Installing XAMPP

XAMPP runs under all versions of Windows. You require 64 MB of RAM and about 110 MB of free hard drive space, which is usually not a problem for conventional computer systems. Simply execute the .exe file in the corresponding directory of the CD. You will now be asked to indicate your language. Then you will see the installation program. Start it by clicking **Continue**. You can then indicate the path in which you want the system to be installed. If you wish to follow the examples in the book exactly, enter *C:\apachefriends* here[1]. Clicking **Install** will start the process. The program creates the folder *[drive]\apachefriends\xampp*, which contains all included components. In addition, the parameters in the respective configura-

[1] This is especially important for setting up *TWikis* in Sect. III.

tion files will be accordingly adapted to the conditions of your system. No entries will be made to the registry and no system variables will be set. Thus, to uninstall the program, you just need to delete the directory in which the software is stored.

After successfully installing the program, you will be asked whether you wish to install Apache, MySQL, and FileZilla FTP server as services. Answer with **No**, otherwise these services will be automatically activated with every system start. Now you will be asked whether you would like to start the XAMPP Control Panel. This allows you to retroactively activate those services.

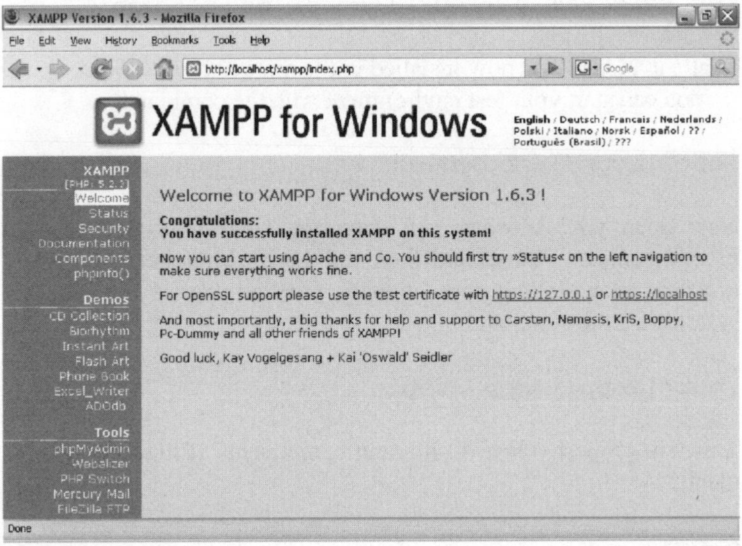

Fig. 2.1

Starting XAMPP

In order to start XAMPP, run the file *xampp_start.exe* in the directory xampp or select XAMPP BASIC START in the Start Menu under PROGRAMS → APACHEFRIENDS → XAMPP. Open a browser and enter the URL *http://127.0.0.1* or *http://localhost*. This is always the local address of the test system. You should now see the start page of the XAMPP environment (see Fig. 2.2). As you have surely noticed, the DOS window that starts the XAMPP environment remains open. A few of the required programs run here. In order to close the test environment, however, we do not recommend simply closing the window, since some of the services running are independent of the window and will continue to run after you have closed it. For "clean" closure, it is thus advisable to run the file *xampp_stop.exe* in the same directory.

2.1.2 XAMPP for Linux

Installing XAMPP

Given the wealth of LINUX/UNIX variants, one should be careful with generalizations, but, in principle, XAMPP should run on all systems. It requires approximately 110 MB on your hard drive. Installation is easy. Transfer the installation package from the CD to your home directory. Open a shell. You should be logged on as an administrator. If this is not the case, switch using `su`. Then, enter the following command to unpack the archive:

Shell

```
tar xvfz xampp-linux-1.6.tar.gz -C /opt
```

That's it. XAMPP is now installed in the directory */opt/lampp*.

Starting XAMPP

You can start your test environment with the command

Shell

```
/opt/lampp/lampp start
```

Now open your browser and enter the URL *http://127.0.0.1* or *http://localhost*. You should then see the XAMPP language selection, and after clicking your language, the start page. To end the test system, use the command

Shell

```
/opt/lampp/lampp stop
```

This will properly close all running components of the test environment.

2.1.3 What's Going on here Anyway?

Interplay of the components

Once you have started XAMPP, a web server will be running on your computer. It waits for queries via the HTTP protocol, which are generally posed by a browser, and answers them with an HTML page or file. In local systems, the web server is always accessible at the address 127.0.0.1 or localhost. Simple homepages are transferred from server to browser in this way.

Tip: If you are online at the same time, any user on the Internet can direct a query to your web server if he knows your IP address. This is of course only the case as long as XAMPP is active.

Tip: You can increase the level of security of your system under Linux by entering the command `/opt/lampp/lampp security`. You will then be asked to assign passwords for the operation of the individual components.

Under Windows, you can find a security check on the XAMPP start page. There you will find a link through which you can assign the necessary passwords.

More complex websites (e.g. wikis) generally require further processing of data. This is done with small programs called scripts. If you request a PHP or Perl script via a browser (usually identifiable by the .php or .pl extension), the web server first runs the program and then sends the generated output back to the browser. Scripts can, in turn, send queries to the MySQL database and thus read and further process data.

XAMPP start page

Once you are at the XAMPP start page, you will be asked to select your language (via a link). Then you will reach the actual XAMPP overview page. For the purposes of this book, only a few options are relevant. Under **Status**, you can see which components are active. Of course, it is important that MySQL and PHP have been activated. If this is not the case, an error has occurred during installation, and you should repeat the procedure. Under the heading **Tools** you will find the program phpMyAdmin, with which you can easily administer your database via the web interface (see Fig. 2.2).

Test environment

The files of your own homepage can be stored in the directory *xampp/htdocs* under Windows and */opt/lampp/htdocs* under Linux. This is the standard directory that Apache accesses when reacting to

Fig. 2.2

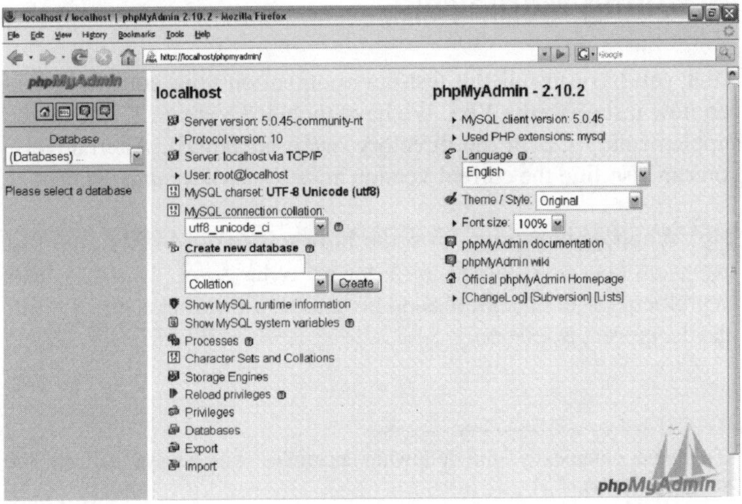

a query. In order to test this, create the subdirectory *xampp/htdocs/test* or *lampp/htdocs/test*[2]. Now, open the text editor and save the following HTML code as *index.php* in the test folder.

HTML

```
<html>
  <head>
    <title>This is a test</title>
  </head>
  <body>
    <p>Your own pages are displayed here
    <p><?php echo "PHP running" ?>
  </body>
</html>
```

If you now access the address *http://localhost/test* in the browser, the file you have just created should be displayed. If the PHP output is also visible, then the installation has been successful.

Caution: Sometimes a file may be saved with an incorrect extension – e.g. with .htm instead of .php or vice versa. Under Windows, when attempting to rename the file, the error often occurs that the operating system automatically adds the old program extension. You can eliminate this in Windows XP, for example, by going to `Control Panel` → `Tools` → `Folder options` → `View` and deactivating (unchecking) the option **"Hide extensions for known file types"**.

2.2 Installing MediaWiki

Copy files

After you have installed a test environment on your computer, you can now install MediaWiki. We have included Version 1.10.1 on the supplementary CD in the directory */wikis/mediawiki*. Alternatively, you can also find the current version at *http://www.mediawiki.org*.

Tip: When downloading, in some browsers (e.g. Mozilla), the file extension may be renamed from .tar.gz to .tar.gz.tar. This may lead to problems with decompression programs. Thus, make sure the file has the correct extension.

[2] To avoid complexity, the following examples will always indicate the "xampp" version.

2.2.1
Version 1: Local System

Copy the compressed file to the directory *xampp/htdocs* and unpack it with FilZip[3] under Windows. Under Linux, use the command

```
tar xvzf mediawiki-1.10.1.tar.gz
```

Shell

The directory *mediawiki-1.10.1* will be created.

Tip: If, instead of finding the directory, you see the file *mediawiki-1.10.1.tar*, just unpack it again.

To facilitate accessing the program, we recommend renaming the directory "mediawiki".

Linux: assign rights

If you are working with Linux, you'll need to make the directory *mediawiki/config* writable. The best way to do this is under *mediawiki* with the command

```
chmod a+w config
```

Shell

Setup via browser

To obtain updated information, first read the *README* file in the directory *mediawiki*. Then, to set up your wiki using the browser of your choice, enter the address of the installation directory; in our case, it is

```
http://localhost/mediawiki
```

URL

This is the address under which we will subsequently access the wiki. You'll first only see the message **"Please set up the wiki up first"**. You can find out how to complete the installation in the section after the next (Chap. 2.2.4).

2.2.2
Version 2: Installation on a Web Host

To install MediaWiki in the Internet, you first need an address (URL) and storage space on the Net. So-called web hosts can provide one. We assume that you have FTP access to your web space. In addition, in order to operate MediaWiki, you will also need to be able to access a MySQL database and run PHP scripts.

[3] You can find this program on the CD under */tools/filzip*.

Unpack the compressed wiki archive to your hard drive, on a temporary directory called *mediawiki*. This creates a directory structure, and the data will be directly stored in the correct location. Now load the entire folder via FTP to the web folder of your web host. This is usually the folder you first access when you connect to your FTP server.

Now check the properties of the *mediawiki/config* folder on your web server. It must authorize writing capabilities for all users. If this is not set properly, you can change the properties directly with most FTP programs and make the folder writable.

For further installation, you will also need the access data to your database. This data includes information on the URL of the MySQL server, the name of the database, the database username and the accompanying password. If you have this information at hand, you can start the browser-supported installation by entering the URL of your homepage followed by "mediawiki", such as in this example:

URL `http://www.wiki-tools.de/mediawiki`

2.2.3 Transferring a Local System to the Webhost

Once you have prepared the wiki locally and want to transfer it to the webhost, you need to execute three steps:

1. Copy the files from the local Mediawiki directory into the webhost directory where the wiki is to be executed.
2. Transfer the database. The easiest way to do so is with phpmyadmin, which you can open locally under *http://localhost/phpmyadmin*. Select the database on the right (probably "mediawiki") and click on the **Export** tab above. Select all tables in the list box directly under **Export** and check the **Send** box. Then click on **OK**. Now you will be offered the option of downloading a file containing the database. In the next step, you have to import the database to the webhost. Most hosts also provide phpmyadmin. Open the target database and click on the **SQL** tab. There, you will find a "File" box where you can insert the database file just created using the **Search** button. Subsequently, click on **OK** and the database will be imported.
3. Now you still need to adjust the settings file *LocalSettings.php* to the new circumstances. You will find the relevant information under `$wgScriptPath`. Here, the path relative to your web directory must be entered. Finally, adjust the database parameters

by entering the data of the new database, that is, server name, database name, user name and password of the database, after `$wgDBserver`, `$wgDBname`, `$wgDBuser` and `$wgDBpassword` accordingly.

Now the page should run on the web server.

2.2.4 Completing the Installation in the Browser

You still have to complete a few settings before being able to work with your wiki. MediaWiki is very user-friendly in this regard, since all entries can be made via the browser. Just follow the link **Please setup the wiki first** with which you can access the installation page (see Fig. 2.3).

Checking the system environment

The script will first test your system environment to determine whether the existing software and its settings are suitable for the operation of MediaWiki. If the message **Environment check. You can install MediaWiki** appears at the end of the checklist, you can continue without worry.

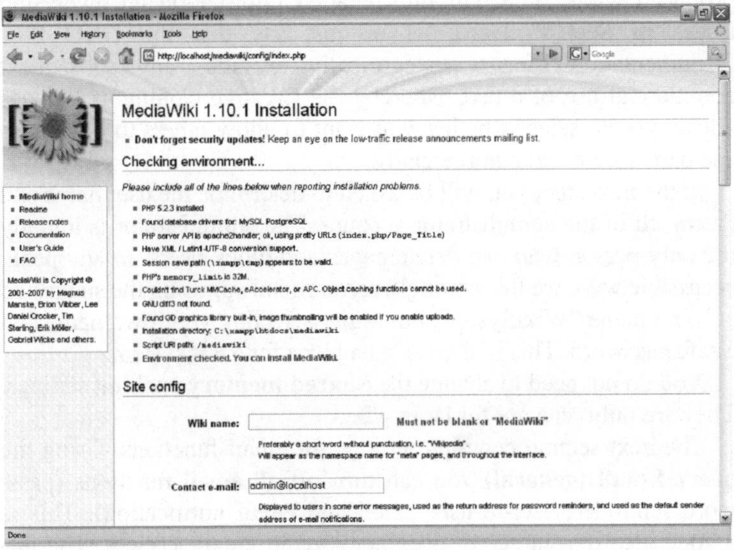

Fig. 2.3

Naming your Wiki
The name of your wiki

In the next section of the installation page, you will be asked to provide some information on your new wiki. Some of these settings cannot be subsequently changed. This especially applies to the name of the wiki. It should thus be selected well. Good names are relatively short and to the point, e.g. TribeWiki. If you wish to use more than one word, you can use a WikiWord, by writing the words together with the initial letters capitalized, which, in the case of MediaWiki, however, only has symbolic meaning.

Caution: Be careful with periods and special characters! Since some of them have special functions in wikis, their use in a title can lead to problems; they should thus be avoided.

Contact

Next, you should indicate an email address as a contact to which the MediaWiki can send a message in the event of a system error. In addition, forgotten passwords can also be sent from that address, meaning it is possible that users will use the address to direct questions to you.

Language

In the next field, you can set the wiki language. Depending on what audience you wish to address and, above all, how international your group is, you may need to consider what language your wiki will be in if English is not your first choice. The character code Unicode (UTF-8) is used for all languages.

License

Now you can decide on the license that will govern your wiki pages. For an open wiki, it is not advisable to leave the question of licensing open, especially so as to avoid abuse of collectively produced wikis. You will find detailed information on ownership issues in Sect. V. Here, let us just say that the GNU Free Documentation License categorically excludes any subsequent commercial use of a text, whereby the Creative Commons License allows you to select whether you want to allow others to be able to use parts of the text commercially.

Administrator account

In the next step, you will be asked to determine the user name and password of the administrator account. The administrator is initially the only person who can delete pages and block users. In an openly accessible wiki, we thus strongly recommend *not* using the suggested account name "WikiSysop", but rather selecting your own name and a safe password. This is also not a bad idea for a test system.

You do not need to change the **Shared memory caching** settings. They are only relevant for large wikis.

The next section contains settings for email functions. Using the query **Email (general)** you can turn off all email functions (password reminder, user-to-user email and email notification). This is a good idea if your server does not support email services. The following queries will allow you to individually activate or deactivate these functions. It is best to leave the default settings as they are.

Email functions

The function **User-to-user email** generally lets you send mail to other users. With **Email notification**, you can allow all wiki users to find out about changes to their private discussion page (user talk) and the pages they are watching. **Email authentication** checks the email addresses of users. Users who enter their email addresses for the first time or alter them will receive a test email containing a link with which they can confirm the receipt of that test email. As soon as this function has been set up, only authorized users can receive email notifications and mails from other users.

Database information

In the last section, you still need to provide information regarding the database. In our case, select **MySQL**. Under **Database host**, enter the address of the database server. In most cases, this will be "localhost". In the following fields, enter the database information. If you are installing the wiki at a provider site, these addresses are pre-assigned. In a test system or if you have access to the administrator account of the database, you can also use these fields to directly set up a new database including users. To do so, enter the name of the new database in the field **Database name** and the name of the user that is to have access to the database in the field **DB user**. It is important to type in and repeat a password for the database to be created (**DB password**). If you are generating a new database, you have to place a check mark in front of **Use Superuser Account** and enter the corresponding data. In the XAMMP system, this is "root" with no password. Now the MediaWiki setup program can easily access the software and generate the necessary database and tables. Of course, the root password should never be left blank on a server on the Net; such an account would have the right to delete you entire database, for instance. An extra **Database table prefix** is only necessary if you wish to run more than one MediaWiki in the same database. The settings pertaining to **Database charset** should be left as they are. The two additional options are still in the experimental stage and can lead to display problems.

Tip: If you do not have access to your own server but are installing Wiki at a web host, you must first set up a database. In this case, you will receive the access data to be entered from your web host.

Complete installation

When you press the **Install MediaWiki!** button, the necessary settings will be made. If this has been successful, a further page will appear showing information on your current configuration. You will see a confirmation message at the end. Now you are almost done! The last task is to copy the file *LocalSettings.php*, which is located in the directory *xampp/htdocs/mediawiki/config*, to the directory *xampp/htdocs/mediawiki*, located one level higher. This step is necessary because, for security reasons regarding scripts under Linux, we have only set up write permissions in the config directory, and thus can only do the automatic settings here.

Open MediaWiki

After you have copied that file, follow **this link** or open the Wiki URL in the browser. You should now see an unadulterated MediaWiki before you with the heading "Getting started" and a few links. These will lead to pages that can provide help in working with your wiki (see Fig. 3.1).

3 First Steps

Before we go into more detail about the opportunities offered by MediaWiki, let us provide you in the following chapter with a general impression of what it is like to work with the wiki.

3.1 The Wiki at First Glance

Description of the main page

At first glance, the start page hardly differs from a normal WWW page. The wiki is in view mode. The display can be divided into four areas (see Fig. 3.1):

Fig. 3.1

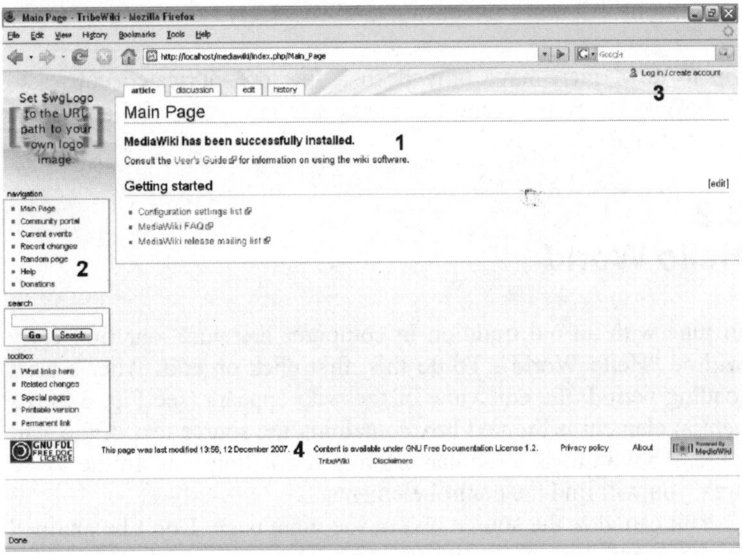

- **Work area (1)**. The core of the wiki. This is where the actual content of an entry, which can be edited by anyone, is displayed. The form in edit mode and the difference and version numbers are also displayed in this area.
- **Navigation, search and tools (2)**. This area enables access to the articles according to various aspects. The image at the top left serves as a link to the main page. A few other functions can also be invoked from here.
- **User area (3)**. Login for registered users. They can enter personal settings or access pages they have edited.
- **Information (4)**. Shows a variety of information about the page, as well as licenses that apply to this wiki.

Work area

Let us have a closer look at the work area. It contains all significant elements of a wiki. Here, all actions take place that can be performed on a page. It can be further divided into:

- **Tabs**. They provide the important functions for editing a page. It is the home of the most important wiki link: **edit**.
- **Page title**. The title describes the content of a page in one or two words. It also indicates which mode is currently active.
- **Content**. All users can design this area freely.

Up to now, there have only been a few pre-fabricated entries to TribeWiki. Now it is time to breathe life into your wiki and make a few changes.

3.2 Hello World

First entry

In tune with an old tradition in computer literature, our first entry will be "Hello World". To do this, first click on **edit**. After a brief loading period, the edit view of the wiki appears (see Fig. 3.2). Its central element is the text box containing the source text of the start page. Above this is a toolbar offering formatting aids. In the lower area, you will find the control elements.

You can alter the source text of the main page. Don't be alarmed by the cryptic look of the existing text. This is simply due to formatting tags. Position the cursor on the place in the text box in which the change is to be made (e.g. between the first line and the first paragraph) and type

```
Hello World!
```

Wiki

If you then click on **Save page**, your entries will be transferred to the wiki, and the normal view will once again appear, only now it will display your text.

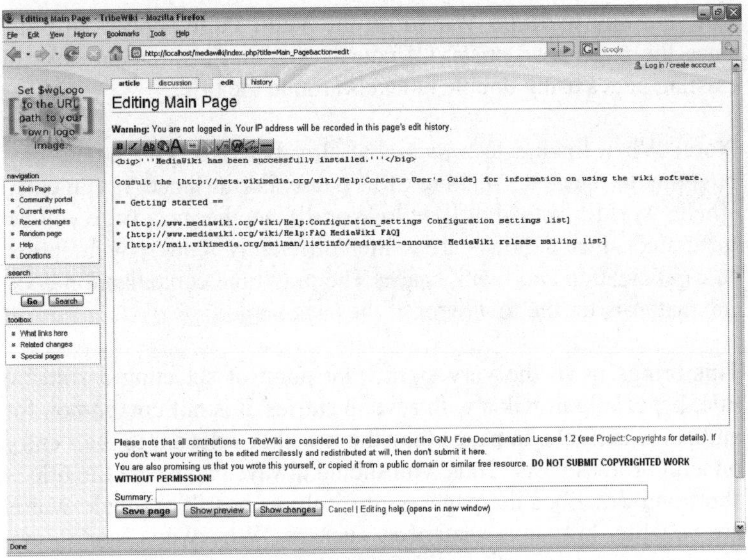

Fig. 3.2

Create new page

One important aspect of the wiki principle is that every user can generate his or her own page. Thus, our next goal is to generate the page *Hello World*. It is not absolutely necessary, but still a good idea, to link a new page with the other pages of the wiki. Thus we will first create a link to *Hello World*. For this, we once again switch to edit mode. Now, enter the following anywhere:

```
[[Hello World]]
```

Wiki

and save the page. The double brackets cause the phrase "Hello World" to be interpreted by the wiki software as a link to the page **Hello World**, and a corresponding link is displayed on the **Main Page**. Since the page does not yet exist, it is colored red. If you now click to switch to **Hello World**, the edit view is automatically displayed. Here, you can once again enter any text. After you have saved it, you will see the newly created page. In order to return to the **Main Page**, click on the sunflower on the upper left, which will subsequently be replaced by a logo of your choice.

Tip: Try to avoid using the Back button as much as possible. Many browsers employ page caches to shorten loading times, so you may receive an obsolete version of the page. In the worst case, the browser may send the form data from the edit mode again, and any new changes would be overwritten.

Now the link to **Hello World** on the **Main Page** appears in blue, since the page now exists. Of course, you can also create links to existing pages using double brackets around the title.

Note: When linking to a page that already exists, you should pay attention to the exact spelling of its name. For instance, if you enter [[hello world]] instead of [[Hello World]], another new page will be generated, since the links are written differently. Thus, pay attention to capitalization and blank spaces.The only time capitalization does not matter is for the first letter of the page name.

Title selection

This brings us to the very significant point of selecting a suitable title. Especially in wikis with several entries, it is not uncommon for authors to set links to pages they think will be relevant to their entry on a hit or miss basis. Thus, you should always make sure the title is short and describes the page as precisely as possible. Single words are suitable, but short sentences, such as "Why wikis work", can also be useful names. In addition, succinct page title names facilitate user orientation and article searches.

3.3 Initial Formatting

Both tasks described above represent the basis for working in a wiki. Principally, you can use them to take part in the generation and editing of a collaboratively administered page. However, the pages we have created up to now still look quite sparse, since we have completely ignored formatting and layout.

Formatting in a wiki

Although wikis are designed such that users need not busy themselves with layout questions, it is of course often desirable or helpful in understanding a text if options for highlighting and formatting text are available. They certainly do exist in MediaWiki. Since, however, entries are purely text-based, formatting cannot be immediately implemented, as is the case with a word processing system in a graphic interface. Rather, you must tell the wiki software that certain words are to receive special emphasis by using special character combinations.

To give you an idea of how the formatting method in a wiki works, first generate a test page as described in Chap. 3.2. We have chosen the name **Format Test** for our test page. Now enter the following text:

```
Flying Sparks Tribal Initiative
The purpose of this page is firstly, to
provide up-to-date information and secondly,
to coordinate our work.
We need YOU!
```

When you save the page as is, you will notice that even the sparse formatting in the text has been lost. This is because in MediaWiki, as in HTML, so-called whitespace, that is, characters that are not displayed (such as blank spaces and line feeds), are initially ignored.

Paragraphs

In order to insert a paragraph, you need to insert an extra blank line in the source code:

```
F Flying Sparks Tribal Initiative

The purpose of this page is firstly, to
```

Italics

To lend the last sentence more verve, let's put it in italics. To mark text in italics, embed it in two apostrophes both before and after the area to be italicized:

```
F ''We need YOU!''
```

Bold

Strongly emphasized words in a text are generally set in bold type. This is done in MediaWiki using three apostrophes:

```
to '''coordinate''' our work.
```

Underlining is not one of the formatting options, because this type of emphasis is used to indicate links on the WWW, and confusion can be avoided by refraining from its use.

Headings

Headings are another simple way to add structure to your text. You can generate them by surrounding the respective text in double equal signs:

```
==Flying Sparks Tribal Initiative==
The purpose of this page is firstly, to
```

Since a heading is always on its own line, you do not need to mark the beginning of a new paragraph by inserting a blank line.

Lists

Lists are very useful layout elements, because they can be employed for quickly generated outlines or brainstorming texts to add structure. Lists are easy to generate. Place a star at the point in the text where a bullet should appear:

Wiki

```
The purpose of this page is
* firstly, to provide up-to-date information and
* secondly, to '''coordinate''' our work.
```

The result of our newly designed page can be seen in Fig. 3.3. Of course, MediaWiki offers many more text layout options, which we will discuss in detail in Chap. 5.

Fig. 3.3

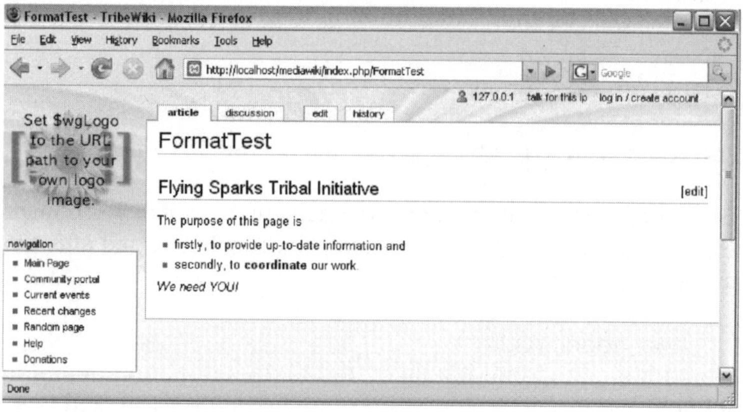

3.4 Vive la Difference: Versions

View history

You probably saved your changes more than once during the last section. If not, make another change to your text and save it. Generally, a wiki enables at least recent versions to be viewed. Click on the **History/Authors** tab. You will see a list of all former versions of the article and who edited them. If you click on a date, the respective version will be displayed. Here, for example, you can access the logbooks containing information on blocked pages, moved pages, rights, etc. for those specific pages. You also can use the History function of a page to undo changes. Simply open the desired older version, switch to edit mode and save it. You will have then performed a so-called rollback and turned the old page into the new page.

View differences

If you click on **current** ("cur") in any line, it will bring you to the difference ("diff") display. This shows you the differences between the current version and the version you select (see Fig. 3.4). Especially in the case of lengthy texts, you can quickly determine which areas have been modified.

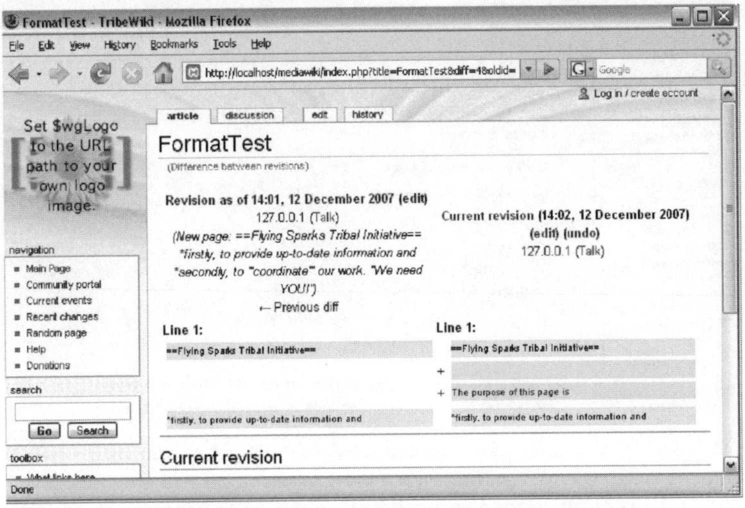

Fig. 3.4

Recent changes

Now, click on the page **Recent changes** in the navigation bar. Our page **Format Test** is also listed here. This function page not only shows the changes to a specific page, but also generates an overview of all articles in the wiki that have been recently revised.

3.5 Registering as a User

On the last stop on our tour, we advise establishing a user account. A few of the actions described below can only be undertaken by registered users. In addition, it is considered proper etiquette in an open wiki to make yourself known if you are editing articles.

Create a user account

In the upper right corner of the screen, you will see a link to create an account or log in. Follow it to reach the registration form. Click on **Create new account**. Under **User name**, select and enter a name, then select a **Password**. You must retype the password on the next line to rule out typing errors. You should also enter your email address under **Your email**, so that your password can be sent to you, should you forget it. If you like, you can enter your real name. If you now click on the button **Create new account**, you will then be registered as a new user, and logged in as well. You can verify this by looking at the upper right where the "Create an account" button had been; in its place is now a series of links, the first one being a link to a page with your user name. (see Fig. 3.5).

Fig. 3.5

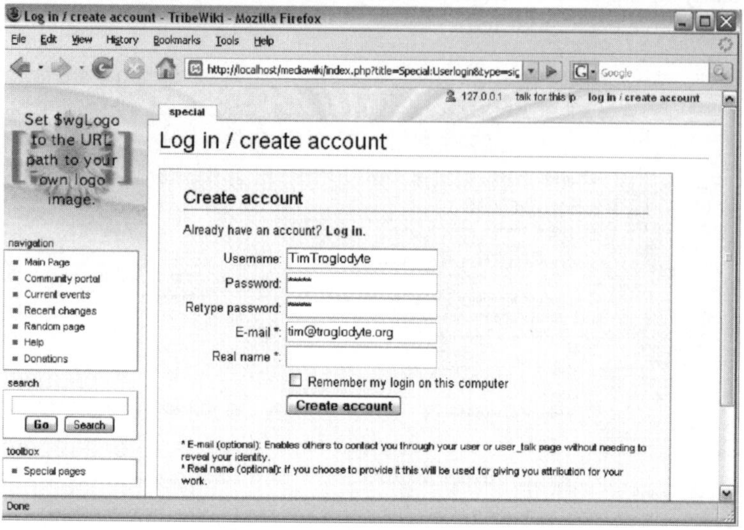

Logging in and out

You will remain logged in until you close your browser or specifically log out (also at the top). On your next visit, you need only to enter your user name and password; the system knows the rest. The setting **Remember my password** is only appropriate if you are the only person using your computer; otherwise, someone else could log in under your name and submit articles to the wiki. When you activate this option, your password will be encoded and stored in a cookie. If you do not place a check mark at this option, you will have to log back in after a certain period of inactivity. To cancel the permanent login option, simply log out explicitly using the **Log out** link.

4 The Core Functions of MediaWiki

The following will illustrate the main functions of a wiki. This will be done step by step, using the tab pages, which enable various types of access to a respective page. Which tabs are visible and thus accessible depend on your status within the wiki. Thus, registered users and administrators have access to more functions than anonymous users.

4.1 Editing

Editing window and toolbox

When you click on the **edit** tab, the edit mode of an article is invoked; that is, the text on the page is loaded along with the wiki-specific format characters ("tags") in an editing window, and can now be manually modified or supplemented.

Note: For lengthy texts, it is also possible to edit it in sections by inserting Level 2 headings into the text (see Table 4.1). In this case, you will find the edit button to the right of the section heading.

Above the window, a toolbox also appears that can be of use when formatting text. It works in roughly the same way as in a graphic word processing program. You highlight the text to be formatted and activate the desired tool. The software initially only sets the corresponding tags around the highlighted text. As in manual editing, you won't see the effects until you select **Preview** or after saving it.

Toolbox functions

The functions of the toolbox are as follows (the second column shows the tag inserted by the corresponding tool):

Tab. 4.1

Image	Replacement	Function
	'''bold'''	Text appears bold.
	''italics''	Text appears in italics.
	[[wiki page]]	Links to an internal wiki page.
	[www.google.de]	Links to an external page on the WWW.
	==Heading 2==	Text appears as a Heading 2.
	[[image: example.jpg]]	Integrates an image previously loaded in the wiki (see Chap. 6.3)
	[[Media: example.mp3]]	Links to a previously loaded media file, e.g. an audio or video file.
	$$	Mathematical formulas in LaTeX can be placed within the set tags.
	<nowiki> </nowiki>	Any existing format instructions are not executed within these tags.
	--~~~~	Depending upon whether you are logged in or not, this function inserts your IP address or user name and a date stamp.
	----	Inserts a horizontal line.

Generally, in the editing window, you also have access to an **Editing help** page, which you can access by clicking on the link of the same name. Unfortunately, this page is not yet filled with content in MediaWiki, and is thus awaiting your constructive assistance (see Chap. 2).

Cancel edit mode

By the way, you can leave the edit mode at any time by clicking on the **Cancel** link. This will display the page in its previous state without integrating any of your changes.

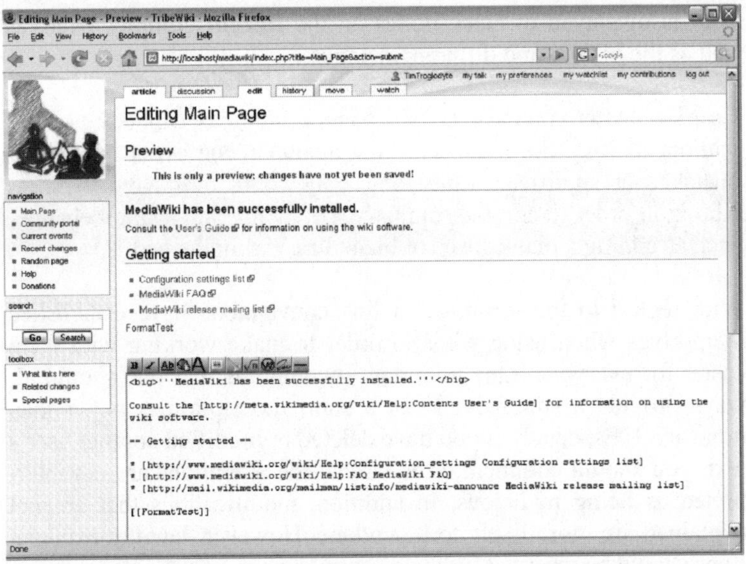

Fig. 4.1

Preview

If you are not sure whether your formatting efforts have had the desired effect, you can view the results with the **Show preview** button without the changes being saved (see Fig. 4.1[4]).

Generally, the preview is displayed above the editing window. That means you might have to scroll up a bit to see it. You can make further changes in the editing area without having to leave the preview mode.

Caution: Do not click on **edit** again while in preview mode, otherwise you will lose your previous changes!

The preview mode has the advantage that the user receives the opportunity to proofread his text in formatted form, as well as that the history page is not loaded up with documents that are edited repeatedly solely due to faulty formatting or careless mistakes. However, note that the versions displayed in the preview mode are not saved versions. Thus, do not forget to save your work in the proper manner once you are happy with the way it looks.

Summary

If you wish to save your text, you can enter a comment on your text or changes in the Summary box under the editing window. This space has a capacity of 200 characters. Anything longer than that, such as when copying and pasting, will not be included. The sum-

[4] Perhaps you have noticed that we have changed the logo. You can find out how to do this in Sect. 8.1.

mary is displayed in black italics on the **Recent changes** page, as well as the history and differences pages.

Caution: After you have saved a page, a summary cannot be edited without altering the main text area again. In the event of serious mistakes or significant omissions, you would thus have to feign editing in order to edit the summary, i.e. by making a small change, such as adding a blank space or blank line within the text.

Conventions

With regard to the summary, a few conventions have established themselves when using wikis in order to make working with them easier for everyone. One important guideline is that one should always provide a summary. Even a short description is better than none at all. Especially if you have deleted or modified another user's text, you should comment on it, so that the alterations are not interpreted as being malicious. In addition, modifications that are not explained are more likely to be undone. However, lengthy explanations should be reserved for the discussion page.

If you have only added a sentence or two to an article, it is advisable to copy them completely into the summary box.

Tip: Think of an abbreviation to use before the summary that will indicate to everyone that the summary includes all of the modified text, so that people will not have to go through the trouble of looking up the page on the **Recent changes** page. For example, one common abbreviation used at Wikipedia is `ft` for "full text".

Minor edit

Registered users additionally have the option of defining their modifications as **minor edits**, i.e. to indicate relatively insignificant changes, such as in correcting a typing error or making any formatting changes. Before saving, simply mark the box next to **This is a minor edit** below the summary.

On the other hand, there are major edits that mainly affect the content of the article. These suggest to the user that it is worthwhile to look at the modifications, since a significant development of the text has taken place. This may even be the case if only one word is changed.

Differentiation between minor and major edits is relevant, since registered users have the option of hiding unimportant alterations on the **Recent changes** page via their personal settings. The decision as to whether modifications are major or minor is, of course, a subjective one, and may lead to readers missing out on important information. That is why you should think carefully about how other users would assess your modifications. It is for good reason that this function is unavailable to non-registered users, to prevent abuse.

Tip: If you have saved alterations as being minor by mistake, we advise just feigning an editing procedure and making a note in the summary that the previous edit was significant.

4.2 Discussions

Discussion page

The content of a respective article can be discussed on the discussion page. When working jointly on a text, the need for a content-based discussion will inevitably arise, especially if participants do not yet know each other: Any misunderstandings must be eliminated or ambiguities debated. Since this communication is very important but – as we know from dealing with forums – can often be very tedious and have little constructive value, it is taken out of the actual text and placed into a discussion page. Furthermore, the content on an article page reflects the current consensus of that topic. Users only wishing to read the article to gain information (such as in the encyclopedic entries of Wikipedia) are usually not interested in a discussion of the further development of the topic.

Taking part in discussions

The discussion pages can be edited in (almost) the same way as the article pages: If you go to **Edit**, you can modify comments already written. However, this function is of little use for discussions that are to be easy to follow for subsequent users and thus must be documented. By clicking on the plus sign in one of the tabs in discussion mode, you can immediately add to the discussion without needing to load all previous comments to the editing window. A subject heading appears under the toolbox. If you enter text here, this heading appears as a second-degree heading to your discussion entry, which is added after the other comments. This creates a structure very similar to that of a forum. However, remember that one of the greatest advantages of a wiki is that you can edit the entire text. Thus, if you have comments regarding a specific entry that has been discussed further up on the page, you should place your comment directly under that entry. Only new ideas or participation in a current discussion should be included with the "+" function.

4.3 Comparisons

History page

When you click on the **History/authors** tab, you can view the development process of a text from the most recent modification to the first time the article was saved, i.e. its history. Deleted pages, which are no longer visible and may only be accessed by administrators, are the exception to this rule (see Chap. 8.2). Each line represents a former version, and includes various additional information, such as the point in time in which the text was saved. The versions can be compared in a variety of combinations.

Fig. 4.2

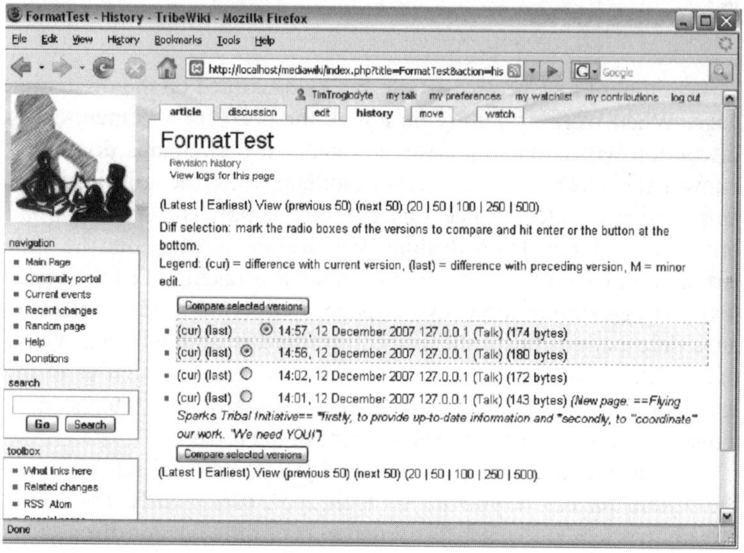

The lines are constructed as follows:

- If you click on the beginning of a line, that is, on **(cur)**, you will get a comparison of the respective version and the current article.
- If you click on **(last)**, you will see a comparison of the version in that line with the preceding version (in the line below it). Thus you will only see the changes made by the participant that generated that edit.
- Using the radio buttons, you can mark any two versions and view the differences between them by clicking on the **Compare selected versions** button at the bottom of the list.
- The radio buttons are followed by the time and date when the edit was saved. They lead directly to the previous version.
- If the originator of the edit is logged in, you can then see his or her name which leads to the respective user page. Otherwise, only the IP address is visible.
- If an author has provided a summary of his edit, it appears at the end of the line in italics and brackets. It is not linked.

Above and below the version list, you will find the button **Compare selected versions**, with which you can compare the versions you have marked to the smallest detail. The result is displayed on its own page (see Fig. 3.4). On the left, the older version is shown, and on the right, the newer one. Only those lines are displayed in which modifications were made, whereby the text highlighted in yellow is deleted data, and the green lines represent newly added text. Under that display, you will find the newest of the two texts again in full.

Diff page

If a page has been moved, that is, if its name has been changed (see below), the entire history of the article before and after the renaming is displayed on the history page, however the act of renaming the article itself is not listed. This is only visible in the history of the page with the old title.

Moved pages

One action often performed is reverting to an older version of an article (e.g. due to vandalism), called a rollback. To do this, on the diff page, open the version to which you want to revert. If you wish to make that version the current article and thus undo all subsequent versions, go to **edit** and then **save page**.

Rollback

Note: The entries to the history page are not deleted; thus a subsequent user could also roll back your rollback.

When you view an old version, you will see two arrows under the heading with which you can jump to the previous or subsequent version.

4.4 Moving and Renaming

Sometimes it is necessary to rename a page, e.g. if the name has been misspelled or does not comply with the stipulated conventions for names, or if the scope of the article has changed. In this regard, the terms **move** and **rename** mean one and the same, because when you change the name of a page, links to that page, which are generated using the name of the page, become invalid. Thus, the page has been moved.

Renaming pages

Open the page you wish to rename and activate the **move** tab. You can enter the new name in the space provided. By clicking on the Options field, you can also determine that the corresponding discussion page be moved, as well. Once you have verified the move by clicking the **move** button, the page is renamed and, at the same time, the old page becomes a **redirect** page, i.e., all links leading to it are automatically forwarded to the new page.

Fig. 4.3

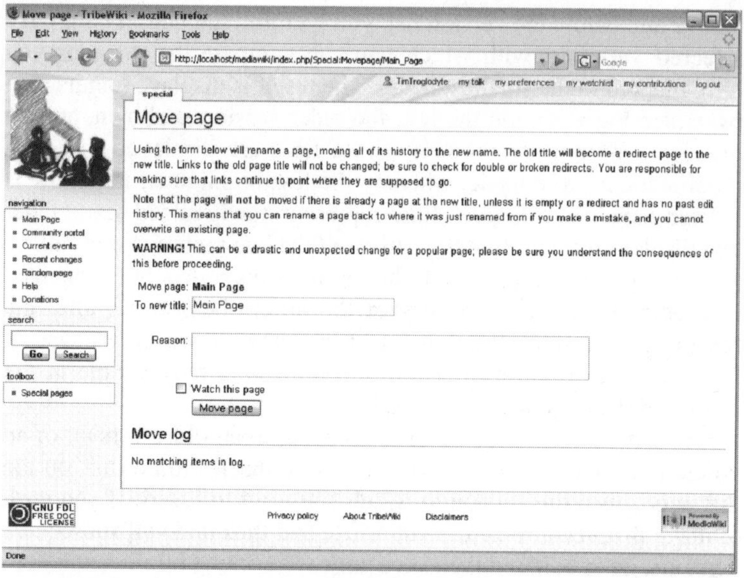

Tip: The **Move** function ensures that the entire history of the page before and after the renaming remains traceable. The alternative, namely cutting out a text and placing it into a new page, has the crucial disadvantage that the previous development of the page can no longer be traced. If this procedure is nevertheless necessary, e.g. if the content of a title is divided, it is advisable to note in the comments where you have obtained the text.

Rolling back a move

If you wish to roll back the move of article A to B, that is, if you wish to give the page its old title, this is only possible if the redirect page has not been edited in the meanwhile. In such a case, move B back to A and have an administrator delete B so that not too many redirects remain in the wiki.

Tip: In order to continue to be able to use the old name of the file for the new content, we recommend a switch. For this, you'll need an interim page which can be deleted once you are finished with it. First move A to Z, then B to A, and finally, Z to B.

4.5 Watching

As a logged-in user, you will see a tab at the top of the wiki pages called **watch**. When you click this tab, the current page and respec-

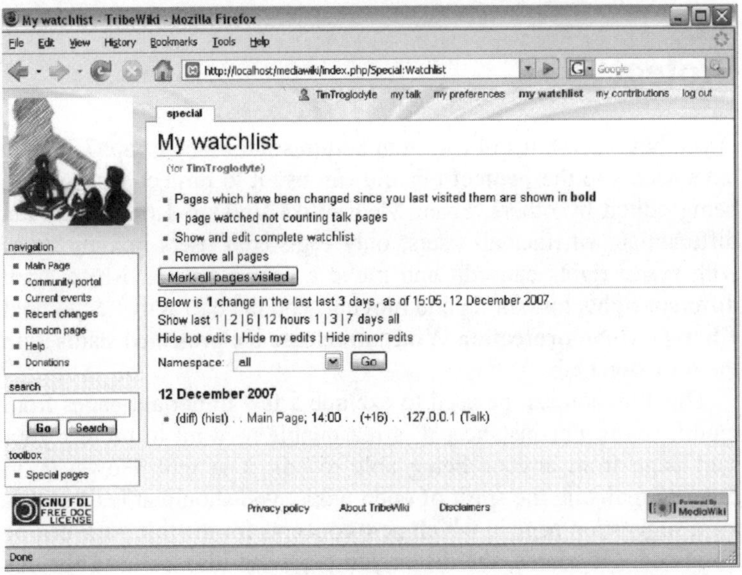

Fig. 4.4

tive discussion page are added to a list of articles in whose development you are particularly interested. The tab then changes to read **unwatch**, and by clicking it, you can delete the page again from your watchlist.

You can open your personal watch page via the Special Pages list or the **my watchlist** link in the top row of links. The watchlist functions the same way as the **recent changes** list, except that only the pages you have selected to watch are included. Modifications to those pages are listed from the most recent edit back to a certain time limit.

Every line shows details about the most recent editing procedure: the date, whether it was a minor edit, a link to the page, the difference to the last version, the user name and summary. Currently, there is no option to hide minor edits here.

Using the link **Show and edit complete list**, you can display all watched pages and edit the complete list.

Tip: In the **Recent changes** list, watched pages are displayed in bold lettering. Thus, even if you never look at your watchlist, setting watch status can still be worthwhile.

4.6 Protect

If you have the status of a system administrator (see Chap. 7.3), you have access to the **protect** tab and can use it to protect a page from being edited by others. From MediaWiki Version 1.6 on, you can differentiate whether all users, only registered users or only those with sysop rights can edit and move a page. If you wish to grant different rights for editing and moving, you have to activate the field **Change Move protection**. You can release the protected status with the **unprotect** tab.

Important pages

This function can be used to exclude a few important pages from modification. For instance, it is reasonable to want to protect your start page from anyone being able to edit it at will. However, in order to maintain the spirit of open wikis, you should at least generate a suggestion page in which new concepts for the title page can be discussed. Of course, the discussion page can also be used for this purpose.

Fig. 4.5

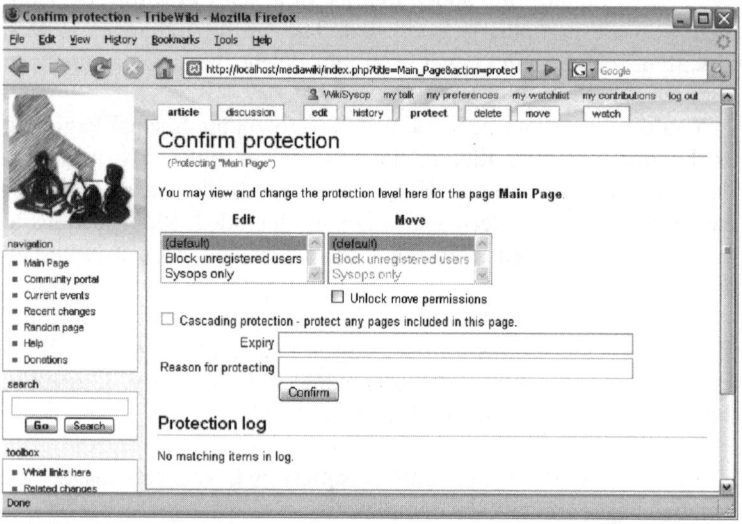

Protection from vandalism

Unfortunately, it is also necessary on occasion to prevent modifications to a page temporarily if differences of opinion on its content have heated to the point where constructive work on the article is no longer possible. Since such blocks are always at the discretion of an administrator, at least two participants should have administrator status, in order to avoid centralist tendencies (the "dual control principle").

4.7 Deleting

Administrators can remove pages and their complete history with the **delete** command. Such pages are placed into an archive and are no longer accessible over the WWW. However, they are only removed from the database when specifically deleted by a sysop (see Chap. 7.2). The deleting of pages should be done with the utmost of care, since one is generally dealing with a work authored by several participants, who, under certain circumstances, would not be happy to discover that their contributions have been removed from the wiki. There is often a page in wikis where potential "delete candidates" are suggested and discussed before an administrator may remove them from a wiki (with "may" we refer to a social, not a technical, limitation). Good delete candidates include the redirect pages mentioned above, which are generated when pages are moved.

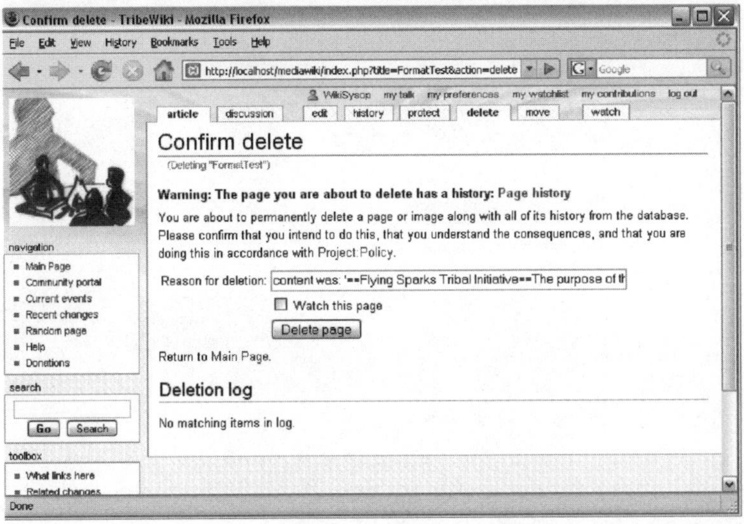

Fig. 4.6

5 Formatting

In addition to standard emphasis in the form of **bold** and *italics* cited above, you can utilize a series of further options in MediaWiki, even if the possibilities of formatting with wikis are clearly not comparable to those of conventional word processing programs such as Word. In addition, there is no WYSIWYG ("What You See Is What You Get") in the standard installation; that is, the formatting is set, as is the case in HTML or LaTeX, in the form of tags, i.e. ASCII characters in editing mode, and is only visible after saving it.

The formatting codes can be divided into two major types. The first are tags that are very similar to HTML codes and work in the same way. That is to say, you place the text to be formatted between an initial and a final symbol, such as `<b>Text</b>`, which displays the word "Text" in bold. On the other hand, one can also set wiki-specific markers that precede the text or surround it. It does not matter which type of symbols you use; the only difference is that the wiki-specific tags cannot be used for text spanning more than one line, whereas HTML tags can.

5.1 Formatting Characters

Bold + italics

As mentioned, two apostrophes before and after the text to be formatted italicizes the text, and three apostrophes around the text allow it to appear in bold. If you want your text to be both bold and italicized, you simply use five apostrophes.

Wiki

```
'''''coordinate''''' our work.
```

With regard to font and size, the selection is not all too great. In addition to the standard font Verdana, you can make your text Courier by setting it between `<tt>`, which imitates a typewriter font and looks fitting especially for technical explanations.

Wiki

```
firstly, to provide <tt>up-to-date
information</tt>
```

If you would like to generate a caption for a picture or a table or use a small font for any other reason, you can use `<small>` to do so.

Wiki

```
firstly, to provide <small>up-to-date
information</small>
```

Underlining/ striking

The tags are also very handy for striking and underlining passages using `<strike>` and. `<u>`, respectively:

Wiki

```
firstly, to provide <strike>old</strike>, no
<u>up-to-date</u> information
```

Superscript/ subscript

For mathematical expressions, the options `<sup>` for superscript and `<sub>` for subscript are available:

Wiki

```
F<sub>square</sub> = s<sup>2</sup>
```

Instead of `s<sup>2</sup>`, you could also write `s²`. However, this only works for superscript formatting, and here only with numbers as exponents.

5.2 Special Characters & Co.

Now we come to the numerous special characters, punctuation marks, symbols and language-specific diacritics, such as a tilde or accents. As in German umlauts in HTML, these symbols are replaced by a type of letter pattern that always begins with an & and ends with a ; such as the Greek letter sigma: `Σ`.

A complete listing of all special characters would be too extensive; thus, we include only a selection of the most commonly used characters.

Tab. 5.1

Symbol	Code	Symbol	Code	Symbol	Code
à	agrave	ã	atilde	ç	ccedil
á	aacute	ä	auml	ñ	ntilde
â	acirc	å	aring	ø	oslash

We wish to call special attention to the space symbol. It is not possible to generate more than one space with the space bar on the keyboard, because the wiki software only registers one space. Thus, if you wish to add several spaces in a row, you must use the special character ` ` as you would in HTML. This symbol also prevents a line break, which can be very useful when generating formulas. *Space*

You should also use special symbols to generate unusual punctuation:

Tab. 5.2

Symb.	Code	Symb.	Code	Symb.	Code
¿	`iquest`	»	`raquo`	¶	`para`
¡	`iexcl`	§	`sect`	•	`bull`
«	`laquo`	†	`dagger`	–	`mdash`
→	`rarr`	←	`larr`	°	`deg`

In our example, we can now add a new line directly under the heading:

Wiki

```
&dagger;&dagger;&dagger; Our fire is being
taken away &dagger;&dagger;&dagger;
```

And, at the end of the page, the following explanation:

Wiki

```
No fire &rarr; no development
```

Especially in the realm of the natural sciences, we often need Ancient Greek letters. For all symbols that cannot be generated using the Latin alphabet, there are the following conventions:

Tab. 5.3

Symb.	Code	Symb.	Code	Symb.	Code
α	`alpha`	γ	`gamma`	Δ	`Delta`
β	`beta`	Γ	`Gamma`	Θ	`Theta`

As you may have noticed, it is not difficult to figure out what the rest of the characters in the table would look like.

The other components of mathematical formulas can also be generated with special symbols. Here is a small selection of them: *Formulas*

Tab. 5.4

Symb.	Code	Symb.	Code	Symb.	Code
∫	`Int`	∑	`sum`	±	`plusmn`
∏	`prod`	√	`radic`	∞	`infin`

For more complex formulas, you also have the option of employing TeX-Tags that are integrated into the text with $Formula$. These are either converted to HTML or – especially if the characters are too exotic – a PNG image is generated.

<pre> and <nowiki>

Using <pre> and <nowiki>, you have the opportunity of suppressing the formatting of text (with the exception of generating special characters), i.e. allow the conventional formatting tags to remain visible after saving the file. These two functions differ only in the fact that <pre> sets the text in Courier and does not ignore line breaks and series of spaces.

Tab. 5.5

Code	Result
<nowiki>no fire → ''no'' [[development]] </nowiki>	no fire → "no" [[development]]

<pre>no fire
→
''no''
[[development]]</pre>
	no fire
	→
	''no''
	[[development]]

Comments

If you want some of your comments to only be visible in the source text by the subsequent authors, you can mask it by identifying it as comment, as in HTML.

Wiki

```
<!-- unnoticed -->
```

5.3 Headings and Paragraphs

You can establish various levels of headings by surrounding them with the respective number of equal signs:

Wiki

```
=Heading 1=
==Heading 2==
===Heading 3===
```

This results in the following display:

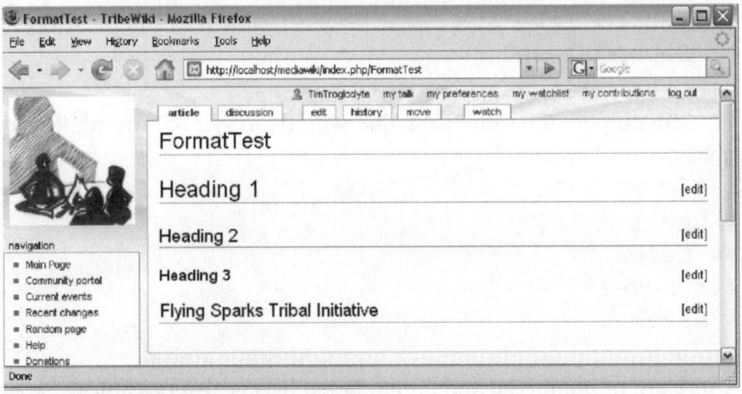

Fig. 5.1

At the same time, headings divide the article into sections which – using the proper setting – can be individually edited and accessed through links.
The headings can be classified in up to six levels, which corresponds to the <hx> tags in HTML. After the headings are formatted, an automatic line break takes place.

Now we can add a little structure to our tribal initiative page:

Wiki

```
= Flying Sparks Tribal Initiative =
== Purpose ==
The purpose of this page is...
== Description ==
no fire ...
== Demands ==
```

Line break/ paragraph

Indent

You can insert a manual line break within the standard text using <br>. This also applies to lists. In order to begin a new paragraph, place a blank space in the source code. You can insert an indentation with a colon at the beginning of the line.

5.4 Lists and Lines

Generating lists in a wiki is much easier than doing so in HTML code.

Unnumbered lists

In the case of unnumbered lists, simply insert a star in front of the corresponding list item. The farther down the level, the more stars are set in front of the paragraph:

Wiki

```
* First level
** Second level
```

```
*** Third level
** Second level
```

Numbered lists

You can employ the same principle with the # symbol for numbered lists:

Wiki

```
# Level 1
## Level 2
### Level 3
# Level 1
```

Mixed lists

A mixture of numbered and unnumbered lists is also possible:

Wiki

```
* Level 1 unnumbered
*# Level 2 numbered
*#* Level 3 unnumbered
*## Level 3 numbered
```

Definition list

If you wish to generate a glossary-like list, the definition list format is the perfect tool. In this case, the term preceding the semi-colon receives special emphasis.

Wiki

```
; Fire: provides energy and light
; Water: can control fire
```

Line

In addition to the possibility of structuring your text with lists, you can also add horizontal lines to your text with the following code:

Wiki

```
Text
----
Text
```

The last lists described are displayed in the following screenshot:

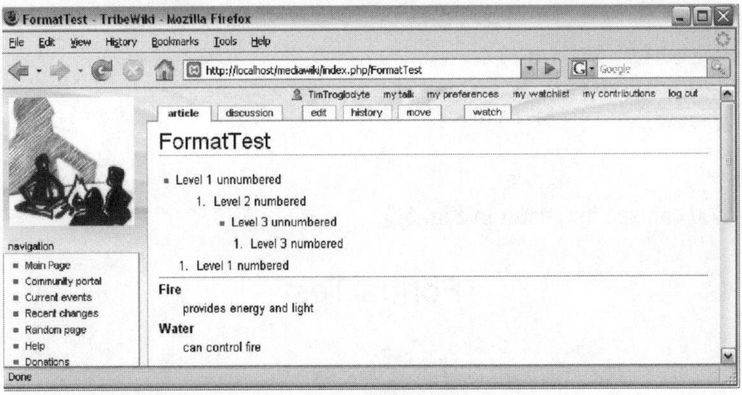

Fig. 5.2

Now we have the means to publish our demands for public access to fire:

```
== Demands ==
# Fire must be accessible to all
# Its exclusive use by
tribal executives is thus not acceptable
# Advanced measures must                       ↵
be undertaken:
** Sufficient supply of fuel
** Hazard control with water
```

5.5 Tables

MediaWiki supports three different kinds of table syntax:

- XHTML
- HTML and wiki-`<td>` syntax
- and so-called pipe syntax

All three methods produce valid HTML code. The following will only focus on the third alternative, pipe syntax, because it is especially simple, space-saving, and it represents an element specific to wiki. Here, the HTML tags are replaced by pipes (|), which results in a table, evident even in edit mode:

```
{|
| cell1 || cell2
```

```
|-
| cell3 || cell4
|-
| cell5 || cell6
|}
```

You can see the result in Fig. 5.3:

Fig. 5.3

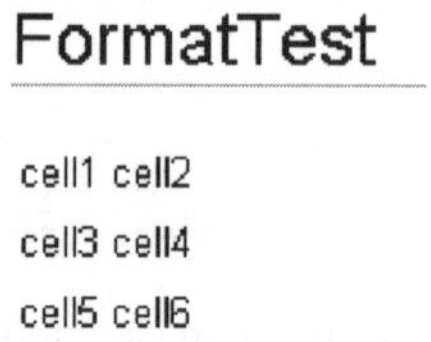

As is the case of HTML, the table is composed of three nesting levels:

Table level: You should always start a table on a new line. It is started using `{| param` and concluded with `|}`. The term `param` stands for optional parameters, such as background color or border thickness.

Caution: You must place a blank space between `{|` and `param`, otherwise the first parameter will be ignored.

Row level: When you initialize a table, the first row is created along with it. Begin the subsequent rows with `|- param`. The row is automatically closed by starting a new row with `|-` or ending the table with `|}`.

Cell level: Cells can be generated in two ways. Either you set two pipes next to each other:

Wiki

```
| cell1 || cell2 || cell3
```

or you combine a new line with the pipe symbol:

Wiki

```
| cell1
| cell2
| cell3
```

The cell parameters, as the table and row levels, are situated behind the pipe symbol, but are separated from the cell content using a further pipe symbol.

```
| param || cell1 || param | cell2
```

Wiki

or

```
| param | cell1
| param | cell2
| param | cell3
```

Wiki

Caution: Every row must have exactly the same amount of cells, so that the number of rows remains constant. You should fill an empty cell with the space code ` `, so that the cell is displayed.

Let us return to the topic of parameters. They are based on HTML and can also be used in their abbreviated forms. Here, too, we differentiate between two levels:

On the table level:

Tab. 5.6

Name	**Function**	**Values**
`align`	horizontal text alignment	left, right, center
`bgcolor`	background color	#000000-#FFFFFF
`border`	border thickness	number
`width`	width	number
`cellpadding`	internal cell spacing	number
`cellspacing`	external cell spacing	number

On the row level:

Tab. 5.7

Name	**Abbr.**	**Function**
`align`	al	horizontal text alignment
`background-color`	bc	background color
`valign`	va	vertical alignment

On the cell level:

Tab. 5.8

Name	Abbr.	Function
align	al	horizontal text alignment
background-color	bc	background color
colspan	cs	several adjacent cells in a row are merged
rowspan	rs	several adjacent cells in a column are merged
valign	va	vertical alignment
width	wd	width

To make your heading or column headings appear in bold, when you open a row, instead of using the pipe symbol, use an exclamation point. Within the row, two pipe symbols before the respective cells are replaced by two exclamation points:

Wiki

```
{|
|-
! Control of !! Water !! Fire !! Both
```

Table heading To give your table a heading, following the table initiation, that is, after the `{|` and any parameters, insert a `|+` and then enter the column names.

Example The following example contains all discussed table elements:

Wiki

```
{| border="1" cellpading="2"
|+Development of Humans
|-
! Control of !! Water !! Fire !! Both
|- align="right"
! primitive
| 70 || 20 || 10
|- align="right"
! average
| 20 || 50 || 30
|- align="right"
! sophisticated
| 10 || 30 || bgcolor="lightgrey" | 60
|}
```

Result:

Fig. 5.4

FormatTest

Development of Humans

Control of	Water	Fire	Both
primitive	70	20	10
average	20	50	30
sophisticated	10	30	60

MediaWiki also allows you to nest tables. To do this, simply start a new table:

```
{| border=1
| Elements ||
{| bgcolor=#ABCDEF border=2
| Fire
|-
| Water
|}
| are especially important.
|}
```

Fig. 5.5

FormatTest

Elements	Fire Water	are especially important.

Let us summarize the most important points regarding tables:

- {| ... | ... | ... |} encloses a table
- |- indicates the begin of a new row
- || separates cells
- `! ... !` displays a table heading
- Parameters following `{|` define the settings for the entire table
- Parameters following `|-` apply to the following row
- Parameters following `|` apply to the individual cell

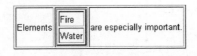

5.6 Table of Contents

A table of contents is automatically generated for articles having more than three headings, unless

- a user's settings are configured differently (see Chap. 7.3)
- the code `__NOTOC__` has been added in the edit box.

The numbering is generated automatically. The table of contents is located before the first heading, yet after any introduction that might be included. However, you can also insert the table of contents in another location with `TOC`.

Fig. 5.6

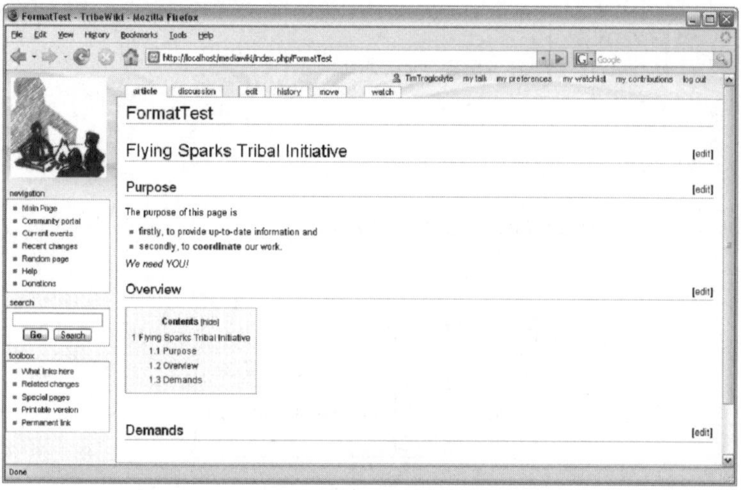

Note: The headings of a template http://meta.wikimedia.org/wiki/template do not appear in the table of contents.

Entries to the table of contents are obtained from the headings of an article.

6 Multi-Page Structures

Up to now, we have dealt with formatting within one page. However, hypertext has the capability of establishing a relationship between various units through links. The type of structuring can vary greatly and has a pivotal influence on the manageability of a hypertext. It facilitates navigation through the pages, since related themes are linked. In addition, embedding an article into a network creates a context that can be helpful in classifying content.

6.1 Linking Methods

There are three levels on which links can be generated in a wiki: "interwiki" links within the wiki, internal links within a page, or external links. We will have a closer look at them below.

Interwiki links

We have already seen interwiki links in Chap. 3.2. They link to pages within a wiki. Thus, it is sufficient to cite the title of a page for such a link. Title pages are always distinct in a wiki; there can never be two pages with the same na me. Remember: An internal link in its simplest form consists of a link target in double brackets:

Wiki

```
[[page title]]
```

Page titles consist of letters and numbers. It is also possible to use special characters. The following symbols, however, may not be used:

```
" # $ * + < > = @ [ ] \ ^ ` { } | ~
```

These characters fulfill special control and layout functions in the wiki source code or in PHP. Spaces may be used. They are stored within the system as an underline. Conversely, this means that underlines that you use in a title will be displayed as spaces.

Naming links

The wiki software takes care of formatting the links. It is assumed that the name of an article is distinct enough to indicate to the reader what the respective page is about. That is why the page title is simply used as the link name. Sometimes, however, it can be useful to have another description. This is the case, for instance, when you have a hierarchical order of pages for which a link "upwards" in the structure facilitates navigation. Also, synonymous descriptions, e.g. "tribe" and "clan", for two different pages should not be used, since they indicate the same thing. The necessary separation between link target and name can be achieved with a so-called "piped link":

Wiki

```
[[page title|description]]
```

As you can see, a horizontal line (pipe symbol) is placed after the page title, behind which you can insert a page description that can consist of one or more words.

Parts of words as links

Within the context of a sentence, a word can have various forms based on the rules of grammar. Since all of these forms link to the same page, the possibility was created to mark only the front part of a word as a link:

Wiki

```
[[Link]]s
```

In Preview mode, however, the whole word is identified as a link. The following construction is a rather exaggerated example.

Wiki

```
[[caves|cave]][[dwelling]]
```

Here, two links are included in a single word. The first part of the word links to "cave", the second to "dwelling". One could surely debate about whether or not such a structure is very useful, especially since, when looking at it, one cannot detect that two different links are embedded in the word. However, the point is that it is possible.

Now it is time to give our wiki example some structure. We can divide the wiki into assorted pages that fulfill various tasks.

Wiki

```
Work areas:
* [[Info booth|Planned information booth]]
* [[Petition|Letter to the chief]]
* [[Summer Festival|Preparation team for the ↵
Summer Festival]]
* [[Material|Link and material collection]]
```

Now, of course, the pages have to be filled with content. Don't forget that, for every page, there is also a discussion page. Thus, on the **Petition** page, you can directly read the current version of the text and make modification suggestions on the discussion page. However, can easily leave that to the members of the tribal initiative.

Internal page links

Especially in large documents, it is a good idea to establish links between elements of the document itself. This is very useful, for instance, when you want to enable readers to be able to jump from an item in a table of contents to the respective portion of the document. Since the page name is the same for internal page links, you will need to define additional link targets within the article. This is a fairly intuitive process in MediaWiki: The sections serve as jump labels. All levels can be used with their names, specified as headings. Internal page links are identified by a hash symbol (#):

Wiki

```
[[page title#section title]]
```

If a link refers to the same page, the page title can and should be left out. Of course, internal page links have the same formatting options as in interwiki links. The only difference is that the wiki software will not verify whether the link target exists on the page. If the target is missing, the link is formatted as such but will have no effect.

MediaWiki article URLs

The wiki is a component of the world wide web. Thus it offers the possibility of external links leading to the wiki, as well as links leading from a wiki to the WWW. As you can see in the address line of your browser, wiki pages are loaded via the URL in which, at the end of the address, in our case following *http://localhost/mediawiki/index.php*[5], a slash is placed and the page name is added. It is also possible to load the edit view of a page directly via URL. To do this, the page title as well as the desired action must be specified:

URL

```
index.php?title=page title&action=edit
```

Please note that, in this case, any spaces are to be replaced with underlines.

External links

To link to an external page from MediaWiki, all you need to do is write the complete URL in the source code. Since it begins with *http://*, the software recognizes it as an external link and will format it accordingly. In links to the WWW, a special character appears behind the text. It indicates to the user that he or she will leave the wiki using the respective link. External links of this type are not limited to the WWW with HTTP protocol. MediaWiki also under-

[5] This path may vary depending on the installation; see Chap. 7.1

stands https, ftp and mailto links, and assigns them their own corresponding symbols.

Formatting a URL

Placing a URL in a text makes the text harder to read and is thus not advisable (except when the exact address is the subject of observation). That is why MediaWiki offers two ways to format external links. The first is to simply surround them in brackets. Such links are consecutively numbered on the page from top to bottom. This is similar to the quotation procedure in scientific texts; however, it also does not facilitate smooth reading. If you wish to provide a description for your link, simply add the description following a space behind the URL in brackets:

URL

```
[http://www.wiki-tools.de The page about the
book]
```

More than one word is permitted. In this way, external links can be embedded in the text flow.

Now we can fill the material page of "Flying Sparks" with content:

Wiki

```
== Links ==
* The [http://www.humanitycouncil.de·           ↵
Humanity Council] publishes development
report
...
```

You can now link directly to these targets on the start page:

Wiki

```
== Statement ==
Tribes without Fire ...
* [[Material#Links|secondary links]]
```

Signing entries

It has become standard discussion style to sign entries with the date and indication of the user's page, so that they can be allocated to participants. To do this, MediaWiki uses the abbreviation

Wiki

```
~~~~
```

When an article is saved for the first time, this code is translated into a link to the internal wiki page of the user and the current time. From then on, this information is stored in the source text. It is replaced even if the user is not logged in; in such cases, the user name is replaced by his or her current IP address.

6.2 Organizing Content

The methods previously described create structures by linking to entries without providing any specific information about why there is a connection between them. MediaWiki also offers the possibility of grouping several pages according to function or content-related aspects. Namespaces and categories serve this purpose.

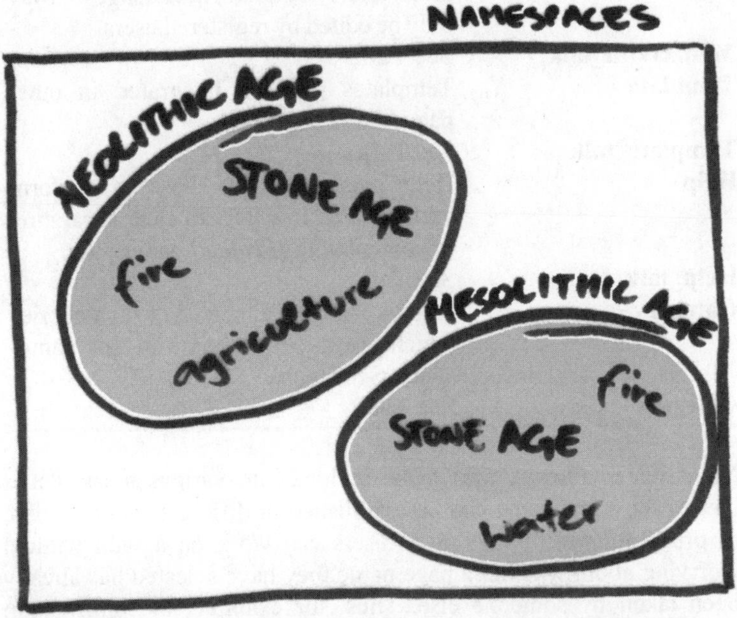

Fig. 6.1

Tab. 6.1

Namespace	Function
Media	Pseudo namespace for uploaded images and files. Is replaced by the file path.
Special	Pseudo namespace for special pages (see Chap. 6).
(Main)	Normal pages. They are indicated without a prefix.
Talk	Discussion pages. They are created for every article (including in the following namespaces), for content discussion. Additional tab (+).
User	User page. Is generated for every registered user.
User_talk	See **Talk**.

Tab. 6.1 (continued)

Namespace	Function
[Project]	Information about the wiki or the current project.
[Project]_talk	See **Talk**.
Image	Description of an image or other files. Is automatically supplied with information regarding version and file sources.
Image_talk	See **Talk**.
MediaWiki	System messages. A complete list is available under *Special:AllMessages*. May only be edited by registered users.
MediaWiki_talk	See **Talk**.
Template	Templates may be integrated in other pages (see Chap. 5.4).
Template_talk	See **Talk**.
Help	Help pages describe how to perform various tasks in wiki. No clear separation of content with ***[Project]*** namespace.
Help_talk	See **Talk**.
Category	Pages can be allocated to categories which are then accessible in this namespace. See below.
Category_talk	See **Talk**.

Function of namespaces

Namespaces allow a wiki to be divided into various areas. Pages having the same name can be established in different areas, so that, in principle, several groups of users can work on a wiki without worrying about whether a page name they have selected has already been taken by someone else. Thus, for example, the information booth and petition groups can each have a separate page in their own namespace with the same significant name **ToDo**.

Namespaces in MediaWiki

However, in MediaWiki, the names of these areas are "hard coded". That means that they have been fixed in the source code of MediaWiki and may not be altered by users. Instead, they serve as a separation between the various types of pages contained in the wiki. Entries with various namespaces may also possess additional functions. For instance, pages in the namespace **Talk** have an additional tab (+) that is automatically set in the articles at the end of the page. In the standard installation, there are 15 namespaces, the standard namespace **(Main)** and 2 pseudo namespaces, which are listed in Table 6.1. A page is allocated to the standard namespace as long as no information has been defined for it. The pseudo namespaces are used like normal namespaces, except that neither can pages be generated nor can existing pages be modified.

Most pages in the namespaces are generated automatically. Special pages are generated by the system before installation, media and image pages are created when a file is uploaded, and user pages when a user is active in a wiki. 'Talk' or 'discussion' pages are also generated along with the respective pages. This leaves only the pages in **Main**, ***[Project]***, **Template**, **Help** and **Category**, which can be designed freely. You can query the pages belonging to the respective categories via the special page **All pages**.

Accessing pages in a namespace

To access a page in a particular namespace or, if it is not yet available, to create one, simply place its name before the page title and separate it with a colon:

Wiki

```
[[Help:How do I set a link|]]
```

In the example, the pipe symbol was also added. It prevents the namespace from being displayed along with the link, which facilitates reading. If you enter a namespace that the wiki does not recognize, the page is generated in the standard namespace **Main**. The portion of the link indicated as a namespace is supplemented by the title of the article and not identified as an area name. A page can only be allocated to one namespace. The same page name in another namespace generates a new page. In addition, namespaces only exist on one level; that is, a namespace cannot be subdivided into further namespaces. That is why a new namespace is created for each discussion page, instead of linking the namespace with the discussion page. In searches (see Chap. 7.2), the search area can be limited to individual namespaces.

Individual user namespaces

Unfortunately, there is currently no way for normal users to receive a listing of all namespaces. The generation of an individual user namespace is also only possible with access to the scripts (see Chap. 8.1.). However, one can use the syntax of the namespaces and simulate an area in the namespace **Main**, by adding an individual name as a prefix followed by a colon to the pages of a desired area. The general advantages of namespaces remain intact. For instance, it is possible to use pages having the same name in various "areas" and thus enable various groups to work on a single wiki. Since this individual "namespace" prefix is a component of the page name, one can now see a display of all pages within the "namespace" by performing a search of the prefix.

These individual namespaces are ideal for our fire project. For instance, we can place all of the meeting minutes in an area with the name **Minutes:** Each entry would be named for its respective date, such as **Minutes:12152004**. A further possible use is for work groups who would most likely want to generate several individual pages. The Summer Festival Group, for example, could generate their task list under the name **SummerFestival:Todo**, whereas the Information Booth Group would call their list **InfoBooth:Todo**, without any conflict between the groups. In addition, the pages are automatically allocated, so we know that every page whose name begins with "SummerFestival" belongs to that group.

Interwiki links

To create links between various wikis, a convention is used that is similar to that of namespaces: The interwiki links. Instead of using the name of a namespace, simply use the name of another wiki. However, the system must recognize these names, so that the URL can be replaced. You can find a few pre-defined wiki links in Tab. 6.2.

Tab. 6.2

Prefix	**Wiki**	**URL**
`TWiki`	TWiki	*http://TWiki.org/cgi-bin/view/*
`Wiki`	WikiWikiWeb	*http://c2.com/cgi/wiki?*
`Wikitravel`	Wikitravel	*http://www.wikitravel.org/en/$1*
`Google`	Google	*http://www.google.com/search?=*

As you can see, you can link to other destinations besides wikis, such as search engines like Google.For example, using [[google: Switzerland]], you can link to Google pages found by a search for "Switzerland". You can find a complete list of pre-defined interwiki prefixes in the file maintenance/interwiki.sql. You can learn how to make your own entries in Chap. 8.2.

Categories

A second type of organizing pages is through categories. This refers to a categorization of page content under a category name. These names are described in the **Category** namespace. Unlike namespaces, any number of categories can be generated and by any user. This is done by creating a page in the namespace Category. All you have to do to allocate a page to a category is insert a link to the category page in the source text.

Wiki

```
[[Category:MyCategory]]
```

Now a note appears at the end of the page indicating under what name the article has been categorized. If you wish to create a link to the category page itself, you must prefix the link with the word "Category" followed by a colon. Just as in the case of creating new pages, you can create new categories with the categorization procedure.

Multiple categorization and position

A page can be allocated to more than one category. To do this, several of these category links are included. It does not matter where the categorization is inserted in the source text. It will always be shown at the end of a page. Thus, you can also insert them in places where they best fit the content. However, the order of the categorizations in the source text determines the order in which they are listed.

Category pages

Category pages function in the same way that normal wiki pages do. That is to say, you can edit them with normal wiki syntax. However, a category page has two further components that cannot be edited because they are generated automatically. The first is an alphabetical list of all pages under this category name. The second is a display of any existing sub-categories. Incidentally, it is also possible to organize categories into categories and thus create a hierarchical ordering system. To do this, insert a subcategory allocation on the respective category page.

Fig. 6.2

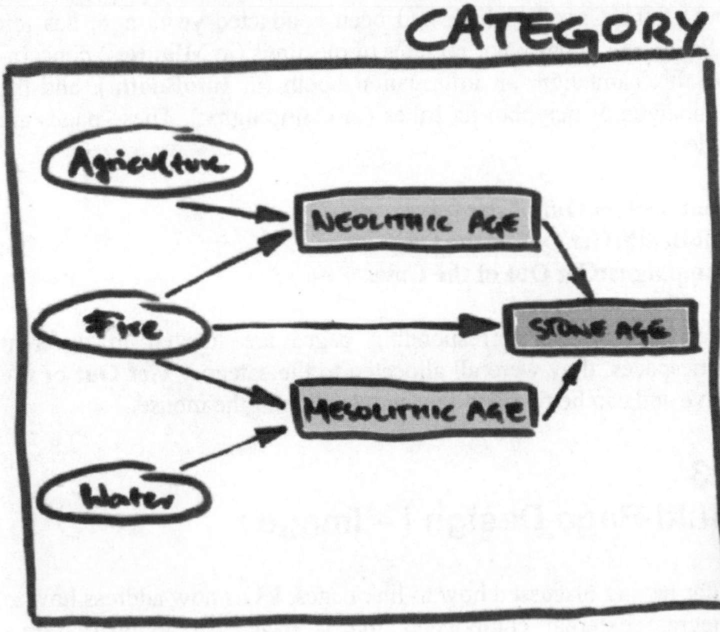

Access to category pages

Access to category pages can be done via the special page **Special:Categories**. All existing category names are displayed on this page. They are ordered such that the categories having the most pages are at the top. This means that the order of the categories changes repeatedly. In addition, categories that have been created but do not yet have any pages allocated to them are not listed here. However, a simple way is to insert a subcategory that contains all of the other groups as elements. Each subcategory thus has a link to that main category, where the individual categories are displayed completely and in alphabetical order.

Using categories

Categories may be used to organize the content of a wiki. Another use is the generation of a hierarchical catalogue which facilitates systematical navigation within a wiki. In addition, in smaller wikis, one could collect a list of highly frequented pages via these category pages (see also Chap. 4.5). The work of several user groups in a wiki can also be organized using categories: Here, each group is allocated a category. As you can see, the category names in MediaWiki offer a variety of application opportunities that stretch far beyond a normal categorization system. But please note that categories are not self-contained; an overlap of names can thus lead to problems.

Categories can help the members of our tribal initiative to maintain a record of all the material gathered during the course of their campaigns, so they can be found more easily. The campaign "Get Out of the Cave!", which had been conducted years ago, has left a few traces in our wiki: minutes of meetings (in **Minutes**:) concerning this campaign, an information booth (in **InfoBooth**:), and the campaigns of neighboring tribes (in **Campaigns**:). These pages are called:

Minutes:Get Out of the Cave
InfoBooth:Get Out of the Cave
Campaigns:Get Out of the Cave

Even though the corresponding pages are located in different namespaces, they were all allocated to the category **Get Out of the Cave** and can be found with a simple click of the mouse.

6.3 Multi-Page Design I – Images

After having discussed how to link pages, let us now address how to integrate external components into a page. An application that should be especially familiar to HTML designers is the displaying of images. Yet that procedure also enables the integration of original texts from other wiki articles.

Internal storage of images

Images can either be saved internally or linked to an external source. Both methods have their advantages and disadvantages. Internal storage ensures that the file is accessible and the address does not change without being noticed. Control over internal images remains in the hands of the wiki community. They can be written over, but the modifications are recorded and can be traced in the same way that page histories can. In addition, internally stored images have their own description and discussion page. The disadvantage of internal storage is obvious: Especially in the case of larger wikis, storage space requirements are enormous, and hard to control, since the size of the uploaded files is unknown.

External storage of images

External images, on the other hand, are in the control of their originator. If an originator does not wish his image to be used further, he can simply remove it, and the external link will lead into emptiness. A great advantage of external images is that they drastically reduce and allow better control of the storage space required for the wiki. In addition, the link, in some cases, leads to the image's original context, or at least reveals its source location. This adds to the authenticity of the image. Yet even for image files that change often, it is advantageous for disk space and maintenance reasons to link them externally. On the other hand, especially in the case of highly-frequented wikis, it may prompt the accusation that one were only trying to save on bandwidth, a valuable commodity on the Internet, by avoiding the need to send large files from one's own server.

Copyright

Especially with regard to images, we must once again specifically stress that linking external sources to your page requires the permission of the originator. While a wiki subjects uploaded files to its free license, this is not the necessarily case for external files. Of course, only those images and files may be loaded that are permissible under the source's license. This especially means that a user who uploads material must possess the respective rights. In order to avoid a great deal of trouble, just remember, when you are not sure: It is better to ask once too often than not enough! It is conventional to allow usage in exchange for a link to the source page.

Uploading images and files

There is a special page, **Special:Upload file**, to upload images and files. You can find it either in the list of special pages or via the **Upload** link in the Tools area. Remember that you can only access the page if you are logged into wiki.

Tip: In the standard installation of MediaWiki, uploading images as well as establishing external links are not allowed. To change this, set the variable `$wgEnableUploads` in *MediaWiki/LocalSettings.php* to `true`. For more information, see Chap. 8.1.

On the Upload file page, you will find a form:

Fig. 6.3

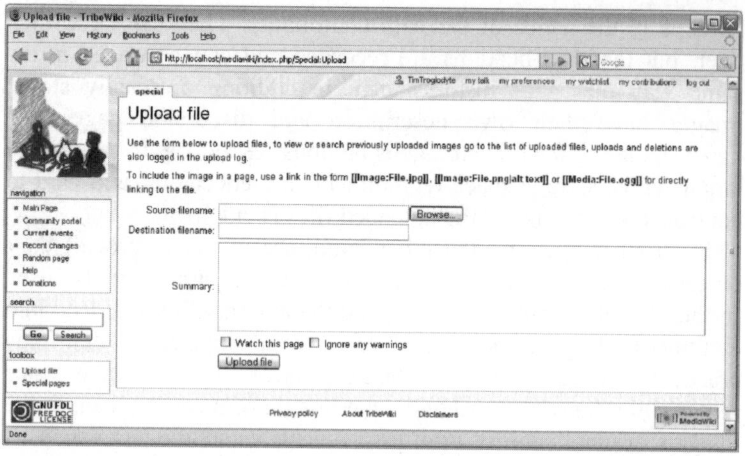

In the **File name** space, enter the path and name of the file you wish to upload. Alternatively, you can click on **Search**. A dialogue window then opens in which you can select a file. The required path information will be entered into the form. In the field **Change file name**, you can give the file a new name. Now you should enter a short description of the image in the **Description** field. This gives potential viewers an idea of whether or not the file is of interest. With the button **Upload files**, the file is then integrated into the wiki. As we have indicated, this procedure applies to all allowed file types. You can find out how to include other file types in this list, see Chap. 8.1. If a file of the same name already exists, you will see a warning page on which you can decide what to do. If you click on **Cancel**, the current action is cancelled and you will return to *Special:Upload*. If you click on **Save file**, the file will be overwritten. However, as mentioned, the old version of the file remains in the history list. You will also be warned if the file size exceeds the limit of 100 KB. Furthermore, any spaces in file names are automatically replaced by underlines in order to conform to wiki page names. If you wish to skip the warning page, activate the **Ignore warnings** field before the upload.

Tip: The name of an uploaded file can no longer be altered. Thus, it is advisable to give the file a significant name.

List of all images and files

A list of all images and files in a wiki can be found under **Special:Imagelist** or under **File list** in the Special Pages menu. In addition to a search function and a selection of displays (see Chap. 2), you will also see a list containing information about the respective files. For each entry, from right to left, there is a link to the image page and to the file itself, information on the size, the name of the user that uploaded the file, the upload time, and finally, a description of the image. If you follow the link **Description**, you will come to the corresponding wiki page with the image.

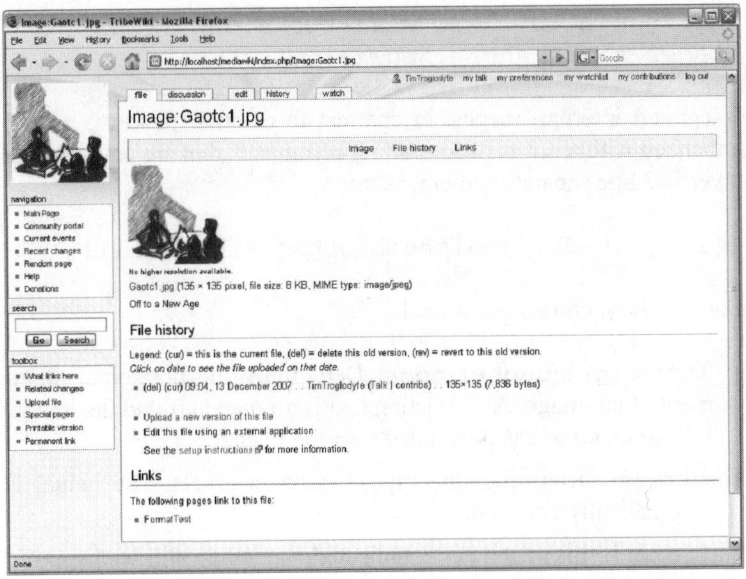

Fig. 6.4

All of these pages are located in the namespace **Image**. Here, you will first see the image itself with a description that you can also modify. Underneath, in the section **Image history**, there is an automatically generated list with the various versions of the image and the corresponding version functions. The section **Image links** is also automatically generated, and displays a list of the pages in which the file has been integrated.

Tip: Remember that the editable description of an image may no longer be applicable if an image has been overwritten; the description may need to be edited accordingly.

Integrating an image

Now we come to the real purpose of our exercise: integrating an image on a page. The (pseudo) namespaces come into play again here. If you only wish to supply a link to the image without actually displaying it on the page, set a link to `[[Image:`*`imagename`*`]]`. To create a link to the image page (with additional information), place a colon before the namespace: `[[:Image:`*`imagename`*`]]`. Both versions that can be displayed on wiki pages can be formatted just like normal links (see Chap. 6.1). To display external images, just enter the URL of the file in the source text. The wiki software will recognize it and insert the original image at that spot. Note that a space must be inserted after the URL; otherwise the end of the address cannot be detected.

Wiki
```
The logo http://www.wiki-tools.de/ ↵
images/title_short.jpg is...
```

Formatting internal images

Integrated internal images, in contrast to external pictures, can be enhanced with a series of formatting commands that are entered with a vertical line separating them, as in:

Wiki
```
[[Image:radh1.jpg|thumb|50px|left|Cave1]]
```

Each of these entries is optional:

- **left/right/center/none.** Determines the horizontal alignment of an image. Any existing text is arranged around the image. For **none**, no text is positioned near the image.
- ***size*px.** Determines the image width in pixels. The height is automatically adjusted.
- **frame.** If this parameter is indicated, the image will be displayed in its original size with a frame and caption (see below). Any size information will have no effect. Standard alignment for the image is along the right margin.
- **thumb.** The image is displayed as a thumbnail for preview purposes and includes a symbol which indicates the tooltip text **enlarge**. Standard alignment for the image is also along the right margin.

The last parameter contains a description of the image. This description is displayed as tooltip text when the mouse is rolled over the image. Texts of this sort are important because they can also be seen by people with vision impairments who surf using voice output. In addition, they provide standard users with further information on the display. In both the **thumb** and the **frame** display modes, the description is added as a caption. Here, it is also possible to add basic formats (e.g. bold and italics), as well as links. However, please note that these formats are translated into HTML code in the normal image display, and thus will appear as tags in the tooltip text.

Tip: If no information is provided for a caption, the last entry in the image link will be displayed instead. Thus, we recommend always indicating the caption explicitly or inserting the pipe symbol at the end. This causes the file name to be used as the image caption.

A few examples will demonstrate the use of images: *Examples*

Image gallery. First, let us generate an image documentation for our "Get Out of the Cave!" campaign that consists of a row of 50-pixel wide thumbnails positioned side by side: *Several images*

Wiki

```
[[Image:radh1.jpg|thumb|50px|left|Cave1]]
[[Image:radh2.jpg|thumb|50px|left|Cave2]]
[[Image:radh3.jpg|thumb|50px|left|Group]]
```

The results are displayed in Fig. 6.5. It is important to indicate an alignment with the left margin. If you fail to do so, or if another alignment is selected, the thumbnails will appear one below another. If you enter more images than will fit on one line, they will automatically break to the next line. This results in a sort of table-like display, such as one would expect from a photo gallery.

Fig. 6.5

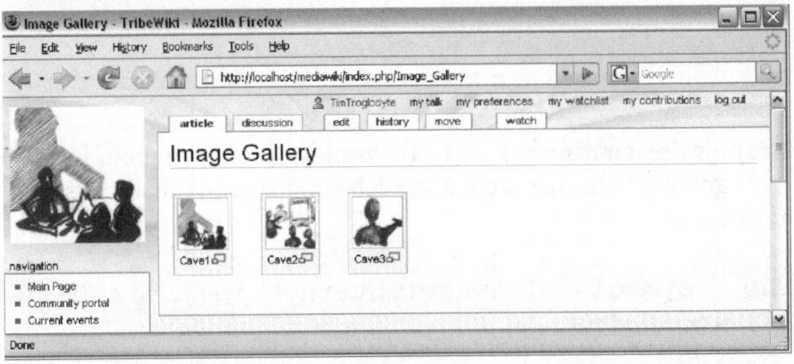

Illustration with a complex caption. Embedding an image in a text for illustrative purposes is probably the most frequent type of application. In our case, our formatted caption will also link to two other pages. *Captions*

Wiki

```
==Flying Sparks Tribal Initiative==
[[Image:radh1.jpg|frame|right|                         ↵
''This'' shows '''(a)''' the                           ↵
[[Infobooth:Caves|information booth]] and              ↵
'''(b)''' reminds you of [[cave campaign|the
campaign]].                                            ↵
]]
The purpose of this page is
```

As you can see in Fig. 6.6, the image is displayed in a frame on the right edge of the page. The text flows to the left. The formatting of the caption corresponds to what we would also expect on a normal wiki page. If you roll over the image with your mouse, you will see that the formats from the caption have correctly not been applied to the rollover text. As a test, delete the attribute `frame` and look at the tooltip again. Now you can see the HTML tags.

Fig. 6.6

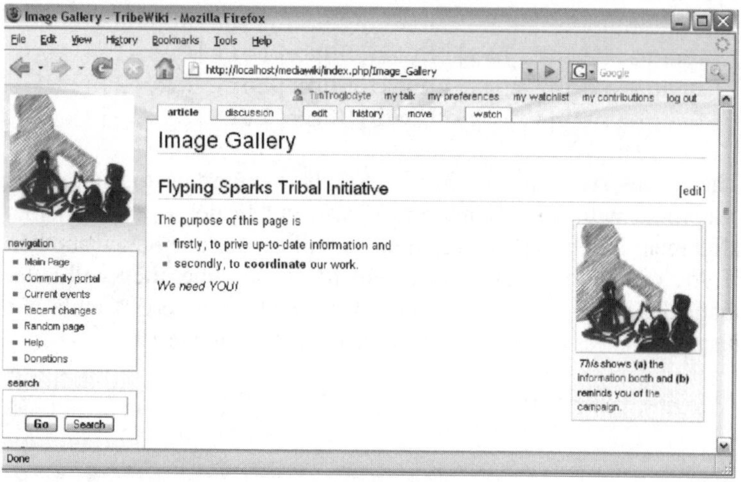

In continuous text

Graphics in continuous text. To display special symbols in text, e.g. lightning bolts that are not available in the set of characters, you must use images.

Wiki

```
The symbol [[Image:Internet.jpg|15px|Image
1]] indicates...
```

The corresponding text excerpt is depicted in Fig. 6.7. The key to smooth embedding in the text flow lies, on the one hand, in leaving out the alignment attribute. This signals that the image is to be displayed directly in the spot in which it is located in the source text. Secondly, the correct size must be selected, so that the height of the image matches that of the text.

Fig. 6.7

Tip: Since the size relates to the width of the graphic, you may need to experiment a bit before finding the correct expansion factor. It is a good idea to work with the preview function instead of saving each attempt.

Aligning images

Aligning images on a page using the attributes `left` and `right` causes the text to flow around these images. There are a few opportunities to influence the positioning of the file. If you want the upper edge of the image to line up with the first line of text, place the image link before the first word in the paragraph. If you insert it after the first word, the first line will be written in full and the image will be attached to the second line. Generally, if an image is announced in a line, it is not displayed until the start of the following line. The end of the paragraph has no effect on the alignment. In fact, the entire subsequent text, including sections and tables, will be displayed next to the image. In order to make the paragraph begin underneath the image, place the following line directly before the respective paragraph:

Wiki

```
<br style="clear:both">
```

The line is then pushed far enough down until it has passed the edge of the image.

Two images at the same height

It is possible to position one graphic image on the left edge and another at the same height on the right edge. To do this, write the links for the images with the varying alignment attributes one directly after the other. The order does not matter. The text will then flow between the illustrations. Text located between the two images is joined with the normal continuous text and thus can, under certain conditions, appear before the first image.

Tipp: The use of areas surrounded by `<pre>` and images in the same paragraph can lead to both elements covering each other; this should be avoided.

Other types of files

Depending on how the wiki is set up (see Chap. 8.1), it is also possible to upload sound and other media files, as well as compressed files, in addition to images. The wiki software will always link them as files and not embed them like images. A link in the **Image** namespace thus links to the description page of the file. If the file itself is to be linked, the link to the file must be put in the pseudo namespace **Media** .

Links to these uploaded files can be collected on one page. You may remember that we set up a Material page for the tribal initiative.

Here, in addition to **Links**, we can also establish a **Downloads** section, through which users can access existing documents (e.g. audio recordings, letters, scanned stone tablets, etc.).

6.4 Multi-Page Design II – Templates

What are templates?

Templates refer to (source) templates that can be integrated in other pages of a wiki. This enables frequently used components, such as form letters or checklists, to be swapped out, so that they do not have to be created all over again every time. Furthermore, templates also serve to provide a certain uniformity. In addition, the use of templates offers a degree of flexibility, since modifications can be made centrally and affect all pages accessing that template. Accordingly, possible applications for templates include the administration of messages, the depiction of uniform navigation areas, or simply the homogeny of a group of pages.

Integrating templates

The namespace **Template** is reserved for templates. You can thus generate your templates with [[template:mytemplate]]. It is integrated into a page by setting the template name in two curly brackets:

Wiki

```
{{mytemplate}}
```

As usual, non-existent templates are displayed with an editing link. Otherwise, the source text in the template is put in place of the link. If you want to explicitly link to a template page (in order to edit it, for instance), you need to place the normal internal link in double square brackets.

Note: If a page contains integrated templates, the latter are displayed in edit mode or below the edit box.

Tip: You can use any page of a wiki as a template. Just enter its complete name (with the namespace). For pages in **Main**, it will suffice to set a colon in front of the name.

However, for reasons of clarity and simplicity, you should use this function sparingly, and use the corresponding namespaces for templates conceived as such.

Possible content

Templates can contain anything that can be on a normal page, including dynamic elements such as links and variables. One possible application for such templates would be the link to the personal page of someone responsible for a particular area. Since this person could change, one could establish a template citing the respective current contact person.

Place of execution

All commands are executed as if they were directly embedded in the page. This is especially true for allocation into categories. Thus, if a template is allocated to a category, all pages using that template will also be allocated to that category. It is possible to nest templates, that is, use a template within another template. This results in an easily maintainable structure of recurring elements of a page.

Variables

Up to now, the use of templates has been relatively fixed and static. When generating a template, either it does not matter in which pages they are integrated or the author must have a relatively precise idea of what kind of pages the template will be used for. For example, for messages of a general nature, it does not matter what content is on a page. In order to offer more flexibility in relation to the article using a template, there are built-in variables. They are placeholders for certain pieces of information on the wiki, the page or the current time. Variables are integrated just like templates, and when a page is accessed, the current values are shown. A list of built-in variables can be found in Tab. 6.3. Note that the names are case-sensitive, and thus writing letters in upper and lower-case makes a difference.

Tab. 6.3

Name	Function
`{{ns:Name}}`	All namespaces have original identifiers in English that are the same in all MediaWikis. Is replaced by the name of the namespace in the language of the wiki.
`{{SITENAME}}`	Name of the wiki
`{{SERVER}}`	Sets a link to the server, that is, that area in the URL from *http://* to the first slash.
`{{localurl:`*Page*`}}`	Displays everything after the slash in the URL of the corresponding page.
`{{localurl:`*Page*`|query}}`	As above, only with the additional indication of parameters.
`{{CURRENTMONTH}}`	Number of the current month
`{{CURRENTMONTHNAME}}`	Name of the current month in the respective wiki language.
`{{CURRENTDAY}}`	Number of the current day.
`{{CURRENTDAYNAME}}`	Name of the current day in the respective wiki language.
`{{CURRENTYEAR}}`	The current year

Tab. 6.3 (continued)

Name	Function
{{CURRENTTIME}}	The time in the format HH:MM
{{NUMBEROF ARTICLES}}	Number of articles in the **Main** namespace that contain at least one link.
{{NAMESPACE}}	Name of the namespace of the page.
{{PAGENAME}}	Name of the page.
{{PAGENAMEE}}	Name of the page as it is displayed in the URL. Generally with underlines instead of spaces.

You can use these variables on any wiki page. For example, using

Wiki
```
{{SERVER}}{{localurl:Hello
World|action=edit}}
```

it is possible to set a link to the editing view of **Hello World**, or using

Wiki
```
{{CURRENTDAY}}.{{CURRENTMONTHNAME}}
{{CURRENTYEAR}}
```

to display the current date. Note that in the first case, the entire URL of the page is generated. This is the only way to access the functions of a page. Using the link

Wiki
```
[[Hello World&action=edit]]
```

you can create a page with the exact name **Hello World&action=edit** and no link to **Hello World**.

Substituting If you place the keyword `subst:` in front of the variable, when you save the content, the variables will be written to the source text at that spot. For instance: If you place the following line in the page **Hello World** and then save it,

Wiki
```
{{subst:PAGENAME}}/{{CURRENTTIME}}
```

you will see when editing the page again that the source text now looks like this:

Wiki
```
Hello World/{{CURRENTTIME}}
```

This mechanism is useful if you want to leave a time stamp on a page. However, it is relatively complicated, since it is a one-time action, and entering the variables is lengthier than just looking at the clock and copying down the time. On the other hand, the same formalism applies to the integration of templates. In this way, the content of a page can be copied to one's own page and then customized accordingly.

The fire initiative wishes to use this mechanism to avoid having to fill out standard text every time the minutes are recorded:

Wiki

```
== Minutes of MM.DD.YYYY ==
===Agenda===
__TOC__
===Attendant===
===TOP1===
===TOP2===
```

In addition, there is a checklist for the information booth which shows what preliminary and subsequent work needs to be done. This is re-entered and customized for every information booth, and checked off in the wiki. The checklist and minutes template are thus simply saved in a template and brought to the target page with {{subst:PAGENAME}}.

Integrate as source text

If you wish to integrate a template without having wiki interpret the text contained in it as source text by the wiki, just position `msgnw:` in front of the name of the template. This causes the entire template text to be enclosed in a `<nowiki>` tag and not processed.

Variables in templates

Variables often appear in templates as well. In such cases, the value of the variables of the accessed page and not those of the template are determined. Thus `{{PAGENAME}}` does not display the name of the template, but rather the name of the page in which it is integrated. This enables a series of page-specific links to be created which primarily lead to functions or special pages regarding the article. For example, the template

Wiki

```
[{{SERVER}}{{localurl:Special:Whatlinkshere| ↵
target={{PAGENAME}}}} Backlinks]
```

creates a link with the name **Backlinks** on the page that displays all incoming links (see Chap. 7.1). Note that the actual URL is generated again here.

Parameters

Especially in the case of templates that dictate layout but not content, it is advantageous to transfer values to the template. You can use your own parameters for this purpose, which can be set when the template is accessed. Transfer of values takes place within the curly brackets that surround the template, and can be done in two different ways:

Wiki

```
{{Templatename|value1|value2|...}}
{{Templatename|name1=value1|name2=value2|...}
}
```

In the first case, the parameters are simply numbered consecutively, and in the second, they can be addressed using a name. The parameters are integrated in the template by setting either its number or name in triple curly brackets. For example:

Wiki

```
{{Salu|Ms|Stone}}
{{Salu1|name=Stone|address=Ms}}
```

Invokes the two templates **Salu**

Wiki

```
Hello {{{1}}} {{{2}}}
```

and **Salu1**:

Wiki

```
Hello {{{address}}} {{{name}}}
```

As you can see, the order of the values in the templates varies. However, the result in both cases is the same; the sentence "Hello Ms Stone" appears. The first version is less complicated when writing it, since you do not need to name the parameters. However, if you have a template with several values, it is simpler to give them names. In such a case, the source text of the template is easier to follow. Furthermore, the order of the entries does not matter; thus, you can be sure that the correct information will end up in the correct spot. This advantage should not be underestimated, especially in large-scale projects!

An example

In the following example, we will further clarify the possibilities offered by templates by working on the design of a uniform participants page for members of a project group of our tribal initiative. We want the page to have a uniform header with a display of current messages, an area where participants can introduce themselves, as well as a section that can be designed freely. The participants are encouraged to make this page their personal start page, and to have a look at it at least every couple of days. The template to be used, **ProjectParPage**, looks like this:

Wiki

```
{{ProjectHeader}}
{{ParInfos|
name=FIRSTNAME LASTNAME|
contact=EMAILADDRESS|
```

```
area=AREA|
image=[[Image:OWNIMAGE|150px|center]]}}
== My responsibilities are ==
* TASK1
* TASK2
== Personal area ==
You can design this area any way you wish
```

As you can see, the information that participants will later customize is written in capital letters to set a visual signal.
The template **ProjectHeader** provides the title, links that are to be on every project page, and an area for important messages that the participants should read. In order to make the layout a bit more attractive, we employed a table:

Wiki

```
{| width=100% style="border:1px solid ↵
  #000000;background:#CCCCFF"
| style="font-size:20pt;font-weight:bold; ↵
  text-align:center" | Fire Project
|-
| <hr>
|-
| Important Links: [[FireProject|Start]] ↵
  {{ProjectContactPerson}}
|-
| Messages: <br> ↵
  '''''{{ProjectMessages}}'''''
|}
```

The cells were formatted using CSS, and they determine the table background as well as the text format and alignment. The name of the project, **FireProject**, has a permanent code, because it will not change during the course of the project. The contact person, however, is integrated in a further template, **ProjectContactPerson**, in which only the link to his page is indicated.

Wiki

```
[[User:ContactPerson|Contact Person]]
```

The messages are also obtained from a separate template. This has two advantages. Firstly, the messages are easy for users to write, because they do not have to search through lengthy code to find the right spot. On the other hand, the **ProjectHeader** template will probably only be able to be edited by administrators. Due to the swapping out of messages, any user can make entries. They are in the form of simple text displays:

Wiki

```
Don't forget: The deadline for suggestions is
Dec.31!
```

Now we have designed the project header. Next, we will turn to the uniform presentation of the participants. As you saw in the template **ProjectParPage**, all relevant information is transferred to the template **ParInfos** in the form of parameters. Ultimately, all we have to do is position the information in an attractive way. To do this, we'll once again use a table:

Wiki

```
{| align="right" style="border: 1px dotted ↵
   #000000"
| colspan="2" | {{{image}}}
|-
| '''Name''':
| {{{name}}}
|-
| '''Contact''':
| {{{contact}}}
|-
| '''Area''':
| {{{area}}}
|}
```

Links, as in the case of `image`, as well as normal text, can be used for the parameter values. It is even possible to use blank spaces, as is done in the case of `name`. MediaWiki correctly identifies them as a value. The same is true for links, which, although they contain the separating pipe symbol | , can still be correctly identified.

Generating a page with a template

Up to now, we have only generated one set of templates. If a user wants to create his own page, he must first make a copy of the prototype **ProjectParPage**. To do this, the first version of the participants page is to be saved with `{{subst:ProjectParPage}}`. Now the participant has his own copy of the page, in which the corresponding placeholder data, such as `first name last name`, just needs to be replaced. Then the uniform page is finished:

Fig. 6.8

6.5 Forwarding with Redirects

A final means of multi-page design in MediaWiki is found in redirects. As the name indicates, they serve to redirect a user from one page to another. This can come in handy when a page has "moved"; that is, when it has been copied to another page with a new title. In addition, several values indicating the same thing can be consolidated in this way. Thus, for instance, you could avoid having double or deviating descriptions of **WikiWikiWeb** and **Wiki**, by forwarding the user from one article to the other. Redirects are installed by placing the following command at the beginning of a page:

```
#REDIRECT [[pagename]]
```

Wiki

Lines below this command are automatically deleted when the page is saved. At the top of the target page, a message appears indicating that the page has been redirected. There is also a link to the original page. Thus, if you wish to cancel the redirection, you can access the old page via the link and edit it. To manually prevent a redirection, you can also add the following parameter to the URL in the address line of the browsers: `&redirect=no`.

7 Components: the Function Pages

Special pages

Although many necessary tasks in a wiki can be completed with the basic functions Edit, History and Search, there are a few procedures that require more complex programming. For example, these involve statistical functions, administrative settings or the categorization of pages according to certain criteria. These functions are carried out by the special pages, which we have already mentioned. These pages are a group of entries in the namespace **Special** whose content is at least partially automatically generated and generally cannot be altered. A few of the special pages can be accessed via the navigation or tool area. A virtually[6] complete list of all special pages is available under **Special:Specialpages**.

Lists

These pages often list wiki articles, such as the special page **New pages** (see Fig. 7.1):

Fig. 7.1

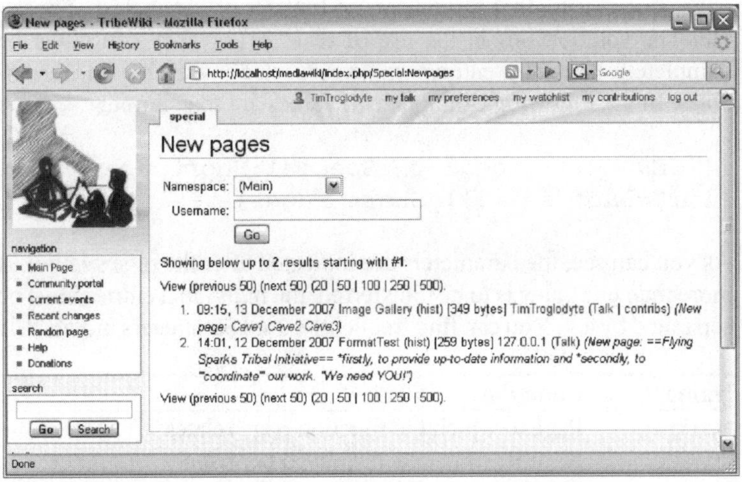

[6] The administrator of the wiki has access to more special pages than the normal user.

They begin with an indication of how many results are displayed, followed by the number of the first result displayed. In the default setting, up to 50 finds are shown on a page. If the number of results exceeds 50, the navigation links **Next 50** and **Previous 50** are activated. You can change the number of articles displayed by clicking on the corresponding number after the navigation link.

Parameter transfer

Information that a function page requires to "know" exactly what it should do, for instance, to what page it refers, is transferred as parameters in the URL. For the page **Links to this page**, which you can find in the navigation bar, it looks like this:

Wiki

```
http://www.wiki-tools.de/MediaWiki/index.php ↵
?title=Special:Whatlinkshere ↵
&target=MainPage
```

If only the `title` and `target` are indicated as parameters, the shortened form can also be used.

Wiki

```
http://www.wiki-tools.de/MediaWiki/index.php↵
/Special:Whatlinkshere/MainPage
```

The main page, the target of the backlink page, is transferred with the command `/mainpage` at the end of the URL. If there is more than one parameter, they are attached and separated from each other by an ampersand (`&`). One result of parameterization via the URL is that one can no longer simply use an internal link to refer to that page, since, using that formalism, no transfer of parameters is possible. The solution lies in the use of real URLs. They can either be completely manually entered or "constructed" with the aid of variables. In the following example, two values are transferred:

Wiki

```
[{{SERVER}}{{localurl:Special:Shortpages| ↵
limit=5&offset=3}} Short Pages]
```

As you can see, the parameters are indicated after the pipe symbol. If more than one value is to be transferred, the individual entries must be separated by a `&`. You can find frequently-used parameters in Tab. 7.1.

Tab. 7.1

Name	**Function**
`target`	Page to which the function page relates
`limit`	Number of results displayed per page
`offset`	Number of the first element shown on the result list

Now let's have a closer look at the individual special pages.

7.1 Navigation

Most of the function pages search the wiki for certain criteria and provide a list of articles as a result. They are designed to improve the navigation, availability and balance of the wiki. Some are considered to be so useful that they have been directly integrated into the navigation area.

Recent changes

The **Recent changes** page lists the subpages of the wiki that have been recently modified (see Fig. 7.2). The most recent changes are at the top. In addition to the display function for lists we have mentioned, there are also two further ordering criteria. You can obtain a list of the changes made in recent days, and a list of changes since the last access to that page. The latter link can be found in the line **Show new changes starting from**. The following date corresponds to the server time at the point when the page was last accessed, and is updated every time. Note that the server time does not necessarily correspond to the time on your computer; for instance, the server might be located in another time zone. The advantage of this function is that you only see those changes that you have not yet viewed. Also, you can see at a glance if no edits have been performed, since the hit list would then be empty. Via a drop-down list, you can filter pages according to namespaces.

Result lines

The individual result lines consist of several links. **Diff** indicates a view of the differences between the latest version of a page and its

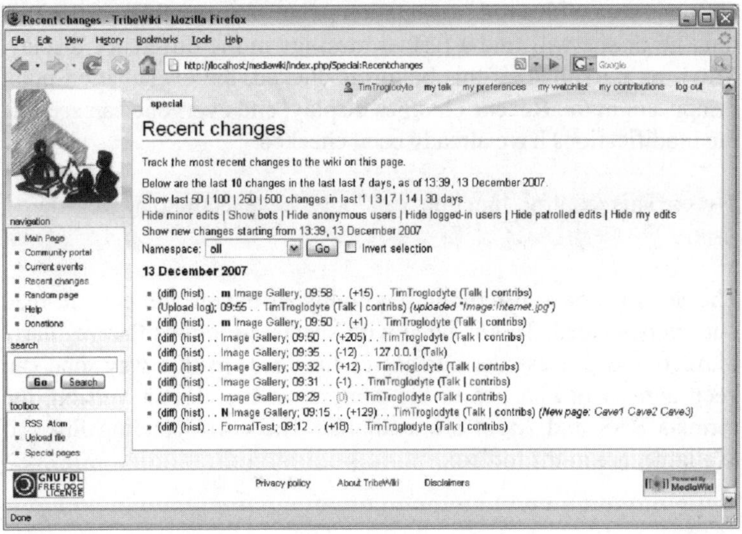

Fig. 7.2

predecessor. This corresponds to the last change. **Hist** provides a list of versions of a page. Next, we see information on how the page was edited. If only two dots are shown, normal editing took place. If there is an `m`, a minor change was made; if there is an `n`, the page was newly created. You will see a red exclamation point in some lines. This is part of a control system, and indicates whether the edit has already been viewed by anyone (see below). The next piece of information is the title of the page that was modified, followed by the point in time in which it was edited. This is followed by the name or IP address, including the talk page, of the user who made the modifications. Last but not least, any comments are shown that were made regarding the edit.

Settings

You can determine whether minor edits are displayed by viewing your personal settings (see Chap. 7.3). You also have the opportunity to activate the extended display of **Recent changes**. This primarily summarizes several changes by a user on the same day. In such a case, an arrow may appear at the beginning of the line. If you click it, the individual edits will unfold below.

Use of the page

The special page **Recent changes** allow you to be at the pulse of the wiki, so to speak. On one hand, you find out what the current hot topics are that are being fervently worked on, since they will have several edits. On the other hand, using that page, you can check new entries to its content. This makes **Recent changes** an indispensable tool for those who have taken on the role of a maintainer in a wiki.

Control system

If several participants take on quality assurance tasks, they have to coordinate their work with each other so that they do not all end up checking the same page. There is a control system for this purpose. Pages that have not yet been checked are marked in the Recent Changes area with a red exclamation point. If a user follows the **Diff** link, he or she will find a further message in the difference display, **Mark as patrolled**. If this button is clicked, the exclamation point disappears in the **Recent changes** display, and everyone can see that the modifications have already been checked.

Note: This control function can only be executed by registered users.

RSS feed

The versions page offers the possibility of having the content read out via newsfeed. This is done with special programs that regularly retrieve and process the content of the feed. In this way, one can keep abreast of changes to the content. In the current version, the formats RSS and Atom are available. The corresponding links, if available, are in the toolbox.

The special page **Random page** does exactly what it says. It displays a random article from the namespace **Main**. This is especially useful in a wiki having an encyclopedic character, because it offers an introduction platform from which to "browse the wiki". This page once again stresses the deliberately playful nature of a wiki.

Random page

The special page **What links here** harbors a very simple, yet just as powerful function. It lists all pages containing links to the current page (backlinks). In principle, this switches the direction of the link; one can now follow it back the other way. This is not always possible on the Web. Pages containing templates linking to the current page are also included here. If you want to view links on another page than the one you are on, you have to change the last value indicated in the URL to the respective page (see the beginning of this chapter).

What links here?

There is an abundance of applications that make this function particularly interesting. For instance, it is possible to obtain an idea of the context in which a page is integrated. When you know what topics link to a specific text, you can draw conclusions as to the direction and perhaps even the quality of the article. Furthermore, you have the opportunity to see to what degree and in what areas an article is integrated in the wiki. If deficits become apparent, remedies may be able to be found.

Use of the page

When employed appropriately, backlinks are a good source of information. Backlinks to a user page list all pages in which the corresponding user has made signed contributions. Since this is particularly common practice for discussions, one can find discussion contributions made by a participant. Templates issuing certain messages function in a similar manner. For example, if you have a template that identifies a page as "urgently requiring editing", you can use backlinks to find all articles carrying this predicate. Similarly, you can establish your own category system using this mechanism, with which you can set a link on the category page for every article belonging to a certain main category. The pages of this group can then be discovered via the **What links here** function. Of course, this is superfluous in MediaWiki, because categorization is possible. However, there are several wikis that have no categorizing function. Yet backlinks are a component of just about every piece of wiki software.

Backlinks for page organization

Recent changes linked displays pages that have been linked from a single page. The use of this special page corresponds to that of **Recent changes**. If you want to be absolutely certain that the list is complete, you should make sure the watch period you select is long enough. One advantage is that the integrated templates are displayed and linked. They can be found and edited more easily than

Recent changes linked

if you first switch to edit mode and then painstakingly search for places that integrate the templates.

Use as a watch page

Establishing a watch page is very similar. You create a page that links to all articles whose development you wish to follow. Via **Recent changes linked**, you can now obtain a list of all edits to those particular pages.

Upload file

If you are logged in, you will find a further special page in the navigation area: **Upload file**. This was discussed in detail in Chap. 6.3.

Navigation pages for readers

Under the link **SpecialPages**, you will find further navigation functions in the namespace **Main**. They can be divided into two groups. The first serves to make interested readers aware of certain articles or facilitate their access to them. This group includes:

- **All pages.** This contains a complete list in table form of all pages in the main namespace of the wiki. Here, you can enter a combination of letters from which point the all articles starting with those letters will be displayed. This is very useful for large wikis. In addition, you can determine from what namespace the articles are to be shown so you can find templates easier, for example.
- **Favorite pages.** The articles are ordered according to frequency of viewing. The number of hits is put in brackets.
- **New pages.** The articles are listed in the order of their creation. Caution: This refers to the first edit. Subsequent edits are ignored here.
- **Categories.** A list of all category pages. Those pages with the most elements are shown at the top.

Navigation pages for authors

The other group of navigation pages represents aids for authors so they can see which articles still need work. These pages include:

- **Wanted pages.** Displays all pages to which links have been set but which have not yet been created. The link in brackets (backlink function!) shows the pages on which these links appear.
- **Orphaned pages.** All pages that are no longer linked by any other page are shown here. They are no longer accessible through normal browsing with mouse clicks.
- **Unused files.** Shows all images and files that were uploaded but not integrated into any page. Since files take up a great deal of disk space, these should be monitored and, if not used for an extended period of time, perhaps deleted.

- **Uncategorized Pages.** Here are all the pages that have not been allocated to a category.
- **Dead-end pages.** These are pages from which no links lead to any other page.
- **Short pages.** The pages are organized according to size in Bytes. The shortest pages are listed at the top.
- **Long pages.** This list shows the longest pages first.
- **File list.** Shows all images and files according to name, size or date as desired, and thus offers an overview of the content of the wiki that does not originate from articles.

A special feature of MediaWiki is the page **ISBN search**. We mention it for purposes of completeness. Here, you can enter the ISBN number of a book to automatically generate links to a few online bookstores where you can order the book.

7.2 Search Function

In the profusion of various pages and their potentially relatively unstructured order, a search function is essential. The MediaWiki search function is designed such that, if you know the name of a page, you can jump directly to it by entering it in the search field.

Go and Search

You will find the search function in its own box under Navigation. As you can see, there are two buttons, **Go** and **Search**. The only difference between them is that **Go** will take you right to the corresponding page without a detour, and **Search** always first brings you to a search results page with a list of all results. **Go** thus offers the aforesaid direct access. Confirming your entry with <ENTER> has the same result as **Go**.

Search display

If, however, the page does not exist, or if you have pressed **Search**, the special page **Special:search** opens. Similar results are not part of the search. You will primarily receive two types of result lists. The top, **matching titles**, shows you what page titles match your search query. If the term appears within the limits of how many lines are displayed on a page, according to preference settings (see Chap. 7.3), it will be displayed along with the line number and its context under the page name. The second list, **matching text**, searches the content of the pages for the desired word. Here, too, their sections are also displayed.

Settings

If your search has not brought the desired results, it may be due to the fact that not all namespaces are taken into account. On the lower part of the results page, you can set which areas are to be searched. There is also a search field here in which the word you have entered is displayed. You can thus conveniently repeat and, if necessary, modify your search.

Possible search items

You can use regular words as search items. The search is not case-sensitive. Only entire words are sought, whereby a dash also counts as a word separator. You cannot search for every word. A query for "the" is virtually useless, since this word appears on practically every page. There is a list of such common words, so-called stop words, that are excluded from the search. Wildcards, as you know them from the Internet search engines, are not permitted. If you enter more than one word, the order is irrelevant; the individual elements are automatically joined by "and". If the order is relevant, put the phrase in quotation marks.

Boolean searches

Boolean searches with "and", "or", and "not" are taken into account in the search. This means that, for instance, it can indicate a list of alternative words if you join the words with "or". In that case, all pages are sought in which either of the two words appear. If you wish to search for pages containing both words, you can join them with "and"; however, that is the default setting. If you want to exclude a certain word from your search, precede it with "not". To determine the order of the joined words, use brackets. For example, in a search for

```
Wiki and (Tool or Tools)
```

we will get "wiki tool" and "wiki tools", but not "wiki wiki". Using these criteria, you can formulate very differentiated searches.

7.3 User Administration

Why register users?

Although one can actually take care of all important work in a wiki on an anonymous basis, most wiki systems offer user administration. There are several advantages to such a system. *Firstly*, it enables a user to make personal settings that will always apply to that person. *Secondly*, the name of the user is added to the version history for every edit, so that other participants can have an idea of who represents what opinion. This, in turn, offers an individual recognition and responsibility, and promotes a certain cohesion in the community. *Thirdly*, there are wikis which, precisely for that reason, make a registration with a user name a requirement for participating in the wiki. The exclusion of anonymous contributions is not possible without a user administration. Note that the real identity of a participant need not be made public, since user names can also be pseudonyms. *Fourthly*, a few wikis offer the possibility of adjusting access rights depending on a respective page and various tasks. However, MediaWiki has only very limited functions in this regard.

Registration

The registration process was described in Chap. 3.5 and can be found under the link **Create an account/log in** in the upper area of the wiki.

Permissions System

The MediaWiki permissions system is relatively straightforward. If you give yourself a user name, you only have "user" permissions. You can now upload files and move pages. Yet there are two higher levels with more rights. These are "administrators" and "bureaucrats". They can protect and delete pages before editing. Furthermore, they also access to a few special pages that deal with the maintenance of the wiki (see Chap. 7.5). The only difference between the two is that only bureaucrats can make other users administrators. Of course, the "WikiSysop" account that we have generated during the installation of the wiki retains bureaucrat rights.

Make a user an administrator

The special page **Makesysoptext** is used to grant other users administrator privileges. Here, just enter the respective user name, select whether he or she is to receive "bureaucrat" privileges like your own, and click on the confirm button. That's it. If anonymous users are not allowed to create a new account, you'll have to also arrange this as an administrator (see Chap. 8.1). In this function, the group "user" does not appear specifically. One automatically belongs to the "user" group if one is registered but not one of the "bots", "administrators" or "bureaucrats".

Bots

"Bots" are a bit out of step with the other categories: They are not a group of people with special rights, but rather small computer programs or scripts that take care of mindless, boring and frequent tasks such as replacing text or correcting errors. Each bot is registered just like a normal user and has its own user page stating the tasks for which it is employed.

User toolbar

Once you have logged in, you will see a series of further links in the top bar that enable you to access your personal pages. There is of course your user page, which bears your user name. On it, you can add information about yourself, for example. As a complement to this page, you'll also find a **user talk** page that serves as a means of communication with other users. In step with the spirit of simplicity, both pages are nothing more than normal wiki pages that are used for a specified purpose. However, this does not prevent you from placing articles on your Talk page or conducting discussions on your user page.

User page Every registered user has his or her own user page. On it, you'll find two new entries in the toolbox on the lower left. **User contributions** lists the edits the user has performed in the wiki. Should it no longer be up to date, you will see a rollback link with which you can restore the version of the page corresponding to the last changes made by that user. Changes to the text made subsequently by other authors are then discarded. For your own contributions, you will find the link **my contributions** in your user toolbar. The second new entry in the toolbox is **email this user**, with which you will arrive at a form that enables you to send an electronic message to the respective user. Of course, this is only possible if the user has supplied his email address.

Watchlist If you have placed one or more pages in your **watchlist** via the **watch** tab, you can monitor recent changes to that page. You will receive lists on a daily basis. Per line, you will find the name of the watched page, a link to the "differences" from the last version, as well as a list of the complete **history**, the participant that made the modifications and, if you have administrator rights, the opportunity to block that participant (see Chap. 7.5). Thus, you have all important administrative functions for a particular page at your fingertips. You could place your own page on your watchlist, in order to observe the reaction of the rest of the wiki community to it. If the list becomes too long, you can delete several entries from the list simultaneously by clicking on **show and edit complete list**. Now you can remove pages by checking them and clicking on the button **Remove checked items from watchlist**.

Preferences In the user toolbar, you will find the tab **preferences**. It will take you to a display in which you can select a number of settings regarding how the wiki should look and behave when you are logged in (see Fig. 7.3). We will discuss the various options in order of appearance below. Once you have indicated all of your preferences, click on **Save preferences** to apply them. Note that old page data may still be in the browser cache and may need to be emptied before you can see the new settings. If you wish to apply the default settings, click on **Reset preferences**.

User data Under **User data**, you can indicate preferences regarding your real name and email address. With the option **Disable email from other users**, you switch off the mail function on your user page. You can also change your password and language selection here as well.

Skin The tab **Skin** allows you to individually determine the appearance of your wiki, thus enabling you to alter its look and feel. Please note that these changes are only visible to you.

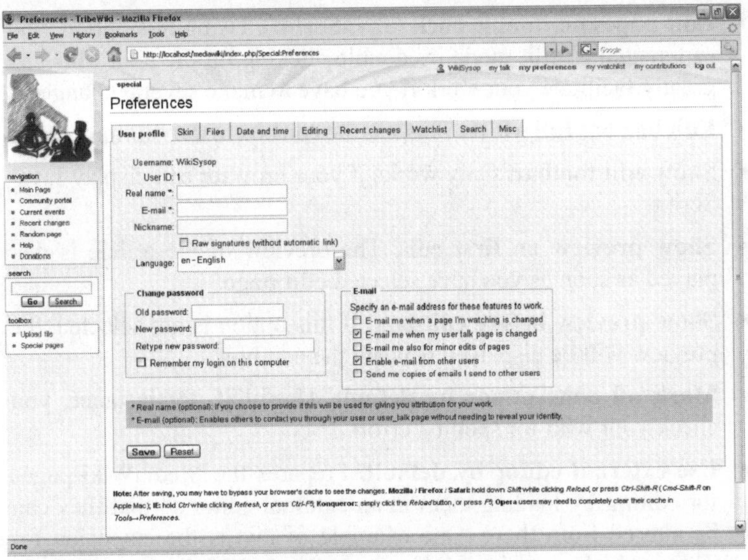

Fig. 7.3

Files

Via **Files**, you can limit the capacities of the image description page by indicating the maximum size of the image display. In addition, you can also determine the dimensions of the thumbnails.

Date and time

The tab **Date and time** gives you the opportunity to set your preferred date format which, for instance, is visible in the signature. You can also set your current time zone.

Files, date format and time zone

Here, you have the option of indicating an upper limit for image sizes that are not to be exceeded on the image description pages. In addition, you can define the size of those thumbnails for which no special dimensions have been set. **Date format** is obvious. **Time zone** enables you to "inform" your wiki of any difference in the time on your server and your local time. All times indicated would then be converted to your time zone.

Editing

A few interesting options can be found under **Editing**. You can set the height and width of the edit box. This is useful if you are working with a very low or very high screen resolution. Further settings include:

- **Enable section editing via [edit] links.** If you deactivate this option, an article can only be edited as a whole.
- **Enable section editing by right clicking on section titles (JavaScript).** This option is independent of the above link display. If activated, you can edit the section by right clicking on the respective section title.

- **Edit pages on double click (JavaScript).** Using this option, you can switch to edit mode by double clicking on the text. This can greatly facilitate your work if you have to make several changes.
- **Edit box has full width.** This sets the edit box to the maximum size.
- **Show edit toolbar.** Only works if your browser can display JavaScript.
- **Show preview on first edit.** The preview of the article is displayed as soon as you have selected **edit page**.
- **Show preview before edit box.** If this option is not selected, the preview will be displayed beneath the edit box.
- **Mark all edits minor by default.** Useful if, for instance, you check your wiki for spelling errors.
- **Use external editor by default.** Prepares the MediaWiki pages for editing by loading them in an external editor so that they can be altered from there. One example of this is the extension for jEdit, which can be obtained under the URL *www.djini.de/software/mwjed*.
- **Use external diff by default.** Enables the use of external programs for the display of version differences.
- **Prompt me when entering a blank edit summary.** Reminds you to comment each edit with a short summary.

Recent changes and stubs

You can determine the amount of pages listed under **recent changes** in the following tab. In addition, you can suppress the display of minor edits. If your browser is JavaScript enabled, you can switch on the enhanced display for **recent changes** (see above).

Watch list

Under **Watch list**, you can design your watch list, i.e. by indicating how many pages are to be displayed and if your edits are to be ignored.

Search results

The item **Search result settings** enables you to determine how many results are displayed per page. **Lines to show per hit** indicates how many lines of context of an article are to be displayed. If you set this number very high, the environment will always be shown with the search item. **Characters of context per line** refers to the length of this context display. Furthermore, you can also indicate in which namespaces a search should take place by default.

Miscellaneous settings

Miscellaneous settings offers a range of options:

- **Threshold for stub display.** The byte value indicated here determines what is to be defined as a stub. Links to articles that are smaller than the indicated value are highlighted in a special color.

- **Underline links.** This makes it easier to recognize links.
- **Format broken links.** If you deactivate this option, links to pages that do not yet exist are not highlighted but rather appear with a question mark that serves as a creation link. Stubs receive an exclamation point after the respective link.
- **Justify paragraphs.** Justified paragraphs are generally more difficult to read and are thus not set by default.
- **Auto-number headings.** Normally, headings are not issued with numbers. This function changes that state.
- **Show table of contents (for pages with more than 3 headings).** This facilitates working with larger texts.
- **Disable page caching.** Do this if you often receive older versions of a page on your display. The disadvantage is that you will have to put up with longer loading times.
- **Enable "jump to" accessibility links.** This activates additional links at the top of a page. They are intended for automated speech generation ("screen readers") and PDAs, and only visible in very old browsers. Thus, this function can generally be deactivated.

Those are all of the settings with which you can personalize your wiki.

7.4 Information about the Wiki

Statistics

A further group of special pages provides information on the wiki software and the state of the wiki itself. Let us first look at the **Statistics** page. In the first section, it shows information regarding the number of pages in the database that are probably legitimate content pages (not including, for instance, talk and special pages), and the number of hits and edits. In the second section, you will find the number of users and administrators, and finally the most highly frequented pages. The **Statistics** page thus actually has a purely descriptive function, serving to measure the size of the wiki and how often it is frequented.

Version

On the **Version** special page, you can view general data on the software used, information regarding copyright and originators of the wiki software, and links to websites of the programs used. Please note that MediaWiki software is always subject to GPL laws.

User list

Two pages provide information on the users of the wiki. The page **User list** displays a list of all registered users and their permissions.

Users who have only registered with an IP address and may have established a user page are not included in this list.

List of blocked users

Time after time, there will be users who do not observe the stipulated rules. To stop such users, administrators can block their IP addresses and thus prevent them from editing pages for a period of time. During that period, the individual's IP address is listed in the **List of blocked IP addresses and usernames**, along with the name of the administrator who blocked that address and the reason. If you are logged in as an administrator, you can also lift a block early. This page, of course, is also interesting if you yourself are among the blocked users. Firstly, you will discover why you have been blocked and secondly, you can contact the corresponding administrator to clear up any misunderstandings.

7.5 Maintenance

A number of pages aids in administering and maintaining the wiki and its community. In MediaWiki versions prior to Version 1.5, there was still a **Maintenance page**, which ironically was not maintained, and which is nowhere to be found in subsequent versions. A few functions have remained intact and can be found quite normally under the special pages. Using them, errors in the structure and content of a wiki can be detected.

Double redirects

The second function, **Double redirects**, searches for all redirects that in turn lead to another redirect. This is unnecessary, since the original redirect can lead right to the target page. One example: Page A links to Page B, which leads to Page C. In practice, automatic redirects only work once. That means that a reader accessing A ends up at B and cannot be redirected automatically. Thus, it is a good idea to eliminate the intermediate step from A to B and redirect from A to C. In the listing of double redirects, you will see the original Page A, Page B to which it links, and in brackets, Page C, so you will know the target. Behind A is a link to the corresponding edit mode, so you can make the correction immediately.

Broken redirects

The link **Broken redirects** brings you to redirects that link to non-existent pages. Since these redirects do not work (see Fig. 7.4), they should be removed or a target generated.

Fig. 7.4

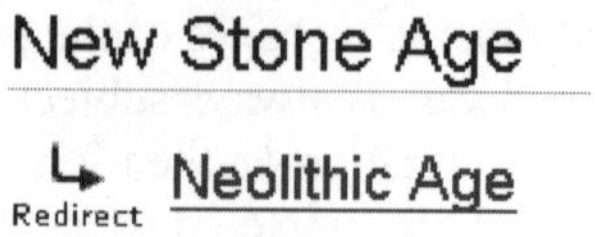

Using the page **Export pages**, you can generate an XML file containing the information on the indicated pages. To do this, you only need to enter the title of the page that you wish to export in the text box on that special page. Each title must be in its own line; otherwise it will be treated as one long title consisting of several words. If you deactivate the field **Include only the current version, not the full history**, all changes will be issued. Caution! This will create very large files. After pressing the button **Export page**, the wiki returns an XML file. You can either view it in the browser (not very useful, since you can see the same information in formatted form on the actual page), or save it for further processing as an .xml file.

Export pages

Note: Page decoration and formatting is not transferred. The information is primarily intended for the exchange of pages between wikis or MediaWikis.

On the whole, the connection of wikis and XML has been treated as a relatively minor topic. With the rising numbers of users and especially wiki systems, and the associated need for swapping between wikis, this is certain to change in the future. After all, there are already efforts underway to create an XML description of the entire MediaWiki formatting and page information under the heading Wikipedia DTD. A conversion function based on XML can be found on the page Wiki2xml *(tools.wikimedia.de/~magnus/wiki2mxl/w2x.php)*.

Wikis and XML

A list showing **MediaWiki system messages** might at first seem to be of little use. Here, you will find a three-column table with all system messages and inscriptions on the right. On the left, there is a link to a page in the MediaWiki namespace. That is an indication of why this area exists. Each edition of the wiki is recorded on one of these pages and can be edited by administrators. Modified messages are highlighted in red. In the middle column, the standard values are shown, such that, in the event of an unjustified modification, they can be easily accessed again. In a few messages, you will notice that variables have been used. These are identified by $ and a number, and are filled directly by the software. The content is usually a page name or number. This should be evident from the context.

All system messages

The page **Logbooks** provides you with the opportunity to follow all changes in the MediaWiki. This refers to uploaded files, deletions and page and user blocks. They can either be shown as a complete list or filtered according to user or page title.

Logbooks

Last but not least, there are four more pages that can only be accessed by users with administrator status. As mentioned earlier,

Block IP addresses

there is the possibility of blocking disagreeable users from editing texts in the wiki for a period of time. This is done via the page **Block IP addresses/usernames**. Here, you can enter an IP number. Note that, in the standard installation, you cannot block known users unless you know their IP (see Chap. 8.1). In addition, it is necessary to enter a block period. You can set this period individually via a drop-down menu or "other". Enter a number and time period in the **other duration** space[7]. Possible variables include "seconds", "hour", "days", "months", and "years". If no deadline is entered, the address will not be blocked. Blocking users should only be a last resort to fight vandalism, and should be reasonably justified.

Undelete pages

Administrators can delete pages. Such pages, however, are only marked as deleted in the database, but they otherwise remain preserved. Thus, in case a page has been deleted by mistake or wrongfully, it can be restored. From the list of special pages, select the **Delete logbook** from the **Logbooks** folder. It contains all pages marked as deleted. Simply select the corresponding file by clicking it. Then you can re-edit the page or view and/or restore a deleted version. For this, follow the corresponding link, select a version and confirm by clicking on **Restore**.

Note: you can also directly access the page **Restore deleted pages** using **Special: restore**. A list of deleted pages is displayed.

The special page **Import pages** is a portal with which to export pages from other wikis to integrate into one's own.

[7] The previous term "indefinite" has remained, but now it is accessible via the drop-down menu.

8 Administration

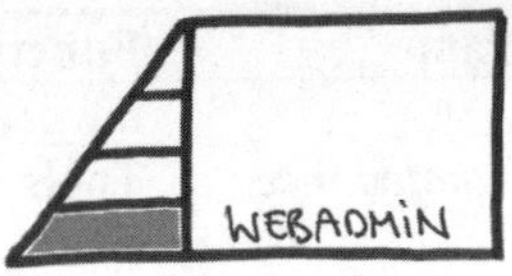

Administration of a MediaWiki, as we have seen, can in part be carried out via the browser. In addition, however, there are a few tasks that can only be performed with access to the server and the files located on it. The following will delve somewhat deeper into the processes and settings significant to the operation of the wiki.

8.1 File Structure and *LocalSettings.php*

To modify the MediaWiki on a file level, it is a good idea to first obtain a rough overview of the functions and corresponding directories, as well as the most important files that determine the performance of the wiki.

Directory structure

The subdirectories of MediaWiki directories and their functions are listed in Tab. 8.1:

Tab. 8.1

Name	Function
config	This is the location of the installation script that was explained in Chap. 2.2. In addition, the file *LocalSettings.php* is generated in this directory during installation.
docs	Documentation offering administrators an introduction.
extensions	Contains extensions of the MediaWiki. Primarily intended for future plugins, which are listed here.
images	Images and files that are uploaded to the wiki are stored here.
includes	The actual core of the MediaWiki. Here, you will find all files concerning the editing and structure of wiki pages.
languages	Translation of wiki messages to the corresponding language. Is read during installation and used for

Tab. 8.1 (continued)

Name	Function
	the generation of the message pages.
maintenance	Tools for administrators primarily for maintenance, updating and exporting of the database.
math	Files required for the integration of mathematical formulas.
skins	CSS files and images needed for the respective skins.
locale, tests, t, serialized, bin	Directories containing the display and test scripts for developers.

Parameters in LocalSettings

Many of the basic settings you can perform in MediaWiki are made via entries in the file *LocalSettings.php*, which is located in the main directory. This is actually a PHP script that determines a few fundamental variables. If you are not a PHP programmer, this should be no cause for worry, since the settings are done using a simple pattern:

CFG

```
$parameter = "value";
```

Lines beginning with a # are marked as commentary and thus have no effect on the software. The value of the parameters are determined during the installation of the wiki and adapted to the conditions of your system. In the following, we will discuss the interesting settings that you can perform more or less without risk. You should only alter the other values if you have experience in dealing with PHP and dynamic websites. In any case, to be safe, you should make a copy of *LocalSettings.php* that you can restore in an emergency. The file can be edited with any editor; however, syntax highlighting is advantageous, because the variables and values can be rendered obvious.

Tip: If during installation you have copied *LocalSettings.php* into the main directory and not moved it, the directory *mediawiki/config* should still contain the original version of the file.

During installation of the MediaWiki, you determined the name and contact email address. This information can be found in *LocalSettings.php* as parameters. The name of the wiki is set in `$wgSitename`. We do not advise subsequently changing the name, because several wiki pages use the set name, especially those in the respective namespace. On the other hand, it is possible that the administrator's email address my change. It is stored in `$wgEmergencyContact` as well as `$wgPasswordSender`. As you can see, both addresses can be different. The first contains that person who receives an email when the wiki software detects a problem. The second indicates from which address passwords are sent. This should be an address to which users can send a reply in the event of questions.

Using `$wgEnableEmail` and `$wgEnableUserEmail`, you can configure the system such that it sends emails (value true) or not (value false) and such that users can send each other emails or not.

Insert logo and adapt interface

The look of the wiki is partially determined by parameters in *LocalSettings.php*. The path containing the image that you see in the upper left corner of the MediaWiki is set in `$wgLogo`. Note that the path must conform to the operating system of the server. Under Linux, slashes are used to separate directories. Entries here are case sensitive. Under Windows systems, case does not matter, and directories are separated by a backslash. For example, our image file is stored in our Tribal wiki in the folder *skins/common/images*. The corresponding entry in the file *LocalSettings.php* is:

CFG

```
$wgLogo="$wgStylePath/common/images/logo.gif;
```

The file indicated should be an image file that does not exceed 135 x 135 pixels. Larger graphics are cut off. The general look of the wiki is determined by skins. The default skin for users not logged in is *MonoBook*. This is set in the parameter `$wgDefaultSkin`. Here, you can enter one of the skins listed. If you misspell it, the default skin will be set. To use your own skins, see below.

Designing the URL

Depending on the configuration of your system, it is possible to design the URL of a wiki page in a different manner. Normally, an article is accessed via a parameter in the file *index.php*:

URL

```
http://localhost/index.php?title=PageTitle
```

The second variation is shorter and nicer. Here, only path and title can be seen.

URL

```
http://WikiPath/PageTitle
```

During installation, the script checks your configuration and sets the variable `$wgArticlePath` accordingly, i.e. if possible, the shorter variation is used:

CFG

```
$wgArticlePath = "$wgScript/$1";
# $wgArticlePath = "$wgScript?title=$1";
```

`$wgScript` is the path, and `$1` the placeholder for the page title. If you prefer the long version of the URL, uncomment the second line by deleting the # and placing a # at the beginning of the first line.

Uploading images and files

Uploading images and files is not possible in the standard installation; thus it must be explicitly allowed. To do this, set the parameter `$wgEnableUploads` to `true`. Note that the value `true` is not contained in quotation marks. Under Linux, you must make sure that the directory *images* is writable. You can also determine what types of files will be accepted for uploading. They are set in the variable `$wgFileExtensions`, which is normally not set in *LocalSettings.php*, but rather in *includes/DefaultSettings.php*. There, it contains the following standard entries:

CFG

```
$wgFileExtensions = array( 'png', 'gif',        ↵
'jpg', 'jpeg');
```

DefaultSettings.php is not modified! If you want to add further file types, you must insert the above line in *LocalSettings.php*. Then you can expand the list however you like according to that pattern; that is, separated by commas and enclosed in single quotation marks. Note that a few file types harbor risks, especially if they are or contain executable programs. Thus, the following types are generally excluded from uploading:

```
html, htm, js, jsb, php, phtml, php3, php4,
php5, phps, shtml, jhtml, pl, py, cgi, exe,
scr, dll, msi, vbs, bat, com, pif, cmd, vxd,
cpl
```

If it should be necessary to upload these types of files, you can permit the uploading of .zip archives, pack the files in question into such an archive, and then upload them to the wiki.

Image sizes

Using `$wgUseImageResize=true;` you can enable the modification of image sizes. The option is switched off during installation, but it is a very good idea to activate it, especially to be able to generate thumbnails. If you have installed ImageMagick, you can use it to modify image sizes. The parameter is `$wgUseImageMagick=true`. The option of integrating LaTeX formulas in a page can be activated using `$wgUseTeX=true`. Please note, however, that this does not work under Windows. A few components are necessary that are issued with Linux distributions. Precise instructions can be found in the directory *mediawiki/math*.

Database access

Settings for access to the database can be found in the parameters `$wgDBserver`, `$wgDBname`, `$wgDBuser` and `$wgDBpassword`. You have already entered these during installation.

Your own namespaces

In addition to the namespaces already configured in the installation, you can add more. To do so, you first need a further variable in *LocalSettings.php* with the name `$wgExtraNamespaces`. All namespaces are numbered, and your own begin at 100. Even numbers indicate normal areas, uneven numbers denote discussion namespaces:

```
$wgExtraNamespaces =
  array(100 => "Flying Sparks",
        101 => "Flying Sparks_Discussion" );
```

You must now determine the behavior of the areas by setting two more variables. In the file *includes/DefaultSettings.php* you will find the entries to the variables `$wgNamespaces WithSubpages` and `$wgNamespacesToBeSearched Default`. Copy both to *LocalSettings.php* and expand the list with the numbers of the new namespaces. The first variable determines that new pages may be generated in the namespace, while the second determines whether the area is to be automatically included in searches:

```
$wgNamespacesWithSubpages = array(
  NS TALK => true,
  NS USER => true,
  ...
  100 => true,
  101 => true );
$wgNamespacesToBeSearchedDefault = array(
  NS MAIN => true,
  100 => true,
  101 => true );
```

Using this procedure, you can add up to 156 of your own namespaces in your wiki.

Limiting page access

The file *LocalSettings.php* can also contain information about who may view and edit pages. This setting is usually performed per user group and action in the form

```
$wgGroupPermissions['group']['action']=value;
```

With the value `true`, the user group is granted a permission; with `false`, it is not. There are generally three relevant groups:

- '*'. All people viewing a site. This also includes anonymous visitors.
- 'user'. All users that have registered in the system with a username.
- 'sysop'. All users who also have administrator status.

You can find all significant actions in Table 8.2.

Tab. 8.2

Action	Function
read	The user group may view all pages.
edit	The right to edit all pages.
createpage	It is permissible to create new pages.
createtalk	It is permissible to create new discussion pages.
createaccount	This right enables new users to be registered in the system.
move	The user group can move pages.
upload	The right to upload files to the wiki.

The default setting is that all users have reading and writing access. If you only wish to allow registered users to edit, you must insert the following line in *LocalSettings.php*:

CFG

```
$wgGroupPermissions['*']['edit']=false;
```

Please note that, with this constellation, it is still possible for all users to open an account in the wiki. If you wish to prevent this, you should also block anonymous users from having this right:

CFG

```
$wgGroupPermissions['*']['createaccount']
   =false;
```

Now the wiki can only be edited by registered users. If you also want to prevent random users from reading pages, because, for instance, the discussion is an internal one, you can also block reading rights:

CFG

```
$wgGroupPermissions['*']['read']=false;
```

Now, however, we are faced with the situation that no more pages are visible at all. This especially includes the homepage and – what is worse – the page for user registration; a seemingly impossible conundrum. Luckily, there is a setting that will save us from this paradox: the read whitelist. It lists pages that may be access despite a read limit. You should include the following pages in that white-list:

CFG

```
$wgWhitelistRead = array(
    "MainPage",
    "Special:Register",
    "MediaWiki:Monobook.css"
);
```

The last page in the list is necessary to also facilitate the correct display of the visible pages for non-registered users.

In order to be able to ban certain users from the wiki not only via an IP number but also via name, you must set the parameter `$wgSysopUserBans` to `true`. Now you can also enter user names on the special page **Block IP Addresses**.

8.2 Database Structure

Database tables

Almost all data created in working with MediaWiki is stored in the database. It is the last resort for edits to the data if no corresponding special page is available for the desired tasks. Thus, we wish to provide an overview of the important tables in the database below (see Tab. 8.3):

Tab. 8.3

Name	Function
archive	Deleted pages are located here.
image	Information on uploaded files.
imagelinks	List of links to images and files.
interwiki	List of known interwiki prefixes.
ipblocks	Information on currently blocked users.
links	List of all functioning links.
math	Information on mathematical formulas.
page	All data on the pages in the wiki. Only the text is saved in the table *text*.
revision	All data on the versions of a page.
recentchanges	List of changes in the wiki.
site_stats	Statistical information.
text	The actual wikitext of the revision versions.
user	List of users.

Tab. 8.3 (continued)

Name	Function
user groups	List of user groups.
watchlist	Entries on the personal watchlists of users.

Modifications to the database aim at the heart of the wiki, and could potentially cause a great deal of damage. When you make changes here, you should have a certain degree of experience in dealing with MySQL to prevent data loss.

A user's last edit

If you have identified a user as a vandal, it may be of interest to find out what pages he or she last edited; that is, for what pages no one has yet rolled back the destruction:

SQL

```
SELECT page.page title FROM page, revision
WHERE revision.rev_user_text='name'
AND page.page id = revision.rev id
```

Your own interwiki links

A list of the known interwiki abbreviations is entered in the table "interwiki". The elements each have three components: First the abbreviation, that is the prefix, is shown. Then the URL appears before an entry, followed by a $1, which stands for a variable for the article name. Finally, a flag must be set to indicate whether the link is local or not. In the former case, the URL of your own wiki is entered in front, in the latter case, the link is considered an independent external link. You can add new entries as follows:

SQL

```
INSERT INTO interwiki
VALUES ("prefix", "URL$1", local)
```

`Local` either has the value 0 for local or 1 for external. In an interwiki link, the prefix is then replaced by the corresponding entry and, in place of the `$1`, the link name is entered.

Empty archive

To reduce the size of the database, you can empty the archive of deleted articles. Only do this if you are certain that none of these articles is needed anymore.

SQL

```
DELETE FROM archive;
```

For some articles, their history only plays a minor role (e.g. if you generate a personal to-do list). To delete the old versions of a page, you can use the script *deleteOldRevisions.php*, which can be found in the directory *mediawiki/maintenance*.

To increase data security, it is advisable to copy and archive the content of the database from time to time. In the event of data loss, at least a portion of the articles can be restored. You can make a copy of the database by entering the following command at the command line level on the server:

```
mysqldump -u user -p db > file
```

Shell

You have already indicated *User* and *Db* (database) during installation. For `file`, you can select any name. It is a good idea to add the extension .sql, because this file is one in a series of SQL commands. You will then be queried for the database password, and after you enter it, the copy will be generated. As an alternative to the command line, you can also use a client such as phpMyAdmin.

Restoring data

To restore data, load the database copy in MySQL.

```
mysql -u user -p db < file
```

Shell

If you wish to import the page from another wiki, all you have to do is retrieve the tables *cur* and *old*. The dump command looks like this:

```
mysqldump -u user -p db cur old > file
```

Shell

The import command remains the same. After you have retrieved the new pages to the wiki, you should execute the maintenance script that refreshes the link tables. This can only be done via the command line level. To do this, switch to the directory *mediawiki/maintenance* and enter the following:

```
php rebuildall.php
```

Shell

Execution of the script can take several hours, depending on the database size. Since a few special pages depend on the data, it is worth the effort for reasons of consistency, because otherwise only incomplete data will be generated.

8.3 Design: your own Skins

Skins

If you wish to utilize MediaWiki as a component of your homepage, it is a good idea to adapt the design of the wiki to your own site. Even as an independent site, you may want to lend your wiki a personal touch. There are two approaches you can use to change its appearance: You can design the skin by altering the CSS files in the directory *mediawiki/skins/common*. Changes to the page structure, on the other hand, are done via the templates in the directory *mediawiki/skins*. The template system has only been in use since MediaWiki version 1.3. Template-based layout, however, is the model for future versions and considerably easier to adapt. In addition, the skin, which is intended to enable one's own settings, is based on a template model. Thus we will concentrate on template-assisted design below. It is of note, however, that the skins *Standard, Nostalgia* and *CologneBlue* use a different system.

Template structure

Let us first have a look at the template *MonoBook.php* in *mediawiki/skins*. The crucial area begins as of the line

PHP

```
class MonoBookTemplate extends QuickTemplate
```

The schematic construction is depicted in Tab. 8.4.

Tab. 8.4

Area	Function
`<head>`	Determines the page title and the stylesheet to be employed.
`<body>`	The entire content to be displayed is located here.
`<column-content>`	Areas in which the article is displayed.
`<bodyContent>`	Article display.
`<column-one>`	All navigation bars and toolboxes are located here.
`<p-cactions>`	The tabs with the various views of a page.
`<p-personal>`	User-specific links.
`<p-logo>`	Logo.
`<p-search>`	Search function.
`<p-tb>`	Tools.
`<p-lang>`	Links to other languages, if activated.
`<footer>`	Content of the footer.

As you can see, we are dealing with an HTML document in which the corresponding content is inserted. The area names, except for `head` and `body`, are each classes (`class=`) or IDs of `<div>` tags that surround an area. In the template, you can now remove elements or add your own HTML components. Of course, you should make a backup copy first.

Entry in the navigation menu

There is one frequently requested change to the design that you cannot perform here: changes to the entries in the **Navigation** box. Let us assume that you do not need the entry "Wikipedia Portal" in your navigation menu; instead, you wish to have a link to the participants list "ParList" of the Fire Project. To access this, open the page **MediaWiki:Sidebar**.

Note: To be able to edit this page, you must be registered as a sysop.

There you will find a **navigation** list with subitems. These lead to pages in the MediaWiki namespace which in turn contain the link target and descriptions of the entries. Thus, to reach our goal, we need to alter the pages **MediaWiki:Portal-url** and **MediaWiki:Portal** accordingy. In the former page, write the name of the target page, i.e. "P-List", and in the latter, "Participants List". Now open the **MainPage**: You should see the new entry in the list.

On the page **MediaWiki:Sidebar**, you also have the opportunity to add an additional box in the navigation bar. To do so, just add a new superordinate point on the same level as **navigation** and add a subitem analogous to the above list.

Editing skins

In order to change the skin design, you can format and position each of the `<div>` elements via its name with a CSS command. We will now edit the skin *MonoBook*. We do not wish to re-invent the wheel here, but rather simply change the design slightly. You can find the stylesheet data in *mediawiki/skins/monobook* under the name *main.css*.

Background

If you now wish to change the background, for instance, look for the entry `body`. This is where the URLs of the background image and color are set:

CSS

```
body {...
      background: #f9f9f9 url("headbg.jpg") ↵
      0px 0px no-repeat;
...}
```

You can change the color by altering the hexadecimal number behind the #. The corresponding values can best be established with an HTML editor or graphic program. To remove the background, delete that part of the entry from `url` to `no-repeat`.

Text color

The text color can also be set in `body` in the attribute `color`. Link colors can be modified a few lines down in the entries `a` and `a.new` for links to non-existent pages. The headings are set in `h1` to `h6`.

Personalized skins

Creating personalized skins is relatively easy. We want to install the skin *FlyingSparks*. Of course, you can use any name you like.

First, make a copy of the file *MonoBook.php* and change its name to *FlyingSparks.php*. You should also copy the directory *mediawiki/skins/monobook* to *flyingsparks*. Now you have to make a few changes to the new file *FlyingSparks.php*:

PHP

```
class SkinFlyingSparks ↵
  extends SkinTemplate {
```

```
/** Using monobook. */
  function initPage( &$out ) {
    SkinTemplate::initPage( $out );
    $this->skinname  = 'flyingsparks';
    $this->stylename = 'flyingsparks';
    $this->template  =                        ↵
      'FlyingSparksTemplate';
  }
}

class FlyingSparksTemplate                    ↵
  extends QuickTemplate {
```

Your skin is now installed. Now you just have to adapt the files of the template, as shown above for *MonoBook*, and your new layout is finished.

> **Note:** Do not forget to set up your new skin as the default in the file *LocalSettings*.php: `$wgDefaultSkin = 'flyingsparks';` you can determine your individual look with the page **Skin** in **Settings.**

List of special pages

Last but not least, let us make one small modification: You can tailor the list of special pages to suit your needs and, for instance, change their order or eliminate unwanted pages. Information on these pages is contained in the file *SpecialPage.php* in the directory *mediawiki/includes*. To remove entries, simply delete the line that begins with the name of the corresponding page. To change their order, move the line to the desired position. However, make sure that, except for the very last entry, all entries end with a comma.

8.4 Design of the Homepage with <div> Tags and CSS

Use sparingly

Nowadays, in many wikis you will find attractive homepages embellished with element boxes and frames. The use of element boxes saves space and lends clarity to the page. They are generated with the aid of `<div>` tags and cascading stylesheets. You can mark part of the source text with `<div>` tags which then read out formatting instructions for all pages from a CSS file and apply them to the area. However, it is wise to use element boxes sparingly. The source code will otherwise become bogged down and scare authors away from participating in the wiki. Besides, authors should have to deal with as few layout questions as possible.

Table as basic structure

First of all, we use a table to create the basic structure for the layout of the page. It consists of one line and two columns, and we assign the columns a width of 400 px each. The element boxes can thus be distributed across the entire page.

Wiki

```
{|
|-valign="top"
|width=400px|
|width=400px|
|}
```

Note: Screen readers for the visually impaired pose a problem for tables. For "barrier-free" programming, you should avoid using tables.

In the next step, we determine the formatting for the element boxes in the CSS. To change the CSS in your MediaMiki, you have two options. One the one hand, you will find the CSS formats in the directory *mediawiki/skins/monobook/main.css* or in the corresponding folder of your individual skin (see Chap. 8.3).

However, only web admins have access to this storage area. Yet MediaWiki provides you with a page at the wiki level with which authors, too, can change the stylesheet:*MediaWiki:Monobook.css*.

Below are two sample formats for two homepage boxes:

CSS

```
.hs-box1 {
    margin: 0;
    margin-bottom:10px;
    border: 2px solid #dfdfdf;
    -moz-border-radius: 1.5em;
    padding: .3em .6em 0em .6em;
    }

.hs-box2 {
    margin: 0;
    margin-bottom:10px;
    border: 1px solid #dfdfdf;
    -moz-border-radius: 1.5em;
    padding: .3em .6em 0em .6em;
    background: #f2f2f2;
}
```

The command `margin` sets a classic margin between the external edge of the element and other elements (which can be specified with `top`, `left`, `right` and `bottom`). The command `border` determines the border around the element; `padding` sets the distance between the frame and the content of the element. The background color is selected in hexadecimal code with `background`. Of course, you can also use all other CSS characteristics (font, text, color, list, height, width).[8] In our case, we selected relative values (em, px). Furthermore, the browser Mozilla can display rounded corners via `moz-border-radius`. However, they are only displayed by Mozilla and no other browser.

Integrate boxes

The formats are now integrated via the `<div>` tags:

Wiki

```
{{|
|-valign="top"
|width=400px|<div class="hs-box"> Text
links</div>
|width=400px|<div class="hs-box1">Text rechts
</div>
|}
```

It can be a good idea to protect this start page from alterations. Should wiki authors still be permitted to alter individual areas, such as **News**, you can still open a backdoor for them with templates. Simply generate the following template in the respective spot:

Wiki

```
{{News}}
```

The authors can then write texts on the page ***Templates:News***, which can then be integrated into the protected page.

8.5 Spam

Spam, that is, automatically generated messages with the goal of advertising a product, is a relatively new problem to the wiki world. Until recently, the email route seemed much more attractive to senders of spam. In addition, spam could be fought in wikis using IP bans or simple rollbacks. However, it is obvious that the frequency of wiki spam (as well as spam in blogs, forums and guestbooks) is

[8] Known HTML references and tutorials for beginners and advanced users can be found at Self-HTML: http://de.selfhtml.org/index.htm and PlanetHTML: http://www.planethtml.de/html/.

on the rise. The reason for this has to do with the ranking of pages by search engines. The more external links lead to a page, the higher up that page is in a search engine's ranking. The assumption is that a page with lots of links is relevant to lots of people. In order to collect as many links as possible, spammers write loads of links to their pages on wikis, blogs, etc. It does not matter that such entries will disappear again soon; it will suffice if a certain percentage of these entries are still online at the point in which a search engine's robot visits the site. Of course, this type of spam is annoying. Not only that, at a certain frequency level, it can also serve to considerably lower the motivation of wiki users, thus posing a serious hazard for the community.

Luckily, operators of the large search engines have recognized this problem, and a solution can now be observed. It comes in the form of a new attribute for the `href` tag which indicates to the search engine that they need not follow a particular link when searching for content to be indexed:

```
<a href="url" rel="nofollow">No Spam</a>
```

HTML

This attribute is attached to all external links. Thus, these links lose their effect for the page ranking. In MediaWiki, this attribute is used by default in versions 1.4 and higher. If you wish to switch it off (its use is disputed), add the line

```
$wgNoFollowLinks = false;
```

CFG

to the file *LocalSettings.php*. Ever since MediaWiki 1.4, there is also an option to install an extension which prevents saving links having certain URLs. These URLs can even be accessed by lists on the Net, to stay up to date. To install the extension, you first need to obtain the SpamBlacklistExtension files at *http://cvs.sourceforge.net/viewcvs.py/wikipedia/extensions/SpamBlacklist/* and copy it to the subdirectory *SpamBlacklist* of the *mediawiki/extension* directory. Then, insert the following lines at the end of *LocalSettings.php*:

```
require_once(
"$IP/extensions/SpamBlacklist/SpamBlacklist.
php" );
```

CFG

Now you still have to indicate from which source the plugin is to obtain its filter information. This is also done in *LocalSettings.php*, directly under the line cited above. You have two possibilities. Either you link to a file or a page in MediaWiki. In the following example, a file was saved as a text file in an extension directory, and an individual blacklist with the name "My Blacklist" was generated in MediaWiki.

CFG

```
r $wgSpamBlacklistFiles = array(
    "$IP/extensions/SpamBlacklist/
        wikimedia_blacklist",
    "DB: wikidb Meine_Blackliste",
);
```

You can find a continually updated list at *http://meta.wikimedia.org/wiki/Spam_blacklist*. The script "load lists" can download this list for you and save it in the file *wikimedia blacklist*. It is advisable to have the script automatically perform this task at regular intervals. The blacklist itself consists of a series of regular expressions that name the blocked URLs. For practical purposes, this simply means that a dot has to be masked with a backslash. The entry might look like this:

```
spammer1\.com
forbidden\.da\.ru   #not allowed in
```

As you can see, it is also possible to include comments. They must begin with a #.

8.6 Security

Generally, operating MediaWiki is as safe as operating your web server. Thus, you should make especially sure that the PHP security settings have been properly set. If you use XAMPP to operate a public wiki, you should definitely switch to safe operation mode (see Chap. 2.1).

Uploaded files

The greatest security risk is posed by uploaded files. They may contain viruses or malevolent code, and should thus be treated with special care and under no circumstances executed unchecked. This especially means that, as described above, a few types of data may not be copied to the server. An additional degree of security is offered by setting the web server to not execute PHP scripts in the upload directory. To do this, add the following commands to the Apache *httpd.conf*:

```
<Directory "path/uploaddirectory">
  php_admin_flag engine off
  AddType text/plain .html .htm .shtml
</Directory>
```

Data in LocalSettings

A further potential security problem is that access data to the database are stored in the file *LocalSettings.php* in plain language. This is risky for two reasons. On the one hand, you must make sure that this data is not passed on unintentionally if you generate a backup of the wiki software and make it available to others. Thus if – for whatever reason – PHP no longer runs, the source text of *LocalSettings.php* can be read via a browser. You can remedy this by storing security-relevant data separately and not releasing it for access from outside.

Thus, create the file *access.php* in a directory which is located on a level higher than the web directory of your Apache server. In the case of XAMPP, this would be outside of *htdocs*. This file looks something like this:

```php
<?php
  $wgDBserver        = "DBServer";
  $wgDBname          = "DBName";
  $wgDBuser          = "DBUser";
  $wgDBpassword      = "DNPassword";
  $wgDBsqluser       = "SqlUser";
  $wgDBsqlpassword   = "SqlPassword";
?>
```

Under Linux, you should make this file readable only for yourself and PHP, that is, the system. In *LocalSettings.php*, you must now also add the access data file after the line in which the default settings are integrated.

```
include_once( "DefaultSettings.php" );
include_once( "path/access.php" );
```

In this way, the web server can be prevented from simply displaying the file. It can only be addressed within the system.

8.7 Update and Uninstall

As and administrator of a wiki, you will most likely be interested in making sure your software is always up to date. This means that you will have to load a new version of MediaWiki to your system from time to time. The risk involved has less to do with getting the program to run than it does with making sure all existing data can be taken over completely.

Update

The developers of MediaWiki have recognized this problem and integrated an automatic update mechanism in their installation program. Before performing an update however, you should save a copy of the database, to be on the safe side. If you now perform an update, just install the new MediaWiki. Instead of the new database, however, enter the access data for the existing one. The wiki will identify it and make the corresponding adjustments.

Uninstall

If you want to uninstall your wiki, you need only do two things:

- Delete the MediaWiki files and the directory in which they are located.
- Delete the database in which the MediaWiki data is stored.

This removes all traces of the wiki.

9 Extensions

The core purpose of MediaWiki development is for the needs of Wikipedia. Many other users, however, have additional needs. That is why the developers have created a possibility to integrate or program extensions into the wiki.

9.1 Integrating Existing Extensions

Download

Extensions allow additional functions to be created in the system. In the meantime, there are more than 200 of these small programs. The range stretches from access controls to editor functions to drawing or exporting a PDF. But be careful: not all of the extensions are not yet technically mature. Often, they represent individual solutions that require a good deal of manual work to adapt them or that are dependent on other programs. Thus it is wise to keep expectations to a reasonable level.

You can find these extensions on two pages on the Internet:

URL

```
www.mediawiki.org/wiki/Category:Extensions
meta.wikimedia.org/wiki/
  Category:MediaWiki_extensions
```

The second URL leads to an old MediaWiki website. In the course of time, all pages located there will have migrated to *www.mediawiki.org*. However, it is a long process, and it is worth it to try both sites in your search for extensions.

Schematic installation

The lists you will find there all lead to a description page for the respective extension. Depending on the degree of enthusiasm with which the author has documented the extension, you will find download links, installation instructions, demos or links to related pages. Usually, the extensions are packed in an archive. To install them, you generally need to perform three steps:

1. Unpack the archive to the MediaWiki directory. The files needed for the extension will automatically be copied to the respective directories. The directory in which the actual program file of the extension is located is *extensions*.
2. Integrate the extension in LocalSettings.php. The best way to do this is by adding the following line at the end of the file:

   ```
   include('extensions/extensionname.php')
   ```

   whereby "extensionname.php" is the name of the file in the *extensions* directory.
3. Frequently, there are still settings to be make or small details to be altered in the MediaWiki code. Do not forget to make a backup of the corresponding file.

The steps listed here only represent the principle procedure. You should definitely read the extension description before you install it, in order to avoid any rude awakenings. Pay special attention to any dependencies the extension might have on other programs which would have to also be installed on the server.

9.2 Employing Bots

Bots

In addition to the extensions described, there are also bots. Bots are programs that, with their own usernames, search a wiki page and make changes according to certain rules. A typical example for this is the standardization of spelling. For instance, a bot could change every instance of "mediawiki" into "MediaWiki".

Setting up a bot user

It is completely understandable that the wiki community would react very sensitively to such automated changes. Thus, before using a bot in a wiki, you should have a good look at the rules valid for that wiki. Normally, bots do not operate anonymously. Thus a first step would be to set up a user under whose name the bot can perform its alterations. On the user page, describe what the bot does and who is responsible for it. Because automated alterations produce a great deal of entries in the list per task, it is advisable to hide the edits of the bot. For this, the bot receives a so-called "bot status". This means it is categorized in the "Bots" group. Changes made by a user with bot status normally do not appear on the Recent Changes list.

Program the bot

Now all you need to do is write the program in WikiCode which is to perform the desired edits.[9] There are a few templates for this

[9] This sentence written with a wink!

that will make the task easier. One example is pywikipedia, written in Python, about which you can find more information at

```
meta.wikimedia.org/wiki/Category:Pywikipedia
```

URL

Using this tool, and assuming you know Python, you can edit texts, move pages, generate redirects, and much more. Unfortunately, a more detailed description would extend the boundaries of this book. The following page will provide a precise explanation of how to configure and employ bots:

```
meta.wikimedia.org/wiki/
   Pywikipedia_bot_on_non-Wikimedia_ projects
```

URL

9.3 Excursion: Making your own Extension

Although the list of available extensions for MediaWiki offers quite a bit, there are usually other wishes, especially when you are trying to adapt a wiki to a particular software environment. Thus, we would like to show you how to write a few extensions of your own. Of course, this topic could fill a book of its own. Thus, this chapter will only serve to get you on your way and provide you with the basic principles and parameters. It will also give you an idea of how to alter (or improve) existing extensions. To write your own extensions, you should possess solid knowledge of PHP and also be familiar with relational databases and the query language SQL.

New Magic Word

We want to make it our mission to enrich MediaWiki by one new MagicWord that provides the number of all articles in a database (the number is higher than that on the MediaWiki statistics list and will supposedly better motivate the community …). MagicWords are integrated in MediaWiki using double curly brackets.

9.3.1 Programming in MediaWiki

Hooks

When you program in MediaWiki, you want to expand the existing functionality, that is, influence the way the program runs when it builds a page. Luckily, the system offers an interface: so-called hooks. Using them, you can "hook" into various spots and include your own functions. The basic struture of these always follows the following scheme:

```php
1  $wgHooks["NameofHook"][] = "MyFunct";
2
3  function MyFunc (parameter)
4  {
5     // Code
6     return true;
7  }
```

The global MediaWiki variable `$wgHooks` manages all functions to be carried out in addition to the normal course of the program. In Line 1, `MyFunct` is registered as such. The subsequent lines define what the function will actually do. The parameters to be transferred depend on the respective hook. We have collected a few of the most important in the following table.

Hook	Task
`EditPage::showEditForm:initial` `(&$form)`	Enables access to the elements and text of the edit form before output; `$form`: object with elements of the edit form.
`LanguageGetMagic` `(&$magicWords, $langCode)`	This hook lets you define your own variables. `$magicWords`: list of keywords.
`ParserAfterStrip` `(&$parser, &$text, &$strip_state)`	Finished wiki text of a page before it is converted to HTML. `$parser`: Access to the object that wiki code converts to HTML. `$text`: the wiki code of the page.
`OutputPageBeforeHTML` `(&$out, &$text)`	HTML text of a page before it is integrated into the template. `$out`: This object contains all data for the output. `$text`: HTML text of the page without navigation, etc.
`userCan` `($title, $user, $action, $result)`	Here, you can manipulate the permissions of a user. `$title`: The page in question. `$user`: The user attempting to perform an action. `$action`: What the user is attempting to do. `$result`: true, if permitted, false, if not.

If an & is situated in front of a parameter, that parameter can be directly altered in the function, and the changes are taken on in the further course of MediaWiki processing. Many of the parameters contain objects with several `characteristics`. The best way to become familiar with them is to print them out using the command

PHP

```
print r($variable);
```

At the end of a hook function, there should be a return value. This determines whether or not further functions are to be edited in this hook. Since it is often the case that several extensions are "hung onto" a hook, it is generally advisable to always enter `true`. One exception is `userCan`. If you have used `userCan` to prohibit an action from being performed by the current user, you should also not permit any further editing.

Global variables

In functions that are integrated into the hook mechanism described above, you have full access to the global variables supplied by MediaWiki. They include information about the title of an articles, the user or data from LocalSettings. The most important are listed in the following table.

Variable	**Content**
`$action`	Is the page being evaluated (**`view`**), edited (**`edit`**) or is the version history being viewed (**`history`**)?
`$wgRequest`	Gives you access to the URL parameters of a page.
`$wgScriptPath`	Part of the URL between the domain name and MediaWiki root directory; important if you want to code URLs.
`$wgTitle`	This enables you to access the current page.
`$wgUser`	Information on the registered user.

Within the functions, these variables must always be globally integrated with a keyword, such as:

PHP

```
global $wgScriptPath;
```

9.3.2 The Framework for Magic Words

Now that we've had enough of an introduction, let's get right to the real code. The framework for Magic Words always follows the following pattern:

PHP

```
1 $wgHooks['LanguageGetMagic'][] = 'ac_magic';
2 $wgExtensionFunctions[] = 'ac_setup';
```

First of all, two entry points are determined. The first registers the keyword such that MediaWiki "knows" that further editing is to be done there. The second is specifically for extensions of MediaWiki syntax and registers a function that is performed when the parser (that part of the program that converts wiki text to HTML) is activated. Let us first have a look at `ac_magic`:

PHP

```
3  function ac_magic( &$magicWords, $lang ) {
4     $magicWords['ac'] = array( 0, 'ac' );
5     return true;
6  }
```

Here, the keyword ac is set for the article count by being added to the variable `magicWords` (an array). Transfer, in turn, is done with an array whose first element indicates whether case sensitivity will matter (`0` means no), followed by the keyword. In further lines, you can indicate further keywords. This is a good idea if you wish to internationalize the extension. The current language is conveyed in `$lang`, such that one could also react to it. The important thing to remember is that there is a difference between the name of the Magic Word (the first `ac`) and the keyword for it. At the end of the function, the value `true` is returned. Otherwise, all Magic Words registered after our extension would be ignored.

Now let's move on to the editing part:

PHP

```
7  function ac_setup() {
8     global $wgParser;
9     $wgParser->setFunctionHook( 'ac', 'ac_render' );
10    return true;
11 }
```

The function `ac_setup` registers the Magic Word "ac" in the parser. For this, the object `$wgParser` must be made accessible in the function with `global`. This object contains all functions as well as the data necessary to convert the wiki text into HTML. In Line 9, the actual registration takes place. Here, the parser is informed that it is to invoke the function `ac_render` if it finds one of the previously defined keywords for "ac".

The actual work happens in the following function `ac_render`:

```
function ac_render( &$parser, $param1 = '') {
    // Code
}
```

The function accepts two (or more) parameters. The first enables access to the parser object and its functions. The second (and subsequent ones) contain additional information included in the wiki text Magic Word. Remember: a Magic Word has the following structure for wiki authors:

```
{{ac|param1|param2...}}
```

In our function, the values separated by pipes end up in the corresponding parameters.

9.3.3 Processing and Database

Access to the database

Now that we have seen the framework of a Magic Word in detail, we can turn to the actual task at hand, that is, counting the entries in the database. The data of the MediaWiki is managed in MySQL in various tables. A list of these tables can be seen in Tab. 8.3. The articles are located in the table called `page`. In order to find out the number of articles, all you have to do is look to see how many entries this table has. For this, we need access to the database. The MediaWiki provides the function `wfGetDB` for this purpose.

```
$db &= wfGetDB( DB SLAVE );
```

With this line, you get an object that will grant you reading access to the database. If you wish to edit entries, you should access this function as follows:

```
$db &= wfGetDB( DB_MASTER );
```

The database object `$db` will now provide you with functions for reading and writing to the MediaWiki database. The generation of the connection and the consideration of any set table prefixes are directly performed by the object, such that you need not worry about it. In addition, at least a rudimentary check for hackers is already incorporated into this routine.

Search tables

The tables can be searched using the `select` function:

PHP

```
$$db->select(table, column, conditions);
```

This function takes three arguments. The first, `table`, indicates the table in which the search is to take place. `Column` determines which table columns will be included in the results list, and `conditions` is a list of limiting conditions for the search result. The results are issued as a two-value array, the first being the column and the second the value according to which selection is to take place.

Let us have a look at the code of the `ac_render` function:

PHP

```
15 function ac_render ( &$parser,                    ↵
                              $param1 = '') {
16    $dbw =& wfGetDB( DB_MASTER );
17    $res = $dbw->select('page', 'page_id');
18    $out = $dbw->numRows( $res );
19    $dbw->freeResult( $res );
20    return array($out, 'noparse'=>1);
21 }
```

In Line 16, access to the database in writing mode is granted. It is a convention of MediaWiki in such a case to label the access variable as `$dbw` for "write" (correspondingly, for reading mode, it would be `$dbr` for "read"). The following Line 17 executes the database search. Since we want to see all of the pages, the third parameter for conditions is irrelevant. The result of the search is stored in `$res`, so that we can subsequently evaluate it. Line 18 simply counts the number of results using the function `numRows`, and stores this number in `$out`. This variable gets its name from the fact that everything is stored in it that will subsequently actually be issued as a result. In Line 19, the search result is deleted from memory in order not to bog down the server. Last but not least, the output stored in `$out` is fed into the further processing of the MediaWiki. The second value, `noparse`, indicates that the returned text no longer needs to be processed by the MediaWiki parser, but rather is already in the state in which it is to be issued.

To activate the extension, first save it as the file *ac.php* in the *extensions* directory.

Tip: Don't forget to label the entire code as PHP. This is done by entering <?php in the first line and ?> in the last.

You now need to integrate this file into *LocalSettings.php*. To do so, add the following to the end of that line:

PHP

```
include ("extensions/ac.php");
```

Now the extension will be activated. To test it, you can use the following code in a page in the wiki:

Wiki

```
{{ac}}
```

After saving, you should see the total number of all pages in place of the Magic Word.

9.4 The HalloWiki

Through the targeted employment of extensions, you can develop the MediaWiki into a true collaboration suite. One example of this is the HalloWiki, which – purely coincidentally – was developed by the authors of this book. We especially tried to improve the aspects of user friendliness and data security.

Fig. 9.1

Source

If you want to test the wiki or practice the codes, you can do so directly from our homepage at the URL

URL

```
www.hallowiki.biz
```

under *Downloads*. For free, of course!

10 Life in MediaWiki

In the previous chapters, you have become familiar with MediaWiki and are now capable of using it creatively. Yet you are not alone in a wiki. It can only unfold its true potential if several persons can work with it together. In this chapter, we thus want to consider what life in MediaWiki can look like. You will find a detailed description of cooperative processes in Sect. IV.

10.1 More than just Text

Wikis generate hypertexts. This form of text, however, is still relatively new. Many people learn it passively by surfing the Net, or reading Help pages, for instance, but only very few have experience in generating hypertext. Yet that is exactly what is required in the wiki.

Peculiarities of hypertext

You should first be aware of the fact that reading hypertext on a screen is coupled with phenomena that are not present with normal text:[10]

- **Content-related unity on hypertext pages.** A page on the Net is generally considered to be a unit.
- **Browsing**. The reader moves through the hypertext by following existing links. This may lead to a text not being read completely.
- **Skimming**. Texts on screen are not read as thoroughly as the printed word. The reader skims the text in the search of relevant information or new and promising links. This is additionally promoted by the fact that links interrupt the text flow due to their format.

---

[10] See Kuhlen, 1991, Chap. 2 and Nielsen, 1996, 309ff.

- **Lost in Hyperspace**. The user happily follows the links as they appear. After a while, he knows neither where he is nor how to get back to the starting point.
- **Serendipity**. On a journey through hypertext, one often discovers things one hadn't been looking for but which still appear very remarkable and helpful.

These peculiarities are translated into concrete reader needs that should be observed. Write everything that belongs together on the same page. However, do not be shy about placing new thoughts in separate articles. This is promoted in a wiki through the necessity of indicating page titles, which lends each article a kind of motto.

Navigation elements

With a history and the **Back** button, browsers already facilitate navigation through the Net. Nevertheless, it is important to set up your links so that they support browsing. For instance, it can be a great help to include a link at the start of the page leading to a superordinate or parent page and can be found under a name such as "Page up" or the like.

Wiki

```
[[Parentpage | Page Up]]
```

If you employ these conventions consistently, the reader will have it much easier. You should also provide information regarding the spot within the wiki in which the reader is presently located. Several Internet pages thus indicate a path to the current article to illustrate the trail through the hierarchy of the website.

Wiki

```
You are here: Main > Stone Age > Development
```

This decreases the risk of your readers getting lost in hypertext.

Link names

In addition, it is important that they can gain an impression of what is behind a link. This means, among other things, that links should not consist of meaningless words, even if they are highlighted and are thus very noticeable. Instead of writing

Wiki

```
You can find the development report
[[development report|here].
```

choose instead to highlight the keyword:

Wiki

```
You can find the [[development report]] here.
```

You should make sure that the links you set have a connection to their information. For instance, in the following text, it makes little sense to set the first link:

```
Humankind in the [[Year]] [[10000]] B.C.
```

Wiki

While it may be of interest to find out what special events occurred in the year 10000, defining "year" as a link is irrelevant. Experience has shown that little thought is given to this point. However, do not hesitate to document unusual associations with links; that promotes the serendipity effect and makes the text more interesting.

10.2 Make Access Easier

An empty wiki is not a pretty sight. Furthermore, every wiki should contain information that specifies what is to be treated in that web. That is why a few important pages must be established right from the start. Our tribal initiative has decided to set up the pages together in a sort of workshop one afternoon, and at the same time, learn how to work with MediaWiki.

Designing the main page

First and foremost, the main page must of course be designed. Describe the orientation of the wiki's content and clarify the status that the published work will have (e.g. discussion, idea collection or finished documents). You should be certain about the target group of your wiki. If you are aiming to allow many strangers to communicate with each other, the description must be a great deal more detailed. In this case, it may be a good idea to allow a separate page for this description. For the tribal initiative, the platform will more likely serve the internal discussion, where the group is more manageable and knows each other. Thus, a description of the site's purpose would not need to be quite so exhaustive.

Editing help

Because we can assume that the members of a tribal initiative do not have much experience in using wikis, it is advisable to place the most important information regarding its use directly on the platform. One important site in this regard is **Wikiname:Editinghelp**. This information can be accessed in edit mode by clicking **Editing help**, and should contain the most pertinent formatting rules. Since syntax in all wikis is the same, it will suffice to use the corresponding text from Wikipedia as an example. In addition, you can establish a separate page on which questions that pop up can be posted and answered, and which can be expanded in the course of the work.

Sandbox

In step with this concept, several wikis offer a sandbox that invites users to experiment. It is not a standard component of MediaWiki; you must generate it yourself. This page has no special functions, which means that it should be cleaned, that is, its contents deleted, manually on a regular basis. A few explanatory lines detailing the purpose of the sandbox can be placed on a separate page and embedded in the sandbox as a template. The advantage to this procedure is that the explanatory text cannot be destroyed by overzealous experimenting.

Establishing conventions

A significant component to every wiki should be the provision of a series of common conventions that promote the organization of the system. It is a good idea to record them on a wiki page, because, during the course of the project, they can be modified and tailored to the needs of the group. These rules, which our tribal initiative will define together, can include items such as work processes or name conventions. Even the "obligations" of the participants are a component of these stipulations, such as, for instance, the setup of an information page which we assume will be read by everyone on a regular basis.

Note: Do not forget that every web presence must include an imprint that cites the contact address, including telephone number and email address, of the provider. Further conditions apply to commercial sites. Failure to provide this information may prove to be an expensive mistake.

10.3 You're not Writing Alone

In conventional forms of publishing, you primarily write your text so that a reader can understand it. In a wiki, you also have to consider that your readers may also be authors. Thus, you are also writing for authors.

Edit conflicts

One central topic in this regard is avoiding edit conflicts. Often, problems materialize when two users edit the same file at the same time without knowing it. MediaWiki actually has a built-in mechanism that detects such conflicts within a certain period of time and makes them known. However, many authors prefer to edit a text on their own computer over an extended period of time (e.g. due to running online costs). In such a case, the automatic protection does not work; in addition, it is very probable that someone else has taken on the text. That is why it is advisable to agree that, when editing a text, one should add a short note to the respective page indicating that the page is currently being edited and will be available again within a certain period of time.

In Wikipedia, there is a prefabricated text module that is placed above an article before extensive edits:

```
'''Attention''': This article is actively
undergoing a major edit. As a courtesy,
please do not make edits to this article
while this message is displayed, in order to
avoid '''edit conflicts'''.
```

This module can be set in the namespace **Template**. Our tribal initiative, for instance, has done so under the name "In Use", and can embed this message on any page indicating

```
{{in use}}
```

Unfinished pages

Once in a while, someone notices that an article is unfinished but does not have the resources at that time to continue work on it himself. To coordinate work on the project, the Fire Group has added two further templates that show that a page urgently needs editing and that its content must be checked. One or two members who are especially attentive in maintaining the wiki have these two template pages on their watchlists, to facilitate quicker access. At regular intervals, they access the pages and use the backlink function. In this way, they receive a list of all pages that contain the corresponding template and thus need editing.

Formatting source text

A second important point to be observed while writing is that other authors must understand your source text. The more complicated the construction of your page is, the more difficult it will be for others to understand, for instance regarding how certain formats can be attained. You only succeed in establishing additional hurdles for participants to the creative process in the wiki.

The readability of a source text can be greatly improved using the following simple means:

- Use **new lines** to separate units. This is, admittedly, at times not easy in MediaWiki, since line breaks in the wrong place will spoil the process. On the other hand, the page breaks are not displayed when the page is formatted, such that, e.g. you can write commands to embed templates or variables in lines.
- **Comment** the source text. To do so, you can use normal HTML comment symbols (`<!--` and `-->`). Describe the structure of the

page, the most important sections and special features that need attention.

- **Store complicated layout elements separately in templates** so as not to confuse inexperienced users, and comment on the way they function.
- Select **meaningful names** for pages, templates and variables that can be understood without a great deal of effort.

Communication between users generally occurs via two means: the user-to-user email function and the user talk function.

User-to-user email

In both cases, you search for the user page of your communication partner. In the navigation bar on the left, you will find the netry **Email this user**. To be able to send email to another user, however, you first have to be registered an have a valid email address. In addition, sending emails must be activated in the wiki.

User-Talk

User talk is nothing more than a the discussion page of a user's page. You can leave the respective user a message on his or her Discussion page. When the user logs onto the wiki, he is automatically informed that his user discussion site has been altered. He receives the message: **You have new messages (last change).** You can directly access the mail by clicking either on new mail or differences to the version before last.

10.4 Usage Examples

This section is intended to serve more as motivation than instruction. Its aim is to demonstrate how the individual elements of the wiki interact and provide an incentive to find your own creative solutions for everyday problems on the web.

10.4.1 Main Page with News

Problem: After the visitor number of the tribal initiative's wiki increased dramatically, it was decided that the main page shall be secured so that only administrators can change it. Only a small area, **News**, is to remain editable by everyone.

Solution: Locking the main page is done by an admin. He or she simply activates the **protect** tab on the main page and indicates as a reason: **Main page requires special protection.** Now, only administrators can alter the page. A small area, however, will remain open.

This is realized via a further page, **News**, which anyone is free to edit. This page is embedded into its respective location on the title page as a template:

Wiki

```
{{:News}}
```

Note the colon, which indicates that the article is located in the main namespace. It thus prevents news from disappearing from the template namespace. The page can thus also be easily accessed separately.

10.4.2 Checklist

Problem: The planning of an information booth always occurs according to the same procedure. Authorizations must be obtained, the material ordered, and the public informed via the press. So as not to forget anything and to learn from experience, we need a checklist that can be expanded if needed for subsequent information booths. Since a few of the items on the list depend on conditions on-site, the respective current checklist should also be able to be adapted accordingly.

Solution: You can probably guess that we can best solve this problem using templates. There is a prototypical list that can be copied to a new wiki page for a corresponding project. First, the page **Templates:checklist infobooth** is generated. It contains a table with the items to be observed in one column, and check marks in a second column:

Wiki

```
== Checklist ==
{|
| Collect material ||
|-
| have authorized by __PERSON __||
...
|}
```

As you can see, there are a few holes here that are marked by underlines. This serves as an optical indication that the corresponding information must be added when the checklist is set up. In order to get your own list, there are two steps you have to take. You must first generate a page, preferably with a link:

Wiki

```
[[Checklist Information Booth in
Neanderthal]]
```

The content of the template is loaded to this page. To do this, the keyword `subst:` is necessary:

Wiki

```
{{subst:Checklist Infobooth}}
```

Now, the blanks are filled in with the information, and the list is ready for use. When an item has been completed, the person responsible for it simply inserts his signature (~~---) instead of a check mark on the list. If, during processing, it becomes apparent that an item to be checked off is missing, it must be added to the actual list as well as the template. This ensures that the information will remain intact for subsequent information booths.

10.4.3 Literature Database

Problem: Now that the tribal initiative has performed extensive research and gathered a good deal of material on the use of fire, a fair amount of disorder reigns. The wiki will be employed to counteract that phenomenon and organize the articles.

Solution: The data must be saved in the wiki in such a way that it can be found again easily. A certain degree of discipline is necessary (unfortunately not one of the tribal initiative's strong points); conventions must be established and, above all, observed. This especially applies to the selection of a title. Since it should be as explicit as possible, it should only contain the title of the work, in its entirety, if possible. The author, year, publisher and a few keywords are set up as categories. Here, you can make life easier for normal users by using a template that displays this information in a uniform way:

Wiki

```
{|
| Author
| {{{author}}} [[category:{{{author}}}]]
|-
| Year
| {{{year}}} [[category:{{{year}}}]]
|-
| Publisher
| {{{publisher}}}
[[category:{{{publisher}}}]]
```

```
|-
| Keyword 1
| {{{keyw1}}} [[category:{{{keyw1}}}]]
|-
| Keyword 2
| {{{keyw2}}} [[category:{{{keyw2}}}]]
|-
| Keyword 3
| {{{keyw3}}} [[category:{{{keyw3}}}]]
|}
```

This template is embedded in the beginning of each entry, and forces authors to provide at least a few fundamental facts about the material:

Wiki

```
{{subst:Literature |
author = Firestone |
publisher = Stone and Chisel |
year = 10000 B.C. |
keyw1 = fire |
keyw2 = water |
keyw3 = use }}
```

The rest of the page can be filled with a summary and any special comments.

There are several possible ways to find a particular article. If you know the title, you can obtain a summary by entering it in a search and pressing **Go**. If you know the author or publisher, you can use the category system for access. For a subject search, you can also use the categories determined by the keywords. If all of that is of no assistance, you still have the MediaWiki full-text search option.

10.4.4 Calendar

Problem: The members of the tribal initiative, all very busy people, must coordinate their appointments and, most of all, maintain an overview of the initiative's events. Because the cooperative platform of the wiki has proven to be successful, let us try using it for this task.

Solution: MediaWiki is stretched to its limits here. A calendar that automatically enters appointments in the correct spots and shows weekends would need more means of automatic editing than MediaWiki can offer. However, you can still generate a simple annual calendar by putting together two tables. The first contains all months. It basically serves to line them up next to each other. The second table displays the respective month. First, let us look at the annual table:

```
{|
| width=16% valign="top" |  January
| width=16% valign="top" |  February
...
|-
| width=16% valign="top" |  July
| width=16% valign="top" |  August
...
|}
```

To make it easier to follow, we can enable the months to be displayed in two columns by selecting a column width of 16%. The respective month tables are then inserted:

```
| width=16% valign="top" | January
{| width=100% border=1
| bgcolor="#FFFFFF" | 1
|-
| bgcolor="#FFCCCC" | 2 appointment
|-
| bgcolor="#FFFFFF" | 3
|-
| bgcolor="#CCCCFF" | 4
|-
| bgcolor="#CCCCFF" | 5
...
|}
| width=16% | February
```

As you can see, the individual days are displayed in various colors. January 4 and 5 are marked as a weekend. This enables the week to be organized easily without having to manually enter the days of the week. Appointments are also highlighted in color. To facilitate editing, we recommend transforming the month names into section headers. Then, every monthly calendar can be edited individually and the desired spot will be much easier to find:

```
| width=16% valign="top" |
{| width=100% border=1
|
=January=
```

```
|-
| bgcolor="#CCCCFF" | 1
```

Don't forget to suppress the table of contents using _NOTOC. You can view the result in Fig. 10.1:

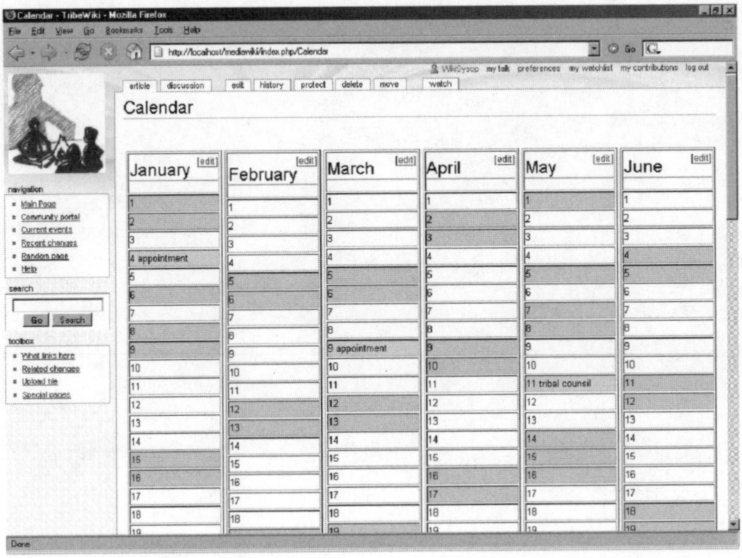

Fig. 10.1

As we have mentioned, a great deal of manual work is required for this process. Thus, MediaWiki is hardly suitable for more complex schedule management.

III. TWiki, the Jack of all Trades

11 Installing TWiki

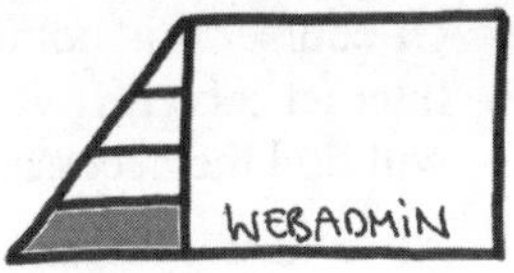

Currently, TWiki is without doubt the flagship of the free wiki variants. It not only offers sophisticated permissions and user administration, various separate areas and its own forms, but also a plugin interface with which the system can be expanded by versatile additional functions, such as drawing, calculation or a database.

Required components

In contrast to MediaWiki, TWiki is written in the script language Perl. It does not use a database to store pages, but rather saves them as files in a directory structure directly on the hard drive. When doing so, it often refers to commands and programs that are present by default on Linux systems. While not impossible, this makes the setup in a test environment under Windows more difficult. For history administration, the tool RCS (Revision Control System) is employed, which records modifications and stores the files accordingly. Since this tool is not present or cannot be installed (in the case of web hosts) on all systems, TWiki has its own version of RCS which, however, is not as high-performance as the original. All required components are listed in Tab. 11.1.

Tab. 11.1

Components	Function
Apache	Web server, administers access to files from the Net.
Perl	Script language in which the TWiki software is written.
Unix Tools	Diverse programs, especially Diff and Grep, that control access to and formatting of pages.
RCS	Revision software to monitor modifications to a file.

Before you install TWiki, you should think about what you would like to do with it:

- If you want to work with a group in TWiki, it is preferable to have your own server. The necessary installation steps are described under the **Linux System** information below.

- Of course, it is not a matter of course that everyone has his own Internet server. If you have stored your site with a **web host**, you will find the necessary information in Chap. 11.2.
- As a test system, it can also be run under **Windows** (see Chap. 11.3); in this case, however, installation is a bit more complicated, because TWiki is tailored to Linux.

In any case, prepare yourself for a somewhat complex installation process. A certain degree of experience in dealing with web administration will come in very handy. For Windows, there are a few preinstalled variants that we will introduce a bit later on in this book.

11.1 Installation under Linux

Installation under Linux is basically the same, but depending on the environment, may vary a bit. You can find more detailed information on the various platforms and webhosting sites at *www.twiki.org* in the **TwikiInstallationGuide** and the link contained therein to the Supplemental Documentation (in the Trouble-shooting section).

We will now take you through the standard installation on your computer and assume that a web server has already been set up. If you have worked through this book up to this point, you should already have a version of XAMPP on your computer. The installation is described in Sect. II.1.

Ideally, you should have root rights to install the program under Linux. Thus, you must log in as an administrator:

Shell
```
su
```

Normally, the two necessary programs, Perl and RCS, will already have been installed under Linux. Verify this by requesting the respective version numbers:

Shell
```
perl -v
rcs -V
```

If you do not get an error message, the programs are installed. If the command is unknown, you must at least install Perl retroactively; there are alternatives to RCS that come with TWiki (see Chap. 11.4).

11.1.1
Copying TWiki

You can find the current version of TWiki under *www.twiki.org* or on the CD under */wikis/twiki*. Copy the file *TWiki-4.1.2.tgz* to a directory to which your server has access, e.g. */opt/lampp/htdocs/twiki*. Unpack the archive with

Shell

```
tar xvzf TWiki-4.1.2.tgz
```

This will generate a directory structure, and the files will be copied to their corresponding locations.

11.1.2
Configuring Apache

Determine executable directory

We first have to adapt the Apache configuration file *httpd.conf* so that the access rights to the individual directories are correctly set. You will find this file in */opt/lampp/etc*. A file comes with the TWiki installation that already contains most of the settings. It must be embedded into *httpd.conf*. To do this, add the following to *httpd.conf*:

CFG

```
include "/opt/lamp/htdocs/twiki/twiki.conf"
```

Set up directory rights

Now open the file *twiki.httpd.conf* located in the TWiki directory. First you need to adapt the paths. Thus, replace all occurrences of /home/httpd/twiki/ with /opt/lamp/htdocs/twiki/. The configuration script must be cleared for the initial settings. Look for the spot where <FilesMatch "^configure.*"> occurs and change it as follows:

CFG

```
<FilesMatch "^configure.*">
  SetHandler cgi-script
  Order Deny,Allow
  #Deny from all
  Allow from 127.0.0.1, 192.168.1.10
  #Require user JohnDoe
  #Satisfy Any
</FilesMatch>
```

If you do not have PHP installed on your server, place a # in front of php_admin_flag engine off. Save that edited file under *twiki.conf*.

11.1.3
Adapting Files

The scripts are designed such that the entire path of the Perl interpreter is called */usr/bin/perl*. You can track down the path on your system using `which perl`. If it should differ from the standard, you will have to modify the shebang lines accordingly. There is a tool for this that you can find in the directory *twiki/tools*. Switch to the *twiki/bin* folder:

Shell
```
cd /opt/lamp/htdocs/twiki/bin
```

That is where the Perl scripts are situated. Enter the following command:

Shell
```
perl ../tools/rewriteshbang.pl
```

You will then be prompted to indicate a new path. Enter the location in which the file *perl.exe* is situated. Confirm the next inquiry with <Return>. Now you should see a list of files that have been changed.

The files in the directory *twiki/bin* must be executable. You can achieve this by entering the following command in this directory:

Shell
```
chmod 755 *
```

The files in the directories *data* and *pub*, as well as the directories themselves, must be writable by Apache. The easiest way to accomplish this is by switching to the corresponding directory and setting the writing rights as follows:

Shell
```
chmod 666 */*
```

They also must be set for the directories themselves, with the following command in the *twiki* directory:

Shell
```
chmod 666 data pub
```

11.1.4
Opening the Configuration File

Now you can perform a preliminary trial run of your configuration. To do this, in your browser, open the URL *http://localhost/twiki/configure*. If you receive an error message stating that access is denied, check the passage in *twiki.conf*. If you see a text file beginning with a shebang line, that is, with #!, your Perl settings are incorrect. Otherwise, you will see an HTML page that starts with the heading **Configuration**.

This concludes the Linux-specific instructions; you can now proceed with the installation in Chap. 11.4.

11.2 TWiki without an Admin-Account

Prerequisites

If you intend to run *TWiki* via a web host, you naturally will not have access to the server configurations. In addition, several web hosts do not offer SSH access, so that the files may not even be able to be edited directly on the server. Nevertheless, you do not have to give up working with wikis. However, one important prerequisite is that your web host offers *Perl* and allows you to use your own scripts. In principle, we proceed exactly as if we were installing a local copy, except that we use the parameters of the web host. We assume that you are familiar with the local installation of TWiki for your operating system.

Required information

You first need a variety of information about your web host.

- **Bin directory**. In which directory are you permitted to execute scripts? Usually, you will find a directory called *bin* or *cgi-bin*, if you log onto your account via FTP.
- **Web directory**. Which directory can be accessed via the Net? Standard names include *public_html* and *www*.
- **Perl**. What is the path to Perl? If you have SSH access, you can find the paths using `which`. Otherwise, a look at predefined Perl scripts may help.
- **Absolute path**. What is the name of the path to the directory of your web folder? Unfortunately, there is no way to guess this path. If you have SSH or Telnet access, you can have the path displayed using `pwd`. Otherwise, ask your host. If you cannot find the path, you can initially work with relative paths.

Unpack the TWiki installation file on your hard drive. If necessary, you will now have to adapt the shebang lines of the scripts in the local directory *bin* to the Perl path of your provider. This procedure is described in Appendix A.

Directory structure

Next, create a directory structure on the web server and copy the files from your local hard drive to the corresponding locations. The following folders are required:

Tab. 11.1

Local Folder	Function	Web Host Folder
twiki	Start files	Master directory of your wiki. It is the one you first access when logging in via FTP.
twiki/bin	Scripts	The bin directory defined above. You can also generate your own subfolders in this directory.
twiki/lib	Function library	This should be in the same directory as the *bin* folder.
twiki/pub	Publicly accessible files	In the web directory defined above or a subfolder.
twiki/data	Pages	Because these pages only need to be modified by the wiki software, it is advisable not to make this directory accessible from the web. If this is not possible, it is no great flaw unless you have secret data on your TWiki.
twiki/templates	Templates	See *twiki/data*.
Twiki/locale	Language files	See *twiki/data*.
Twiki/tools	Tools	See *twiki/data*

You can now open the test script *configure* in a browser as described above. If you now see an HTML page with the heading **Configure**, your efforts were successful.

11.3 Installation under Windows

Since TWiki has been tailored for use on Linux systems, we strongly advise against running public wikis under Windows. However, it may be useful to set up a version under Windows for testing or editing purposes.

As mentioned above, there are several variants. We will start off by introducing the two simplest versions. These are pre-configured systems that can be used immediately. The third variant walks through the installation. Which variant you choose ultimately depends on your requirements and knowledge. The first two variants are relatively easy to install. For the first variant, you have to put up with a few small limitations, but for a start, it is probably the best solution. In the second variant, you have a fully functional TWiki, but you need to be familiar with Linux in order to configure the files. This is especially necessary from time to time in subsequent chapters. The third variant illustrates the installation for the hard-boiled among you, but the payoff is that it also enables you to use (almost) all features of TWiki in Windows as well.

11.3.1 Variant I: TWiki for Windows Personal

TWiki for Windows Personal is a package that contains an entire test environment and installation script. You can find the file on the CD in the directory *wikis/twiki-WP*. Unpack the content of the archive *TWiki-WP-4.0.5.zip* to the directory *C:\twiki* on your hard drive.

Caution: When unpacking the files, they may be copied into a further *twiki* folder within *C:\twiki*. If this happens, you need to copy the content of the inner folder to the outer folder.

Once there, execute the file *run.bat*. This will start the web server. Now you can open the TWiki in the browser with

```
http://localhost:8765/cgi-bin/view.pl
```

URL

That's it. When you want to close the TWiki, simply close the browser. This will not however shut off the web server. To do so, you need to end the process **tinyweb** in the task manager.

As in all simple things, there are some limits to TWiki for Windows Personal. For example, it is not possible to perform user registrations with this system. Thus, you cannot change the pages that are blocked for anonymous editing.

In addition, this distribution contains a TWiki of the version 4.0.5, which can deviate slightly from the newest version, 4.1.2.

Note: TWiki for Windows Personal uses the extension *.pl* for Perl scripts. This is different from the other installations described in this book. In URLs that lead directly to scripts, such as to *configure*, you must always indicate the extension, too, thus, for instance: *configure.pl*.

11.3.2 Variant II: TWiki VMWare Virtual Machine

A virtual machine is a type of computer within a computer. With it, you can start a second system (guest system) within your operating system (host system), such as Linux under Windows. That is exactly what TWiki VMWare Virtual Machines does. It is a complete installation that you can start if you own the VMWare Player, which can be obtained free of charge at:

URL

```
http://www.vmware.com/products/player
```

Copy the virtual machine found on the CD under *wikis/twiki-VM* onto your hard drive. Open the player, load the virtual machine and start it. Please make sure that, under the menu Devices – Ethernet, the point **NAT** (not **bridged**) is marked. Now you can simply open a browser in the host system and launch TWiki via the URL

URL

```
http://twiki-vm
```

When you want to close the system or edit the TWiki file, you need to log onto the guest system. For this, log onto the system of the virtual machine with the username "root" and password "root". To end the program, enter the following command at the console:

Shell

```
shutdown -h now
```

The system will then shut down.

TWiki VMWare Virtual Machine is a fully functional wiki. Its only disadvantage: A system within a system requires a good deal of resources. Accordingly, in weaker computers, page generation may take somewhat longer.

This distribution, too, is supplied with an "older" TWiki, Version 4.0.4, which may deviate slightly from the newer 4.1.2.

11.3.3 Variant III: TWiki with IndigoPerl

Starting the installation

In order to install TWiki itself under Windows, we first need to generate another test environment. To do so, we use IndigoPerl. Like XAMPP, it is a collection of programs necessary to operate a web server. However, the Perl variant supplied with IndigoPerl works better with TWiki than that supplied with XAMPP.

You will find the latest version of IndigoPerl as of this printing, Version 2005.02, on the CD included with this book in the directory *\indigoperl*. Unpack the archive to *C:\IndigoPerl*. Now switch to that directory and start the file *setup.bat*.

Note: Make sure that no application is using port 80 during installation. This especially applies to Skype, which you should switch off, since it could lead to conflicts.

You will see the message **Enter installation directory**. You will be instructed to enter a dot in order to install IndigoPerl in the **current directory**. Once you have done this, Apache will be set up and started as a server. You will see a symbol in the task bar in the lower right with which the server can be controlled.

Tip: Apache is set up such that it is automatically loaded when Windows is started. If you do not want it to start automatically, access System Administration (Start → Control Panel → Administrative Tools → Services) and switch the start mode for "Apache 2" from **automatic** to **manual**. This can be done via the properties page, which you can access by right-clicking the service.

Setting environment variables for Windows NT, 2000 and XP …

In order for Perl to be detected, you must include the path in the Windows environment variable PATH. You can define PATH under Windows NT, 2000 and XP by clicking on the **System** symbol in the **Control Panel** (for XP, located under **Performance and Maintenance**), then selecting the **Expand** tab and clicking on the **Environment variables** button. A list of existing variables will appear. Highlight PATH and click on **Edit**. If the variable does not exist, you can add it with **New**. Put the path to Perl at the beginning of the variable value:

```
C:\IndigoPerl\perl\bin;
```

Pay attention to the closing semicolon. It separates this path from others that are important to the system.

Trial run

Now you can test whether Perl is functional. To do so, start the DOS box. At Start → Run …, enter `cmd`. If you now enter the command

Shell

```
perl -v
```

you should see information about the current Perl version. If not, check the PATH variable. In a subsequent trial run, restart the DOS box.

11.3.4 Copying TWiki

Finding installation files

After having tweaked only the test environment, we can now venture installing TWiki itself. You can find the current version at *http://www.twiki.org*. We have included Version 4.1.2 on the CD, which is located in the directory *\wikis\twiki*. Create a directory for TWiki, if possible under the IndigoPerl directory, that is: *c:\IndigoPerl\twiki*. Unpack the files of the archive *TWiki-4.1.2.zip* into that directory.

Tip: If you should use paths whose names have spaces (e.g. *My Files*,) you may have to perform the following steps to be able to use DOS paths: Enter the first six letters, a tilde and a consecutive number starting at 1 to indicate the differentiation. In this case, it would be `myfile~1`.

It is in the nature of Perl scripts that they contain information where that Perl interpreter is located that is to perform a task. They are contained in the so-called shebang line at the beginning of the document. After TWiki has been optimized for Linux, this line must be edited under Windows. This can be done with a small program included in TWiki. Open the DOS box and change to the directory in which the scripts are located using

Shell

```
cd C:\IndigoPerl\twiki\bin
```

Once there, enter the following command:

Shell

```
perl ..\tools\rewriteshebang.pl
```

You will now be asked to enter a new path. Type in the place where the file *perl.exe* is located. In our case, this is

Shell

```
C:\IndigoPerl\perl\bin\perl.exe
```

Confirm the next inquiry with <Return>. Now you should see a list of files that have been changed.

Tip: If you have made a typing error, you can simply run the script again and replace the error with the correct path.

11.3.5
Configuring Apache

Determine executable directory

Next, we have to adapt the Apache configuration file *httpd.conf* such that the access rights of the individual directories are properly set. A file comes with the TWiki installation that already contains most of the settings. It only needs to be embedded into *httpd.conf.* This file is located in the program directory, *c:\indigoperl\apache\conf.* It is best to reopen that file via Windows Explorer. Add the following line to the end of the file:

CFG

```
include "C:/indigoperl/twiki/twiki.conf"
```

Setting directory rights

You may have noticed that the file *twiki.conf* does not exist yet. Thus, we have to create it now. Open the file *twiki.httpd.conf* in the TWiki directory. You first need to adapt the paths that are preset for Linux. To do so, every time you see `/home/httpd/twiki/` replace it with `c:/indigoperl/twiki/`. The best way to accomplish this is using an editor with a replace function. For the initial settings, access to the configuration script must be granted. Search for the line `<FilesMatch "^configure.*">` and change it as follows:

CFG

```
<FilesMatch "^configure.*">
  SetHandler cgi-script
  Order Deny,Allow
  #Deny from all
  Allow from 127.0.0.1, 192.168.1.10
  #Require user JohnDoe
  #Satisfy Any
</FilesMatch>
```

Since IndigoPerl does not include PHP, you should add comments to the corresponding entries. For this, simply set a # in front of `php_admin_flag engine off`.

Save the file thus edited under *twiki.conf.* Now you have to restart the Apache server. The easiest way to do so is via the symbol in the task bar. In the context menu, you will find the entry Open Apache Monitor. Then a window appears listing all running Apache servers. Normally, only one Apache server is running. Highlight it and press the **Restart** button. This loads all changes. If problems arise here, check the changes made in *twiki.conf.*

11.3.6 Retroactive Installation of Perl Modules and Grep

In order for TWiki to operate smoothly, we need two more components that are not included in IndigoPerl. Firstly, two Perl modules are missing. There is a program with which we can easily retroactively install them.

Note: To retroactively install the Perl modules, your computer must be connected to the Internet.

Just enter the following commands, one after the other, in the DOS box. It does not matter which directory you are in:

Shell

```
ipm install Algorithm::Diff
ipm install CGI::Session
ipm install Error
```

Furthermore, you need the program Grep. You will find it on the CD under *tools/grep*, or you can download it from the website *gnuwin32.sourceforge.net/packages/grep.htm*. Install the software in the directory *C:\IndigoPerl*. The file grep.exe should now be in the directory *C:\IndigoPerl\GnuWin32\bin.*

11.4 Completing TWiki Installation

Configure

The script *configure* is intended to be a setup tool with which to view the current configuration and find any errors present. You can access it in the browser via the URL

URL *http://[hostname]-/twiki/[binpath]/configure*

thus, for example:

URL *http://localhost/twiki/bin/configure.*

The first time you access the configuration pate, click on **next** to save the file for the first time. Save it without assigning a password (we'll do that later on) and return to the configuration.

You now see a page on which you can find all information regarding the current configuration of the TWiki. As a general rule: No errors should appear on the list (they are marked red) and as few warnings as possible (marked yellow). If you click on one of the headings on the list, that particular section opens, and you can make the necessary changes. There are a few things you should check right from the start.

Paths, languages, plugins

1. **General Path Settings -> TempfileDir.** Here, the path should be *C:\Temp*.
2. **Store Settings -> RCS.** If you are not working under Linux or do not have an rcs installed, use RSCLite here.
3. **Store Settings -> EGrep Cmd:** Here, you must enter the path to the program Grep. Normally the settings are correct under Linux. Under Windows, replace the line with `C:\indigo~1\GnuWin32\bin\grep.exe %CS{|-i}% %DET{|-l}% -H -- %TOKEN|U% %FILES|F%`.
4. **Store Settings -> FGrep Cmd:** Proceed as with FGrep Command.
5. **Plugins -> WysiwygPlugin/Enabled:** If you check this option, an editor is activated that facilitates editing of TWiki pages.

Save the settings by clicking on **Next** at the bottom of the page. You will now be asked to enter a password. The default here is an empty password. However, since the data here are critical to the system, we advise setting a new password in the lower area. Then click on **Change Password and Save**. If you do not wish to change the password, just directly click on **Save**. If you open *configure* again, you should not see any more red errors.

Opening TWiki

Now, the moment of truth has come: It is time to start TWiki for the first time, to verify whether all of the proper entries have been made and all components are available. Open the wiki with *view*. It has the same URL as *configure*, with the exception that "view" is at the end of it. If you now see an interface as depicted in Fig. 12.1, your installation has been successful.

11.5 Viewing TWiki Pages

Checking RCS

Now would be a good time to have a look around your TWiki to determine whether the installation has been executed correctly. At the end of a page, you will find the version of that page under **History**. Note the version number of any page. Edit that page with a click on **Edit**, and save it with Save. The number should now have gotten larger. If it has not, check the last entries in the error report of the Apache server to see if the program RCS has been found. If this is not the case use RCSLite.

Click on **Changes** in the menu bar to the left. This will display a list of all pages in this web that were last edited. If errors crop up here, you should have another look at the paths to EGrep and FGrep in the configuration file.

Write permission

Finally, load a file into TWiki. This is done via the tab **Attach** in the upper right. On the following page, enter a file and click **Upload file**. You should then see a table of attachments at the end of the entry. If it is not possible to upload files, this is probably due to the fact that the server in the directory *twiki/pub* has not received write permission.

Once all tests are successful, you then have a functional TWiki that you can work with.

12 Working with TWiki

12.1 What Are Webs?

Before getting to the components and functions of the start page of TWiki, that is, the first page displayed when the program is opened, we would like to provide a brief explanation of a special feature in TWiki: the webs.

A TWiki is divided into several webs. These are self-contained areas in which the pages are located. The nice part about them is that you can more or less operate several small wikis for various project groups, and yet only need a single TWiki installed on your web server.

The disadvantage is that, at least at the beginning, it may be a bit confusing – because, once your TWiki is installed, you already have a series of standard webs at your fingertips that exist equally and parallel to each other, but perform diverse functions. For instance, the **Sandbox** Web enables uninhibited experimentation, while in the **TWiki** Web, one can determine important settings for the layout, among other realms.

Standard webs

Here is a brief overview of the standard webs:

Tab. 12.1

Web	Use
Main	Starting point in the TWiki. The user and group pages are also located here.
TWiki	Documentation of the TWiki and general settings and templates that apply to the entire wiki.
Sandbox	Playground in which wiki users can try out various functions without needing to worry about causing damage.

You can add any amount of your own webs to these pre-installed ones. Instructions for doing so are detailed in a subsequent chapter (17.1).

Topics

There is another noteworthy little TWiki quirk: The pages are not called "pages", but rather "topics", which, especially regarding page names such as **WebTopicList**, may lead to confusion. So remember:

topic = a TWiki page.

We should also mention one notation convention. When we refer to a topic in a certain web, we write *Web.Topic*.

12.2 A Website

Where is everything?

We are now in the **Main** web, which is invoked when you open the TWiki URL. All subsequent explanations, however, also refer to all other webs.

Fig. 12.1

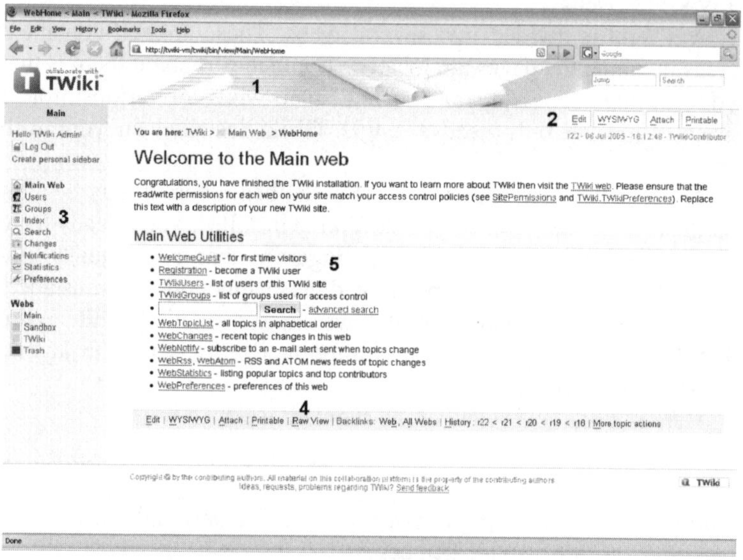

We can divide this page into four general parts:

- At the top is the **Header (1)**, normally highlighted in color and containing a logo. It serves as an orientation and permits fast access via "Jump". Directly underneath it we have a small
- **Information bar (2)** with central functions and information.

- On the left, there is a **Menu sidebar (3)** containing the most important links and functions pertaining to the entire web. You can also add your own links or diverse functions (see Chap. 16.1).
- The **Function bar (4)** offers options you need to edit the content.
- The **Body (5)** is situated between header and footer, and can be filled with content via the edit box.

12.2.1 The Menu Sidebar

We will now have a closer look at the most important components of the menu sidebar:

Register

If you wish to edit a page, you must first register in the login box that appears when you click the **Edit** button. You can register via a "borrowed" account, that is, as a "TWikiGuest" with the password "guest", or you first register as a regular user by filling out the registration form with a TWiki name and password. For the sake of consistency, your TWiki name should be a WikiWord, such as a first and last name without spaces, as in: *TimTroglodyte*.

When you register

- an account will be opened for you. Using your **TWiki name** and password, you can now make yourself known at any time. Other users can see who is responsible for the edits you have performed.
- TWiki creates an additional user page with your TWiki name as its title and the further information in the registration form as its content.
- your name will be entered on the **TWikiUsers** user list.
- you will receive confirmation via email.

If you would like to verify whether your entry has been successful, click on **Users** in the menu sidebar. You should find your Wiki name in the appropriate spot in the alphabetical list of users. The names are linked to their respective pages. Behind that entry, the registration date is also indicated.

Note: Registration is not yet activated for the out-of-the-box installation; that means you can edit all pages without registering (see Chap. 16).

For now, we will skip over the menu option **Groups**, which we will examine subsequently in Chap. 16.4 in the context of access control.

The next menu option, **Index**, leads you to the page **WebTopicList**. As mentioned above, the term "topic" means the same as "page". Accordingly, the **Topic list** is a list of all pages currently in the web in alphabetical order. These include:

- Pages created by you and the community
- User pages automatically generated upon registration
- Configuration pages
- Documentation pages of TWiki developers.

The next important option in the menu sidebar is the search function **Search**. There, you can enter one or more search items in the text box. Using the radio button, you can determine whether the key words should be searched in topic names, in the content, or both. In addition, you can set whether the current web or all public webs in the TWiki are to be searched. This limits the search scope, thus speeding up the search process.

The customary rules apply to the search function:

- Words lined up next to each other are linked by a logical AND, meaning the function only finds those pages containing ALL of the search terms.
- If words are sought in a specific order, they must be placed in quotation marks, such as "Eric Raymond".
- To exclude certain terms from a search, place a minus sign in front of that particular key word.
- However, if your entire search begins with a minus sign, you should mask it in quotation marks, such as "–nowarns".
- Filler words such as adjectives and conjunctions are not taken into account during the search unless you place a plus sign in front of them. These so-called stop words are defined on the page **TWiki.TWikiPreferences** under the item `SEARCHSTOPWORDS`.

Here is another brief search example:

```
flame -romance
```

Here, all pages are searched having the word "flame", but that have nothing to do with romantic encounters.

Advanced Search

If you want to further specify your search, use the advanced search services. In addition to detailed selection criteria regarding the web and additional sorting functions, you also have the opportunity of entering your search as a regular expression. This is a notation convention especially popular with programmers for very flexible and thus powerful searches. You should observe the following "ground rules", which differ slightly from a simple search:

- The search patterns are either linked with a semicolon (AND) or a pipe symbol (OR).
- To exclude a word, do not use the minus sign, but rather an exclamation point before the word.
- Semicolons and exclamation points are to be masked with a backslash.

Here is the above example of a simple search as a regular expression:

```
flame;!romance
```

RegEx

Are you wondering why one would perform a search with regular expressions when a simple search would have the same result? Well, then just try to obtain the result of the following search pattern with a simple search:

```
(torch(|es))?light(|s)?;!electric
```

RegEx

Here, we are looking for "torch" in the sense of a flaming torch, either in the singular or plural, and "torchlight", in the singular or plural, but not the word "electric", because we are not looking for a flashlight, whose British counterpart is an "(electric) torch".

We should briefly mention here that you can embed your search into a page using the `%SEARCH%` variables. We will examine this option closer in Chap. 13.

On the page **WebChanges**, which you can access via the menu option **Changes**, you will get an overview of all pages that were recently edited. The currently last edit is situated at the very top. However, you cannot access the older versions of a page from here. To do so, you must utilize the revision option (**History**) of that respective page.

Note: The focus of this function is on the name of the pages that are edited. That is why only the very last edit to a page is taken into account.

Fig. 12.2

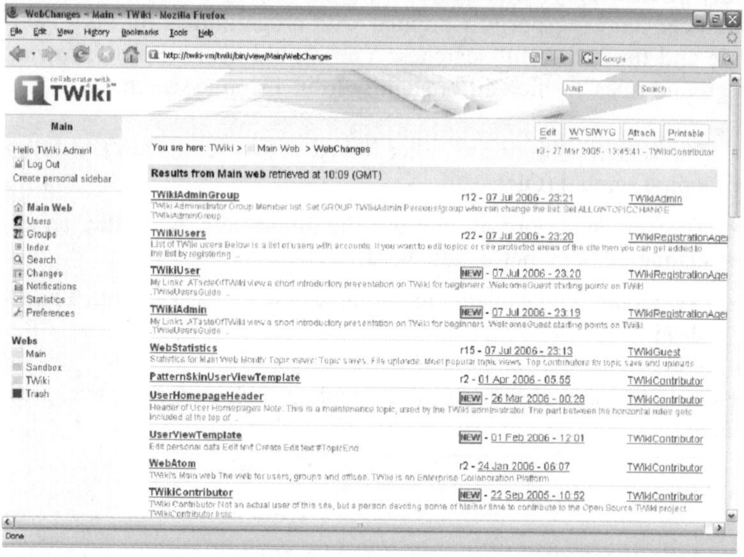

The structure of **WebChanges**: To the left, you see the name of the edited page, in the middle the version number and the date. To the right is the author of the edit. Under this line, the beginning of the page's text is displayed in a pale gray for orientation purposes.

Further entries

The following entry, **Notifications**, has to do with being notified via email of changes in the web. We will discuss this in more detail in Chap. 15.5, since this tool is important in the administration of a TWiki.

The **Statistics** page is self-explanatory, while the configuration of the statistics is not. That is why we will not discuss it further in this chapter.

The menu option **Settings** configures the web; especially in the case of granting reading and writing rights, each web can be assigned different rights (see Chap. 14.4). We will return to the topic of **Settings** when we need them.

Create personal sidebar

Last but not least, we will examine the option **Create personal sidebar**. However, you can only see this option if you have not yet used it, because once you activate it, you enter the edit mode of the **WebLeftBar** page. Here, you can design the lower area of the menu bar as you wish by, for instance, adding your favorite links. Even if you change none of the text at all, you still have your own small section of the menu sidebar in which at least a link to your user page appears. Do not be confused by the many preset variables in the source text; rather, try to set a further link by entering the following in the "My Links" list behind a star:

```
http://twiki.org
```

URL

Once you have saved the page, you will not only be able to notice the changes on that page itself, but also in the menu sidebar.

Note: A **TWikiGuest** can also individually design this section of the menu sidebar, even if there really is no point in doing so, since various people can log in as a **TWikiGuest** and change the entries.

This concludes our examination of the menu sidebar. We can now move on to the next component of the window.

12.2.2 The Information Bar

The information bar below the header functions as a header: It tells you what page you are currently visiting, which version you are looking at, when it was last modified and by whom. In addition, you will find a couple of TWiki tasks, such as **Edit, WYSIWYG, Attach** and **Printable**, which are also located in the lower toolbar and will be discussed in detail below. The advantage of this doubling up becomes evident in long texts, because you do not need to scroll to the end of an article to access them.

12.2.3 The Toolbar

The function toolbar contains the most important tools for **TWiki** authors. There is the core function **Edit**, which opens the edit window (see Chap. 12.3), and the link **WYSIWYG**, which opens the Kupu editor (see Chap. 13.8). If you want to first edit a page, you can skip directly to those two chapters and come back here later.

Attach

If we follow the toolbar further to the right, we can use **Attach** to attach all types of files to the page. This is a truly valuable instrument with which you can perform several functions.

For instance, it is possible to attach files of any format to a certain TWiki page for opening and saving. Along with a complete revision control, it facilitates cooperation between participants in a document, since any needed data located outside of the wiki can easily be made available to everyone.

These functions represent prime prerequisites for file sharing: Well documented and categorized, you can make available multimedia files, drivers, patches, etc.

In addition, you only need to upload the file once; you can use it on a particular page, in that web, or in the entire TWiki.

Attaching files

To attach a file, click on the **Attach** link. You will then access a dialogue page where you can make more specific settings before uploading the file.

For instance, you can enter a comment or determine that a file will be attached in "hidden" mode, so that it is not indicated on the page as being attached. It can still be integrated into the page. However, the advantage is that at the end of the page, it does not appear in an attachment table. If you activate the **Create a link to the attached file** option, it enables the attached image to be viewed in the editable text of the page. If it is not an image file, a simple link to the file is established.

Generally, any type of file can be uploaded. However, if the files are program files that might pose a risk, TWiki disarms them by adding an additional .txt, for instance to the name of a .php file.

Note: You can limit the size of the attachment in the variable `%ATTACHFILESIZELIMIT%` on the page **TWikiPreferences** on the TWiki Web. The default value is set to 10000 KB. Larger files are not recommended anyway, since loading time would be considerably slowed or a timeout produced. For such cases, use an FTP site.

When you return to the page view, you will see the following table on the bottom, unless the file was hidden when uploaded:

Fig. 12.3

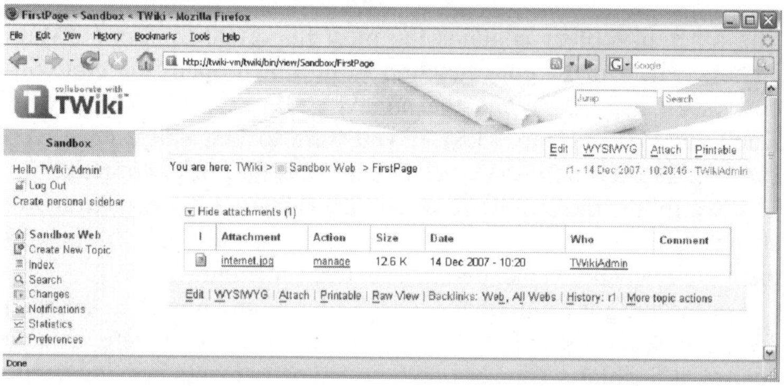

Here, anyone having authorization to edit the topic has the opportunity to download the file. In addition, you can use the **manage** link to access a page in which all important settings regarding the attachment can be made and/or modified, including moving and deleting a file:

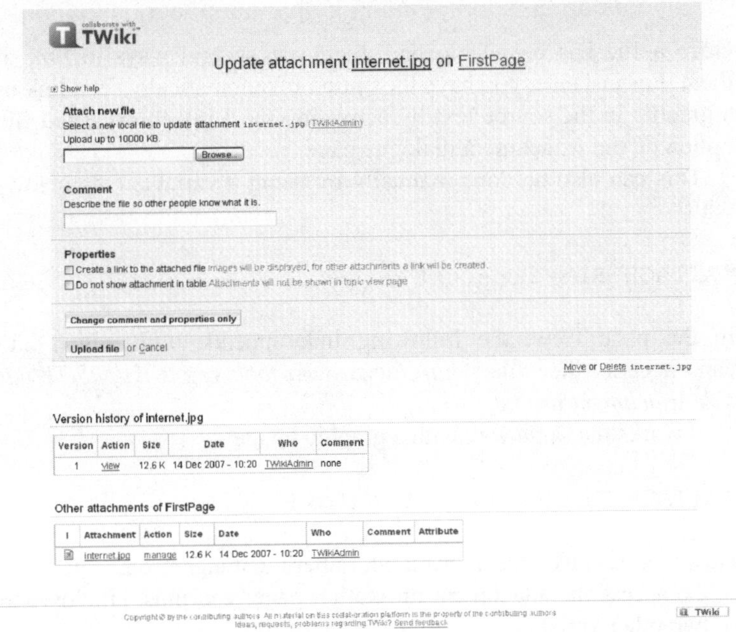

Fig. 12.4

The first table lists the various versions of a file. For every new upload, the revision number increases by one. To evaluate a certain version, you must click on the respective **view**.

The second table shows all attached files, including their attributes. An h, for instance, means that the file is hidden.

If you only change the attachment attributes, e.g. **hidden**, it will suffice to confirm the change with **Change properties**.

There is one small detail to observe: If you have entered or edited a comment, the new comment will only be visible in the page view; in the revision table, the comment will continue to appear as it did when the file was uploaded.

Tip: In contrast to TWiki pages, uploaded files are not locked when you work on them. To avoid storage conflicts, you should thus note in the comment that you are currently working on the file.

Moving/ deleting files

To move a file, activate the **Move** link at the outer right. In the dialogue box that appears, you can either move the attachment to another page (even one in another web), or delete it completely by selecting the web **Trash** and the page **TrashAttachments**. However, it is faster to simply click the **Delete** link to the right of it.

Note: You can only attach files if you have editing rights for that page. However, this limit does not apply to moving files!

Linking to attached files

Once a file has been uploaded, there are several ways to link to them. For instance, you have the option to automatically set a link or a graphic in the source text by activating the **Link to attached file** option on the Attachment dialogue page.

This can also be done manually by using a variable (see below) with

Wiki

```
%ATTACHURL%/fire.txt
```

In the page view, the following link appears, with which one can access the file: *http://www.wiki-tools.org/twiki/pub/TWiki/FileAttachment/fire.txt*.

It works the same way with a graphic image:

Wiki

```
%ATTACHURL%/cavepainting.gif
```

However, no link appears here, but rather the image itself.

To access the attachment of another page, you must employ one or two other variables.

If the page is located in the same web, you need:

Wiki

```
%PUBURL%/%WEB%/OtherPage/fire.txt
```

If the page is in another web of the same TWiki, use:

Wiki

```
%PUBURL%/OtherWeb/OtherPage/fire.txt
```

There is also the possibility of directly integrating an attached HTML file into the source code using:

Wiki

```
%INCLUDE{"%ATTACHURL%/fire.txt"}
```

Embedding HTML files

To do so, however, the script *configure* (under **Security setup – Miscellaneous**) must allow the embedding of URLs, which, on the other hand, is only advisable in environments protected from denial of service attacks. The content of the file, that is, the HTML code, is then seamlessly embedded in the edit box and processed when saved.

Tip: There is no access control for the individual attachments. If you wish to protect a certain file, attach it to a separate page and apply an access control code to it.

All attachments are saved in the web server directory *twiki/pub*. A separate folder is created for each web which, in turn, contains a folder for attached files.

Printable version

Let us now continue with the toolbar. There is not much to say about the function "Printable version:" When it is activated, all TWiki menu bars disappear, and you can print the page without all of the superfluous bordering elements.

Raw Text

The option "Raw text" lets you have a look at the source text of a page without having to switch to edit mode. This is especially necessary if you are not authorized to edit a topic but want to see how certain areas have been generated, and e.g. if you want to adopt them with the copy & paste function.

Backlinks

"Backlinks" lists all pages that link to the current page. Thus, we can obtain important information about the content network of our wiki. Backlinks are especially interesting if a site is to be renamed or deleted. Also, the TWiki allows us to conveniently select either the display of all backlinks within a certain web or the backlinks from all webs.

In contrast, the display of various page versions is somewhat unsystematic and takes some getting used to. "History" lists the concrete changes ("Diffs") of a current page. To the right, you can then choose to display the individual edits of a page ("Revisions") as a whole. Click on the corresponding version number or, to compare two versions, on the greater than/equals sign between them. If the older page can no longer be found in the bar, you need to click on "More topic actions".

More topic actions

Be sure to remember this somewhat hidden page, because it offers you access to a great deal of very useful functions:

- **Edit topic preference settings:** Here, you can configure the page using TWiki variables (see Chap. 12.7), such as to set access control on the page level. The parameters set here do not show up in the text of the topic.
- **Rename or move topic:** Moving or renaming pages is very easy here. You can have the links on the page be automatically updated. However, you should only select the **Trash** web if you wish to delete the page. You can always easily undo a page move

by clicking on the "Put back" link on the corresponding page below the toolbar.

- **Delete topic:** This function is set to move pages into the **Trash** web for deletion. If the page name is already in there, you have to first rename the page. When deleting it, you will receive the option to update links on the page being deleted, which means that they will then link to the **Trash** web. You can perform this update in the current web or in all public webs of the TWiki.
- **Select new topic parent:** A topic parent is that page from which another page has originated. Since the parent topic is indicated in the information sidebar as a path, it is sometimes useful to be able to rename it for organizational purposes.
- **Child topics in *Main* Web:** Lists all pages in the current web (in this case *Main*), that were generated from this page.
- **View previous topic revision:** If you know the number of a version you are interested in, you can directly search for it here and have it displayed in the page view or source text. For older versions, however, there is neither an edit nor a save option. Thus, you can no longer modify the page.
- **Compare revisions:** If you are interested in comparing the differences between two revisions, you can have them displayed here. Just indicate the revisions you wish to compare.
- **Backlinks:** From here, too, you can obtain an alphabetical list of all links referring to the current page.

12.3 The Edit Window

If you are logged in as a user and would like to edit a page, when you have clicked on the **Edit** button, you see the content of the page in its source text, and can then make any modifications or additions you like. All menu and information bars normally visible in normal view are hidden. You only see the options that apply to the current mode.

12.3.1 Storage

Underneath the edit window, you will find the new checkbox **Force new revision**. TWiki does not generate a new version if one and the same user edits a particular page within a certain amount of time. This saves on storage space and keeps things more organized. Over

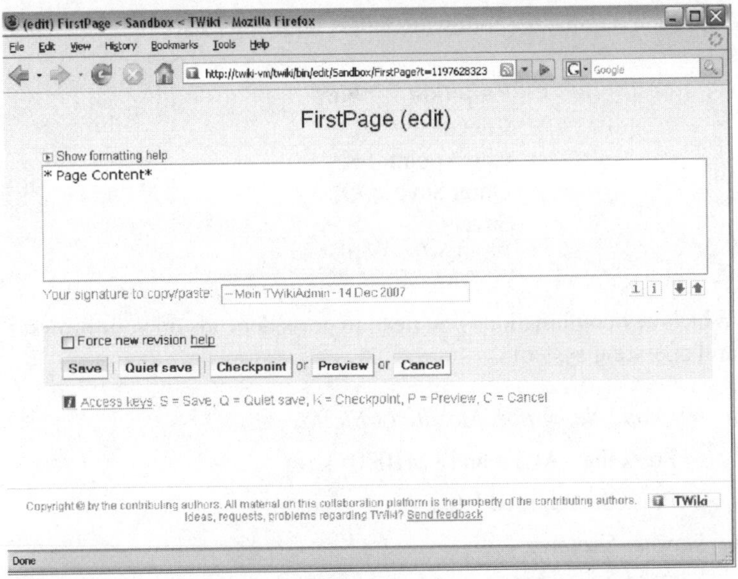

Fig. 12.5

the checkbox, you can now instruct TWiki to save every edit, no matter how small, as a new version.

You have three easy ways in which to save your work:

- **Save:** The regular way to save pages. When you use this method, the edit lock is set.
- **QuietSave:** You may remember this option from MediaWiki: It identifies edits as minor. This means that in TWiki no message about an edit is generated by the **WebNotify** service (see Chap. 17.5).
- **Checkpoint:** This is a kind of interim storage. The page is visible to all in this state. However, you do not leave edit mode, but, after such a save, can continue working on the page.

Before final saving of the page, you can have another look at it using the **Preview** function. However, do not forget to save the file afterwards; otherwise your edits will be lost! If you want to get back to edit mode, for whatever reason, you need to use the **Back** button of your browser.

If, for some reason, you wish to cancel the editing procedure, just press the **Cancel** button.

Access keys

Access keys are key combinations enabling the advanced user to work more quickly. Using them, it is no longer necessary to first grab your mouse and then click on buttons.

You can combine the following letters with other keys:

Tab. 12.2

Function	Key
Cancel	C
Checkpoint	K
Quiet Save	Q
Save	S
Preview	P

Which key combinations you need to press depends on your browser and operating system:

- *Netscape Navigator*, *Mozilla* or *Firefox*
  - Press the <ALT> and <SHIFT> keys
  - Press the required letter
- *Internet Explorer*
  - Hold the <ALT> key down
  - Press the required letter
- *Mac*
  - Hold the <CTRL> button down
  - Press the required letter.

Formatting aids

At the top edge of the edit window, by the way, you can allow a short overview of formatting commands in TWiki to be displayed, e.g. how to italicize text.

Adjusting the edit window

On the right edge of the edit window of the new TWiki, you will find a couple of buttons with which you can alter the look of the edit window. The window itself can be enlarged or made smaller with the arrow buttons. In addition, you can use the letter icons to select whether a font is to have proportional or fixed spacing. The latter is important if, let's say, you want to make an indented bullet list and have the letters directly below each other.

And what about **Add form**? Well, we have dedicated an entire chapter to that topic (15): Structured Data with Forms.

13 Formatting in TWiki

In principle, formatting in TWiki is done in exactly the same way as in MediaWiki. Each wiki, however, has its own conventions. Thus, you must get used to a few new formatting symbols.

13.1 Formatting Text

Generating a page

The best way to test formats is to use a separate page, which we will now generate in preparation for our formatting tasks. To do this, set a link to **FormatTest** on the page **Main.WebHome**:

```
FormatTest
```

You will then see that there is a question mark after the link. This is TWiki's way of indicating that the page does not yet exist. When you click on the question mark, the page will be created. The page of origin will be entered as the parent page. You can recognize this by the fact that, after saving it, the parent page appears in the top information bar in the path **You are here**.

Headings

TWiki headings always begin with three minus signs, and are followed by plus signs and then the heading text. A heading of level one, that is, the most important heading, has one plus sign, a heading of the second level has two plus signs, etc. No additional format indicators must be placed after the heading.

```
---+Heading 1
---++ Heading 2
---+++ Heading 3
```

Headings can be nested in up to six levels.

Formatting text

You can view the other formatting options in the following table:

Tab. 13.1

Description	Example	Result
Bold	`*Text*`	**Text**
Italics	`_Text_`	*Text*
Bold + italics	`__Text__`	***Text***
Fixed font	`=Text=`	`Text`
bold + fixed font	`==Text==`	**`Text`**

Fixed font text is written in a font with a fixed width (usually Courier) and displayed in another font color.

If you wish to prevent the source code from being interpreted (e.g. HTML), place it between <verbatim> tags. For instance, this is useful if you are describing an HTML formatting procedure. Such a description should be readable to the user and not interpreted in the display:

Wiki

```
<verbatim>
  <b>makes bold text</b>
  <i>makes italics</i>
  <a href="test.htm">linked</a>
</verbatim>
```

Caution: Do not put any spaces between the format indicators and the text; otherwise the formatting will not take effect!

You can see a display of the previously discussed formatting procedures in the following screenshot:

Fig. 13.1

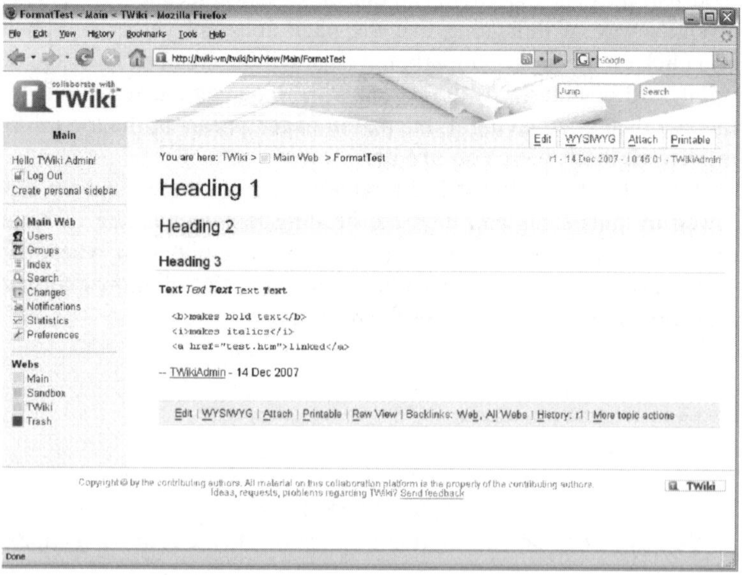

With a bit more effort, you can change the font color of your text. In TWiki, there are variables (see below) for the most popular colors:

Text color

```
%YELLOW%, %RED%, %PINK%, %PURPLE%, %TEAL%,
%NAVY%, %BLUE%, %AQUA%, %LIME%, %GREEN%,
%OLIVE%, %MAROON%, %BLACK%, %GRAY%, %SILVER%
```

To lend color to a paragraph, write the respective variable before the text, and follow it with %ENDCOLOR% to end the color mode.

```
%RED% red color %ENDCOLOR% and %GREEN% green
color %ENDCOLOR%
```

> **Note:** If you wish to switch from one color to another, you must still end the active color with %ENDCOLOR%, e.g. %RED% red color %ENDCOLOR% %GREEN% green color %ENDCOLOR%.

Now that we have reviewed the text formatting options, let us turn to structuring options. You can start a new paragraph – as in Me-diaWiki – simply by inserting a blank link before it.

Paragraph

If you want to structure your content in the form of lists, there are several options, displayed in the following table. Please note that three blank spaces must be inserted before each corresponding format indicator.

Lists

Tab 13.2

List	Example	Result
Simple list	`···*·Fire`	• Fire
Nested list	`···*· Fire` `······*·Embers`	• Fire ○ Embers
Numbered list	`···1.· Fire` `···1.·Water` `···A.· Fire` `···A.·Water` `···i.· Fire` `···i.·Water`	1. Fire 2. Water A. Fire B. Water i. Fire ii. Water
Definition list	`···$·Fire:··hot` `···$·Water:··wet`	Fire hot Water wet

13.2 Tables

The following three methods can be used to generate tables in TWiki: using a wiki convention, in normal HTML and with the aid of the <verbatim> tag. These three procedures will be explained below.

13.2.1 Wiki Convention

In the wiki convention, each line represents a row in a table; any spaces at the beginning of the line are ignored. The row can consist of several cells. Each cell begins and ends with a pipe (|). That is basically it!

In addition, however, there are also several formatting options available:

- `| *Content* |`: This cell is interpreted as a table header and thus – depending on the browser – is more strongly emphasized than the other cells.
- `|  Content  |`: (Two spaces on the left and the right) The cell content is centered in the cell.
- `|  Content |`: (Two spaces on the left) The cell content is aligned with the right margin.
- `| Content ||`: The cell is combined horizontally with subsequent cells to make multi-span columns. If you only want one empty cell, you must place a space between both pipes. You can also join several cells by entering the corresponding number of |.
- `|^|`: The cell is joined vertically with the cell above it to form multi-span rows. It is also possible to join several cells in this way.

The following example table illustrates the TWiki table conventions:

Wiki

```
| *Culture* | *Primitive* | *Developed* |
| Mesolithic Age |||
| Fire |  -  |  X  |
| Agriculture |^|  -  |
| Neolithic Age |||
| Fire |  X  |  X  |
| Agriculture|  -  |^|
```

The final result looks like this:

Fig. 13.2

Culture	Primitive	Developed
Mesolithic Age		
Fire	-	X
Agriculture		-
Neolithic Age		
Fire	X	X
Agriculture	-	

13.2.2 Tables in HTML

You can also use plain HTML notation to make your tables. Here is a simple example:

Wiki

```
<table border="1">
  <tr>
    <th> Mesolithic Age </th>
    <th> Neolithic Age </th>
  </tr><tr>
    <td> flint </td>
    <td> metal working </td>
  </tr><tr>
    <td> settlement </td>
    <td> agriculture </td>
  </tr>
</table>
```

Here is the result:

Fig. 13.3

Mesolithic Age	Neolithic Age
flint	metal working
settlement	agriculture

As you can see, the automatic formatting found in tables employing wiki syntax is not used in this case. This means that you can determine the look of the table regardless of the skin of the TWiki, which, of course, is coupled with a certain degree of additional effort.

13.2.3 Tables with the <verbatim> Tag

The `<verbatim>` tag mentioned above is not only handy when formatting programming code; it can also be of assistance when generating simple tables.

Wiki

```
<verbatim>
  Culture   Primitive  Developed
  ------    --------   ----------
  Meso      wood       fire
</verbatim>
```

The text between the tags is displayed on a 1:1 basis. This notation can be useful if, for instance, the table is to be exported to another program as ASCII text.

13.3 Links

CamelCase

In contrast to MediaWiki, we can work with the famous, wiki-specific CamelCase in TWiki. Words written together with their initial letters capitalized, such as `SponsorContacts`, will generate a link to a new page called **SponsorContacts**. It is tagged with a question mark, indicating that the page has not yet been created. Of course, the link is also generated if the topic does already exist. If you wish to link to a topic in another web, you must first specify the web before the topic name: **OtherWeb.SponsorContacts**.

To prevent automatic linking of a WikiWord, place it between the `<noautolink> </noautolink>` tags, or add an exclamation point or `<nop>` without a space in front of the word.

Note: `<noautolink>` also works with entire tables. Make sure, however, that there is a space between the table end and the `</noautolink>` (this is a TWiki bug).

External links

Of course, you can also link to pages outside of the TWiki. The following Internet services are automatically recognized and linked accordingly: `http://`, `https://`, `ftp://`, `gopher://`, `news://`, `file://`, `telnet://`, `mailto:`.

Alternative with brackets

If you do not like CamelCase, but prefer notation using brackets, you can also use this method to produce links: The link `[[History of humankind]]` will still generate a page with a CamelCase name: **HistoryOfHumankind**. The advantage to notation with brackets is that you can separate the link text from the link reference; i.e. while, in the case of `[[Main.HistoryOfHumankind]]`, you could have this complicated phrase appear in the middle of your article without the brackets, if you use `[[MyWeb.HistoryOfHumankind][History of humankind]]`, your link, appearing as "History of humankind", can fit better into the flow of the text. In the case of external links, you do not even have to separate the link reference and link text with brackets. A simple `[[mailto://tim.troglodyte@web.de Tim]]` will suffice to only have "Tim" displayed on the page.

Note: In order to be able to display square brackets, which normally constitute a link, you have to mask them with an exclamation point before the phrase.

Jump labels

For very long pages, it is a good idea to set jump labels at various points on the page containing internal page links. To do this, define an anchor by placing the anchor name after a hash mark, e.g. `#Summary` at the beginning of the line to which you want the browser to jump. As you can imagine, the anchor name should also be a WikiWord. To then set a link to a certain jump label on a page, just add the anchor name with the hash to the page name:

Wiki

```
[[HistoryOfHumankind#Summary]]
```

If you link to a jump label on the current page, you do not need to add the page name.

13.4 Integrating Images

You have already indirectly seen how to integrate images in the text of your article in Chap. 12.2.3. However, let us review it once again briefly: To integrate an image, you first have to attach it to your page using the **Attach** function. In the options on the dialogue page, you can then determine that a link to the attachment be included in the text. If you are integrating a graphic image, this means that it will be visible in the page view mode at the end of the article; the following line would be added to the source text:

```
<img src="%ATTACHURLPATH%/image.gif">
```

To place the image in another spot on the page, put the line in the corresponding spot in the source text. By the way, you do not necessarily have to use the link function to integrate an image: You can also manually add the above line to the source text. As an alternative, the following expression also works:

```
%ATTACHURL%/image.gif
```

Images attached to other pages or even other webs can be accessed via

```
%PUBURL%/webname/pagename/image.gif
```

13.5 HTML in TWiki

All HTML tags can be used in TWiki. However, in a cooperative project, you should refrain from doing so when possible and use TWiki formats instead to keep the source text easy to follow and thus easier to edit. In addition, uniformity in formatting is no longer ensured if you employ HTML. Remember, too, that the text, which is surrounded by tags, is still interpreted by TWiki and converted by it to HTML anyway. This could lead to unwanted side effects.

If, however, you do use HTML, you must follow a few rules:

- Keep to the standards of HTML 4.0 and XHTML 1.0 as far as possible, since you would otherwise lose compatibility with various browsers.
- Refrain from stretching an HTML tag over several lines. The greater/less than signs that surround the tag must be on the same line.
- Remove all blank lines, since TWiki would otherwise make new paragraphs out of them, which could pose problems in certain areas, such as in tables.

13.6 TWiki and JavaScript

Employing JavaScript with your TWiki application is also practically effortless. To circumvent TWiki formatting, the JavaScript code should be masked with an HTML comment and <pre> tags. Here is an example:

```
<script type="text/javascript">
  <!-- //hide JavaScript
    //<pre> suppress TWiki formatting
      window.alert("JavaScript is active");
    //</pre>
  // -->
</script>
```

Every time the page is accessed, a message box appears indicating that JavaScript is active.

13.7 TWiki Variables

TWiki variables fulfill two functions.

- *Firstly*, they stand for certain data that is only employed when the page is invoked and the source text is displayed in its normal form. For example, the placeholder `%DATE%` displays the current date. This can save the author a great deal of effort, and it makes the page more dynamic.
- *Secondly*, a few variables have a switch function. They enable several settings to be determined in TWiki. For instance, the `%NOAUTOLINK%` variable determines whether CamelCase is active or not.

You can identify a variable by the fact that its name is enclosed in percent signs; depending on the variable, comments can be inserted in curly brackets after the name, e.g. for an embedded search for `%SEARCH{"fire"}%`. There are pre-defined variables that are set when the TWiki system is installed or that access information from the server. Others can be set by the user. Here, we differentiate between the following options with regard to the area of validity of the variables:

- Variables applicable to the entire TWiki. They can be defined and edited on the page **TWikiPreferences** in the **TWiki** web.
- Variables set for a certain web. They can be found in the respective **WebPreferences** page.

- Variables pertaining to individual topics. They are inserted directly into the source text of that page.
- Variables that the individual user can determine. They are found on the respective user pages.

The variables of the lower levels overwrite the values set in the superordinate instances. If you wish to suppress this for certain placeholders, you must assign them to `%FINALPREFERENCES%`. This is a variable that prevents settings outside of the current level from being altered. For the entire TWiki, the code looks like this:

Wiki

```
···*·SET FINALPREFERENCES = PREVIEWBGIMAGE, ↵
WIKITOOLNAME, WIKIWEBMASTER, SMTPMAILHOST, ↵
SMTPSENDERHOST, ALLOWWEBMANAGE, ↵
READTOPICPREFS, TOPICOVERRIDESUSER
```

These settings can only be made at **TWikiPreferences**.

The following lists a few of the many variables available. You can find a detailed list on the page **TWikiVariables** of the **TWiki** web.

Pre-defined variables

- **%WEB%:** names the current web.
- **%TOPIC%:** names the current page.
- **%INCLUDE{"*ATopic*"}%:** includes the topic of another web.
- **%INCLUDINGTOPIC%:** cites the name of the page that integrates the current topic.
- **%INCLUDINGWEB%:** cites the name of the web into which the current topic is integrated.
- **%SEARCH{"*searchtext*"}%:** the search result is integrated into the page text.
- **%TOC%:** generates a table of contents for the page. The entries are composed of the topic headings.
- **%WIKIUSERNAME%:** cites the name of the user currently logged in.

Preferences variables

Now we will discuss a few variables whose content you can either edit on the TWiki, web, topic or user level, or across all levels. The most important settings are **TWikiPreferences** and the web-specific **WebPreferences**:

- **%WIKILOGOIMG%:** Found in **TWikiPreferences**. Determines the image displayed in the upper left portion of the TWiki.

- **%WEBBGCOLOR%:** Sets in **WebPreferences** which background color certain elements of the page will have.
- **%WEBCOPYRIGHT%:** Determines the copyright text at the foot of the page on the individual web level.
- **%EDITBOXHEIGHT%** and **-WIDTH%:** With this, users can set the size of the edit box on their page.
- **%RED%:** Determines what color value in hexadecimal notation "red" is to have. This of course also applies to all other colors.

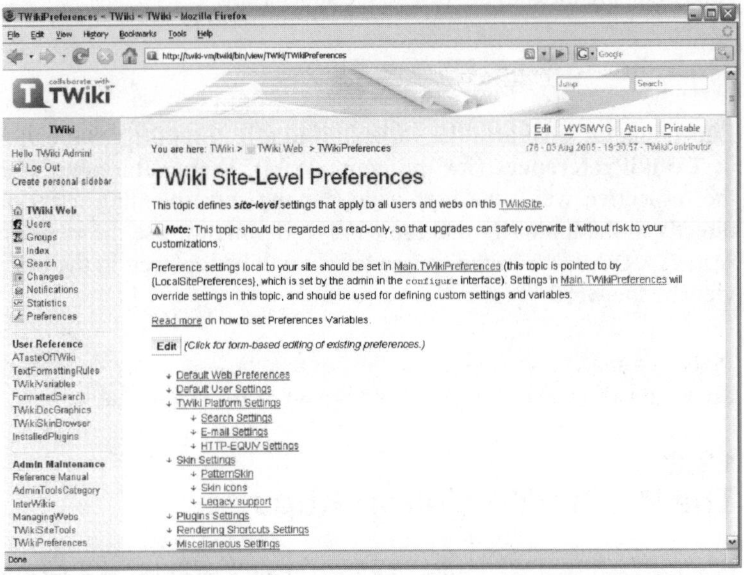

Fig. 13.4

Changing values

A set variable generally has the following structure:

Wiki

```
···*·Set VARIABLENNAME = value
```

These definitions are often located on a lower level of a list. Depending on the variable, the corresponding value can be set by simply editing a page and changing the `value` to suit your needs. Usually there are explanatory notes on the page to assist you. To avoid redundancy, we will only discuss individual variables at the point where they are employed. This especially refers to Chaps. 14 and 16.

In the lines below and above the settings, you can use normal Wiki code; only the sections having the form displayed above are recognized and interpreted as value settings.

Tip: Often the parameters on the page will disturb the overall look of the page and you may want to hide them. To do so, you can utilize HTML comments (`<!--` and `-->`) that you can insert in the lines above and below the parameters. They will still be visible in your browser's source text view mode. A more elegant solution is to swap out the variables: in the **Edit topic preference settings** under **More topic actions** in the function toolbar!

Creating your own variables

It is also possible for users to create and assign their own placeholders by placing them in the respective spots using

Wiki

```
···*·Set OWNVARIABLE = Test
```

Depending on what area the variable is to affect, set the value either in **TWikiPreferences** (for the entire Wiki), **WebPreferences** (for the respective web), the user page (for the corresponding user) or directly in the topic (for that topic only). If you now use the variable `%OWNVARIABLE%` in the source text, it will be replaced in the page view by the word "Test".

Note: To mask a variable, it is best to use the procedure described above in which an exclamation point is set before the variable.

13.8 The WYSIWYG Editor: Kupu

For the installation of TWiki, the Kupu Editor has been the default editor installed along with the product since Version 4.0.

Using this editor, it is possible to jazz up the graphic depiction of the text a bit, as with a simple word processing program. However, remember that an editor is always just an attachment designed to make working with TWiki simpler. Not all functions can be achieved with it. Basic knowledge of TWiki syntax is still required, and the Kupu Editor can only implement what your version of TWiki can enable. For instance, the editor, as in the case of the TWiki in general, only has one font.

The editor knows text and paragraph formats, for instance. Text formats are applied to highlighted text; correspondingly, paragraph formats are applied to the paragraph in which the cursor is situated. Via the header, you can format text with a click of the mouse. The following functions are available in the header:

Icon	Function
	Save.
	Cancel.
	Undo last command. Does not function very reliably as yet.
	Undo the undo command. Also not very reliable.
Heading 2	Assign headings up to six outline levels or highlight a quotation with Formatted.
	Make highlighted text bold.
	Make highlighted text cursive.
	Assign a color to text.
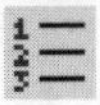	Numbered list.
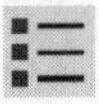	Non-numbered list.
	Decrease left indent.
	Increase left indent.
	You can insert a table with this button. Enter number of columns and rows in dialogue box.
	Select a topic from a list to which a link is to be created.
	Insert an external link.
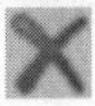	Remove a link. Only appears if a link is highlighted.
	Extendable list with icons.
	You can upload and insert an image or file here.
	Inserts a set character string.
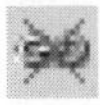	Defines an area that is not to be processed by the wiki.
	Switches between source code and edit view.
	Increases the editing area to the whole page.
	Shows the Help page of the WYSIWYG editor.

Tab.13.3

Tip: Using the **Edit Source** button, you can directly edit the source code, thus utilizing all possibilities of TWiki syntax. For example, when copying and pasting or working with tables, there is often data in the source code that either has no function or is bothersome. This data can be found in the **Edit Source** view and corrected.

Setting links

Objects – text, images or symbols – can be supplied with a link. Mark the respective object and click on one of the symbols to insert a link. Please note that there are various links:

- Links which lead to a page outside of TWiki ("external links"). Enter the desired URL in the dialogue box under **Link the highlighted text to this URL**, e.g. *http://www.stoneage.com*. Using **Preview**, the page will be displayed in the preview area beneath the entry. Confirm with **OK**. The link text will now be displayed in blue and underlined.
- When setting a link to a target within the TWiki ("internal links"), a similar method is used. Once you have marked the link text and clicked on the corresponding button, select one of the topics of the current web in the dialogue box (**Main, Sandbox …**). You can now select the respective TWiki page from a list. After you have confirmed it with **OK**, the internal link will be placed in a blue box.

The main page would appear as follows using Kupu:

Fig. 13.5

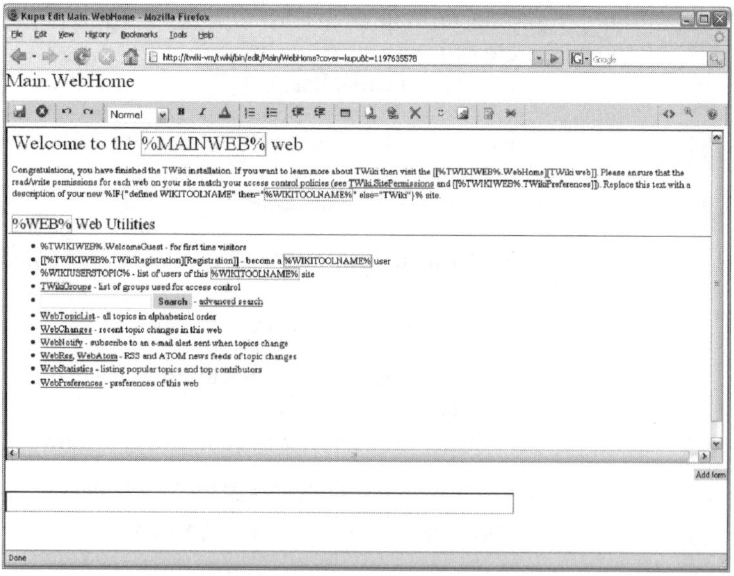

Inserting attachments

Furthermore, the Kupu Editor also enables easy administration of attachments, hidden behind the button to insert images. This function is self-explanatory: You can enter a data path in the **Local file** box or search for the desired file with the **Search...** function. In the **Comment** field, you can also add a comment. The file is attached to the TWiki page by clicking **OK.**[1] Images are displayed immediately, and links are generated for files.

Inserting tables

The table function is just as simple. Simple tables can be inserted into text. Place the cursor in the spot where the table is to be situated. Click on the **Table** button and select the desired characteristics in the dialogue box. Confirm with **Add Table**. If you click on the table in the edit view, anchors appear that you can pull while depressing the left mouse button to adjust the size of the table. Clicking the right mouse button with the cursor on the table opens a dialogue box with which you can perform actions such as adding or deleting lines.

[1] To delete attachments or use the "hide" function, see Sect. III.2.2.

14 Searching in TWiki

A well-developed wiki is a sizeable knowledge database. However, it is largely filled with freely generated text, i.e. the data is not present in a structured form and thus not divided into various types and individually labeled. This results in the problem that stored information is hard to find.

One possibility is to consistently classify articles right from the start and link them such that a type of catalogue is created in which one can click through subject headings and subheadings until one has arrived at the desired spot. However, this would mean additional effort that would not be able to be performed consistently when editing wars heat up.

You have already seen another possibility, that of having all pages listed alphabetically with the **index** function. Yet, in order to get a handle on the (dis)order in the wiki, the search function is ultimately the best, if not only, opportunity.

14.1 The Search Function

You will find the search function under **Search** in the navigation sidebar. When you click on it, the search form already discussed in Chap. 12.2.1 will appear.

If you search for, let's say, "leftbar", in all public webs (the search is not case sensitive), you will get a list of results. The results are categorized according to webs. Per hit, you will see the title of the topic, the date of the last edit and the name of the user who last edited it. At the bottom of the list, the number of topics found is indicated.

Advanced search

The advanced search offers more possibilities for displaying the result list and limiting the search. It can be found under **Advanced Search** or in the topic **Main.WebSearchAdvanced**.

Fig. 14.1

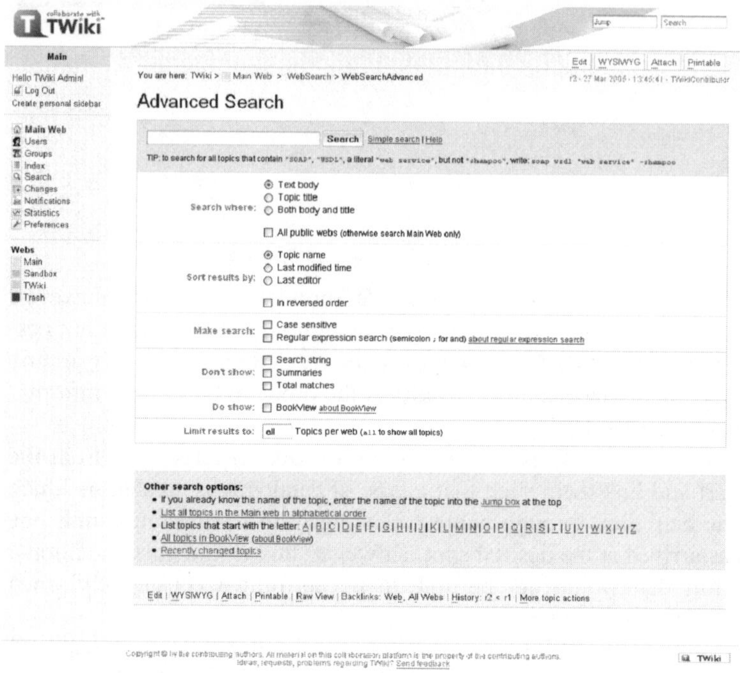

Here, you will find a wealth of additional settings:

- **Sort by …** The results can be sorted by topic name, last modified time, or last editor. If you select **in reversed order**, the order is reversed.
- **Make Search …** If you would like the search to be case sensitive, put a check in front of the first option. With **regex**, or **regular expression**, you inform the system that the series of characters you type in is to be interpreted as a special search formulation. You can find more information in Chap. 14.3.
- **Don't show …** Here, you can determine what information is to be displayed in the results list. A check in front of **search string** suppresses the display of the search item before the list, **total matches** the number of results. The most interesting option is probably that of hiding the **summaries** content lines and thus enabling a clearer overview.

- **Do show ...** With **BookView**, not only the titles of the articles found, but also their content, is shown. This name was chosen because the function can be used to print out collections of articles.
- **Limit results to:** If you enter a number in place of **all**, only that amount of hits per web is indicated.

14.2 Effective Searching

Two factors are crucial to the quality of a search result. The first is the question as to how many of the relevant documents are found and how many remain in the dark. This value is called the recall. The second factor is how many documents are found that are not really desired and are left as "data trash". This value is called precision[2]. The selection of search items can considerably influence the quality of the search. The best types of words are those that most clearly describe the desired subject, yet still occur relatively frequently. If a word is used too rarely, you will only find a small portion of possible results. If the word is too frequent, too many documents will be found, and the result will be virtually useless. To avoid the latter, there is a so-called stop word list (`SEARCHSTOPWORDS`) located in **TWikiPreferences**. All words on that list are simply ignored during a search.

Search method

The search method normally employed is based on simple comparison. That means all pages are displayed that in some way contain the word without sensitivity to case. This also applies to word fragments. If you enter more than one word, all words must be present in the document. The order is of no significance. Possible operations have already been covered in Chap. 12.2.1.

This search mode does not accommodate the display of various search items as alternatives (but see below). Note, too, that the search program does not perform any replacements. The search for "leftbar" results in several hits, but a search for the plural, or "leftbars", results in none. This is also an issue with regard to foreign diacritical marks; if, for instance, you search for "Dusseldorf", the German spelling "Düsseldorf" will not be found, and vice versa.

[2] See Ferber, 2003, Chap. 1.3.7.

14.3 Searching with Regular Expressions

If the quick search methods mentioned above are not enough, you have another powerful tool in regular expressions (RegEx), to extract information from articles in a very precise manner. Regular expressions actually come from the world of programming, and refer to search patterns compared with a character string. RegEx is a complex topic that would fill bookshelves. However, we nevertheless want to try to give you an idea of what the term means.

Boolean operations

In a RegEx search, there is also the option of using Boolean operations:

Tab. 14.1

Expression	Result
`Term1;Term2`	AND operation. Both terms must be present. This operator is specific to TWiki.
`Term1|Term2`	OR operation. At least one of the terms must be found.
`!Term1`	NOT operation. The term entered must not appear in the document.
`(expression)`	Collection of several expressions to make a single unit having processing priority.

There are a few more points to remember. First of all, make sure you do not insert any spaces. They are not ignored in RegEx, but rather processed along with the rest. That means if there is a space before a term, the character string "term" (preceded by a space) will be searched. Secondly, as the above table shows, words can be collected into a single unit using parentheses; these will be processed first. The order of the expression priority is PARENTHESES before NOT before AND before OR. Thirdly, employing brackets also enables unlimited nesting of expressions. This option facilitates very complex searches.

Examples

A few examples will illustrate the functions described. For instance, the word

RegEx

```
torch|torches
```

is not only searched in the singular, but also the plural. We can also combine them to search for torchlights as well:

RegEx

```
torch(light|lights)
```

Note that the entire term will be searched as one unit. Thus, pages containing just “torch” or just “light” will be ignored. A search for a torchlight from a flaming torch, excluding light from a flashlight, which in British English is called an (electric) torch, might look like this:

RegEx

```
torch(light|lights);!electric
```

You can also make a search take into account differences in orthography is well, as in:

RegEx

```
neighb(o|ou)r(s)
```

which effects a search for the American “neighbor” as well as the British “neighbour” in singular and plural.

Letter patterns

The real advantage to regular expressions is that you not only can look for words, but also letter patterns. For instance, you can use them to search for email addresses or telephone numbers in TWiki. The basic unit of such patterns is information on permissible letters:

Tab. 14.2

Expression	Significance
`[acf]`	One of the letters indicated.
`[a-g]`	A letter between (and including) `a` and `g`.
`[^a]`	All letters except the one indicated.
`.`	any character.
`[\-]`	The minus sign. The backslash functions as a mask, indicating that the following character is not a function (as in the normal function of a backslash as an area sign).

Instead of letters, you can also use numbers or other characters. If such characters have a special function in RegEx, you must “disarm” them with a preceding backslash. Then, for instance, you can search for links to films and audio files in TWiki:

RegEx

```
\.mp[g3]
```

Determine frequency

It gets even more interesting when you can also indicate how often a certain character pattern may occur in a row:

Tab. 14.3

Character	Frequency
*	Never, once or more than once
+	At least once
?	At most once
{*n*}	Exactly *n* times
{*n*,}	At least *n* times
{*n*,*m*}	Between *n* and *m* times

The characters indicated are placed behind the expression whose size is to be determined. Now we can express a search for singular and plural words in the following way:

RegEx

```
Page(s)?
Box(es)?
```

URL search

You can find a normal URL with the following pattern:

URL

```
http://[a-zA-Z0-9._%-]+\.[a-zA-Z]{2,4}
```

A character string is searched beginning with `http://`, followed by an arbitrary number of alphanumerical characters and numbers and ending with a period or a series of two to four letters.

Email address search

The next regular expression search concerns email addresses, and works in a very similar way:

RegEx

```
[a-zA-Z0-9._%-]+@[a-zA-Z0-9._%-]+\.                    ↵
[a-zA-Z]{2,4}
```

Remember that a search via RegEx always produces the entire article containing the respective search pattern.

14.4 Embedded Searches

A sophisticated search, such as that for email addresses, may need to be performed more than once. Furthermore, the user may want the result displayed on a separate page. This can be achieved with an embedded search, which produces a freely formattable hit list in any location in a topic. Thus one can create free and dynamic pages, since they are generated from the version of the TWiki existing at any respective point in time.

Parameters

The embedded search is invoked with the variable `%SEARCH%`, which accepts a series of parameters:

Tab. 14.4

Parameter	Function
`"text"`	Search string in quotation marks.
`web="..."`	Name of the web to be searched. Several webs are separated by commas. If you want to search all webs, enter **all**.
`topic="..."`	Only the topics indicated are searched. Here, too, you can indicate more than one, separating them by commas. In addition, you can use the star as a placeholder for an arbitrary number of characters.
`excludetopic="..."`	The opposite of `topic`. The topics indicated are not searched.
`type="..."`	▪ **keyword**. Normal search. ▪ **regex**. Search with regular expressions.
`scope="..."`	Searches ▪ **topic**. Only the title. ▪ **text**. Only the content. ▪ **all**. Everything is included.
`order="..."`	Results displayed in order of ▪ **topic**. The title. ▪ **created**. The date of creation. ▪ **modified**. The date of the last edit. ▪ **editby**. The last author.
`limit="..."`	Limits the number of results displayed.
`reverse="on"`	The results are shown in the reverse order.
`casesensitive="on"`	For a case sensitive search.
`nosummary="on"`	Only the titles of the resulting articles are shown.
`bookview="on"`	The entire text of a topic is shown.
`nosearch="on"`	The search string is not included in the result display.
`noheader="on"`	The search title is not displayed.
`nototal="on"`	The number of results is not displayed.

So, let us assume the gods want an overview of all settings in the wiki in addition to fast access to all **Preferences** pages. Since new projects and new webs are continually being added, a static page for this purpose would not make much sense. Thus, we generate a page called **PreferencesOverview** and put in a title and the following search:

Wiki

```
---++ All Preferences
%SEARCH{"Preferences" scope="topic" ↵
web="all" nosummary="on" nosearch="on" ↵
nototal="on"}%
```

Thus, all pages in all webs are displayed that have **Preferences** in their title. Special information is excluded, with the exception of categorization into webs. If that, too, is annoying, it can also be suppressed using noheader="on".

Fig. 14.2

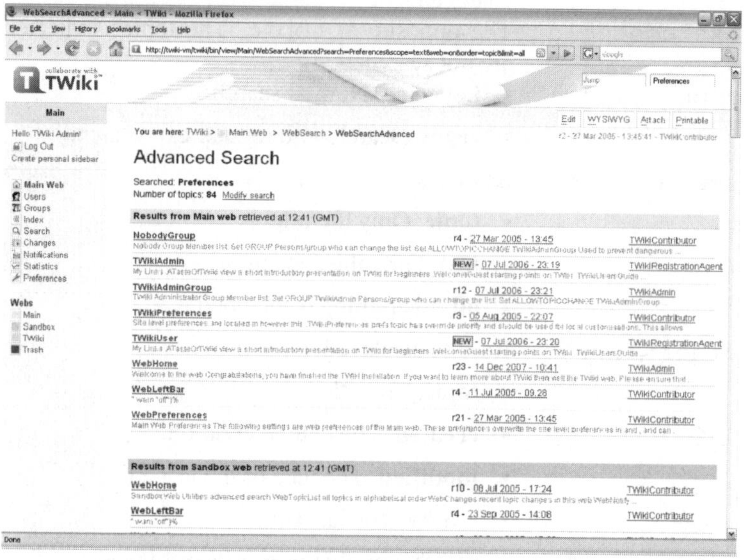

Format result

And yet, the integration of the search into a page can go even further. Using formatted searches, you can determine which information is shown on a page. This can even be taken to the point where you only have certain passages displayed from the pages found. This can be done with the parameter format, in which the desired display can be determined. If, for example, you want to display the above list of Preferences pages in a list, just include the format parameter:

Wiki

```
format="···*·$web: $web.$topic "
```

The web and the link to the topic are displayed. Note that the header is now automatically suppressed. This function can be individually set (see below). As you can see, the web and the topic title were replaced by variables that are appropriately filled in by the system. There is a whole list of such variables; we have included a few in Table 14.5.

Tab 14.5

Variable	Function
`$web`	Name of the web in which the topic found is located.
`$topic`	Name of the topic found. Using the formalism `$topic(`*n*`, ...)`, the first *n* characters of the topic title are displayed followed by three periods. Instead of the three periods, you can have any series of characters displayed, e.g. . They will be inserted after *n* characters in the topic name.
`$parent`	Name of the parent topic. Formatting as in `$topic`.
`$text`	The formatted text of the topic.
`$rev`	Number of the last revision of the topic.
`$date`	Date of the last edit.
`$wikiname`	Name of the last author.
`$createdate`, `$createwikiname`	Date and author of the first version of the topic.
`$summary`	The first 162 characters of the topic as a summary.
`$pattern(`*reg-ex*`)`	In this spot, a regular expression may be employed to extract a certain text from the topic found.
`$percnt`, `$dollar`, `$n`	The percent sign, dollar sign, etc. and new line.

The following search string displays all skin files, their web and parent element in a table:

Wiki

```
| *Name* | *Parent* |
%SEARCH{ "Skin" scope="topic" web="all"          ↵
nosummary="on" nosearch="on" nototal="on"        ↵
header = "| *$web* ||"                           ↵
format="| $topic | $parent |"}%
```

The header of the table is first entered manually with two columns. The search result will also be entered in two columns. One blank line spanning both columns is issued per web. This is indicated in the `header` parameter.

Display individual results

Using a formatted search, data can be easily extracted from articles. This can be done with regular expressions that are processed with the variable `$pattern`. To be precise, the variable contains the text that corresponds to a certain expression. For example, to find the email addresses in TWiki, and only have these displayed, all you have to do is use the pattern cited above for email addresses. Since we are searching all topics containing these addresses, and at the same time wish to extract these addresses from the topics, the regular expression must occur in the search and as a pattern. So don't be shocked – it looks worse than it actually is. For simplicity's sake, we have limited the possible addresses to small letters without special characters.

Wiki

```
%SEARCH{
  "[a-z.]+@[a-z]+\.[a-z]{2,4}"                          ↵
  scope="text" nosearch="on" nototal="on"               ↵
  web="all"                                             ↵
  regex="on" separator=", " multiple="on"               ↵
  format="                                              ↵
  $pattern(.*?([a-z.]+@[a-z]+\.[a-z]{2,4}).*)           ↵
  "                                                     ↵
}%
```

As you can see, three parameters have been added. The parameter `regex` activates the search with regular expressions, and `separator` indicates the symbol with which the individual results are separated. The parameter `multiple` makes sure that a page is processed more than once if more than one result for the search pattern is detected. Otherwise, only one email address per page would be found.

Search patterns

The additional characters inserted before and after the expression in `$pattern` are required for internal processing. The expression `.*?` results in the first and not the last result found being used. The text in the inner parenthesis is utilized. It often happens that one wants a display of text located between two known characters. There is a fixed regular expression for this purpose:

RegEx

```
$pattern(.*?(from here.*?to here).*)
```

The starting and end point are included. If the end of the line is to be the end point, add the expression `[^\n\r]+`. This type of search is often used to display data stored in lists, e.g. on the user pages. The expression for this is as follows:

RegEx

```
$pattern(.*?\*.*?label\s*([^\n\r]+).*)
```

As you can see, the position of the interior parentheses has changed. This results in a display of only that which comes after the label. The expression `\s*` stands for any number of spaces.

There is also the possibility of performing a further search within the search results. In principle, the internal search is indicated as a part of the parameter `format`. However, it must be reformatted so that the command is not executed too soon:

Nested search

- Replace the leading `%` with `$percnt`.
- Mask the quotation marks: `\"`.
- Replace all `$` with `$dollar`.
- Deactivate the final sequence: `}$nop%`.

We have now hidden the word "fire" in various places. A search of all pages that link to pages containing the word "fire" would thus look like this:

Wiki

```
%SEARCH{ "fire"                                          ↵
  nosearch="on" nototal="on"                             ↵
  format="···*·$topic:$n······*·                         ↵
  $percntSEARCH{ \"$topic\"                              ↵
    format=\"$dollartopic\" nosearch=\"on\"              ↵
    nototal=\"on\" separator=\", \"                      ↵
  }$nop%"                                                ↵
}%
```

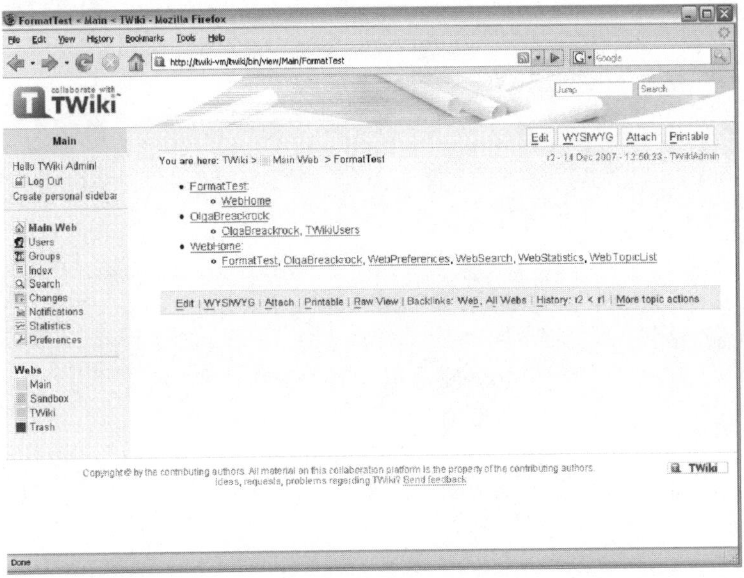

Fig. 14.3

You now see the pages containing fire, and separate from those, the pages linking to the pages with hits. Search requests can be nested in up to sixteen levels – but don't worry: We neither have an example of this nor any conceivable application.

15 Structured Data with Forms

Normally, the articles written in wikis are so-called free text. This type of text is different from information found in databases. Such structured data is characterized by the fact that, for the individual units of information, the type of entry is also indicated. For example, let's take an address. In a wiki, they look like this:

Wiki

```
Stony Way 23
Caveberg 08166
```

Structured data

Now imagine that we have an entire series of such entries. It makes sense that one would want to search for specific data. In the previous chapter, we already broached this subject. A conventional search, however, soon reaches its limits. The relatively simple query of having all known towns listed can only be solved with a complex regular expression. The task would be much easier if the available data were already classified:

```
Street       -> Stony Way
House number -> 23
Town          -> Caveberg
Zip code     -> 08166
```

This makes it possible to search for all data with the classification of "town".

Applications

Why do we need structured data in wikis? In addition to the variant just described, in which a wiki is used as a type of database, we can also use such entries to store so-called metadata about a page. For instance, this may include the edit status: work in progress vs. stable version, or the allocation of a page to defined categories.

15.1 TWiki Forms

In Twiki, structured data is achieved in so-called forms. For this, the system divides the description of the data and the actual entries. This makes sense, because then a defined data set can be used in different topics. In the example of the categories, then, the groups available would not have to be reinvented every time, but rather could be centrally stored. The separate description of the data thus leads to a standardization of data sets.

Form templates

In order to be able to use forms in a TWiki, a form template must first be generated which stipulates what data are to be stored and what possible values this data may have. If there is one or more of these templates, they can be linked with individual topics. When editing them, an additional field is displayed below the edit area in which the corresponding data can be entered. If you are in view mode, the form data is shown at the end of the topic.

Metadata in a topic

Technically, the storage of data is done in the topic itself, in special variables:

Wiki

```
%META:FIELD{name="category" value="person"}%
```

As you can see, the data here consists of a classification (name) and the actual value (value). However, you do not need to nor can you enter metadata by hand. The form takes over this task for you. The variables are not displayed in the normal view and edit area, yet they are included in the versioning process. This means that you also receive a new page revision, even if you only edit the metadata.

15.2 Generating a Form

Describing metadata

The first step in using structured data is generating a description of it. For this, you need a separate topic in the TWiki. You can generate such topics in the web where it is to be used, or you can create it in a general web, such as **TWiki**. In our example, the template is to be situated in the **Main** web. Thus, generate a page called **CategoryForm**. The structure of the data is described in a simple TWiki table having six columns with defined labels. (see Tab. 15.1).

Tab. 15.1

Column	Use
`Name`	Name of the field. The data is later addressed under this name. It must be explicitly in the form.
`Type`	Type of entry field in the form.
`Size`	Size of the entry field in a form or number of predefined entries.
`Values`	Possible values of the field.
`Tooltip message`	This text is displayed when the mouse rolls over the field.
`Attributes`	Defines the field as "hidden" (`H`) or "mandatory" (`M`).

The type field defines how the data can be entered into the form. There are various possibilities (see Tab 15.2).

Tab. 15.2

Type	Display
`checkbox`	Specifies one or more checkboxes. Several values may be selected.
`checkbox+buttons`	Like `checkbox`, except that it will also display buttons for setting and clearing checks.
`date`	Field to enter a date. Next to it, there is a calendar button with which the date can be selected.
`radio`	One or more radio buttons. Only one option can be selected.
`label`	Pure label text, read-only.
`select`	EA list of selection options, either as a drop-down box or scrollable list.
`text`	A single-line text field.
`textarea`	A multiple-line text field.

Depending on the type, the field size and values also have varying significances (see Tab 15.3).

Tab. 15.3

Type	Size	Values
`checkbox`	Number of entries per line.	A list of selectable entries separated by commas.
`checkbox + buttons`	See `checkbox`.	See `checkbox`.

Tab. 15.3 (continued)

Type	Size	Values
`date`	Width of the text field.	Default date.
`radio`	See `checkbox`.	See `checkbox`.
`label`	Is ignored.	The label text.
`select`	1: Drop-down. 2: Multi-line list.	A list of selectable entries separated by commas.
`text`	Width of text field in characters.	Default text.
`textarea`	Columns x lines of the text field, e.g. `20x5`. Default setting is `40x5`.	Default text.

A form for categories

A form enabling allocation into categories can be displayed in various ways. If the number of categories is modest, you may want to use the `checkbox` or `radio` option (if only one element can be selected). If, however, there are several possibilities, it is better to work with the `select` function. Let us try to incorporate both into a single form. With a small box, we can indicate whether a page is already in stable condition or if more editing is needed. The categories themselves are selected in a selection field. The code looks like this:

Wiki

```
| *Name* | *Type* | *Size* | *Values* |              ↵
  *Tooltip message* | *Attributes* |
| condition | radio | 2 | beta, stable |            ↵
  edit condition of the page |    |
| category | select | 3 |                           ↵
  Stones, Society, Hunt |                           ↵
  Page allocation |    |
```

The data set consists of two fields. The first is displayed as a control switch with the labels "beta" and "stable". The second is a list of predefined entries from which one can be selected.

However, there is often the need to allocate more than one category to a single page. This can be done relatively easily by altering the type to make it `select+multi`.

Note: This feature is only available from Version 4.1 on.

Of the fields for form definition, only the columns Name, Type and Size are mandatory. The others are optional.

Swapping out data

As in the case of categories, especially when dealing with very long lists, it is easier to follow and maintain them if you administer them on separate pages. For instance, one might allow these pages to only be edited by a single structure group, while a technical group takes charge of the form itself. Do you still remember our search from the previous chapter? That is going to help us out here. First of all, generate the topic **Categories**. It should contain the following content:

Wiki

```
Stones,
Society,
Hunt
```

Now, replace the values in the Values column of the form template with a search:

Wiki

```
%SEARCH{ "Categories" scope="topic"                    ↵
nosearch="on" nototal="on" format="$text" }%
```

This causes the entire text from **Categories** to be inserted at that spot.

A second, simpler variant is to select as a label for a field the name of another topic and leave the `values` column blank. TWiki will then automatically take the content of this topic in its entirety as a value list. The disadvantage in this case, however, is that the name of the field is set and, for example, cannot be internationalized.

15.3 Topics with Forms

Now that we have used the form template to set a uniform data storage method, the next step is to attach this data set to individual topics.

Activate a form in a web

To do so, the form must first be activated in the web in which it is to be utilized. Without activation, it cannot be used. So, in our case, go to the **WebPreferences** of the Main web. There you will find the variable `WEBFORMS`, which contains a list of active forms. Enter the form we have just generated:

Wiki

```
···*·Set WEBFORMS = UserForm, CategoryForm
```

You need to generate this entry for every web in which the form is to be used.

Note: Unfortunately, automatic activation using the search function is not possible here.

Allocating a form

Now we are ready to work with structured data. For this, create a test topic in the Main web, e.g. **FormTest**. If you are in edit mode, you will see the link **Add form** under the text field.

Fig. 15.1

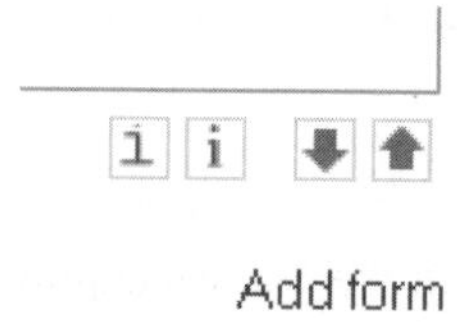
Add form

If you follow this link, you will arrive at a selection field listing the forms available in the current web.

Fig. 15.2

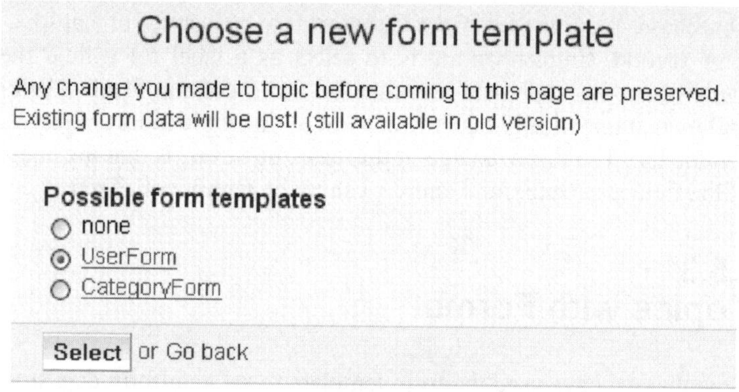
Choose a new form template
Any change you made to topic before coming to this page are preserved.
Existing form data will be lost! (still available in old version)
Possible form templates
none
UserForm
CategoryForm
Select
or Go back

Here, use the radio buttons to select **CategoryForm**.

Note: When you click on the title of a form, the entry is not selected, but rather you directly access the definition, that is the page of the form template.

Confirm your selection with **Select**. This brings you back to the edit mode. Below the edit window, there is now a template with additional entry elements corresponding to the pattern you set in the form template.

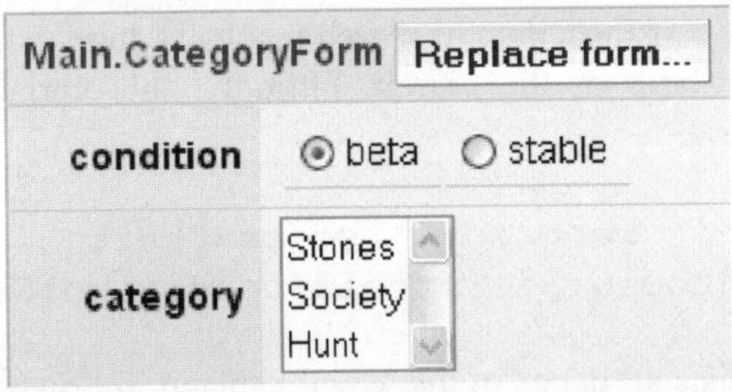

Fig. 15.3

Here, you can now enter the data according to your wishes. When saving the topic, the metadata is saved along with it, such that altering this data is subject to the revision process and will be stored in the History.

Change forms

In the form, you will also see a button to **Change** forms. With it, you can allocate a new form template to the topic.

Note: Only one form can be allocated to each topic.

When a form is switched, the data of the old form is not taken over in the new revisions. As of that point, they are only accessible in the old versions.

In the view mode of a page, you will now see a table at the end of the topic containing the data entered. An exception is fields in which the attribute "H" for "hidden" has been set.

15.4 Working with Structured Data

Display metadata in a topic

One considerable advantage to structured data is its easy and targeted access. For instance, you can access data within a topic using variables. To do this, use `FORMFIELD`:

Wiki

```
%FORMFIELD{"condition"}%
```

In place of the variable, the current value of the field is displayed in the text. Thus, you can display data in a formatted manner and also read out hidden fields.

Search for metadata

Naturally, the question of how we can access data via a search is extremely interesting. We have to differentiate between two types: One the one hand, there is the issue of how to display metadata on the topics we have searched, and on the other, we also want to search for topics that have certain values in their metadata.

The display of form data in search results is done via a variable in the form attribute of the search. Fittingly, this variable is called `$formfield`:

Wiki

```
%SEARCH{"*" web="Main" scope="text"                    ↵
format="$topic:$formfield(condition)$n"}%
```

Selecting topics by metadata

This search lists all pages in the Main web and, followed by a colon, indicates the value of the form field **condition**. However, as you can see, those topics are also listed that do not even have a form allocated to them. Thus, we must perform a second step to limit the topic search.

After the metadata has been internally stored directly in the text of a page, it is possible to simply search for keywords in the form. Using

Wiki

```
%SEARCH{"name=\"condition\"" web="Main"               ↵
scope="text"                                           ↵
format="$topic:$formfield(condition)$n"}%
```

to search only for the word "condition", the risk would be too great that this term would also appear in the body text. The indication "`name=`" is a part of the metadata variable as discussed in Chap. 14.1. Note that the quotation marks around "condition" have been masked with a `\`, because they would otherwise be interpreted as the end of a search term. If you now additionally want to search for a certain value of the form field, you can do so with `value=` :

Wiki

```
%SEARCH{"condition.*value\=.*stable"                  ↵
regex="on" web="Main" scope="text"                     ↵
format="$topic:$formfield(condition)$n"}%
```

As you can see, the search term was modified slightly in this example. We are now using a regular expression. This gives us greater flexibility and enables us to find the desired value even if several entries in the form have been selected. We use the placeholder `.*`, which stands for random characters, between the important words. Please also note that, when using this method, the evaluation of regular expressions must be activated with `regex="on"`.
A second, somewhat easier variation of metadata search can be had with the variable `%METASEARCH{}%`:

Wiki

```
%METASEARCH{type="field" name="Category"              ↵
value="Stones" format="$text"}%
```

It has three new parameters: Type determines in which metadata the search is to take place. In our case, it is always `field`. The attribute name determines which field is to be read out. Using `value`, you can then set values which are to be searched. Hits are normally issued as lists of topics separated by blank spaces; however, with the parameter `format`, you have the opportunity to influence the display, as in the search.

Note: The format parameter is only honored for metasearches as of Version 4.1.

16 Installing TWiki

Up to now, anyone has had access to all pages. This is not always desirable, especially for project work where there is urgent need for a space for internal meetings and the exchange of information. TWiki distinguishes itself from other wikis in that it possesses a relatively reasonable user administration system with which access to certain pages can be specifically controlled. This is not yet activated in the standard installation, but can be activated in a few simple steps.

Caution: For user administration, TWiki requires the additional Perl module Digest::SHA1.

16.1 Authentication vs. Access Control

Concepts for user administration

Generally, there are two concepts when working with users: authentication and access control. The former means determining who is currently in the system. This requires a registration by name, and a login. Users are then identified, and actions they undertake in the wiki are associated with their name. However, authentication does not necessarily mean that the system is closed to the public. For one thing, you can offer and promote guest access that anyone can use to log in to test the wiki. In the standard installation of TWiki, this is done via *TWikiGuest* with the password *guest*. On the other hand, you can give all visitors of the site the option of registering as a user in the system. In such a case, there is a publicly accessible registration page with which users can obtain a user name and password.

Access control

If a user is known to the system, you can allow or prohibit him or her from doing certain things. This is what is meant by access control. For example, some areas are blocked to normal wiki users such that they cannot even see them (e.g. preferences pages). Or, you can limit the editing of pages affecting the public (e.g. the title page) to a certain circle of users.

As you see, there is a variety of possible combinations of user and access controls. We will first have a look at how to activate and set authentication and access control. Subsequently, we will give some thought to access models and their sense or nonsense in the wiki.

16.2 Activating User Registration

Registration page

Before you activate the authentication, it is advisable to set up your own user account and register as an administrator. To do this, go to the page **TWiki.TWikiRegistration**.

Fig 16.1

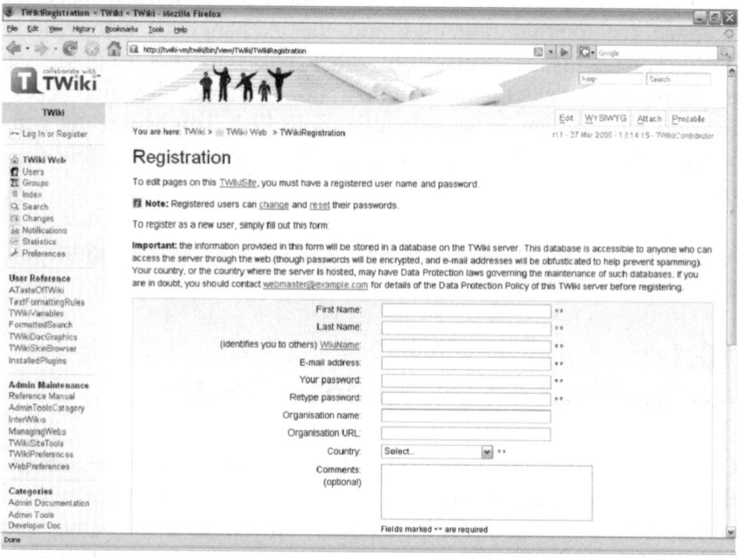

Caution: You should see a form here containing, among other things, a box to enter your password. If this is not the case, you have accessed the registration page for intranet users. If so, move that page to **TWikiRegistrationIntranet.** Search for the page **TWikiRegistrationPub** and move it to **TWikiRegistration.**

It is a general convention in TWiki to use real names. If you do not wish to do so, you are of course free to select a pseudonym. You can find out if the registration has been successful by looking at the page **Main.TWikiUsers**. Your name should now be on the list.

Note: If you have not set up the email function (see Chap. 17.5), you may receive an error message telling you that the confirmation email could not be sent. However, this message will not interfere with the registration process.

Now, make yourself an administrator. To do so, access the topic **TWikiAdminGroup**. Alter the line in which the members of the group are indicated by entering your name:

Defining administrators

Wiki

```
···*·Set GROUP = YourUserName
```

Several users are categorized in a single group who then all have the same TWiki permissions. You can find out more about groups in Chap. 16.4.

You can also modify the template with which the user page is generated. It is saved in the topic **TWiki.NewUserTemplate** and can be edited like any normal page.

16.3 Setting up Password Protection

In order to enable registration, you must activate this function in the configuration tool. To do so, go to the section Security setup and open it. It is important to set the authentification method, facilitated by the field **Login Manager**. Here, you have three options from which to choose:

- **None.** There is no login. Every user has the opportunity to edit pages. The pages explicitly blocked (see below) are the exception. They cannot be edited at all.
- **TWiki::Client::ApacheLogin.** Users are authenticated via the web server. Apache can protect a few or all scripts from unauthorized access.
- **TWiki::Client::TemplateLogin.** Users are identified via a login site and logged into a session. TWiki takes care of administration.

The selection of the authentification method has practical consequences. If the web server takes charge of registration, it is possible to log in, but Apache will not support a logout. Thus, the login is valid as long as the browser window is open. This poses a security risk in places like Internet cafés, and also makes a switch between two users more difficult, which especially administrators frequently require. Furthermore, the server can only verify scripts on one level. If, for instance, you block the edit script, all users must register before editing. A solution which would free up parts of the wiki for anonymous use is either impossible or extremely difficult to achieve.

You may be wondering why anyone would even want to use the ApacheLogin method at all. There are two possible reasons: Firstly, authentification via the web server is considered to be very reliable, making unexpected security gaps unlikely. Secondly, if you are familiar with Apache configuration, you have the opportunity of checking user data against an authentification server already present in the computer environment, thus conducting central user administration.

We also use the *TemplateLogin* method, since it offers the largest possible room for access control. To make the most of this option, however, an additional setting in the configuration script is necessary: Delete all entries from the line "AuthScripts" in the section "Security setup". If you do not do this, the TemplateLogin will act exactly like the ApacheLogin with regard to scripts, which is precisely what we are trying to avoid.

If you now enter the TWiki, you will see two links in the left navigation bar: **Log In** and **Registration**. You are already familiar with the latter. The former button asks you for your user name and password. Enter these and click **Log In**. You are now logged into the system, which you can recognize when you look at the navigation bar again: You will see the greeting: "Hello <your name>". Perhaps you have also noticed that your name is highlighted like a link. This leads to your personal user page in the TWiki, which contains a link to change your password, among other things.

16.4 Access Control

Access to the files in TWiki can be controlled very precisely. The users are identified by their user names, which are known to the system via authentication. Since it would be very cumbersome to continually list all authorized users for every action, we can categorize users into groups. In keeping with TWiki logic, these, in turn, are also only topics in which the corresponding users are listed. A list of all existing groups can be found under **TWikiGroups**. Here, in a new system, you should only see the **NobodyGroup** and the **TWikiAdminGroup**.

NobodyGroup

The first group has no members, and for good reason: Using it, you can completely prohibit certain actions that are potentially hazardous (so that nobody has permission to execute them). Such actions include, for instance, renaming **TWikiPreferences** or **TWiki-**

AdminGroup. As you will see, this does not offer complete protection, since these permissions may be changed by anyone having editing rights to a page. However, it is an effective means of protection against accidental actions.

TWikiAdmin Group

The second group is the Administrator Group. By default, admins have editing permissions for all pages and may generate new webs. Of course, this too, can be changed. The members of a group are defined with the variable GROUP. In the standard installation, you will see that the developers of TWiki are still listed as admins. You will also see that several users are simply written one after the other, delimited by commas. Your user name should definitely be here as well, if you are responsible for the TWiki.

Creating new groups

The easiest way to add a new group is by filling out the form on the **TWikiGroups** page. Here, you just have to enter a fitting name. Make sure that the name ends with "Group". A new page is generated that already contains all of the elements the group needs. Importantly, you are already listed as a registered user in the GROUP variable.

You will also see a second variable here, ALLOWTOPICCHANGE. This determines who can modify entries on a page. Admittedly, it would be rather ridiculous to limit certain actions to the Admin Group while at the same time allowing everyone the opportunity to make themselves admins.

Allow vs. deny

This brings us to the access authorizations. There are two ways to define them. Either you explicitly define who may not execute an action, which makes it accessible to all the rest. This is an open security strategy with which you can exclude certain persons who, for example, have become conspicuous due to vandalism. The other method is to indicate who may execute certain actions. This is useful in actions critical to security, where you would like to know the circle of authorized persons by name. The two key words are "DENY" for the exclusive strategy and "ALLOW" for the inclusive approach.

Protecting individual pages

The two most frequent limitations relate to changing and renaming topics. The corresponding variables are:

Wiki

```
···*·Set ALLOWTOPICCHANGE = User, Groups
···*·Set DENYTOPICCHANGE = User, Groups
···*·Set ALLOWTOPICRENAME = User, Groups
···*·Set DENYTOPICRENAME = User, Groups
```

Of course, you only have to make the entries that you need. If you only wish to enable inclusive access, you do not need to make any DENY entries. The first two variables relate to the editing of a topic and also include the option of attaching files. Thus, users prohibited from editing a topic may also not upload anything to that topic. The second pair of variables relates to renaming or moving a topic.

Hiding access variables

If you do not want to make it possible for everyone to immediately see who has access to a page and who does not, you can place the settings in HTML comments that begin in the line above the variable settings and end in the line below it. By doing this, you won't prevent users experienced in HTML source text from reading and nevertheless finding out this information. However, it is also a question of aesthetics to refrain from making such technical information immediately obvious to everyone in normal browser viewing.

Limiting viewing access

You can also limit viewing access to an article. The respective variables are `ALLOWTOPICVIEW` and `DENYTOPICVIEW`. The TWiki documentation describes this type of access control as "insecure"; however, we have been unable to reproduce the objections listed there.

Combining strategies

`DENY` and `ALLOW` can also be combined to exclude individual users of a group for a certain topic. Let us assume that the user *TimTroglodyte* is a member of the group *StoneAgeGroup*. However, recently, this user has conducted himself in a rude manner on a certain page to which he is obviously attached. The community decides to block him temporarily. This is done by setting the following permissions:

Wiki

```
···*·Set DENYTOPICCHANGE = TimTroglodyte
···*·Set ALLOWTOPICCHANGE = StoneAgeGroup
```

This does not change anything for the other members of the group, and you do not necessarily have to change the group structure to define permissions for a particular topic. Principally, the cross section of both settings is permitted.

Note: In the default settings, members of the **TWikiAdminGroup** have access everywhere (see below). If you wish to test the access controls, you should do so with users who are not in that group.

Web-level access control

Regulating access for each individual topic would not only take considerable effort during generation, but it would also easily lead to inconsistent settings if several people worked on them. Thus, there is the opportunity to set web-level controls that define which actions may be performed in a particular web. This is done via the respective **WebPreferences**. The corresponding variables for editing, renaming and viewing are:

```
   * Set ALLOWWEBCHANGE = User, Groups
   * Set DENYWEBCHANGE = User, Groups
   * Set ALLOWWEBRENAME = User, Groups
   * Set DENYWEBRENAME = User, Groups
   * Set ALLOWWEBVIEW = User, Groups
   * Set DENYWEBVIEW = User, Groups
```

Wiki

If you wish to protect your web from unauthorized viewing, it is also a good idea to set the parameter

```
   * Set NOSEARCHALL = on
```

Wiki

Otherwise, the web will be included in a full-text search. With regard to viewing restrictions, remember that a search requires registration as soon as blocked content is to be displayed. If a visitor does not have a user name, he or she cannot use the search in this case. The same applies to viewing topics and editing.

If you decide to protect a web from unauthorized access, you should also define the permissions of the preferences page. This is done, as usual, with the parameter ALLOWTOPICCHANGE, since it pertains to a single page.

Priorities in issuing permissions

This also means that a priority list must be generated for the event that topic and web settings are different. Normally, topic settings have priority. Thus, as you can see, decisions regarding access to individual topics are in the hands of the respective authors.

Wiki-wide permissions

The only setting that pertains to the entire TWiki is the permission to generate new webs. It is defined via **TWikiPreferences**. If you prefer not to have access limits in your TWiki, you should remove the following entries:

```
   * Set ALLOWWEBMANAGE = User, Groups
   * Set DENYWEBMANAGE = User, Groups
```

Wiki

since you otherwise will not be able to add new webs.

SuperAdmin Group

Now, there is still one serious security problem: An inexperienced user who tries to change settings changes the ALLOWTOPICCHANGE for a topic. In doing so, he makes a typing mistake or, if acting malevolently, knowingly enters a non-existent user. From then on, nobody can edit the page! One would have to lift the password protection temporarily in order to manually fix the problem. However, this would lead to considerable problems for users logged in at the time, because their permission verification only works through authenticated pages. To avoid such problems, a SuperAdmin Group can be set up that always has edit permissions for all topics. This group is activated by default and can be set up at **TWikiAdminGroup**. If you do not want such a group, or would like to grant another group these rights, you need to make changes to the configuration script *configure* in the area **Security setup**. The relevant parameter is **SuperAdminGroup**. This defines the name of the Super group.

16.5 Strategies for User Rights

At this point, we should briefly contemplate possible access control strategies and their implications. Generally, the whole appeal of a wiki lies in the fact that there are relatively few hurdles regarding access and editing. Access control is diametrically opposed to this concept. On the other hand, in TWiki, we are confronted with the fact that many system settings are self-defined and can be modified. It is understandable that you may not want these pages to be edited by just anyone, because the rest of the community would have a lot at risk (e.g. with regard to pages for skins).

Closed system

A completely closed system offers the advantage that you have fairly precise control over who may view and edit content. In addition, there are no guest users, so you can always track which individuals have performed what edits. Closed areas in the Net, however, generally make an unfriendly and thus uninviting impression. Such a wiki would make sense if it only concerns the internal matters of a group. On the other hand, these wikis are often operated on an intranet, such that the public is excluded anyway. General wikis, accessible via a known URL, should at least have an accessible start page that explains the purpose of the wiki.

Viewing permitted, editing upon registration

The default setting of the TWiki user administration is to permit anyone to view pages but require a login to edit them. As we have seen, this creates the opportunity to target individual pages for limitations or grant privileges to certain users/groups. Although in this version, anyone is permitted to edit pages via the guest login, the request to register sends a clear message: "This is a self-contained area; you are intruding into our wiki." Often, this is the decisive hurdle in participating in a joint project.

Editing partially permitted

Since we have determined above that not every user should be able to edit every page, it is a good idea to only limit access to those pages in the TWiki that require authentification of users. We made this setting when we decided on the *LoginManager*.

17 Administering TWiki

As an administrator, you are responsible for the operation of TWiki; thus, you will have a few duties that do not directly concern the "normal" user. For instance, you are especially responsible for the smooth operation of the system. This includes helping users with password problems, assuring security, and notifying users before any planned big changes.

To obtain admin privileges, you must be a member of the **TWikiAdminGroup** (see Chap. 16.4). You can find a list of the most important sites needed for administration work in the topic **TWiki.AdminTools**.

17.1 Administering Webs

If you have various groups in your TWiki, you cannot get around providing them with their own webs. However, separation into a variety of areas can also be useful for content purposes, since the individual webs are completely encapsulated. In the standard installation, only one member of the **TWikiAdminGroup** has permission to create new webs and edit existing ones. You can find this setting under `ALLOWWEBMANAGE` in **TWikiPreferences**.

17.1.1 Setup

Name

To create a new web, you only need to fill out the form in **TWiki.ManagingWebs**. It is depicted in Fig. 17.1.

Fig. 17.1

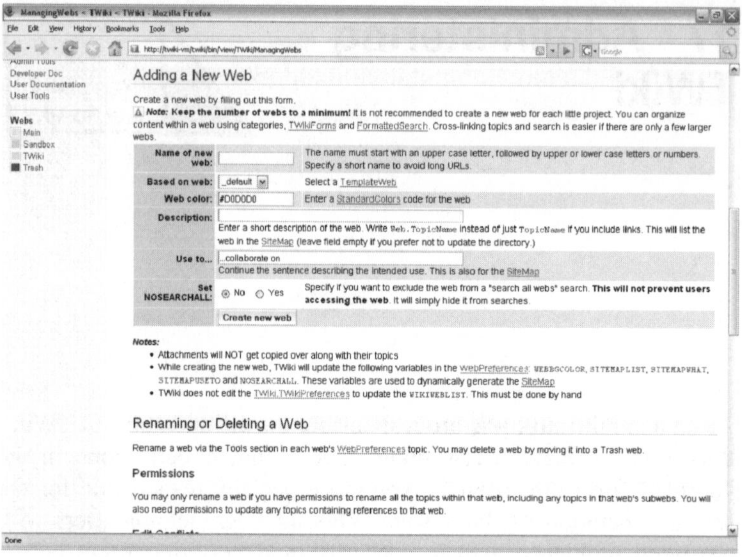

First, enter the name of the new web. A WikiWord can also be used here.

Note: This may lead to undesired side effects, since a WikiWord is also interpreted as such. However there are generally no pages in a web having the same name, leading to the web name being shown with a question mark. In page templates, you can avoid this by placing <nop> in front of the web name.

Template

Next, you have to select a template web. As the name indicates, this is a template for the web. Normally, you would use the template "_default" which, along with the web, also supplies a basic configuration of pages. These include all pages that start with "Web", thus **WebHome**, **WebChanges**, **WebIndex**, **WebNotify**, **WebPreferences**, **WebSearch**, **WebStatistics** and **WebTopicList**.

Tip: You can also create your own template web. To do this, generate a directory in *data* that starts with an underline, and copy all topics to it that you would like to have in the template.

The other possibility is to build the new web up on an existing one. When this is done, all pages from the old web that start with "Web" are taken over. However, make sure that any attachments are not copied along with the pages.

Color and description

Indication of the color of the web varies depending on the skin. In the *Pattern* skin, the tile of the navigation bar is displayed with the corresponding background color. In the *Classic* skin, you will see the title bar with the toolbar in the respective color. The content of the two description boxes **Description** and **Used to ...** are displayed in the topic **SiteMap**, which is integrated in the start page of the **Main** web, among others.

Search

Finally, you can determine whether the new web is to be searchable with the search function. Generally, you should permit this. However, if the web contains hidden pages, it is better to exclude it from searches, since such a search may access the hidden pages.

Create

If you now click on **Create new web**, the web will be generated, and you can now fill it with content. If you use a skin that accesses `WIKIWEBLIST` (e.g. *Classic*), you have to manually add the new web to this variable in **TWikiPreferences**.

17.1.2 Renaming, Deleting, Archiving

Finding links

There is a tool for renaming or deleting webs. You can find it in the corresponding web on the page **WebPreferences**. There is a link at the bottom called **Rename/more/delete this web ...** It appears on a page on which you can enter a new web name and parent web. You can delete a web by selecting **Trash** as the parent topic. Otherwise it will be renamed. Under it, you will find a list of the corresponding topics. You can now place a check in front of any topic for which you wish to update edits. If you rename a web, you should mark all topics. If, instead, you wish to delete it, we recommend removing all marks: if not, the corresponding links in the entire TWiki will be placed in the trash. These changes are made with **Rename/move**.

Archiving webs

To archive webs, you only need to pack the contents of the respective web directories from *data*, *pub* and *templates* into an archived file. Under Linux, you can use the following command:

Shell

```
tar czvf ↵
archivpfad/archivname.tar.gz ↵
twikipath/data/web ↵
twikipath/templates/web ↵
twikipath/pub/web
```

At regular intervals, you should also first archive and then empty the contents of the **Trash** web, into which deleted pages are placed.

17.1.3 RSS Feeds

TWiki also offers the possibility of monitoring recent changes via RSS. This news service is provided by the page **WebRss**, which is available in every web. If you look at that page in TWiki, you will only find a collection of URLs and a few comments. To obtain the actual RSS document, you have to have it displayed in the *Rss* skin. This is the URL under which an RSS reader can pick up its information:

URL

```
Web/WebRss
```

This feed contains all pages that are also found in **WebChanges**, including a short description. The newest pages and most recent edits are listed first.

Adapted feeds

You can also create an adapted feed that only monitors a selection of pages containing a particular key word. To do this, add to the URL the additional parameter `search`:

URL

```
Web/WebRss&search=keyword
```

Now, only those edits to pages are shown that can also be found with a normal text and title search under that key word. Of course, it is also possible to generate a page of links to specialized feeds. Such a link can be integrated into a wiki page with the following command:

Wiki

```
[[%SCRIPTURL%/view%SCRIPTSUFFIX%/Web/                 ↵
WebRss?skin=rss&search=keyword]                       ↵
[Feed to keyword]]
```

17.2 Topic Templates

When you generate a new topic, you will see that there is already text on the page, consisting of your user name and the current time. This text is defined in a topic template, and adopted when a new page is generated. Templates of this kind are generated for various purposes; you can find an overview in Tab. 17.1:

Tab. 17.1

Name	Application
`TWikiGroupTemplate`	Generating new groups.
`NewUserTemplate`	Setup of a new user.
`WebTopicEdit Template`	Generating a new page.

Name	Application
`WebLeftBarPersonal Template`	Setup of the user navigation sidebar.
`TWikiFaqTemplate`	Generating a new entry in **TWiki.TWikiFAQ**.
`ATasteOfTWiki Template`	Template for the slideshow **ATasteOfTWiki** (see Sect. IV.5.3)

Tab. 17.1 (continued)

Special variable treatment

Except for the **TWikiGroupTemplate**, all templates are located in the **TWiki** web. Of course, you can alter these sample pages according to your wishes, just like any other wiki page. However, there is a slight difference. The variables you see listed in Tab. 17.2 are not adopted, but are replaced by the values when the page is generated:

Tab. 17.2

Variable	Function
`%DATE%`	Current date.
`%USERNAME%`	Login name via the browser.
`%WIKINAME%`	Wiki user name, e.g. *TestUser*.
`%WIKIUSER NAME%`	User name with indication of web, e.g. *Main.TestUser*.
`%URLPARAM {"name"}%`	Value of the parameter `name` transferred in the URL.
`%NOP%`	Variable is simply removed. Can be used to mask other variables.
`%NOP{...}%`	As above, but spans more than one line.

Personalized templates

You can also use templates for your own purposes, such as to generate uniform agenda pages for every project group. To do so, first create your own template page, e.g. **ProjectAgendaTemplate**. To now create new pages out of the above, you need a form with which the *Edit* is invoked. This might look as follows:

Wiki

```
<form name="ProjAg"                                   ↵
      action="%SCRIPTURLPATH%/                        ↵
              edit%SCRIPTSUFFIX%/                     ↵
              %INTURLENCODE{"%WEB%"}%/">
  <input type="text" name="topic"
         value="Project#CHANGE#Agenda" />
  <input type="hidden" name="templatetopic"  ↵
         value="ProjectAgendaTemplate" />
  <input type="hidden" name="topicparent"    ↵
         value="%TOPIC%" />
```

```
   <input type="hidden" name="onlywikiname"   ↵
          value="on" />
   <input type="hidden" name="onlynewtopic"   ↵
          value="on" />
   <input type="submit" value="create" />
</form>
```

The form is depicted here:

Fig. 17.2

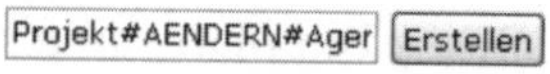

As you can see, the name is already suggested to the user, which he or she just needs to adapt. If the user presses **Create**, the page is generated. The possible parameters of the form are explained in Tab. 17.3

Tab. 17.3

Parameter	Function
`topic`	Name of the topic
`templatetopic`	Name of the template used
`topicparent`	Name of the parent topic
`onlywikiname`	Only permits WikiWords as topic names
`onlynewtopic`	Only permits topic names that do not yet exist.

Wiki variables can be allocated to the form parameters, since the parameters are filled with the corresponding values when the page is displayed, i.e. including when the form is displayed. If you wish to disable `onlywikiname` or `onlynewtopic`, you need to delete the corresponding lines. It is not enough to simply set the value to `off`.

17.3 Interwiki Links

Much like MediaWiki, TWiki also enables you to establish simplified links between various wikis and other websites. For this, place the abbreviation of the corresponding wiki or page in front of the actual link. The following link, for instance, invokes a Google search:

Wiki

```
Google:Wiki-Tools
```

You have surely noticed that, since the spelling was originally intended for wikis, you cannot use blank spaces. However, you can use `%0E` instead; thus, to search for the inventor of the Wiki concept, type

```
Google:Ward%0ECunningham
```

Wiki

Create your own

A list of all compatible abbreviations can be found on the page **TWiki.InterWikis**. You may be wondering if you can also define your own interwiki abbreviations on this page, and you would be right. Simply expand the respective table. It has three columns: the abbreviation, the URL to be invoked, and any corresponding tooltip text. You can insert the variable part of the URL using `$page`. A link to *Wikipedia.org* will serve as an example:

Wiki

```
| WP | http://de.wikipedia.org/wiki/ |          ↵
$page on Wikipedia |
```

As you can see, `$page` can also be left out if the variable part is at the end of the URL.

Tip: The tooltip function is switched off by default. It can be activated by setting the variable `LINKTOOLTIPINFO = on` in **TWikiPreferences**.

17.4 User Administration

Because administrators are responsible for access control, they are also confronted with the administration of users. A few tasks, such as registering and changing data, can be performed by the users themselves. Others, such as administering groups, are taken care of by a community of users on its own. This leaves questions that must be answered by an administrator: How can forgotten passwords be reset and users deleted? Let us briefly look at the answers to these questions.

New passwords

Resetting passwords works in two steps. On the page **TWiki. ResetPassword**, enter the user name and new password.

Deleting users

If a user has permanently left the TWiki community, or simply wishes to obtain a new name, it can be useful to delete that user from the database. To do this, you first need to remove the account from the password list. The location of this list is indicated in *Twiki.cfg*; it is normally found in *data* and is called *.htpasswd*. There, delete the line beginning with the user name to be removed. The remaining traces can be directly removed from the TWiki. The page **Main.TwikiUsers** lists all registered users. Just remove the corresponding entry here. The topic of the users can also be deleted, if desired. If, however, the user was active in the wiki, several links marking his or her edits will then lead to nothing. You should also have a look at permissions administration. If the user was granted special rights, you should delete the corresponding entries on the pages. Otherwise, someone could register under the same name and automatically have the same rights. The best way to find these entries is through a search (see Chap. 14).

17.5 Email

Contact data

Emails are sent to inform users about page edits and to confirm the registration of new users. The corresponding parameters can be found on the configuration page under the heading **Mail and Proxies**. Set the `"WebMasterEmail"` to the email address of the wiki administrator. In any case, you should make sure that the address indicated is accessible, since it will be distributed as a contact address during registration for any questions users may have. You can also indicate the name of the responsible person in `"WebMaster-Name."`

Mail program

To send emails from TWiki, you naturally need to specify in what way and via which server the emails are to be distributed. There are generally two possibilities for this, either via the Perl module *Net::SMTP* or an external mail program such as *sendmail*. If you want them to be sent via Perl, enter the name of a mail server in the parameter `Mailhost`. If it is on the same computer, `localhost` will suffice. Accessing an external mail program is defined in the variable `MailProgram`. In this case, the `Mailhost` must remain empty. In `Senderhost`, you can also indicate from which URL the email was sent. If you use a proxy server for your Internet connection, enter the corresponding data in the variables `Host` and `Port`. Now your TWiki is configured to automatically send emails.

email notification

You can verify whether your setup has been successful in two ways. You can register yourself as a new participant in wiki, for one. Unfortunately, this may lead to a series of unused dummy users if the email does not function right away. Therefore, it is better to test the notification of changes function. To register for that, just add your name to the list on the page **Main.WebNotify**:

Wiki

```
···*·Main.Username - your@email
```

This page exists separately for every web. When you add your name, you change a page in the **Main** web. Now, go to the command line of your server, switch to the *bin* directory, and add the following line:

```
mailnotify -q
```

Shell

You have just manually started the email notification service. If the mail settings are correct, you should now receive an email at the address indicated containing recent changes in the TWiki.

Automating notification

Of course, in order to run a decent notification service, you must automate the scripts. Under Linux, so-called Cron Jobs take care of this.

```
crontab -e 0 2 * * *                                  ↵
  (cd path/twiki/bin; mailnotify -q)
```

Shell

With this command, an email is sent every night at 2:00 a.m. (server time). The order of the time indicated is minute, hour, day, month and weekday. A star means "every time". So, if you want to issue a notification every day, the "day" space must have a star, such as in the above example. Under Windows, there are a number of programs offered by third parties that simulate Cron. Microsoft lists a few under the URL *http://www.microsoft.com/ntserver/partners-/findoffering/serversolutions/Maintnce.asp*.

Tip: One possibility with which to send all users (whether registered or not) general information are so-called broadcasts. These are messages that can be seen on every TWiki page via the toolbar. You can define its content in **TWikiPreferences** by making an entry to the variable BROADCASTMESSAGE. In the subsequent lines, you will see two examples that you can simply copy and adapt accordingly. The second method is only possible when the *Pattern* skin is used. Broadcasts are especially useful if you wish to inform users about large-scale maintenance work or changes to the TWiki.

17.6 Security Aspects

One could generally say that TWiki is relatively secure if you set access rights to the scripts and raw data very carefully. The scripts should only be executable by the system. In addition, except for the script directory, no other directory should be able to be accessed from outside via a web browser.

Holes in the security function

If you are using the TWiki, however, you should still have a look from time to time at the site *http://twiki.org/cgi-bin/view/Codev-/SecurityAlerts*. There, the most common security problems for the respective TWiki version are documented and solutions offered.

You will also find a mailing list on the page, with which you can always be kept abreast of developments.

Free use of HTML and scripts

One problem which is more aggravating than dangerous is the use of HTML and script languages. Free HTML can cause side effects with template tags and render a page undisplayable. This means one can no longer enter the edit mode from a browser to eliminate the error. Of course, you can always manually start the edit mode via the URL, but this requires a level of technical know-how that you cannot assume inexperienced users have. You can also bring about unpleasant effects with JavaScript as well. For instance, you could integrate a script that automatically closes the browser when a page is accessed. As in the previous problem, the normal user is at a loss. These problems are not hazardous; however, they can spoil the fun of the TWiki.

That is why there is a variable in the configuration realm "Security setup" called *allowInlineScript*. Remove the check mark from it if you want to work with an open TWiki and cannot be sure that all users have benevolent intentions.

Log files

TWiki keeps a record of requests made via the web. You can define which actions are included in this report in the configuration realm "Log files". Here, you will find a list of actions that are logged. You can find the log files in *twiki/data*; they are arranged by month and named according to the year and month, consistent with the following pattern:

```
logYYYYMM.txt
```

An entry in the log file contains the following tabular information (separated by | pipes): the date and time, user, invoked script, web and page, miscellaneous information such as whether the storage process was "quiet", that a requested page does not exist or that a page has been revised, as well as the IP address. This information can give you an idea of what sensitivities and errors may exist during processing.

17.7 Backing up Data

Any computer system is susceptible to technological failure. When this happens, total data loss is possible. That is why it is advisable to back up data in your TWiki at regular intervals and save the copies in a separate location.

Save all pages

Page data is stored in the directory *data*. To back it up, simply copy the entire directory or archive it. When this is done, the current versions as well as the history of the files are saved. Uploaded files are saved in the *pub* directory, which you should also back up. Under Unix, the command to back up data is as follows:

Shell

```
tar czvf backup_data.tar.gz */*
```

You must be in the respective directory. Form data does not need to be backed up separately, since it is saved as metadata in the respective topics and thus included in your backup.

Restoring data

To reload the data, unpack both archives to the directories *data* and *pub*. If you want to be extra careful, you should first empty those directories. This is especially true if you want to restore an older state of the wiki because, for instance, in the meanwhile, vandals have left their marks. This is the only way to make sure that no unwelcome remnants are still lurking in the webs.

17.8 Upgrading and Uninstalling

Since a new version of TWiki is released from time to time, it may happen that you may want to update your installation. Unfortunately, there is no comprehensive recipe for this task. However, you will find detailed information for every combination of versions at *http//twiki.org/cgi-bin/view/TWiki/TWikiUpgradeGuide.*

To upgrade from *TWiki 01-Sept-2004* to *TWiki-4x*, you must perform the following steps:

- Install the new version of TWiki in a new directory.
- Install the extensions in the new TWiki that you also used in the old wiki. Remember to use the respectively newest versions.
- Copy the old webs from the directories *data* and *pub* to the new TWiki. Make sure that, for the standard webs (especially the TWiki web), no standard pages from the new web are written over. They may contain new settings or templates that are necessary in the new wiki.
- Copy the users. The page **TWiki.TWikiUsers** must be adjusted manually. Copy the old *htpasswd* file into the *data* directory.
- Transfer the changes of the skins and settings. This must be done manually.

If you should actually need to uninstall TWiki for some reason, for instance because you are switching servers, you must do so manually; there is no uninstall routine. This is no big deal, however, because the TWiki stores all of its data in the *twiki* directory. Thus, if you delete that directory, all TWiki data will be removed. You should then undo the adjustments made to the Apache configuration file *httpd.conf*. To do so, remove the link to *twiki.conf*. That will remove all traces of TWiki.

18 Designing a TWiki

Especially in your own online presence open to the public, it is a bit frustrating to only be able to use predefined, standard layout options. This is especially true if you intend to integrate the wiki as only one component of your homepage, or if you have already gone public with a specific corporate identity. Luckily, TWiki offers simple options to alter the layout. You can also achieve functional changes to the community using plugins.

18.1 Designing the Look

Setting skins

As in the case with MediaWiki, TWiki also offers the opportunity to control the look of the page using skins. The default skin that is active is the version of the **Pattern** skin that we use. Of course, you are free to change it; this is done, as in the case in so many other TWiki functions, via a topic. You will find the corresponding entry in **TWikiPreferences**, in the section "Skin Settings" under the name `SKIN`. You can see how the installed skins look in the **TWikiSkinBrowser**.

Fig. 18.1

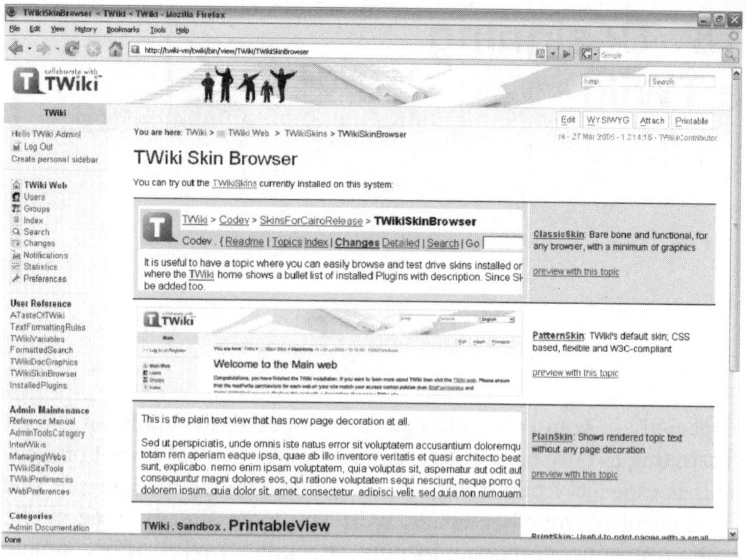

To activate one of the templates in the skin browser, set `SKIN` to the name of the desired skin, without using the word "skin;" thus, if you want **ClassicSkin**:

Wiki

```
···*·Set SKIN = classic
```

However, perhaps you initially only wish to give a few pages a new skin before you decide. To do this, attach the parameter `&skin=skinname` to the URL of the page you are currently viewing and thus access the page. Now the selected layout will be shown.

Installing new skins

Admittedly, the selection of skins in the standard installation is rather sparse. However, you can install additional skins. A list of current skins can be found under *http://twiki.org/cgi-bin/view/Plugins/SkinPackage*. From there, you can go to the respective page of the skin and download an archived file which is present as an attachment. Unpack the file to the *twiki* directory.

Note: The procedure described here may vary somewhat for individual skins. Thus, you should read the installation instructions indicated for each skin.

Caution: Before you set up a newly installed skin, you should first test it on a single page to avoid any unpleasant surprises. For instance, sometimes you must first define the edit buttons. If you forget to do this, you can only obtain the edit mode of the preferences page directly through the URL (`edit` instead of `view`).

In the **Pattern** skin, it is relatively easy to put together a menu bar. In every web, there is a topic with the name **WebLeftBar**, which is integrated into the page as a template on the left side of the article. If you access the page, you will see that a complete copy of the menu sidebar is located there. You can edit that sidebar just as you can any other page in the TWiki. For example, if you want to add a link to our homepage, just add the line

Adapting the menu sidebar

```
*[[http://www.wikitools.org][WikiTools]]*
```

Wiki

This will insert a link in bold lettering. After you save it, you will notice that the changes have been immediately adopted.

Tip: In the template issued with the software, all entries are elements of a list. This is irrelevant to the display on the left side of the screen and can just as easily be left out.

18.1.1 Functional Elements

The most important question that crops up with regard to creating your own layouts is about functional links. How can one access the various views of a topic via links? You may have guessed that the scripts in the *bin* directory play an important role. These scripts are accessed with the corresponding page as a parameter. For a few functions, there are a few further entries to be made. You will find a list of scripts and their functions in Tab. 18.1:

Tab. 18.1

Script	Function	Parameter
`view`	display	▪ **skin**: Display of the page using a particular skin. ▪ **raw**: "on" displays the source code, "debug" additionally shows the meta information. ▪ **topic**: Name of the article to be displayed.
`edit`	edit	▪ **t**: Displays the time at the start of editing.

Tab. 18.1 (continued)

Script	Function	Parameter
search	search	▪ **scope**: Area in which the search is to take place. Possible options are "topic" for a search of the title, "text" for a full text search and "all" for both. ▪ **search**: The actual search string.
rdiff	revisions	To show all old versions: ▪ enter no parameters. To show old versions: ▪ **rev**: number of revision to be displayed. Comparing revisions: ▪ **rev1**: number of first revision. ▪ **rev2**: number of second revision.

Accessing the View script

Since we want to conceive our scripts for all pages, it is advisable to proceed as generally as possible. This primarily means replacing statistical information with the corresponding variables when possible. For instance, the *View* script is then invoked as follows:

Wiki

```
%SCRIPTURL%/view%SCRIPTSUFFIX%
```

The path to the script, as well as any defined file endings in *configure*, are derived from the TWiki settings. The name of the topic to be accessed is clearly defined by the following variables:

Wiki

```
%INCLUDINGWEB%/%INCLUDINGTOPIC%
```

Note that the skin files are actually embedded in the article. That is why it is not enough to use the placeholders `%WEB%` and `%TOPIC%`, since they would always point to the skin itself. The list of parameters begins with a `?`, and several parameters are separated by an `&`. Thus, if you wish to have a link on every page which will display that page in the *classic* skin, use the following lines:

Wiki

```
[[%SCRIPTURL%/view%SCRIPTSUFFIX%/                 ↵
%INCLUDINGWEB%/%INCLUDINGTOPIC%                   ↵
?skin=classic]                                    ↵
[in Classic Skin]]
```

The print view can also be generated with this link, since it basically opens the same page with **Print** skin. So, you only have to replace `classic` with `print` in the above commands and change the label.

Edit link

The edit script additionally requires the current time as a parameter. You can use the variable `GMTIME` for it:

Wiki

```
[[%SCRIPTURL%/edit%SCRIPTSUFFIX%/                ↵
%INCLUDINGWEB%/%INCLUDINGTOPIC%                  ↵
?t=%GMTIME                                       ↵
{"$year$mo$day$hours$minutes$seconds"}%]         ↵
[edit]]
```

As is the case for all TWiki pages, for a complex layout, it is indeed possible to write it directly in HTML.

Revisions

Unfortunately, it is not possible to display the revisions view with skins that are controlled by TWiki pages in the way that you are familiar from the **Pattern** skin. You can only have all edits displayed at the same time. To do so, simply open the *Rdiff* script with the corresponding page.

Tip: You can integrate the revisions view via the templates. The templates for this display are located in the *template* folder, and are called *view.[skinname].tmpl*. The variable `%REVISIONS%` is available in these files, which displays the revisions view.

Backlinks

You can generate a list of backlinks with the aid of the built-in search function (for more detail, see Chap. 13). To do so, use the following command:

Wiki

```
[[%SCRIPTURL%/search%SCRIPTSUFFIX%/              ↵
%INCLUDINGWEB%/SearchResult                      ↵
?scope=text                                      ↵
&amp;regex=on                                    ↵
&amp;search=%SPACEDTOPIC%%5B%5EA-Za-z%5D]        ↵
[Backlinks]]
```

Do not be distracted by the many cryptic characters. Those are circumscriptions for the special characters `&` (`&`), `[` (`%5B`), `^` (`%5E`) and `]` (`%5D`), that would otherwise disturb processing of the wiki page. Principally, this command searches for all pages on which the page name occurs in square brackets, that is, as a link. Those are the backlinks.

Attachments

The function for attaching files is activated via a separate script. You only need to open the page using `attach` instead of view, and the upload dialogue will start.

Extended functions

To integrate extended functions (renaming, deleting, etc.), you need to access the *Oops* script. It actually produces the TWiki messages (including error messages). Since a wide variety of messages must be issued, it is invoked with its own templates that contain the corresponding message. This concept is also used for displaying extended functions:

Wiki

```
[[%SCRIPTURL%/oops%SCRIPTSUFFIX%/                  ↵
%INCLUDINGWEB%/%INCLUDINGTOPIC%                    ↵
?template=oopsmore]                                ↵
[extended functions]]
```

The last functional link we will add is a field for direct access to our skin. The *View* script can be invoked using the parameter `topic`, which will take us directly to the page indicated or, if it does not yet exist, display a search dialogue. The parameter `topic` can also be issued via a form. To do so, the following HTML code will suffice to display direct access:

Wiki

```
<form action="%TOPIC%">
  <input type="text" name="topic" size="16"/>
</form>
```

Of course, this is only a minimal version. The form is sent by pressing the <ENTER> key. You can achieve greater user friendliness by inserting at least one button.

List of all webs

Now, let us have a look at two dynamic components of the navigation sidebar. As you can see, a list of those webs that are created in the wiki is displayed in the **Pattern** skin. This list can be displayed via the variable `%WEBLIST{""}%`. Without indicating any further formatting information, the names of the webs are simply written one after the other. That is why you have the opportunity to make detailed comments on the display in square brackets. You can enter any text you want here. In the spot where the name of the corresponding web is to be displayed, insert `$name`. In this way, you can display the webs as a linked list, for example:

Wiki

```
%WEBLIST{"···*·[[$name.%HOMETOPIC%]·                ↵
[$name]]"}%
```

When the script puts the page together, it displays the line indicated once for each web, whereby the corresponding name is inserted in each case. `%HOMETOPIC%` links to the start page of the web.

Highlight the current web

The %WEBLIST% variable also offers the possibility of highlighting a certain web. To do this, you first must define which web is to be marked using $selected. Then, use $marker to determine how the highlighting will look. Now, you just have to place $marker in the right spot in the display. For instance, to display the current web (stored in %WEB%) in bold, use the following code:

Wiki

```
%WEBLIST{                                        ↵
  "···*·$marker[[$name.%HOMETOPIC%]              ↵
  [$name]]$marker"                               ↵
  selection="%WEB%"                              ↵
  marker="*"                                     ↵
}%
```

The star indicating bold lettering is only shown if the web currently being processed ($name) matches the current web.

As a drop-down element

TWikis, in which several groups work simultaneously and thus have a number of webs, can quickly become complex if the entire list of all webs is always issued. A more elegant solution would be the integration of drop-down menus. For this, we need an HTML form that is filled with a <SELECT> element:

Wiki

```
<form action="">
  <select size=1 name="selection">
   %WEBLIST{                                     ↵
   "<option value="%SCRIPTURLPATH%/              ↵
   view%SCRIPTSUFFIX%/$name.%HOMETOPIC%">        ↵
   $name</option>"}%
  </select>
</form>
```

Unfortunately, we still have another hurdle to clear. Nothing happens when you select a web. This is due to the fact that the form is not sent out. A small JavaScript can come to the rescue here. The following attribute loads the URL indicated in value as soon as anything changes in the selection box:

JS

```
onChange=                                        ↵
"document.location.href=                         ↵
this.form.selection.options[                     ↵
this.form.selection.options.selectedIndex        ↵
].value"
```

Add the line in the `<SELECT>` element after `name="selection"`.

Now we still have the problem that the **Main** web is always displayed. Yet it would be nice if the current web in which we are located would also be preselected. For this, the HTML command `selected` must be inserted in the corresponding option. The `%WEBLIST%` then looks like this:

Wiki

```
%WEBLIST{                                            ↵
"<option $marker value="%SCRIPTURLPATH%/             ↵
view%SCRIPTSUFFIX%/$name.%HOMETOPIC%">               ↵
$name</option>"                                      ↵
selection="%WEB%"                                    ↵
marker="selected"}%
```

List of topics

Similar to the list of webs, you can also have a list of topics generated that enables quick access to existing topics of a web as long as there aren't too many entries. The variable in which all topics are stored is called `%TOPICLIST%`. Here is a printout of the source code for a drop-down list:

Wiki

```
<form action="">
  <select size=1 name="aw"                              ↵
   style="width:100px;"                                 ↵
   onChange="document.location.href=                    ↵
    this.form.aw.options[                               ↵
      this.form.aw.options.selectedIndex                ↵
    ].value">
     %TOPICLIST{                                        ↵
       "<OPTION $marker                                 ↵
         value="%SCRIPTURLPATH%/                        ↵
         view%SCRIPTSUFFIX%/%WEB%/$name">               ↵
         $name                                          ↵
       </OPTION>"                                       ↵
       selection="%TOPIC%"                              ↵
       marker="selected"}%
  </select>
</form>
```

The changes in comparison to the listing of the webs are highlighted in bold. Because the length of the entries in the topic list may vary greatly, it is a good idea to limit the width of the drop-down list. Thus, a `style` attribute has been inserted in the `<SELECT>` element.

18.1.2 Advanced Options

Templates

If the previous adjustment possibilities are not enough for you, an all-around solution can only be offered by writing your own templates. You can find templates on the server in the directory *twiki/templates*. They all follow the same name convention:

```
scriptname.skinname.tmpl
```

For scripts to which no templates have been allocated in the current skin, standard templates are employed, so that you do not necessarily have to generate all templates. You can write normal HTML code in the template files, but also use certain variables.

Standard template

The system is divided into two levels. On one hand, there is the standard template *twiki.tmpl*. It defines elements that other templates can access. A few of these predefined elements are already visible in Tab. 18.2:

Tab. 18.2

Name	Content
`sep`	element separator.
`htmldoctype`	Standardized <head> area.
`standardheader`	Standard layout header.
`simpleheader`	Simplified header of the standard layout, e.g. for the *Edit* and *Attach* script.
`standardfooter`	Standard layout footer.
`oops`	Error message skeleton.

You can integrate these elements using the command

CFG

```
%TMPL:P{"variablename"}%
```

If you wish to adopt entire swapped out files, you can do so with the following code:

CFG

```
%%TMPL:INCLUDE{"filename"}%
```

The extension *.tmpl* can be left off. As in the case of the other templates, the standard master template is replaced when there is a file *twiki.[skinname].tmpl* that matches the skin. In this master template, you of course have the possibility of defining a few elements:

CFG

```
%%TMPL:DEF{"elementname"}%
    elementtext
%TMPL:END%
```

Script templates

The second level is that of the concrete scripts. They are the ones that ultimately determine which HTML code is issued. To be able to use the elements from the master template, you have to integrate them with `%TMPL:INCLUDE{"TWiki"}%`. It suffices to indicate "TWiki" as the file name. The respective skin version is automatically searched.

Tip: If you define a few elements in the script templates, you can link to them in the embedded master template. This gives you the opportunity to parameterize the master templates. An example: In the standard template, the function toolbar is placed in the footer. This is defined in the master template. However, the commands that are supposed to be there are defined in the respective script template as `%TMPL:DEF{"topicaction"}%`. Thus, you can basically use the same footer for all scripts.

Placing text

Of course, one important question is how to place the actual topic text. This is stored in the `%TEXT%` variables. In addition, there are several other variables containing content components. A selection of them is listed in Tab. 18.3:

Tab. 18.3

Name	Content
`%TEXT%`	The actual content of the page. In the edit and preview modes it appears in raw form. Caution – the corresponding text box is not included in the variable.
`%EDITTOPIC%`	Edit link.
`%REVISIONS%`	Link to the last three versions of the topic.
`%TOPICPARENT%`	Name of the article from which the page has been generated.
`%PREVIEW BGIMAGE%`	Path to the background image of the preview mode.

Note that not all variables are always filled with content. If you create your own templates, you should always start from an existing template and adapt it to your wishes. In this way, you will also see what variables contain the functions you need.

Metadata

In addition to the source text of the topics, TWiki also saves so-called metadata. This is information about the page itself, its attachments, the parent page, and any related moves or forms. It is generally not shown when a page is edited.

Tip: You also have the option of having the metadata displayed along with the source text. To do so, open the page with the URL parameter?`raw=debug`.

The metadata is stored in meta variables. They are listed in Tab. 18.4:

Tab. 18.4

Name	Content
`%META{"parent"}%`	Name of the topic from which the current page has been created. In contrast to `%TOPICPARENT%`, you can also enter further options here: ▪ **dontrecurse="on"**. Only the immediate predecessor is displayed. ▪ **nowebhome="on"**. The web homepage is not included in the display. ▪ **prefix=""** "and **suffix=""**. Text that is to appear before and after the display. ▪ **separator=""** Separator in the event that there is more than one predecessor.
`%META{"moved"}%`	If the page has been moved, a report of the move is found here.
`%META{"attachments"}%`	Display of the files that are attached to a page. ▪ **all="on"** also shows the hidden attachments.

You cannot use these variables on normal pages. In your templates (e.g. **WebLeftBar**) and in the other templates, however, they are used according to the same principle as all other variables.

Your own parameters

In Templates, you even have the possibility of adopting four of your own parameters from the URL. They have to be transferred in the address line using `&param1` to `4`, and can be accessed in the script with `%PARAM1%` to `4`.

18.2 Plugins and Add-ons

TWiki achieves its special degree of power and flexibility with the aid of so-called plugins. These are small, add-on modules that you can install to supplement your existing software. A great advantage is that the core wiki remains relatively trim, which means that it does not drag around any unnecessary program code. Every TWiki operator can integrate those particular modules that are truly necessary. Furthermore, programmers of plugins can easily and cleanly expand TWiki and adapt it to their needs without endangering the stability of the core wiki. Plugins are often developed from a concrete necessity in using TWiki, so that there is a whole series of very useful supplementary functions. In addition, plugins enable programmers to react relatively quickly to new developments without having to issue completely new versions of TWikis. Thus, it is worthwhile to have a look at the page *http://twiki.org/cgi-bin/view/Plugins* every once in a while[3].

As you can see, there are two types of add-ons found there. Generally, add-ons are independent from the existing functionality, and are executed as independent scripts or small programs. Plugins, on the other hand, expand the possibilities of existing scripts by enabling additional TWiki formatting elements, for example. You cannot directly use contributions; they are used by plugins.

Plugins

In Tab. 18.5, we have included a list of especially useful and interesting plugins, to give you an overview of what they can accomplish. To find a plugin at *twiki.org*, you have to add "plugin" to every name:

Tab. 18.5

Name	Function
Calendar	Display of a calendar and appointments.
ActionTracker	Task planner for a project group.
Database	Database access from TWiki.
TWikiDraw	Cooperative generation and editing of drawings (requires Java).
SpreadSheet	Spreadsheet in TWiki.
SlideShow	Generate and display presentations.
Toc	Table of contents of *TWiki* webs.
Pdf	Generates a PDF document from a TWiki page.

[3] The plugins discussed in the book can also be found on the CD under /wikis/twiki/plugins.

Tab. 18.5 (continued)

Name	Function
Comment	Add comments to a page without having to edit it first.
Peer	Enables pages to be evaluated.
Poll	Conduct a poll in TWiki.
ProjectPlanner	Manage time and scheduling plans for projects.
SectionalEdit	Targeted editing of sections (see MediaWiki).
Session	Session-based authentication to circumvent the browser's mechanism.
TagMe	Social tagging for TWiki.

So just how are these plugins accessed? In principle, they simply add new variables to the existing ones. They are inserted in the topic source text, just like normal TWiki variables. A few are already included in the standard installation, so we can test the concept right away using a concrete object. The list of installed plugins is found on the page **TWiki.InstalledPlugins**. You should also see the smilies plugin here. Edit any page, and add

```
:cool: and :)
```

Wiki

You will see that the characters from the smilies plugin have turned into smilies. You can find a more detailed list of possible graphics in the description page having the name **TWiki.SmiliesPlugin**. This kind of documentation is issued with every plugin, and we recommend looking at it before using the plugin.

Installing Plugins

Because there is such a wealth of add-on programs for TWiki (currently more than 250), we cannot discuss all of them here. A few are needed in Sect. IV, where we will have a closer look at them. However, our primary focus right now is the process of installing new plugins. It is a relatively easy task. On the overview page *http://twiki.org/cgi-bin/view/Plugins/PluginPackage*, you will find the entire list of installable plugins. Each one has its own topic. There, you can find directions for using the plugin, updated tips, and, most importantly, the installation instructions. Generally, you only need to download the archived file attached to the end of the topic and unpack it to the TWiki installation directory. This procedure will automatically copy the files to their correct directories. Cautious webmasters can also unpack the files to a temporary directory. A directory structure will be generated that is analogous to that of the TWiki directory, and you will know which files are to be copied to which directories.

Caution: A few plugins must additionally be configured on the file level. To do this, carefully read the corresponding installation instructions.

All plugins are activated automatically as soon as they are installed. However, you can prevent a plugin from being activated by adding it to the list of `DISABLEDPLUGINS` in **TWiki.TWikiPreferences**.

Unfortunately, we cannot provide a universal recipe for the installation of add-ons. Often, they are simple programs that you can execute either from your computer or server. A few of these programs require Java J2EE to be installed on your computer. You can download it at *http://java.sun.com*. Just follow their installation instructions.

FirefoxExtension

We would like to highlight one particular add-on, since it can make working with TWiki much easier. It is the *FirefoxExtensionAddOn*, which can be found at the URL *http://twiki.org/cgi-bin/view/Plugins/FirefoxExtensionAddOn*. If you use Firefox as your browser, this add-on gives you the option of inserting several TWiki formatting commands via a toolbar or context menu. You can install the add-on directly from the page indicated from Firefox. Then you just need to restart the browser, and you should see the TWiki bar. Now you can either insert formatted text in the edit mode (tables, images, lists) or format highlighted text.

IV. TWiki as a Project Kit

19 Preliminary Thoughts: What is a Project?

How can wikis contribute to the improved organization of groups? Let's assume that we want to organize a project. What benefits would we garner from a wiki? How would we have to work with it? Using the example of TWiki, we want to demonstrate that wikis, in comparison to other systems (e.g. CMS), offer a number of advantages as an integrative organizational and communicative medium. They are just as appealing for companies as they are for political, social and cultural organizations. At the same time, we wish to introduce a few attractive TWiki features.

In the principles of project management and the wiki philosophy, two opposing concepts meet: a predefined goal, clear definition of work steps, resources and participants on the one hand, and on the other, self-determined goal definition, self responsibility for work methods and steps and an open number of participants. Yet, when we take a closer look, there are several similarities. It is worthwhile to make use of experiences from the realm of classic project management for wikis and the wiki philosophy.

Project management

The literature on project management attempts to define a project using three characteristics:[1]

1. It is a one-time event with a predefined result.
2. There is a predefined scheduled start and a predetermined end to the project.
3. The amount of people, financial means, production means and equipment available are planned in advance.

[1] See. e.g. Portny 2001, 26.

However, these characteristics can be used to describe just about any project: from construction projects worth millions to moving furniture around in an office. Its presumable clarity leads to the use of the term in daily language to refer to any random human activity. After all, the word "project" only describes the fact that a person predefines his activity in his head ("plans"), implements them and evaluates the altered reality for further action.

Taylor's Division of Labor

But contemporary use of the term is not arbitrary. "Regardless of what your project looks like, you always define it on the basis of the three same elements: output, start and end date, and resources", observes Portny.[2] The word "project" in project management is related to Taylor's principle of internal division of labor. According to this principle, all work steps are divided into their individual components (in project management, into "projects" and "work packages") and standardized. The individual work steps can thus be re-assigned and resource usage more precisely planned. As a result, efficiency and productivity of mass production can be increased considerably. However, prerequisite to this success is the exact observance of schedules and the extensive elimination of coincidence. Project and personnel alike are under central control.[3]

A project as a concept

The project concept, as it also forms the base of the wiki philosophy, counters that of the original meaning of "project". The older term "project", stemming from the 17th-century French word "projet", has a much broader target and is far less technocratic. It means something like "design", "urge forward", "push out", "throw forward", and "thrust out;"[4] all more reminiscent of the English verb "to project". The wiki philosophy, too, deals with reformulating systematic action, but with the intent of moving from simple reaction and optimization to planning, attempting and designing. Questions of efficiency and cost-benefit issues also play a role, but the wiki philosophy is based on the notion of "people in free cooperation" (Spehr). This means not exposing oneself to apparent system obligations, but rather promoting the construction of self-administrating structures and direct control of central decisions by the pool of participants. Participants themselves decide on goals, milestones and deadlines – thereby running the risk of areas

---

[2] Portny 2001, 27.

[3] The boom of "projects" in the working world fits in with a redesigning of production, right up to greater flexibility of employment relationships with the goal of a reduction in wage costs and a simultaneous integration of the immediate producers with more responsible autonomy (see Candeias 2004, 179).

[4] See Kluge 2002, 722.

not being processed and the production process running less directly.

Project: free planning?

In keeping with the wiki philosophy is the wish to achieve target-oriented action and concrete results. Yet, at the same time, decisions regarding the course of the project are to be as democratic and open as possible. The wiki philosophy promotes freedom of movement and freedom to be able to decide for or against participation in a project.

Project phases

Wiki software, then, can provide assistance in certain project phases (Tab. 19.1) or be employed as a supplement to existing systems. Yet they can also serve as the central medium with which to manage all phases.

Tab. 19.1

Phase	Goal	Concrete examples
1 Concept	The idea is developed.	▪ Establish start group. ▪ Collect ideas. ▪ Write project drafts.
2 Delimitation	Composition of the project plan.	▪ Define goals. ▪ Plan work. ▪ Plan costs. ▪ Plan procedure.
3 Start	The team is put together.	▪ Allocation of important tasks (admin, moderation, finances, PR work…). ▪ Define rules.
4 Execution	The work is accomplished.	▪ Query sponsors. ▪ Do publicity work. ▪ Occupy rooms.
5 Conclusion	The project is concluded.	▪ Accounting. ▪ Documentation. ▪ Transfer to subsequent projects. ▪ Evaluation.

Phase overlap in wiki philosophy

The phases in conventional project management are relatively strictly separated from one another. If, in comparison, one employs the wiki philosophy, there is overlap between the first and third and the fourth and fifth phases. The construction of the team starts as early as the idea collection phase, and the circle of participants does not remain static, but rather can and should increase. This philosophy ranks volunteerism as its top priority. The “two foot” principle rules: Team members can also walk away from such projects. It nevertheless makes sense to establish responsibilities and clear rules after the second phase, at the latest. There is overlap toward the end of the project, as well. For instance, materials need not be collected for closing documentation, since, ideally, all necessary information is available on the wiki network.

20 Conceptual Phase: Collecting Ideas and Outlining the Project

20.1 Establishing a Base

Define the assignment

A project begins with your idea or an external assignment. If you receive an external project assignment, clarify as precisely as possible what the goal of the project is, what expectations the client has of you, and why the project was assigned. Also discuss at an early stage the resources at your disposal, and don't be afraid to reject the project if you have the impression that financial or conceptual support will be lacking.

Example: Conference on the Neolithic Age

We wish to illustrate the possibilities of wikis using the example of a conference preparation process. We will assume that our Stone Age people want to call a conference on the future, in order to discuss life in the Neolithic Age. To organize a conference, we will conform to the general phases of project management (see Tab. 17.1).

To wiki or not to wiki?

Because the use of a wiki for the character of the conference is a fundamental decision, the group should decide as early as the conceptual phase if and to what extent they wish to work with a wiki. Excluding factors would be if the majority of participants or superiors – for instance, the old shamans – do not agree to the procedure and will not support the results because they fear having to surrender control, although they are crucial to the implementation of the project results. It is vital that ideas that are developed "from below" ultimately have the chance to be implemented they way they were intended.

Choosing TWiki

In answer to the question as to which of the wiki clones to use, we have decided on TWiki. Our most important criterion was its variety of application options. TikiWiki, bitweaver and TWiki stand out in this regard. As we mentioned in the preface, TWiki represents a technically greater challenge for admins. We nevertheless chose it because this clone remains true to wiki technology, whereas Tiki-Wiki contains the wiki only as one of several communications applications.

Introducing wiki

Therefore, immediately before or directly at the start of the conceptual phase, a separate wiki introduction meeting should be arranged. In our case, we are introduced to TWiki, and the participants are made familiar with the wiki philosophy.

This meeting concerns the integration of the wiki. Furthermore, it serves to eliminate any existing reservations and conduct a few practical experiments with TWiki. It is also a chance to discuss the classic wiki questions – regarding vandalism, etc. The occasion serves to point out that wiki is not a miracle technology, but that adopting it can be well worth it, and that its adoption is a decision that the participants themselves must make.

Tweaking TWiki

Especially TWiki, in the condition in which it is supplied to users, needs a bit of preliminary tweaking, for instance, by creating an HTML start page that offers an overview, and by generating a few webs and topics with initial content. Furthermore, the sandbox is to be activated and the most important syntax made available at a glance. Computer skills can never be assumed, so it is advisable to publicly discuss what skills and experiences participants have. It is a good idea to appoint a contact person that can provide support in the case of technical problems.

Constructive criticism

Another good reason to hold an introductory meeting is that some people wince at the thought of expressing their thoughts in writing, compressing the content, and exposing themselves to criticism. Many prefer to communicate orally, because they can be certain that the right people receive the information. Such needs should always be taken seriously, and can be addressed accordingly at such an event. Yet reciprocal constructive criticism and cooperative discussions take practice. By constructive, we do not mean avoiding conflict and stressing harmony, but rather criticism that is always paired with suggestions for alternatives. We are talking about assuming a position of respect for the work of others, since they identify with it.

Establishing rules

Let us get back to the hunters and gatherers. Basically, they need to lay down a few rules for interaction. Points to be considered include:

- Is there a check mechanism if, for instance, a part of the project gets behind schedule because certain content could not be generated? Who is responsible?

- It has to be determined how and according to what rules the project is to be moderated. Which procedures exist to solve internal conflicts?
- How do you regulate the power differential that exists between admins, maintainers and moderators and normal users? A separate page should definitely be generated for such discussions. To prevent someone from blocking the project, a backup should be made at regular intervals and saved to a neutral server. To do this, at least one additional person is required who is familiar with the technology and has full access rights.
- Setting up central contact points has already been addressed. This includes establishing pages such as "News" or "Conventions".

Tip: Don't put too many expectations in your wiki. Not everything is going to function properly right off the bat. Never forget that, with all of the spontaneity, you are dealing with group processes and learning processes that take time. Associative thinking, creative seizing of ideas and cooperation are not prevalent in our form of society, nor are insight and understanding in organizational issues.

20.2 Collecting Cooperative Ideas and Generating Project Outlines

Project outlines

The hunters and gatherers must first collect ideas and ultimately formulate a draft paper (project outline). They already have several suggestions. A possible title would be "Get Out of the Cave. Prospects for the Future in the Neolithic Age." The advantages of sedentariness could be thematicized, or new techniques in cross-country plowing. Workshops on band ceramics are to provide a cultural supplement to the conference.

The draft paper describes the beginning and end, the title, goal and possible content of the conference. By making the ideas more concrete and compact, we can achieve more clarity for ourselves, and the paper can be presented to sponsors for their decision. Thus, we can already utilize two advantages of the wiki.

- More ideas can also be collected for the paper between meetings. They would be immediately worked into the paper and available online to all participants.

- The draft paper can be further developed in a cooperative way. Cooperative writing will also come into play for the subsequent organizational planning, applications, goal descriptions, task planning and invitational texts.

Collecting ideas

Now we can already start collecting ideas or query people's expectations on a wiki page for the next meeting, to summarize them in a text on a new page. The involvement of the people concerned in the formulation process increases the chance that the draft paper will be read and agreements will be better understood and accepted by everyone. Any modifications can vary greatly, from the correction of minor typing and grammar errors to the editing of long passages.

Brainstorming

Wikis can also serve as a private notepad on which impressions, inklings, tips, questions, etc. can be noted down at random intervals. The hypertext structure can reflect and promote basic networked thinking. However, you can also use the wiki for cooperative forms of writing, such as collaborative brainstorming and other playful types of idea collection. One popular variation is to have the first person write one sentence, and the next person add a sentence to it spontaneously, and so on. For brainstorming, "fantastic" or "imaginary" ideas are also welcome, since they motivate participants to abandon habitual thought routines and think innovatively. "Food that won't run away", may have been one such invented idea on the verge of the Neolithic Age. Only after such a thought is expressed, has caused friction or prompted objection can it be seized by others and modified.[5] We are thinking such general considerations through here because experience has shown that this process is extremely important and, in day-to-day life, are quick to be ignored. Several wiki projects fail not because of technical problems, but because of the forms of communication, or rather: of non-communication.

Seize ideas and new thought processes

Thus, cooperative and associative thinking is a must. Initial fuzziness is not a hindrance; on the contrary – even if one does not agree with a point of view, an important impulse may be triggered that sheds light on aspects that had been previously ignored. This requires an attitude in which one asks what someone else had really been trying to say. A relaxed atmosphere means unusual ideas and half-baked thoughts can also be expressed, which can be the source of innovative thinking as well as "criticism".

Creativity is learnable

Cooperative writing occasionally requires spontaneity and creativity. It is an artistic process that triggers the interaction of rational

[5] Which may possibly have developed from the desire for food that would not bite back.

thought and emotional perception in both hemispheres of the brain. Many people generally think they are not creative and that cooperative forms of writing are not "their thing". However, they overlook the fact that people basically do nothing more than think associatively. Thus, everyone is creative in some area: in landscaping, mixing music or even in destruction (for instance, some wiki "moths"). In creativity research as well as education science, the realization has meanwhile taken hold that creativity is learned and, for example, can be promoted with combinatorial analysis games and mind maps.

Blocks

Writing has always also had a psychosocial component. Here are just three tips in that regard:

1. Individuals, not least, seek to obtain attention from others. The fact that their own ideas are perceived and discussed plays an important role in interactivity, dynamics, creativity and motivation. That is why so many management guidebooks recommend good old backslapping to more or less manipulate employees. When it is about cooperation and creativity, not only open and goal-oriented criticism is required, but also truthful statements regarding what one liked or found helpful.
2. A hostile climate encumbers creativity by instilling a fear of disgrace. Also, open, associative thinking in a group is prevented by social blocks. Cave painter Hanna will think twice about what she says if her teacher or the cult community supervisor is within earshot – and vice versa.
3. Everyone has writer's block from time to time. The thought that a text must first be finished before being published is paralyzing. In such cases, it can be helpful to start writing as early as possible and begin with small articles. The wiki philosophy assumes that starting is more important than waiting for the perfect version.[6] "Ignore all rules", is the call Wikipedia makes to its new authors to illustrate the fact that they should not shy away from what has in the meantime become a mountain of conventions, but rather release texts as quickly as possible for further processing.

Visuals

We must admit that computers are not the best tools for creative processes, since they indeed prescribe technical behavioral patterns and set limits. However, you should still take advantage of any existing room for design in creative processes. Especially when ideas are sought, the forms of design can differ greatly and consciously stretch beyond the scope of traditional structures, such as when images are

[6] Just think of Linus Torvald's method of releasing texts early and often.

also integrated because colleagues express their ideas and utopias via images or other data formats. Thus, include pictures and graphic images, and submit sketches and mind maps from team meetings if they serve to substantiate your ideas. However, before you rush off and integrate a bunch of images into your page, you should frequently ask yourself if the visuals are truly fitting, and what functions they are to serve. As you know, too many pictures can be overwhelming.

20.3 Keeping a Log with Wikis

Keeping a log with wiki

All possible sorts of texts can be generated in a cooperative effort: project outlines, invitational texts, blurbs or reports. Naturally, logs and reports also play a vital role in projects. After a meeting, the minutes of the meeting can be submitted to the wiki, either as a downloadable file, or, even better, as normal text.

In this regard, wikis offer the advantage that modifications can be made after the fact. Team members have another week's time to think things over. If, for instance, it was agreed that the "Finances" group will subsequently submit the cost estimate of the cave operator, it can be directly entered on the group's own wiki page. Similarly, unclear formulations can be corrected or existing ambiguities debated using all available texts. Such discussions can prevent misunderstandings at an early stage that otherwise would only crop up once execution of the project has already begun and that would endanger the success of the project. That is why it can also be of assistance to highlight new entries in a different color and specifically inform the project management of such entries.

During the meeting

Of course, meeting minutes can be entered in the wiki during the meeting itself, if the technical requirements are available. In addition, a video projector would provide visualization. However, the experiences of facilitators and lecturers have shown that these measures are not optimal for a wiki project. *Firstly*, such technology assumes that the keeper of the minutes has sufficient experience in dealing with TWiki. Technical problems could quickly hamper the discussion flow and ruin the meeting's spontaneity, productive atmosphere and content context. *Secondly*, minute takers hide behind their laptops, making it all the easier for them to withdraw from the discussion. This may be interpreted by the other participants as a lack of respect, since they are not sure whether the minute taker is taking part in the discussion or not. *Thirdly*, we must not forget the power of formulation. As soon as more than just the facts are recorded, it has a great influence on the course of the discussion and the direction of thoughts. In contrast to other moderation techniques, the other participants cannot directly influence the visuals. The minute taker may thus cause some individuals to feel insecure. *Fourthly*, wikis without WYSIWYG systems are not suitable for video projection presentations of this sort.[7]

[7] There is a very useful SlideShowPlugin for presentations; see Chap. 23.3.

21 Composing the Project Plan

21.1 Preparing Work Packages

Project structure diagram

Once the initiators of the conference "Get Out of the Cave" have conducted basic discussions with friends, colleagues and stakeholders about the execution of the project, concrete individual planning can begin. In traditional project management, the next step involves first developing the project structure. In planning meetings,

Fig. 21.1

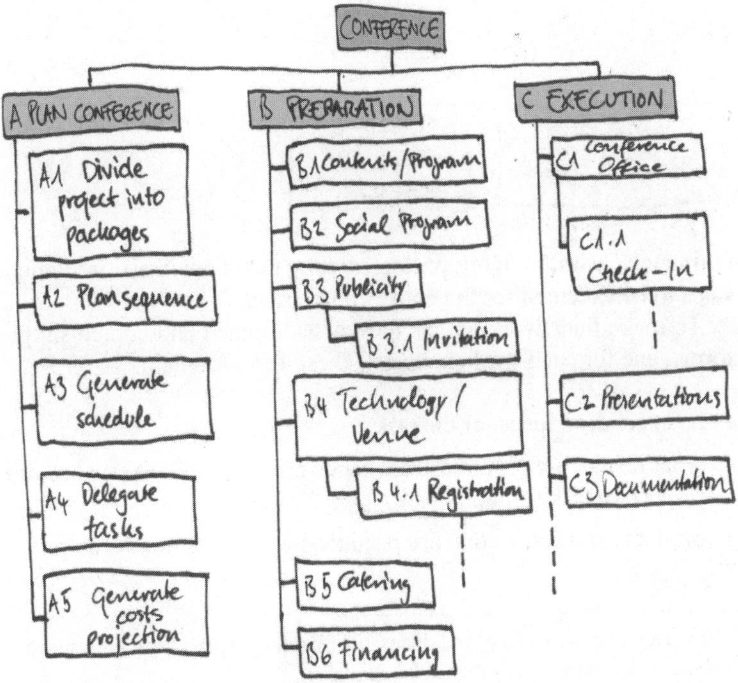

individual tasks are specified, divided into subtasks and individual steps (work packages) (see Fig. 21.1 and Fig. 21.2). This detailed and hierarchical division will help in the subsequent assessment of how much time is required for the individual project steps and when which tasks are to be completed. Thus, organizers are forced to develop a clear picture of the overall project.[8] Our hunters and gatherers first roughly define which subtasks they must complete in the course of the entire project. Their structure diagram for the conference looks like this:

Forms for work packages

With the aid of the project structure diagram, the project is then thought through, step by step, and all necessary work steps are noted in detail. The subtasks are further divided into individual tasks, known as work packages:

Fig. 21.2

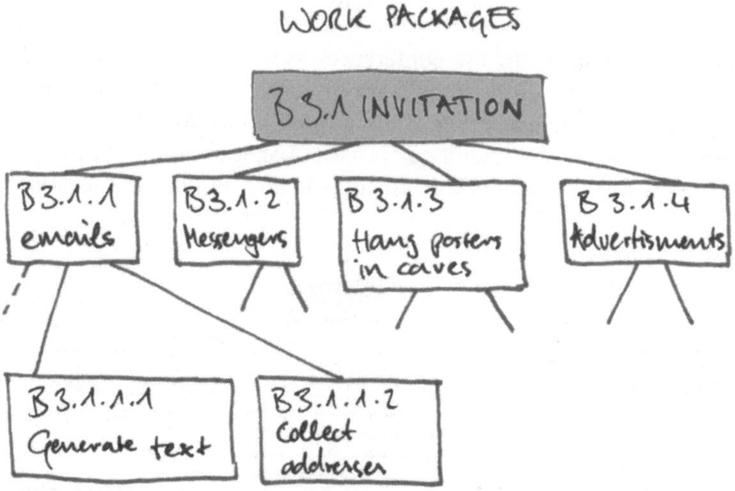

Ultimately, with the work packages, they then have small individual steps to be executed for the entire conference.

Forms

To make their work easier, they first designed and copied simple forms, one for each work package. These forms contain

- an exact description of the task
- what results are required from other tasks in order to perform the respective task (inputs)
- products and results that are produced with this subtask (outputs)

---

[8] You can find assistance and ideas on planning work steps in respective technical literature, e.g. Portny 2001, 69–91.

- roles and responsibilities for the package
- the timeframe of the individual task and
- the required resources.

Often, the direct predecessors and successors of the respective task are noted. The paper forms are ideal for sorting on a wall and subsequently developing the procedure, deadlines and financial plans.

To-do list

A great deal of information can be filtered from these forms: overall cost, material requirements, time schedules, etc. Now TWiki comes into play again. The hunters and gatherers first transfer the work packages to a to-do list that can be viewed by everyone involved in the organization. The groups involved can note the status of their respective subtasks there. This results in an updated report on the status of the project.

The groups must clarify how detailed the list is to be. A graduated list works well. Numbering can help in order to define precisely which work package is being addressed in discussions. It is possible, for example, that the publicity group and the content group both have a work package called "Send emails".

Note: These numbers must be assigned in a fixed manner and may thus not be generated with the numbered list function.

Project number list

The best thing to do is create a separate wiki page on which the project numbers can be clearly noted. It might look like this:

Fig. 21.3

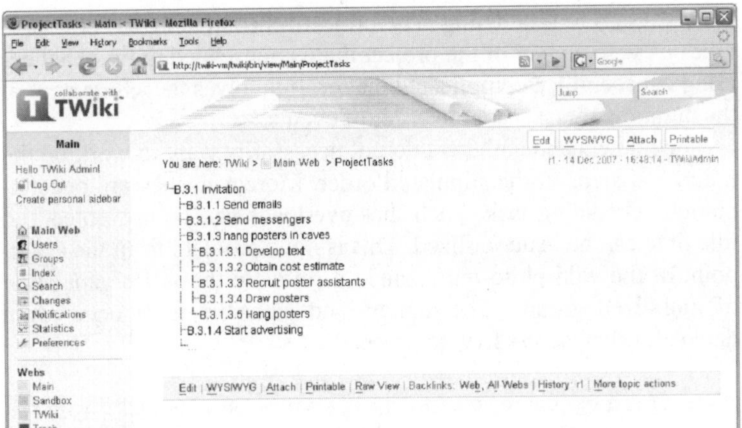

RenderList plugin

The RenderList plugin comes into play for this list, which we will only explain briefly. The plugin, which should already be installed, enables lists to be formatted with either predefined icons or your own. We have selected the standard format `thread`, which we indicate in the variable `%RENDERLIST%`. Our list looks as follows in code view:

Wiki

```
%RENDERLIST{"thread"}%
B.3.1 Invitation
  * B.3.1.1 Send emails
  * B.3.1.2 Send messengers
  * B.3.1.3 hang posters in caves
     * B.3.1.3.1 Develop text
     * B.3.1.3.2 Obtain cost estimate
     * B.3.1.3.3 Recruit poster assistants
     * B.3.1.3.4 Draw posters
     * B.3.1.3.5 Hang posters
  * B.3.1.4 Start advertising
  * ...
```

As of TWiki version 4.0, you need to activate the plugin on the configuration page under Plugins.

21.2 The Project Schedule

Project schedule

Now we turn to scheduling. The project schedule diagram only provides us with a view of the project that is not related to time. Scheduling is generally a complicated matter. It involves the assessment of the duration of tasks and the order of events.

The hunters and gatherers do not necessarily want to work on the individual steps in the stipulated order. Moreover, they are contemplating scheduling tasks such that overloads can be prevented and idle time can be better utilized. This is not a problem from the standpoint of the wiki philosophy, since it refers to the self-organization of mobilized groups. The hunters and gatherers must once again decide for themselves how to proceed.

Note: It is a typical mistake to calculate project schedules "from the back" and thus incorrectly estimate the real time needed or resource requirements. The schedules are then embellished instead of modifying the projects. Do not be tempted to develop the schedule according to this "backing in" method. It is better to do without some project content, since projects tend to need to fill too many expectations at once anyway.

Bar graphs

In our case, we will offer a visual in the form of a bar graph to depict scheduling. The bar graph organizes all elements in their order of performance along a time axis, such that the duration and time differences are also visible graphically. Such graphs are the same kind as those used to depict vacation scheduling in companies.

Unfortunately, TWiki as yet does not offer any solutions to achieve such a bar graph, generated in a group meeting, using the wiki principle. We can only generate the graph in another program and then load it into the wiki system as a finished graphic image. It would not be able to be edited using TWiki.

Integrating graphics

By and large, graphics and images are still employed conservatively in wikis. The integration of existing graphics is practical in that they also stimulate the right half of the brain, which is responsible for visual and spatial thought. Images are absorbed quickly, spark curiosity, and can improve clarity. In combination with the text, they can promote new ideas. Our group, for instance, has integrated images of the planned venue. On their wiki, they also display statistics. It is also conceivable to transfer flowcharts, workflows or mind maps to the wiki. In classic project management, for example, procedural node network plans have been very helpful in depicting work packages and their dependencies (see Fig. 21.4).[9] The next section will explain how to draw these graphic images directly in the TWiki using a flowchart.

Calendar function

Similarly, neither MediaWiki nor TWiki offers a sufficient calendar function that can be integrated into the schedule and used autonomously by the work groups. TWiki does have a calendar plugin, but the effort needed to install it is not worth the functionality it offers. That is why we would need to rely on other programs for this service.

---

[9] There, procedural node network plans are used to develop project strategy ("network plan technique"). These are graphic or tabular depictions of procedures and their dependencies. More detail on this topic would extend beyond the scope of this book; the illustration supplies a rough idea of the procedure.

Fig. 21.4

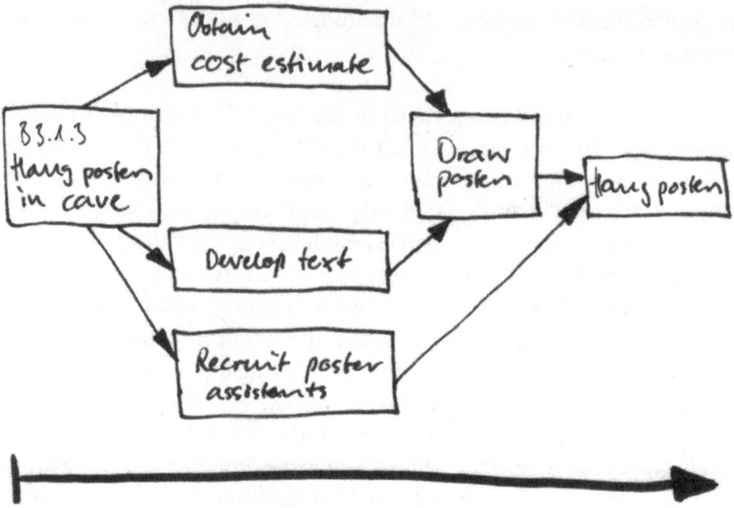

21.3 Distributing Tasks and Forming Groups

Distributing tasks and forming groups

In the next step, participants accept a variety of tasks (work packages) and, if necessary, form work groups. Furthermore, it is advisable to appoint responsible persons for subtasks (finances, technology, catering, social program, content, and so on) who can help with the coordination when there are tie-ups, contribute their professional expertise, and keep an eye on the overall project. There are several different models for this job. Responsibility for subtasks can change hands in the course of the project, as is the case with moderation. The important thing is that responsibilities are frequently defined at certain points in time – just as in any democratic system.[10] In the end, all tasks and responsibilities must be clearly distributed so that the project can begin with a prospect for success.

Delegating tasks?

Some proponents of self-organizational processes may object at this point. They make the transfer of tasks dependent upon interests, the "passion" and self-motivation of participants. When this method is employed, tasks that are not assumed are also not delegated. It is true that there is Linus Torvald's principle urging to "delegate everything that can be delegated", but here, the explicit accent is on voluntary assumption of tasks. Pekka Himanen goes the same route when he presents the thesis that the hacker ethic is a new work ethic that represents an alternative to the "protestant work ethic" of Max

[10] In self-organized systems, "hierarchy" develops through authority toward which one has worked, or through the election of responsible persons.

Weber.[11] Accordingly, in self-organizing relationships, only those tasks are fulfilled that people want to execute. Thus, it is possible that some subtasks will initially be left undone. For a long time, Linux was to a large extent an insular system for experts, because the needs of the "normal" user were completely ignored. The open-source community refers to the successes of this method, since ultimately all central subtasks were taken on.

We cannot unfold the advantages and disadvantages of self-organized processes here. Each individual group must decide which principles to follow in the distribution of jobs and subtasks. It is obvious that our conference cannot take place if central tasks are not completed on schedule. The ideal of self-determining schedules does not necessarily have to contradict this goal.[12] However, it matters, of course, who defines the goals. Thus, in self-organized projects, too, there is a much discussed "inherent necessity" problem and routine work that is not linked to recognition. Also, there are "deadlines" – even if they come about for other reasons.[13]

Setting up group webs

Now work groups can be provided with their own webs in the TWiki, as described above, that they may design independently from other groups. In our case, let us take a couple of organizers of the Neolithic Conference on the Future. For instance, if Walter has volunteered to get water, and Daniel has offered to catch the mammoths, and Lea has taken charge of the roasting skewers, they can come together in a work group called "Catering", and upon request receive their own web, in which, without worrying about the work style and requirements of other work groups, they can develop their file structure as desired. We need to differentiate between two types of webs:

- Function webs, e.g. individual webs for registration
- Group webs, e.g. a web for the work group "Catering".

[11] See Himanen 2001, who explains in detail the motivation of hackers and free software projects.

[12] Whether or not the article "Hacker Ethics" will appear on the Net today or in one month is naturally less of a problem than the regular supply of staple foods (the "bread roll question").

[13] Beware of the danger of falling back into romantic, pre-capitalistic societal utopias. Further differentiated division of labor and systematic project coordination does not automatically lead to a limitation of human self-determination, as Marx thought when he criticized the fact that relationships created by humans rise above them. To be precise, division of labor is the actual prerequisite to self-determination.

While function webs are available to all participants, insofar as this is possible with regard to data protection regulations, group webs tend to only be accessible for their respective members.

Granting permissions

Traditional content management systems offer very detailed permissions management. In such systems, permissions are often bound to existing functions and hierarchies. According to their original intention, the first wikis had no user administration. In the meantime, newer wiki clones offer possibilities to grant various degrees of user permissions. This can be practical because not every memo has to be open to the whole web, or because private data must also be protected. The hacker ethic puts it as follows: Information should be free, but personal rights and private data are to be protected. When establishing user permissions, you should consider their effect:

- Some may interpret user rights as resembling a bouncer hindering access at the door. For others, the step of registering is also an instance of conscious decision for active participation in a relationship of work and discussion.
- Rooms that are limited are seldom opened again. Experience has shown that discussions shift to the limited rosters, and the open lists lose significance.

In any event, the dual control system should apply and not only be accessible to a single admin. Supporters, observers, helpers and those concerned with the project should be integrated into the wiki project to as great an extent as possible.

21.4 Outlining Structures and Procedures with the TWikiDraw Plugin

Organization charts

In very dynamic, self-organized projects it is also, and even especially, necessary to appoint contact persons and advisors for certain areas, so that the groups can make arrangements between themselves. We want to combine the sensible with the beneficial, and thus introduce a tool that is very easy to use: the TWikiDraw plugin. Using it, we can create visuals of structures and procedures, for example, such as in the form of workflows and organization charts.

Mode of operation

The plugin is based on a Java Applet that was developed by Peter Thoeny from the original JhotDraw. With it, you can place ready-made lines, shapes and text in a drawing window, similar to MS PowerPoint and MS Word, and supply them with links to pages within or outside of TWiki.

You should first install the plugin, since it is not a standard component of TWiki (see Sect. III.7.3). Again, you must activate the plugin for versions from 4.0 and higher on the configuration page under Plugins. Once you have moved the files to the correct directory, the plugin will be visible in three places on the **TWiki** web:

- on the web homepage under "TWiki User's Guide"
- on the InstalledPlugins page
- as the new topic **TWikiDrawPlugin**.

On the page of the plugin, you can test the drawing program and – if desired – make other settings (see below).

Syntax

Now, in order to draw on another page, just integrate the variable `%DRAWING%` to the respective spot in the source code. With the attribute `name`, you can give your drawing a `name` that, however, need not contain CamelCase; for example:

Wiki

```
%DRAWING{name="Drawing_one"}%
```

If only one drawing is planned for that topic, it suffices to simply name the variable `<%DRAWING%`.

Starting

In page view, you should now see the following switch:

Fig. 21.5

If you click on the switch, a drawing window opens with the tools you will need to edit your drawing:

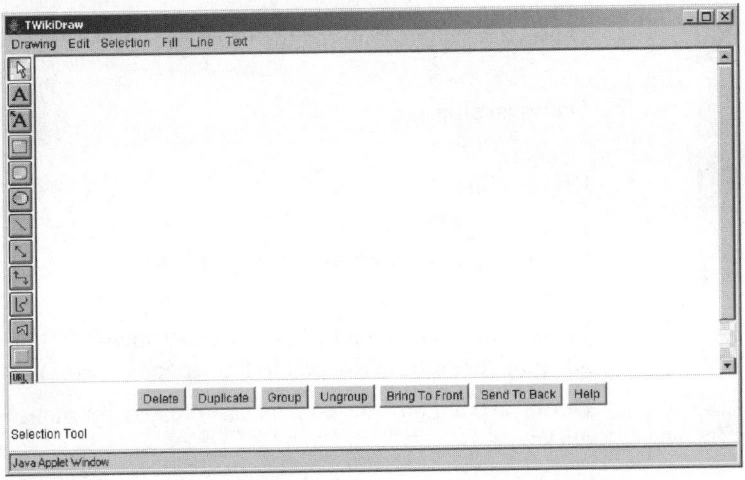

Fig. 21.6

Closing

To leave the drawing program and return to the page, press either **Exit without Saving** or **Save and Exit** in the **Drawing** menu, depending on whether you wish to save your work or not. The drawing will now be attached in a frame on the page. If you wish to edit it and thus open the drawing program, click on the drawing. In the event that there are links in your drawing that you may activate by mistake, we recommend clicking on the drawing frame or on the **Edit** button.

Note: There is the usual X icon in the upper right corner of the window, but you cannot close the window with it. To close, you must use a menu option.

21.5 The Tools

On the left side of the interface, there is a toolbar offering the following functions:

Tab. 21.1

Icon	Function
	Selects, moves and edits the clicked object.
	Inserts text.
	Inserts text and attaches it to the object.
	Draws a rectangle.
	Draws a rectangle with rounded corners.
	Draws an ellipse.
	Draws a line.
	Creates a connection between two objects.
	Creates an elbow connection (hold left mouse button and pull cursor from the first to the second element).
	Draws a polygon; the corners are created by mouse clicks.

Tab. 21.1 (continued)

Icon	Function
	Enables freehand drawing.
	Decorates the clicked object with a frame.
	Adds a link to the clicked object.

Hot Spots

The last function listed in the table needs some explaining. In order to turn a figure, for instance a circle, into a so-called hot spot, that is, to supply it with a link, click on the URL icon in the toolbox and then mark the desired object. A small input window opens in which you can enter the URL or page name. When you leave the window by simply clicking on another spot in the drawing window, the path of the link will appear in red. However, this label is no longer visible in the page view.

Note: If you wish to edit or remove the link, you must once again activate the URL icon and then click on the red path. In the input box, you can edit the link. This also applies to text boxes as well.

Attributes

You can change the attributes of an object, such as the fill text color or the shape of an arrow tip, primarily through the entries **Fill**, **Line** and **Text** in the menu bar.

Move/ delete/ align

The buttons underneath the drawing window provide a few more important functions, such as cutting, copying, duplicating, deleting and grouping, which are also in the menu. You should have highlighted the respective object first, though.

Hold points

When marking the object, hold points become visible in various colors, depending on the figure. You can manipulate the figure with the mouse on these points:

- **White**. Changes the size of rectangles, lines and ellipses.
- **Yellow**. Changes the font size of text and the degree of rounding in rectangles with rounded corners. Also, the elbow connection lines can be shaped here.
- **Green**. Moves a connection arrow to another object.

Sample organization chart

To be able to present a drawing made with the plugin, we have designed an organization chart for our conference. It shows the various work areas of the conference planning and who is available as a contact person for questions.

Fig. 21.7

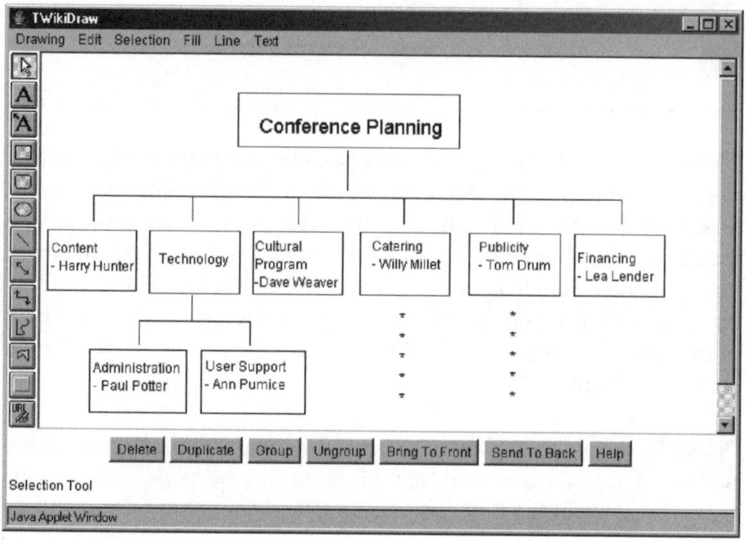

Default settings

On the **TWikiDrawPlugin** page, you will find a few variables that you can set there and then apply globally to the entire TWiki:

Tab. 21.2

Variable	Significance
`%EXTRA_ COLORS%`	Includes additional colors that can be used in the drawing. Example: `Set EXTRA_COLORS = Aquamarine = #70DB93`
`%EDIT_ BUTTON%`	Set to "1", this variable adds an Edit button over every integrated drawing. Example: `Set EDIT_BUTTON = 0`
`%EDIT_ TEXT%`	Designs the initial link in a drawing not yet saved. Example: `Set EDIT_TEXT = Edit drawing`

21.6 To-do List with EditTable Plugin

Status of individual tasks

It is a great help when every group can report the status of its work to the other groups. Conversely, groups and individuals need information regarding how far along the parallel tasks have progressed. For instance, the group responsible for recruiting poster assistants has to find out whether or not poster production is running or has slowed, so they can inform the glue mixers of the delay in a timely manner.

In a further table, the current status of the tasks can thus be depicted. The preinstalled *EditTable plugin* enables a table to be generated without a great deal of prior skills and without any confusing source code.

Mode of operation

With the aid of the plugin described above, you can enter content to tables in a simple manner. In the page view, nothing much changes at first: A button and a table appear that are connected with the plugin. By clicking on this **Edit** button, a special edit view is generated. However, you do not then get table code written in ASCII text in which you first must search for the correct cell, but rather a user friendly interface with text boxes, drop-down menus and/or date boxes. In addition, there are buttons with which you can conveniently add rows, undo changes or save your work. There can be more than one editable table on a page, but only one of them can be edited at a time.

21.6.1 Formatting the Entire Table

Formatting tables

To create and editable table, first set the variable `%EDITTABLE{...}%` in the corresponding place or insert the variable directly before an existing table. The parameters are now defined within the brackets for the edit view of the table.

Here is a very simple table with only two parameters as an example:

Wiki

```
%EDITTABLE{                                          ↵
  format="| row, -1 | text, 20, init |               ↵
  select, 1, one, two, three, four |                 ↵
  label, 0, %SERVERTIME{"$day $mon $year             ↵
  $hour:$min"}% |"                                   ↵
  changerows="on"                                    ↵
}%
```

```
|*No*|*Text Field*|*Drop-Down Menu*                ↵
|*Time Stamp*|
| 1 | init | two | 07 Jan 2005 14:55 |
```

The page view then looks like this:

Fig. 21.8

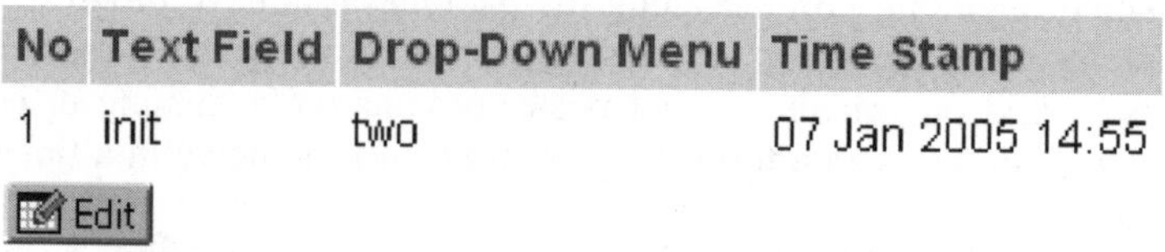

The same in the edit mode of the table looks like this:

Fig. 21.9

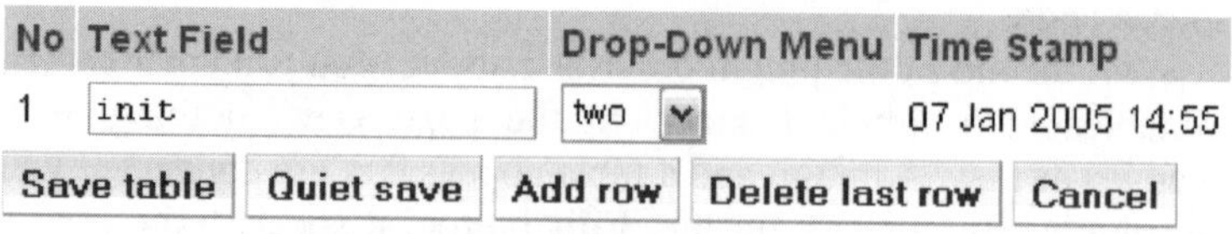

In the %EDITTABLE% variable, the input options of our table were first defined. Then we entered the content of two lines, namely the header and the first line, directly in the code, although it is not necessary to fill the table with content at the code level. However, the user deserves at least an explanation if he or she sees an **Edit** button but no table.

21.6.2 Parameters

The most important parameter for the structure of the table is the `format` parameter. It defines the type and look of the input boxes for the entire table based on one line. All lines newly added follow that established pattern.

Using the remaining parameters, you can define the operating options of the edit view. Here is an overview of all parameters:

Tab. 21.3

Parameter	Description
`header`	Determines the text of the header, e.g. `|*Stone*|*Weight*|`; only matters if the table is still empty and is to be initiated with the **Edit** button.

Tab. 21.3 *(continued)*

Parameter	Description

`format`	The following input boxes are possible (words in italics are to be replaced with the corresponding values):
	
	▪ text box (one line):
	`| text, `*`size, standard value`*` |`
	▪ text box (several lines):
	`| textarea, `*`rows x columns,`*
	`<standard value> |`
	▪ drop-down menu:
	`| select, `*`size, entry_1,`*
	`entry_2,`` etc |`
	▪ radio buttons:
	| radio, *`number buttons`*, *`entry 1`*, *`en-`*
	`try 2`, etc |
	▪ check boxes:
	| checkbox, *`number boxes`*, *`entry 1`*,
	`entry 2`, etc |
	▪ fixed label:
	`| label, 0, `*`label text`*` |`
	▪ row number:
	`| row, `*`offset`*` |`
	▪ calendar box:
	`| date, `*`size, standard value`*` |`

`changerows`	If `"on"`, lines can be added and removed. The opposite is `"off"`.
`quietsave`	If `"on"`, a **QuietSave** button is added.
`include`	Integrates the `%EDITTABLE%` variable of another topic. It accesses the first variable of the page cited.
`helptopic`	Inserts a link to a help page.
`headeris-label`	Headers are only readable, i.e. cannot be altered when the variable is set to `"on"`.
`editbutton`	With this, you can define the text on the **Edit** button, e.g.: "Edit this table".

Here is another fact about the `format` parameter `date`: When you utilize this input option, the user can navigate within a calendar to select the desired date.

Escape symbol

If there are variables in the standard value parameters, they will be replaced with every save. This feature is useful for a time stamp, for example (see above). If you do not want the values to be replaced, mask the critical symbols. Thus

```
%SERVERTIME{"$day $mon $year $hour:$min"}%
```

becomes

```
$percntSERVERTIME{$quot$dollarday $dollarmon ↵
 $dollaryear $dollarhour:                   ↵
 $dollarmin$quot}$percnt                    ↵
```

Let us briefly review:

Tab. 21.4

Code	Replaces:
`$quot`	Double quotation marks
`$percnt`	Percent sign
`$dollar`	Dollar sign
`$nop`	Prevents the dollar sign variable from being replaced

In addition, it is possible to place the "literal" % variables in a drop-down menu, for instance, by supplementing them with a `<nop>` after the percent sign, such as in

```
select,1,%<nop>X%,%<nop>Y%.
```

As you can see from the above example, in the table edit mode, several buttons are automatically added, some of which you recognize from the normal edit mode. You can influence a few of them via the `format` parameters:

Tab. 21.5

Button	Description
Save table	Save table.
Quiet save	Save without notifying another WebNotify user.
Add row	Insert row.
Delete last row	Eliminate last row.
Cancel	Return to page view without saving.

Example: To-do list

Armed with this knowledge, we can now design our To-do list. Here, we enter the task and responsible contact person under the respective project number. Furthermore, there are input boxes for the scheduled start, scheduled end, status, and estimated end of a task.

```
%EDITTABLE{
  header="|*Project no.*|*Responsible*|        ↵
   *Task*|*Planned Begin*|*Planned            ↵
   End*|*Status*|*Finished by*|"              ↵
  format="|text,10|text,15|textarea,3x15|     ↵
   date|date|select,1,not begun,              ↵
   begun, stopped, finished | date|"          ↵
  changerows="on"                             ↵
}%
```

Wiki

Fig 21.10

Project no.	Responsible	Task	Planned Begin	Planned End	Status	Finished by
B.3.1.3.1	Dwayne Drummer	Develop Test	12 November 2007	5 December 2007	begun	21 November 2007
B.3.1.3.2	Dwayne Drummer	Obtain cost estimate	5 November 2007	9 November 2007	not begun	8 November 2007
B.3.1.3.3	Dwayne Drummer	Recruit poster assistants	6 November 2007	29 November 2007	begun	23 November 2007
B.3.1.3.4	Olga Stonehack	Draw posters	26 November 2007	6 December 2007	not begun	30 November 2007
B.3.1.3.5	Homer Sapiens	Hang posters	3 December 2007	21 December 2007	not begun	20 December 2007

Edit

21.6.3 Determining the Format of Individual Cells

Up to now, formatting commands made in %EDITTABLE% applied to the entire table and thus for all cells. However, if you want to format an individual cell differently, e.g. if you want to define another input box, you can overwrite the table formatting with the variable %EDITCELL{"..."}%.

To do this, set the variable directly after the content of the cell, e.g. to define a text field:

```
| cell content %EDITCELL{"text, 20"}%  |
```

Wiki

All of those input boxes are supported that you also recognize from the format parameter.

Caution: The %EDITCELL% variable only functions in connection with %EDITTABLE%.

Cell formatting is especially useful if your table is more vertical than horizontal and, for instance, consists of so-called key/value pairs. Here is a brief example:

Wiki

```
%EDITTABLE{ format="| label | text, 40 |" }%
|*Key*|*Value*|
| Name: | Jane Public |
| Gender: | F                                        ↵
  %EDITCELL{select,1, ,F,M}% |
| Occupation | Gatherer                             ↵
  %EDITCELL{select,1, ,Gatherer,Hunter}% |          ↵
| Town of residence: | Marble Valley |
```

Table edit view:

Fig. 21.11

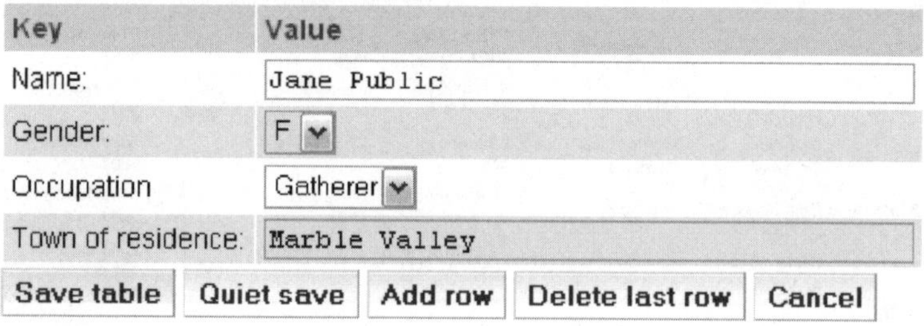

Problem zones

However, in a few ways, the plugin is stretched to its limits. We will name a couple of them here:

- It does not support a few formatting options, such as multi-span (connected) cells (`| ... ||`) and text alignment values within the cell (e.g. `| centered | right |`).
- From about the fifth row on, there could be processing problems.
- It is not possible to include two `%EDITTABLE{}%` expressions within a single code line.

Global settings

As is typical of all other plugins, you can also make global settings on the **EditTablePlugin** page regarding the following variables:

Tab. 21.6

Variable	Significance
`%CHANGEROWS%`	Opportunity to delete or remove lines. Example: `Set CHANGEROWS=on`
`%QUIETSAVE%`	Defines whether a **QuietSave** button should be set as a default. Example: `Set QUIETSAVE=on`
`%EDITBUTTON%`	Labeling of the **Edit** button. Example: `Set EDITBUTTON=Edit table`

For internal use, TWiki offers its own ProjectPlanner plugin. In a separate web, report pages are generated for every project and subtask. Team members provide information on their project page regarding the status of the subtasks and work packages (project begun, estimated duration, time already invested …). Using this information, an overview page is generated that presents a brief summary of the status of the individual tasks using simple bar graphs. Due to the current stage of development, we will not go into this plugin any further, because we think that the effort required to install it does not merit its worth. You can largely generate its functions yourself using a few central overview tables.

ProjectPlanner plugin

21.7 Planning Costs and Financing with Tables (Spreadsheet Plugin)

Determination of requirements and cost projection

Using the estimated materials requirements of the individual work packages, the overall requirement for a project can be calculated. We can now generate a cost projection plan for our conference. Similarly, the requirements of the individual cost units can be determined; that is, we can estimate what expenses the "Catering" group or the "Content Planning" group will have. These groups can then manage their funds themselves.

Who, what, when

For smaller projects, such an overall cost projection, split into cost units, is completely satisfactory. In the case of larger projects, further temporal overviews are necessary. When are which expenses due? When will which personnel be required? What equipment and materials must be available where and when? Technical literature cites a variety of terminology (financial plan, operating resources plan, etc.) and methods. Admittedly, the limits of reification of human relationships can be quickly exceeded. Bureaucratic control concepts of "human resources", for instance, express themselves in the fact that said human resources are evaluated according to their work capacities, which need to be optimized and controlled.

Spreadsheet

Spreadsheets are an invaluable aid in maintaining an overview of finances. Although wikis cannot provide a highly developed spreadsheet program, its Spreadsheet plugin nevertheless enables us to work reasonably with tables in TWiki. Once again, the advantage of a wiki is that the data can be collected centrally in a document that is available to everyone and can be independently updated by the individual project groups. Thus, in the area of financial planning and control, new trails can be blazed with regard to transparency and self-determination.

Mode of operation

This plugin is included in the standard installation. It equips TWiki with conventional spreadsheet options. You can perform calculations based on entered formulas or existing functions, process strings – for instance, turning upper case letters into lower case – and formulate logical queries. To do this, in the edit view, add a variable to your calculation that will be replaced by its solution in the page view. This works within as well as outside of the table, which basically distinguishes this plugin from others. For example, you can display the individual items of a table column as a sum in a continuous text.

21.7.1 Syntax

The plugin is triggered by the variable `%CALC{"..."}%`. This variable can be situated within a table cell or in a normal continuous text, whereby several functions only make sense in connection with tables. The result of the function between the quotation marks is issued when the page is opened. For example, let us say you wish to calculate the average number of participants of three workshops visited by 14, 21 and 12 people respectively:

Wiki

```
%CALC{"$AVERAGE(14,21,12)"}%
```

In the page view, the result 9 is displayed.

Note: Calculations are always based on functions. Even an easy expression such as 1+1 must be expressed as a function: `%CALC{"$EVAL(1+1)"}%`.

Functions

Functions have the following schematic structure:

Wiki

```
$FUNCTIONNAME(parameter)
```

Its interpretation is done from left to right. It is possible to nest several functions, e.g.:

Wiki

```
%CALC{"$AVERAGE(14,21,$SUM(4,8))"}%
```

whereby the calculation in this case is done from the innermost to the outermost function.

The parameters of a function can be depicted as text, a mathematical formula, a cell address or cell area. This depends on the function itself. So, for instance, the sum function processes concrete values or information in cell areas.

Cell reference

If you wish to refer to the possibly changing content of fixed table cells, you can do so via the following coordinates:

Fig. 21.12

R1:C1	R1:C2	R1:C3	R1:C4
R2:C1	R2:C2	R2:C3	R2:C4
R3:C1	R3:C2	R3:C3	R3:C4

The R stands for row and the C for column.

To now be able to calculate with the content of one of these cells, you must enter the cell coordinates in the function `$T`:

Wiki

```
%CALC{"$AVERAGE($T(R2:C3),$T(R3:C4))"}%
```

Caution: The convention of cell references only works in pipe tables, but not in HTML tables!

Table range

It is also possible to include an entire table range by indicating each of the top and bottom corner cells and separating them by two periods ("`..`"); e.g. `R1:C1..R3:C3` would completely include the first three columns of the above table.

In this case, it is not necessary to use the `T` function; you can transfer the table range directly as a parameter:

Wiki

```
%CALC{"$SUM(R1:C1..R3:C2, R1:C4..R3:C4)"}%
```

Note: The cell data in the formulas can only relate to the cells in the current row and previous cells in the table. All cells below the current row cannot be addressed with that formula. If you insert a formula with cell data outside of the table, they will refer to the previous table.

Lists

If a parameter consists of several elements (of the same kind), e.g. in the calculation of an average, a list of values is transferred whose components are separated by commas, such as `%CALC{"$SUM( 3, 5, 7)"}%`. Also, there are a few functions that were conceived specifically for editing and processing lists. Thus, for instance, the function `LIST` can be used to transform a cell range into a list and then further processed.

If it doesn't work ...

When using the plugin, you may frequently make mistakes, especially at the beginning, since you first have to get used to the conventions of the program. However, the causes of the following undesired results can be found relatively quickly:

- In the page view, the code of the formula is displayed but not calculated. The plugin is probably either incorrectly installed or not installed at all.
- Parts of the formula are displayed. The syntax of the formula is incorrect. Perhaps a dollar sign was left out?
- A 0 ("zero") comes out as a result. Your cell references may be referring to an HTML table.

Note: Remember that command lines in the plugin must have a period, not a comma. Thus, it would be 3.14 and not 3,14.

21.7.2 Important Functions

The plugin contains about 65 functions, the sum of which we unfortunately cannot present here. However, we will present the most important functions as follows.

Caution: Please do not forget that when using a function, the dollar sign must be set before the name!

All examples with cell data refer to the following table:

Fig. 21.13

	Content	Catering	Advertisement
Cost of personnel	-5000	-1000	0
Costs for equipment and material	-500	-3000	-2000
Income	0	5000	100

`ABOVE()`
Addresses the cell range above the current cell.
Example: `%CALC{"$SUM($ABOVE())"}%`
Result: Displays the sum of the values above the current cell.

`ABS(`*`number`*`)`
Absolute value of a number.
Example: `%CALC{"$ABS(R3:C2)"}%`
Result: 1000

`AND(`*`list`*`)`
Logical And of a list
Example: `%CALC{"$AND(1, 0, 1, 1)"}%`
Result: 0

`COLUMN(`*`offset`*`)`
Return of the column number under consideration of a possible off-set.
Example: `%CALC{"$COLUMN(2)"}%`
Result: current column number +2

`EVAL(`*`formula`*`)`
Calculation of simple operations such as sum, difference, product, division and modulo. Nesting is also possible. The general rules of calculation apply.
Example: `%CALC{"$EVAL( (5/2) *3 - 1.2 )"}%`
Result: 6.3

`EXACT(`*`text1, text2`*`)`
Comparison of two character strings; returns 1 when both are the same.
Example: `%CALC{"$EXACT(cave, cove)"}%`
Result: 0

`EXISTS(`*`page`*`)`
Tests of *page* exists or not.
Example: `%CALC{"$EXISTS(DoesNotExist) "}%`
Result: 0

`IF(`*`condition, value if true, value if false`*`)`
Branching using a condition
Example: `%CALC{"$IF($T(R2:C2) > 0, profit, loss)"}%`
Result: loss

`LIST(`*`range`*`)`
Transforms a cell range into a list.
Example: `%CALC{"$LIST(R1:C2..R1:C4) "}%`
Result: Content, Catering, Publicity

`LISTSORT(`*`list`*`)`
Alphabetical sorting of a list.
Example: `%CALC{"$LISTSORT(R1:C2..R1:C4)"}%`
Result: Catering, Content, Publicity

`MAX(`*`list`*`)`
Returns the largest value of a list.
Example: `%CALC{"$MAX(R2:C2..R3:C4"}%`
Result: 0

`MOD(`*`number, divider`*`)`
Modulo operation; returns a division remainder.
Example: `%CALC{"$MOD(15,4)"}%`
Result: 3

`PROPERSPACE(`*`text`*`)`
Inserts blank spaces in a WikiWord.
Example: `%CALC{"$PROPERSPACE(WebHome)"}%`
Result: Web Home

`ROUND(`*`number, decimal places`*`)`
Rounds off floating-point number to the number of decimal points indicated.
Example: `%CALC{"$ROUND(2.323256, 2"}%`
Result: 2.32

`SUM(`*`list`*`)`
Sum of a list.
Example: `%CALC{"$SUM(R2:C2..R4:C2)"}%`
Result: -5500

`T(`*`cell reference`*`)`
Returns the cell content.
Example: `%CALC{"$T(R1:C2)"}%`
Result: Content

`TODAY()`
Returns the current date (server time).
Example: `%CALC{"$TODAY()"}%`
Result: current date

`UPPER(`*`text`*`)`
Transforms text to upper case.
Example: `%CALC{"$UPPER(Mammoth)"}%`
Result: MAMMOTH

Default settings

You can naturally also define default settings in the Spreadsheet plugin as well. Here are the variables you will need:

Tab. 21.7

Variable	Significance
`%SKIPINCLUDE%`	In integrated pages, the `%CALC%` variable is not processed. Example: `Set SKIPINCLUDE=1`
`%DONTSPACE%`	Indicated pages are excluded from the `PROPERSPACE` function. Example: `Set DONTSPACE=WikiWord`

21.7.3 Exporting/Importing Excel Files

When you work with tables in TWiki, sooner or later you will want to know whether you can transfer tables between office programs, such as MS Office or Open Office, and TWiki. There are several methods with which to do so. We would like to present a very simple program for that purpose that will enable you to

- import tables from office programs, HTML editors and texts structured via tabs to TWiki.
- conversely, export TWiki tables to office programs.
- perform table formatting and sorting tasks within the program.

Installation

The program, written in Delphi, presently only runs under Windows. You will find it at *http://www.twiki.org* in the Plugins web under the Add-Ons as **Copy Table from/to Spreadsheet/table Programs Add-On.** Download the file *CopyTWiki.zip* and unpack it to a local directory on your computer. When you then open the .exe file in the folder created, the program's interface will appear.

Mode of operation

The spreadsheet that you now see in front of you functions as a sort of clipboard, and is the interface between the various formats. For instance, you can copy your Excel table onto the sheet, edit and format it as desired and then copy it to your TWiki – or vice versa.

Fig 21.14

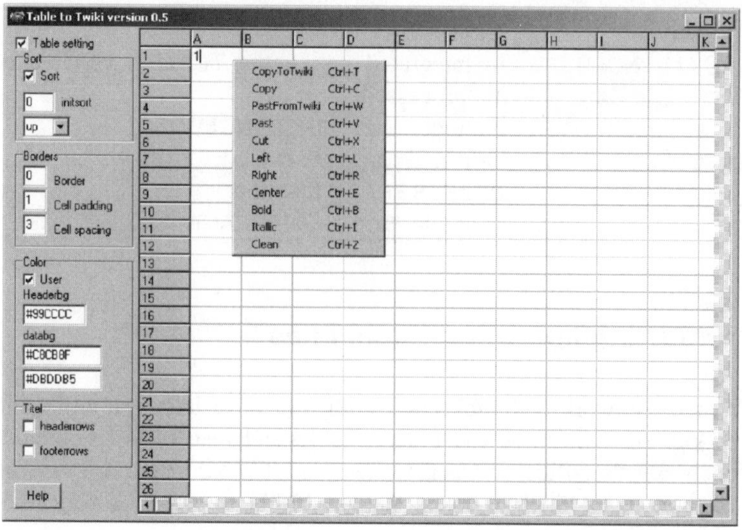

The context menu plays an important role in the program; that is, the menu bar that drops down when you press the right mouse button. There, you will find the various transfer actions as well as a few formatting options. You have the following possibilities:

Tab. 21.8

Menu Entry	Function
CopyToTWiki	Copies the highlighted cells to paste to the TWiki.
Copy	Copies the highlighted cells to paste to an office program.
PasteFrom TWiki	Inserts cells that were copied from the TWiki source code.
Paste	Inserts cells that were copied as an HTML table (not in the source code).
Cut	Cut out.
Left	Left cell alignment.
Right	Right cell alignment.
Center	Centered cell alignment.
Bold	Bold.
Italic	Italic.
Clean	No format.

On the left, you have further options for formatting and sorting by activating **Table Settings**. These include background color and cell spacing. However, they are largely self-explanatory.

22 Preparing for your Event

22.1 Planning Your Event

Public relations

The preparations for your conference are already in full swing. The lecturers have been invited, the program put together, and advertising has begun. TWiki will help keep all participants up to date. It serves as a bulletin board. The forte of wikis in this phase of the project lies precisely in this double duty: It is an organizational tool as well as the basis of public relations and the integration of the outside world, e.g. by enabling the external viewing of spatial planning. In our specific case, it is helpful to involve participants as "collaborators" at an early stage.

Accordingly, you can present further web offerings:

- Separate discussion forums
- Feedback pages
- Carpooling and accommodation exchanges

Abstracts

This dual function can also be utilized to have lecturers integrate their abstracts into the pages themselves. Also, participants can write their questions and ideas right underneath, so that lecturers can better attune themselves to their queries.

22.2 Conference Registration

Registration procedure in the TWiki

A few weeks before the conference, participants should be able to register for the conference over the Internet. Unfortunately, TWiki lacks a type of form plugin with database integration. To enable our visitors to nevertheless register for the conference, we are limited to existing features, and we can adjust them a bit. We will create our own registration form. Based on the registration data, we will then generate various queries (or calculations) that a database management system would ordinarily perform. The suggested solution is only one of several options.

22.2.1 Modifying the Standard Registration

Registration procedure

Before going into more detail on creating the conference registration, we should first clarify how a normal TWiki registration process works. This illustration will elucidate the procedure somewhat:

Fig 22.1

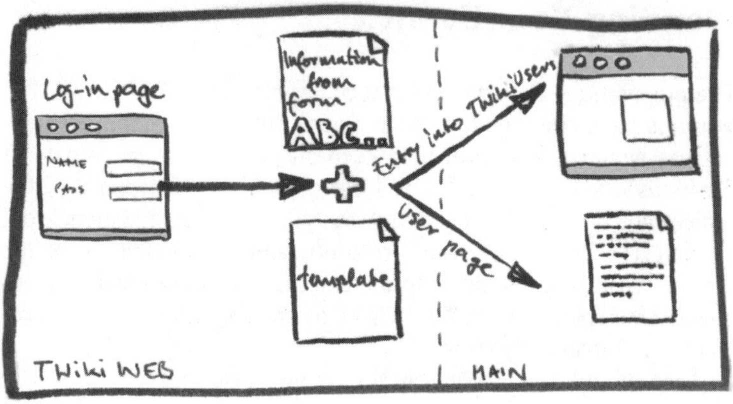

Firstly, you register in the **Main** web. The data indicated is integrated into a template. This combination is stored as a user page in the **Main** web. In addition, an entry is made to the overview of all users (**Users** Topic in the **TWiki** web).

Modifying the registration mechanism

Since it is not possible to generate a normal form with data integration using PHP/MySQL, we will now “misuse” the user registration form normally located in the **Main** web and the registration mechanism upon which it is based for our own purposes.

22.2.2 Designing the Registration Form

Copy form

We will design the registration page (in the **Main** web) according to the requirements of the conference. Users register themselves for the conference as well as for the TWiki, meaning a user page is generated for them. However, additional data, such as what fees are due, will be obtained via the conference registration form.

When a user registers for the conference, he or she should receive the corresponding feedback, such as error messages if incorrect entries are made or a confirmation page if registration has been successful.

We thus have two registration options within TWiki: One is the standard user registration in the **TWiki** web, which generates a page for the user and allows him or her to make modifications in the TWiki; the other registration option is done in the **Main** web, and registers the user for the conference as well as for the TWiki.

The standard registration could be used by users who move about within the environment of the conference, such as assistants, but do not belong to a group of official visitors and thus do not need to provide any information regarding prices, accommodation, etc. Thus it should be possible for these people to not need to register.

General design

For the conference registration, first create a new topic in the **Main** web with the name **ConferenceRegistration**. One possibility is to transfer the text from the **TWiki.TWikiRegistration** into this new topic. To a great extent, you can now modify the copied form as you wish.

We can go into the edit view and alter the layout by adding a fitting heading with explanatory text or images such as a logo. Any language changes should be made here. Formatting is done according to the standard TWiki rules.

Adapting input fields

Then it is necessary to alter the form input fields according to requirements, i.e. fields not needed should be removed and any additional ones inserted. As you can see in the edit view, the form syntax is pure HTML. The values entered are stored in the `name` variables that you indicate in the respective HTML tags. However, there are two things to remember. First of all, you cannot delete all input fields: **WikiName**, **Name**, **Password** and **confirmation of the password** should definitely be part of the form, which is sensible for the registration process. If you delete the fields or alter the defined names, the visitor will receive an error message when trying to register, and the registration will fail.

Secondly, we must differentiate between optional and obligatory input fields.

Setting up obligatory input fields

The optional fields may, but do not have to be, filled out. The obligatory fields, on the other hand, are usually displayed in the page view with two red stars, and must be filled in by the user to facilitate registration. As the designer of the form, you can achieve this differentiation by beginning the names of the variables for obligatory fields with `Twk1` and with `Twk0` for optional fields. Thus, a registration page for our conference might look like this:

Wiki

```
<div class="twikiPageForm">
<form action="%SCRIPTURLPATH{"register"}%/
%MAINWEB%/%HOMETOPIC%" method="post">      ↵

<div class="twikiFormSteps">
<div class="twikiFormStep">

<table border="0" cellpadding="0"
cellspacing="6">
<tr>
<td align="right"> First name:</td>
<td><input type="text" name="Twk1FirstName"  ↵
 size="40" class="twikiInputField"/> =<font  ↵
color="red">**</font>= </td>
</tr>
<tr>

<td align="right"> Last name: </td>
<td><input type="text" name="Twk1LastName"   ↵
size="40" class="twikiInputField"/> =<font   ↵
color="red">**</font>= </td>
</tr>

<td align="right"> Your <nop>WikiName: </td>
<td><input type="text" name="Twk1WikiName"   ↵
size="40" class="twikiInputField" value="" />↵
 =<font color="red">**</font>= </td>
</tr>
<tr>

<td align="right"> Password: </td>
<td><input type="password" name=             ↵
"Twk1Password" size="40" /> <font color=     ↵
"red">**</font> </td>
</tr>
<tr>
<td align="right"> repeat password:          ↵
</td>
<td><input type="password" name="Twk1Confirm"↵
 size="40" /> <font color="red">**</font>    ↵
</td>
</tr>
```

```
<tr>
<td align="right"> email address: </td>
<td><input type="text" name="Twk1Email"        ↵
 size="40" class="twikiInputField"              ↵
 value="" /> <font color="red">**</font>        ↵
 </td>
</tr>

<tr>
<td align="right"> Your organization: </td>
<td><input type="text" name=                   ↵
"Twk0OrganizationName" size="40"               ↵
class="twikiInputField" value="" /></td>
</tr>
<tr>
<td align="right"> Street: </td>
<td><input type="text" name="Twk0Address"      ↵
 size="40" class="twikiInputField"             ↵
value="" /></td>
</tr>
<tr>
<td align="right"> Postal code and town:
</td>
<td><input type="text" name="Twk0Location"     ↵
 size="40" class="twikiInputField"             ↵
 value="" /></td>
</tr>
<tr>
<td align="right"> Country: </td>
<td> <select name="Twk1Country" size="1">      ↵
 <option selected value="">Select...           ↵
</option>
<option>Euphrates</option>
<option>Levante</option>
<option>Andalusia</option>
<option value="Other Country">Other
country</option>
</select> <font color="red">**</font>
</td>
</tr>
<tr>
<td align="right"> Fee: </td>
<td> 30 dollars (discounted)
```

```
<input type="radio" name="Twk1Fee"                ↵
 value="30 dollars (discounted)" /> 50
dollars <input                                    ↵
 type="radio" name="Twk1Fee" value="50
dollars" />Free ticket<input type="radio"
name="Twk1Fee" value="Free ticket" />
 <font color="red">**</font> </td>
</tr>

<tr>
  <td  valign="top"  align="right">  Comments:
</td>
  <td><textarea name="Twk0Comment"               ↵
 wrap="virtual" rows="2" cols="38"               ↵
 class="twikiInputField"></textarea></td>
</tr>
<tr>
<td> </td>
<td> (Boxes marked in <Font color="red">**      ↵
</font> are obligatory)                         ↵
</td>
</tr>
</table>
</div><!-- /twikiFormStep-->

<div class="twikiFormStep twikiLast">
<input type="hidden" name="rx"                    ↵
value='%BLACKLISTPLUGIN{ action="magic" }%'      ↵
 />
<input type="hidden" name="Conference"            ↵
 value="RADH" />
<input type="hidden" name="topic"                 ↵
 value="%TOPIC%" />
<input type="hidden" name="action"                ↵
 value="register" />
<input type="submit" class="twikiSubmit"          ↵
 value= "send" />
</div><!-- /twikiFormStep-->
</div><!-- /twikiFormSteps-->
</form>
```

Visual identification of obligatory fields is not done automatically, so you should add it. Otherwise, however, you are free to design the page as you like. For example, you do not have to limit yourself to simple text input fields, but can utilize the entire palette of form fields offered by HTML, such as radio buttons, drop-down lists, etc. We have simply taken the entry of an email address from the standard registration. In a hidden field at the end, we have also included the conference name, which facilitates searches and enables a separation between normal TWiki users and conference participants.

Here, you can see the finished registration form for our Conference on the Future, for which a Mr. Stonecake would like to register:

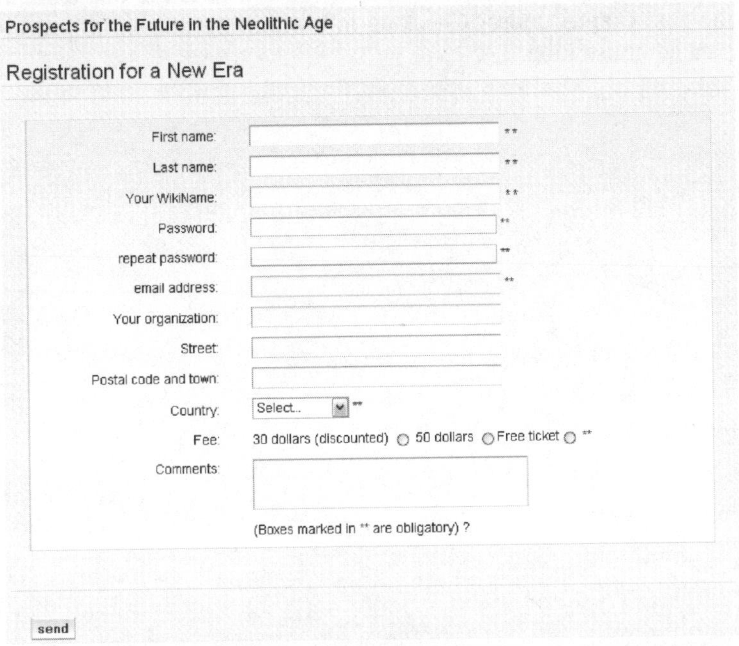

Fig. 22.2

Prospects for the Future in the Neolithic Age

Registration for a New Era

First name:	**
Last name:	**
Your WikiName:	**
Password:	**
repeat password:	**
email address:	**
Your organization:	
Street:	
Postal code and town:	
Country:	Select.. **
Fee:	30 dollars (discounted) ◯ 50 dollars ◯ Free ticket ◯ **
Comments:	

(Boxes marked in ** are obligatory) ?

send

The solution depicted here takes almost all data from the **UserForm** of the user page. The fees (a new field), however, are not included in the table of user information, but rather shown underneath as a list. In order to change this, the **UserForm** would have to be modified, which we unfortunately cannot show due to space limitations.

22.2.3
Navigation

Now we can create a link in the navigation bar to our own user page. To do this, access the page **WebLeftBar** via the address input in the **MainWeb**, and enter, for instance

Wiki

```
[[%WIKIUSERNAME%][My userpage]]
```

If the user is not yet logged in, the link of course will not work. The user would be transferred to the **TWikiGuest** page. That is why the user must be forced to log in. We can achieve this by blocking the **WebHome** of the **Main** web for anyone not logged in. Then, the login window opens automatically. Here, the user can log into the system or be transferred to the registration form via a link.

The registration is thus complete. We will return to this topic in the next chapter under "Checking in", within the context of participant administration.

23 Executing and Documenting an Event

23.1 In the Event Office

Crisis management

With the start of the conference, the organizers have their hands full to ensure that the lectures, workshops and podiums run smoothly. In the process, they have set up the usual event office on site. Despite all of the preparation, improvisation and continual crisis management are now the order of the day. People cannot find their rooms, there is no change left in the cash box, one of the video projectors has disappeared, and one of the lecturers has forgotten to bring the scripts she needs for her presentation. Since people at the conference will be speaking directly with each other, the computer takes a back seat as a means of communication. However, we would still like to point out a few aspects of TWiki that can be of assistance in executing your event.

Bulletin board

At first, the wiki is the central bulletin board for organizers and participants alike. The event office, for instance, can announce room changes via the wiki by projecting the program on a wall with a video projector. Participants can find out about the current event program at home or on the go. The current nature of this function makes wiki not only a publication medium, but also the central organizational medium. Any assistant can easily maintain an overview of room assignments with a corresponding EditTable plugin.

Note: Remember that additional assistants – such as during check-in – should be introduced to the software in a timely manner.

Workshop TWikis

After the workshops, participants can immediately supplement texts and publish their results. For instance, in "open space" conferences, short summaries are written directly after an event, which are posted in a central location. This makes it easier to pick up on ideas from other events. Furthermore, it offers the possibility for participants to centrally collect addresses and exchange ideas via the wiki.

23.2 Participant Administration/Registration Status

Checking in

The bottleneck of a conference is the check-in. Participants must definitively register, pay the fee and receive conference materials.

Adjusting the RegistrationWeb

To be able to complete as many of the formalities of the registration office as possible in TWiki, let us return to the **Main** web. Just to remind you, the registration form and user pages of registered participants are located on that web. It will now be expanded by three more pages: **InternalAdministration**, **Receipt** and **ParticipantList**. They primarily serve to take the load off of employees in registering the expected rush of visitors on the first day as quickly as possible while still keeping an overview of participant numbers and finances – because nothing is more frustrating for visitors than standing in line for hours right at the start of the conference all because registration is not optimally coordinated.

23.2.1 The InternalAdministration Page

Internal Administration

First we will generate the page **InternalAdministration**. It represents the central contact point from which all activities originate during the check-in procedure. We recommend simply generating a link to this page in the left side menu bar of the **Main** web.

Identification

The first step is entering visitors in the data management system. The page **InternalAdministration** must now be prepared for two scenarios:

1. A visitor is not yet registered and must thus be entered in the TWiki system with all of his or her data.
2. A participant – in our case Mr. Stonecake – has already registered.

For the first case, the page contains a link to conference registration, where an employee can enter the new person's data in the registration form at check-in. He or she then returns to the **InternalAdministration** page.

Search form

If a visitor has already registered, he has to be found in TWiki. To do this, a formula with a search function is generated that already contains a couple of parameters that you otherwise would have to generate from scratch in a normal search, such as the setting of the `scope` parameter, which effects a search of the page title as well as within the page itself.

The form, with a text box for entering the search item and the subsequent search function, looks like this:

Wiki

```
<form name="Check1"                            ↵
    action="%SCRIPTURL%/                       ↵
           view%SCRIPTSUFFIX%/                 ↵
           %WEB%/%TOPIC%"                      ↵
    method="get">
  <input type="text"                           ↵
      name="query"                             ↵
      value="%URLPARAM{"query"}%">
  <input type="submit">
</form>

%SEARCH{search="%URLPARAM{"query"}%"           ↵
      scope="topic"                            ↵
      type="keyword"                           ↵
      noheader="on"                            ↵
      web="Main"                               ↵
      nosearch="on"                            ↵
      excludetopic="%TOPIC%,                   ↵
                   TWikiUsers"                 ↵
}%
```

If, during check-in, Mr. Stonecake's name is entered in the search, a link to his user page should appear.

Receipt

The next section of the page leads to the receipt that is to be printed out for every participant. Of course, you can simply generate a link to this spot. However, the receipt should already be filled out with the individual details of the participant, including name, address and fee paid, which is why the link must already include the identity of the participant, so to speak, using the `%URLPARAM{"query"}%` variables. Technically, this is done using another form with a text box in which the TWiki name of the visitor should be entered:

Wiki

```
<form name="Check2"                            ↵
      action="%SCRIPTURL%/                     ↵
            view%SCRIPTSUFFIX%/                ↵
```

```
                    %WEB%/Receipt"                    ↵
          method="get">
     <input type="text"                               ↵
            name="query"                              ↵
            value="%URLPARAM{"query"}%">
     <input type="submit"                             ↵
            value="Generate receipt">
</form>
```

Further links

Before getting into what exactly happens on the receipt page, let us have a brief look at the rest of the **InternalAdministration** page:

```
RegistrationForm

ParticipantList
```

As mentioned above, the first link is primarily required in cases where the visitor is not yet registered in TWiki. The second link leads to the **ParticipantLink** page, where employees are to enter all visitors that have checked in and paid. This gives conference management an overview of which visitors have actually arrived at the conference and how much money should be in the cash box. We will get into more detail about this page later.

This completes the **InternalAdministration** page. The page view would look like this:

Fig. 23.1

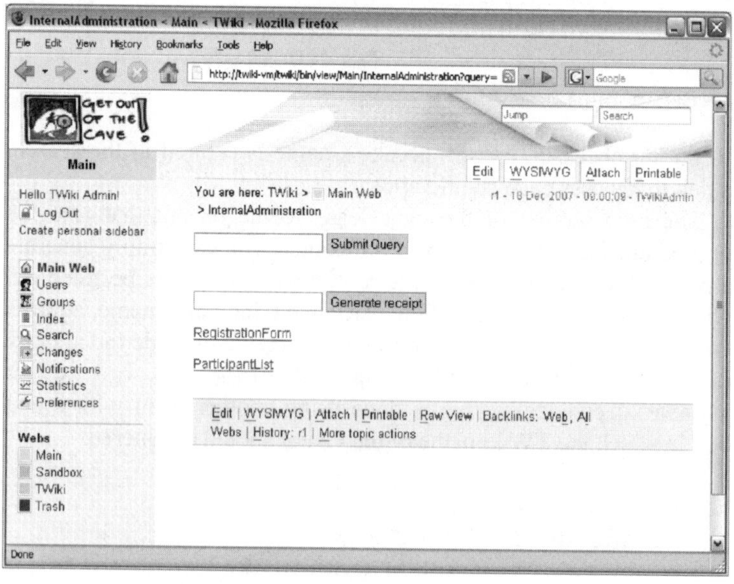

23.2.2
Generating Receipts

The *Receipt* page, as we have mentioned, already has access to a Wiki name, via the data in the URL, and thus to the user page of the respective participant. The receipt is now to be filled out in the right spots with the content from the user page, specifically the address of the user on the upper left, his or her last name in the salutation, and the conference fee that was paid in the text portion. This is done using the %SEARCH%- variable with the corresponding regular expressions. You now have the opportunity to use the skills you learned in Sect. IV.4 or simply take on the three expressions. Directly under the heading "Receipt", however, in the same table row, the logo of the conference is entered which then appears on the right side in page view.

Wiki

```
---++ Receipt
<table border=0 width="100%">
<tr>
  <td align="right">
    %PUBURL%/%TWIKIWEB%/                              ↵
    TWikiLogos/wiki-logo-roll.jpg
  </td>
</tr>
</table>
%SEARCH{search="%URLPARAM{"query"}%"                ↵
        scope="topic"                               ↵
        web="Main"                                  ↵
        noheader="on"                               ↵
        nosearch="on"                               ↵
        nototal="on"                                ↵
        format="                                    ↵
$formfield(FirstName)                               ↵
$formfield(LastName)%BR%                            ↵
$formfield(Address)%BR%                             ↵
$formfield(Location)                                ↵
"                                                   ↵
}%

Dear
%SEARCH{search="%URLPARAM{"query"}%"                ↵
        scope="topic"                               ↵
        web="Main"                                  ↵
        noheader="on"                               ↵
```

```
        nosearch="on"                              ↵
        nototal="on"                               ↵
        format="                                   ↵
$formfield(FirstName)                              ↵
$formfield(LastName)"                              ↵
}%,

In accordance with your registration for "Get
out of the Cave" from June 15-17, we hereby
charge you a participation fee:

   * conference fee:
%SEARCH{search="%URLPARAM{"query"}%"               ↵
        scope="topic"                              ↵
        web="Main"                                 ↵
        noheader="on"                              ↵
        nosearch="on"                              ↵
        nototal="on"                               ↵
        format="                                   ↵
$pattern(.*?\*.*?fee:\s*([^\n\r]+).*)"             ↵
}%

Best regards,

Your Conference Manager, Harry Hunter
```

Tip: In order to avoid superfluous navigation elements from being included on the printout, you can apply the Plain skin to the Receipt page (see Sect. III.7.1). This skin is set so that none of the elements before and after the page text are printed.

Mr. Stonecake receives the following receipt after he has paid:

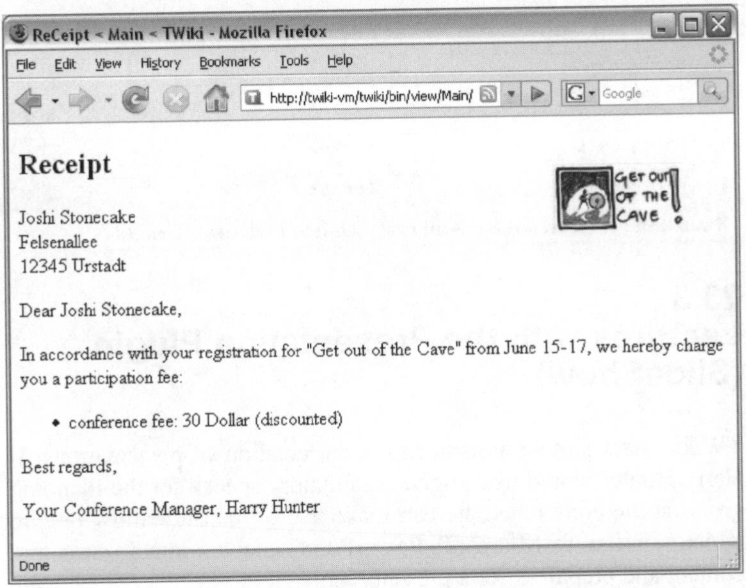

Fig. 23.2

23.2.3 Participant List

The last page that we are adding is the **ParticpantList**. Its primary purpose is to provide an internal overview of the visitors that have already checked in, by entering their names in a table. In addition, the fee paid is to be recorded, to facilitate checking the status of the cash box.

The EditTable plugin can be of great assistance (see above). Using it, we can design a user-friendly form that also makes the employees' work easier. It backlinks to the **InternalAdministration** page, and might look like this:

```
%EDITTABLE{header="|*No*|*Last name*|                   ↵
                  *First name*|*fee|"                  ↵
          format="|row, -1| text,25 |                  ↵
                text,25 |select,1,35,50 |"             ↵
          changerows=on                                ↵
}%

[[InternalAdministration]]
```

Here you see the table after a few visitors have arrived:

Fig. 23.3

No	Last name	First name	fee
1	Stonecake	Joshi	50
2	Venus	Gesine	35
3	Forestcalm	Markus	50
4	Berryheimer	Lothar	35

Save table | Quiet save | Add row | Delete last row | Cancel

23.3 Lectures with the Presentation Plugin (SlideShow)

Presentations and lectures

TWiki offers simple assistance for the creation of presentations. If Harry Hunter would like to give a salutatory speech for the Planning group at the conference, he can make use of his SlideShow plugin, which, similar to Microsoft PowerPoint, enables him to structure content and prepare it for a presentation.

Mode of operation

The SlideShow plugin is included in the standard installation. It is not a separate program interface: Each page or part of a page divided by headings can be turned into a presentation. Of course, the plugin cannot be compared to professional presentation software that includes animation and other multimedia effects. However, it is an easy way to present content in TWiki for a lecture.

To prepare a presentation, write the content of the presentation on a page and divide it by headings. Each heading and the text following it is displayed as a slide. The format of the slides is based on a slide template that you can format at will and fill with contents as well as navigation buttons.

23.3.1 Syntax

You begin the presentation in edit mode with the variables

Wiki

```
%SLIDESHOWSTART%
```

Then the slide content of the presentation is entered. The slide title should be identified as a second-level heading using `---++`. You can also use headings of other levels, but they should be used consistently for each slide of the presentation. The text following a respective heading is interpreted as slide content. Usually, it is structured in unnumbered lists, but you can also integrate tables and graphic images.

If you wish to add a comment within the presentation, start a slide with a third-level heading and call it "Comments". The text underneath it and up to the next slide will be interpreted as a comment, and will not appear in the presentation view.

You can define the end of a presentation with

```
%SLIDESHOWEND%
```

Wiki

After you save your work, you will then see the slide breakdown of your presentation.

Harry Hunter's draft for the presentation of his salutatory speech looks as follows in the edit view:

Wiki

```
%SLIDESHOWSTART{                                        ↵
     template="ConferenceLaunch"}%
---++++ Conference: Prospects for the Future ↵
in the Neolithic Age
%BR%
<center>
by Harry Hunter, Conference Manager
</center>

---++++ Salutation
   * Promotion of a "Neolithic                          ↵
     Revolution"
   * Conference as a first step?
   * Status of the debate: Doubt as to
whether a new era is even possible.
   * Example: sedentariness

---++++ Sedentariness: Cons
   * Humans are not intended for agriculture
   * Health concerns
   * Humans will become soft
   * Shamans prophesize the decline of                  ↵
     culture

---++++ Sedentariness: Pros
<table width=100% border=0>
<tr>
  <td>
    %PUBURL%/Main/DiaGram/                              ↵
    _ChartPlugin_bar_graincultivation.png
```

```
  </td>
</tr>
</table>
   * Agriculture creates jobs
   * Better nutrition
   * More variety on the table
   * More time for family

---++++ Conference Program
   * Workshops
   * Cultural Program

---++++ Finally: Technical tips
   * Events Office
   * Room changes: How do I find my          ↵
     "cave"?
%SLIDESHOWEND%
```

As you may have noticed, Harry Hunter has integrated an image, specifically a diagram, on the third slide. You can find out how to generate diagrams in Chap. 23.4.

Let us get back to the presentation: Before each slide title, the number of the slide is indicated. In addition, a button is inserted that starts the presentation:

Fig. 23.4

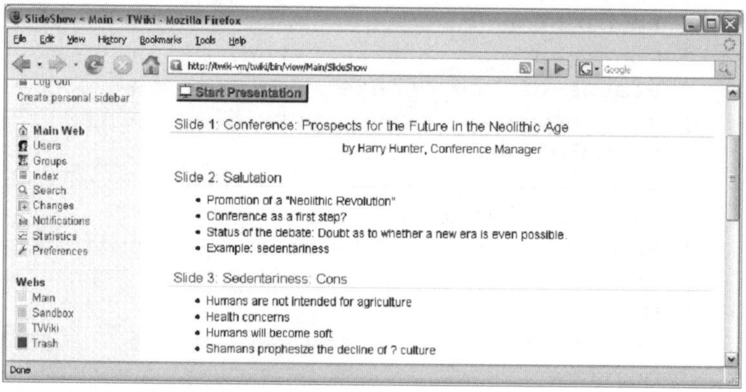

Presentation

When you press the button, TWiki begins your presentation: It accesses a template and inserts the slide title and contents you have provided. If you have not yet created your own template, the TWiki presentation template is used, which is defined in the topic **SlideShowPlugin**. Using the included navigation buttons, you can jump back and forth from slide to slide.

You can exit the presentation switch via the slides with the button **End Presentation**.

23.3.2 Your Own Template

You most likely do not want to employ the TWiki test template for your presentation, but would rather use the opportunity to create your own layout. It basically does not matter where you define your template: You can generate a separate topic for it, or insert the template on the page in which your presentation is also located. However, there should only be one template per topic, since it is integrated via the topic title.

Surround the template with the variables `%STARTINCLUDE%` and `%STOPINCLUDE%`. Between them, use an HTML table that defines the design of your slide. Thus, for instance, you can define the first row as your slide title by inserting the logo and the placeholder `%SLIDETITLE%`.

The following variables are available for the template:

Tab. 23.1

Variable	Significance
`%SLIDETITLE%`	Slide title.
`%SLIDETEXT%`	Slide text.
`%SLIDENUM%`	Current slide number.
`%SLIDEMAX%`	Number of the last slide.
`%SLIDENAV%`	Navigation buttons for the **first**, **previous**, and **next** slide.
`%SLIDENAVALL%`	Navigation buttons for the **first**, **previous**, **next** and **last** slide.
`%SLIDENAVFIRST%`	Navigation button **First slide**.
`%SLIDENAVPREV%`	Navigation button **Previous slide**.
`%SLIDENAVNEXT%`	Navigation button **Next slide**.
`%SLIDENAVLAST%`	Navigation button **Last slide**.

Of course you can also utilize all other design options of HTML tables, such as background color, text alignment, and so on.

On the other hand, it is easiest to alter the standard template on the page **SlideShowPlugin** or copy and edit it. That is what Harry Hunter has opted to do. However, there are a few settings that need to be defined on the copy of the template, in addition to the new logo: For instance, the graphic file *clearpixel.jpg* is integrated in the standard template, which the altered template will continue to want to be able to access. To allow this, the following path to the topic **SlideShowPlugin** in **TWiki** web must be set:

Wiki

```
<img src="%PUBURL%/TWiki/                              ↵
  SlideShowPlugin/clearpixel.gif">
```

Here you can see the complete template of the salutatory speech on the page **ConferenceLaunch**:

Wiki

```
%STARTINCLUDE%
<table width="100%" border="0"                         ↵
       cellspacing="0" cellpadding="0">
<tr bgcolor="#003399">
  <td valign="middle" width="2%"></td>
  <td valign="middle">
    <font size="+3" color="#FFFFFF">
      %SLIDETITLE%
    </font>
  </td>
  <td align="right" valign="middle">
    <img src="%PUBURL%/TWiki/TWikiLogos                ↵
              /wiki-logo-roll.jpg"                     ↵
         border="0"                                    ↵
         alt="Get out of the Cave" />
     
  </td>
</tr>
</table>
<table width="100%" border="0"                         ↵
       cellspacing="0" cellpadding="3">
<tr bgcolor="#FFFF99">
  <td width="1">
    <img src="%PUBURL%/TWiki/SlideShowPlugin/↵
              clearpixel.gif"                          ↵
         width="1" height="480" alt="" />
  </td>
  <td valign="top">
    %BR%
    <font size="+2" color="#003399">
      %SLIDETEXT%
    </font>
  </td>
</tr>
</table>
```

```
<table width="100%" border="0"                        ↵
       cellspacing="0" cellpadding="0">
<tr bgcolor="#FFFFCC">
  <td valign="middle">
    %SLIDENAVALL% 
  </td>
  <td valign="middle" align="right">
    <font size="-1" color="#666666">
      Slide %SLIDENUM% of %SLIDEMAX%
    </font>
  </td>
  <td valign="middle" align="right">
  </td>
</tr>
</table>
%STOPINCLUDE%
```

The following image results when displayed in the page view:

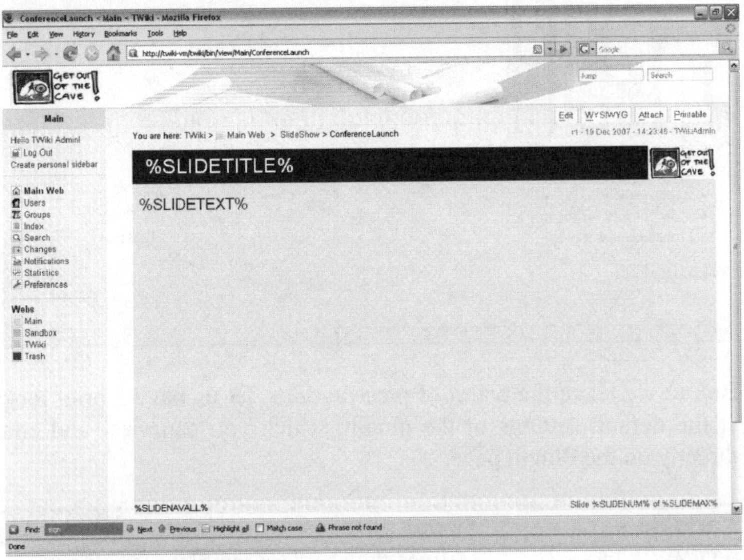

Fig. 23.5

There are now two ways to allocate the template to a presentation. You can define it as a standard template in the variable `%TEMPLATE%` on the **TWikiDrawPlugin** page, e.g. with

```
Set TEMPLATE=ConferenceLaunch
```

Wiki

In this case, the template is automatically allocated to every presentation in the TWiki.

Alternatively, you can integrate the template once in a single presentation by transferring it to the variable `%SLIDESHOWSTART%` as a parameter. In our example, we need to add the following:

Wiki

```
%SLIDESHOWSTART {template=
   "ConferenceLaunch"}%
```

The third slide of the launch speech looks as follows after we integrate the template:

Fig. 23.6

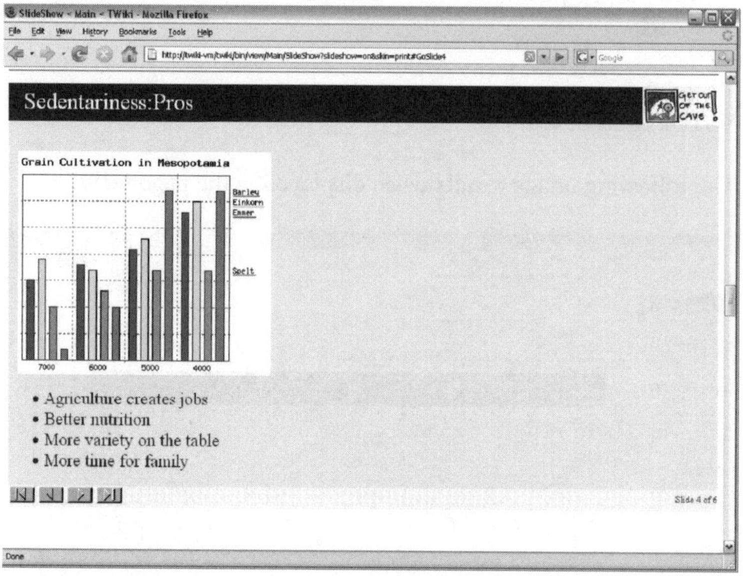

Default settings

Before we leave the realm of presentations, let us have a brief look at the default settings of the plugin, which you can view and edit directly on the Plugin page:

Tab. 23.2

Variable	**Significance**
`%TEMPLATE%`	Defines the standard template for all presentations in TWiki Example: `Set TEMPLATE = ConferenceLaunch`
`%HIDECOMMENTS%`	Activates or deactivates the option of including comments in the presentation Example: `Set HIDECOMMENTS = on`

23.4 Generating Visuals for Statistics using Diagrams (Chart Plugin)

Statistics

Diagrams are irreplaceable in providing visualization. The depiction of trends and statistics are essential in projects, including our conference. Perhaps you wish to portray the number of visitors over the course of the conference, for instance. Now that we are nearing the end of our Wiki project, we would like to present the Chart Plugin. It can be used to generate very simple diagrams in the wiki.

Mode of operation

This plugin provides a function that is often familiar from spreadsheets: The program generates a diagram based on the identified database.

In the TWiki, the database consists of a table that by default should be in the same topic. However, there is also the option of citing tables from other pages. There are five different types of diagrams that can be selected, which can also be combined with each other. Furthermore, it is possible to set several diagram parameters, such as the color combinations. The generated diagram is created in jpeg or png format. All diagrams on a page are located in the open folder of the corresponding web. Thus, others also have access to the diagrams.

Note: For the Chart plugin, you will also need the additional Perl module GD. You also have to install it retroactively with CPAN. GD, in turn, requires the graphic library gdlib to be in your system. You can obtain further information at *http://www.boutell.com/gd/*.

23.4.1 Syntax

To generate a diagram on a page, insert the variable `%CHART{...}%` in the appropriate spot. The diagram type, data source and diagram attributes are to be defined inside the curly brackets.

A few parameters, such as `xlabel`, expect information on the table ranges. This information corresponds to the data with which you are already familiar from our discussion on spreadsheets: A cell is defined by a row and column entry, e.g. `R1:C1` for the cell in the first row and first column. A table range, in turn, is defined by two cells; e.g. `R2:C1..R5:C7` refers to the corresponding twenty-eight cells.

Here is a brief example:

Fig. 23.7

	Hunters	Gatherers	Shamans
Day 1	40	59	11
Day 2	32	62	9

The source text of the above is as follows:

Wiki

```
%TABLE{name="Example_1"}%
| | Hunters | Gatherers | Shamans |
| Day 1 | 40 | 59 | 11 |
| Day 2 | 32 | 62 | 9 |
```

Table plugin

The reason that we make reference to the source code again here is the `%TABLE%` variable in the first row that belongs to the so-called Table plugin, which we must mention here. This plugin is part of the standard installation, and enables formatting and sorting parameters, such as a background color, to be defined in a table using pipe syntax. However, it also enables you to name the table, which is vital to generating our diagram, so that the desired database can be distinctly named in the `table` attribute. That is why only the parameter name is relevant here, that we have allocated with **Example_1**. We will not go into more detail about further options of the plugin.

We would now like to portray the data from the **Example_1** diagram as a bar graph. The code line for this procedure is as follows:

Wiki

```
%CHART{ type="bar" name="Bar_1"                   ↵
  table="Example_1" data="R2:C2..R3:C4"           ↵
  xaxis="R1:C2..R1:C4" legend="R2:C1..R3:C1"      ↵
  ymin="0" width="225" title="Visitors"           ↵
  height="200"
}%
```

It is used to generate the following graph, *Bar_1.png*, which is saved in

Wiki

```
%PUBURL%/%WEB%/%TOPIC%/                           ↵
   _ChartPlugin_<type>_<name>.png.
```

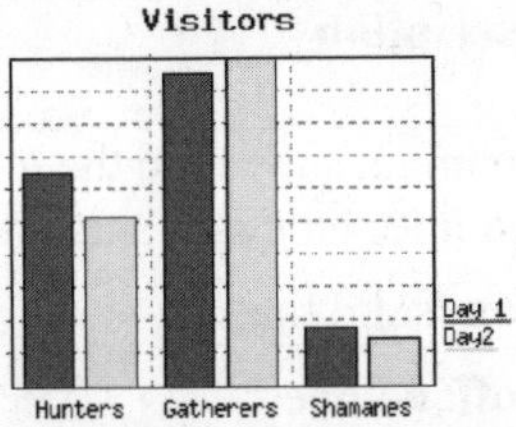

Fig. 23.8

The list of possible parameters for the diagram is extensive. However, the only necessary ones are **name, table** and **data**.

Tab. 23.3

%CHART%-Parameter	**Description**
`type`	Primary diagram type ▪ **area** = area diagram ▪ **bar**= bar graph ▪ **line**=line graph ▪ **scatter**=scatter diagram ▪ **combo**= combination diagram
`subtype`	Diagram types of the remaining data series for the primary type combo; possible combinations: `area`, `bar`, `line`, `point`, `pline`. Area and bar graphs should not be mixed in a single diagram.
`scale`	Linear or semi-logarithmic.
`name`	Name that distinctly identifies the diagram.
`web`	Web in which the topic with the base table is located.
`topic`	Topic containing the base table.
`table`	Base table
`title`	Diagram title; appears above the diagram.
`xlabel`	X-axis label.
`ylabel`	Y-axis label.
`data`	Value range of the table that is to be depicted.
`defaultdata`	Default value if a cell is empty.
`xaxis`	Values of the X-axis; is indicated as a cell range.
`xaxisangle`	Angle at which the values of the X-axis are shown; O means horizontal, and all other numbers are vertical.
`yaxis`	Values of the Y-axis; **off** means they are not displayed.
`ymin`	Minimum shown on the Y-axis.

Tab. 23.3 (continued)

%CHART%-Parameter	Description
ymax	Maximum shown on the Y-axis.
xgrid	Grid lines on the X-axis level: ▪ **on**: solid lines ▪ **off**: no lines ▪ **dot**: dotted lines
ygrid	Grid lines on the Y-axis level; values as in xgrid.
numygrids	Number of grid lines on the Y-axis level.
numxgrids	Number of grid lines on the X-axis level.
datalabel	Individual data points are displayed: ▪ **on**: Values are displayed ▪ **off**: Values are not displayed ▪ **box**: Values are displayed in the box ▪ **off,off,box**: Every third value is displayed
legend	Legend displayed on the right of the diagram; is defined via a table range.
width	Width of the diagram in pixels.
height	Height of the diagram in pixels.
colors	Colors used for the data rows.
bgcolor	Background color of the diagram.
gridcolor	Color of the grid lines.
linewidth	Line width of the curve in pixels.
pointsize	Width of a data point in pixels (in the direction of the X as well as the Y-axis).

23.4.2 Sample Table

The following diagrams have been generated with the data of this table:

Fig. 23.9

	7000	6000	5000	4000
Emmer	20	23	26	33
Einkorn	24	22	28	35
Spelt	15	18	22	22
Barley	7	15	37	37

Here, you can see the Chart plugin in action:

Tab. 23.4

Area diagram:

```
%CHART{ type="area"
name="Grain_
cultivation_area"
table="Cultivation"
data="R2:C2..R5:C5"
xaxis="R1:C2..R1:C6"
legend="R2:C1..R5:C1"
width="250"
height="200" }%
```

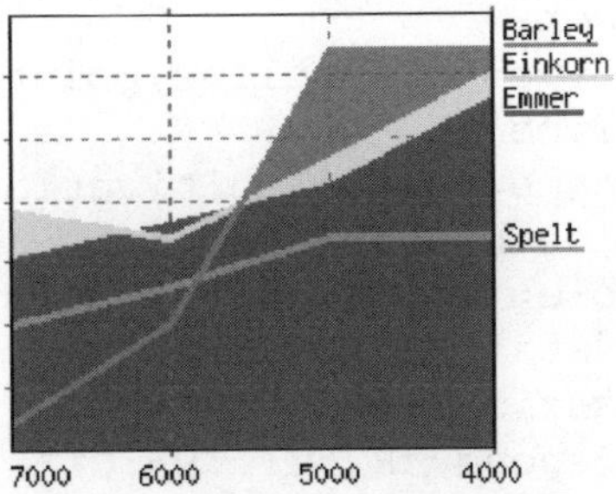

Bar diagram:

```
%CHART{ type="bar"
name="Grain_cultivation
_bar" ta-
ble="Cultivation"
data="R2:C2..R5:C5"
xaxis="R1:C2..R1:C5"
legend="R2:C1..R5:C1"
width="250"
height="200" }%
```

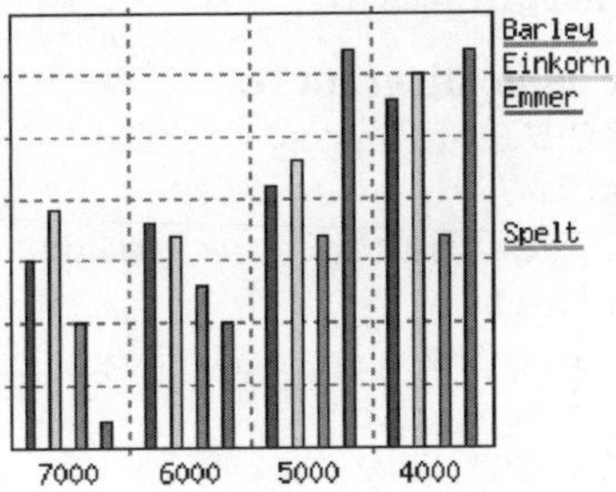

Line graph:

```
%CHART{ type="bar"
name="Grain_cultivation
_line" ta-
ble="Cultivation"
data="R2:C2..R5:C5"
xaxis="R1:C2..R1:C5"
legend="R2:C1..R5:C1"
width="250" datala-
bel=”on” height="200"
}%
```

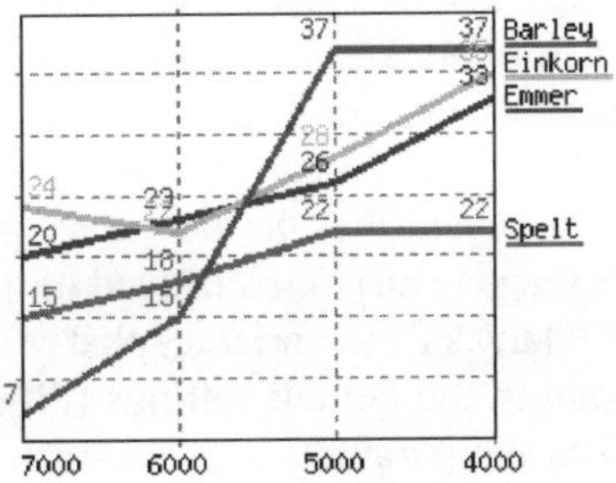

Scatter diagram:

```
%CHART{ type="bar"
name="Grain_cultivation
_scatter" ta-
ble="Cultivation"
data="R2:C2..R5:C5"
xaxis="R1:C2..R1:C5"
legend="R2:C1..R5:C1"
width="250"
height="200" }%
```

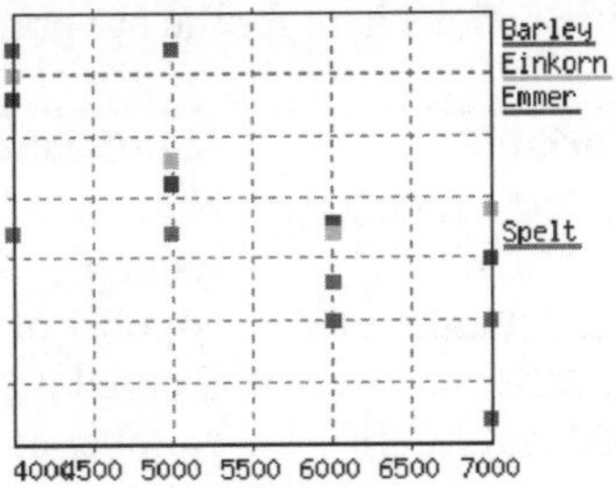

Tab. 23.4 (continued)

Combo diagram I:

```
%CHART{ type="combo"
sub-
type="area,pline,point,
line"
name="Grain_cultivation
_combo_one" ta-
ble="Cultivation"
data="R2:C2..R5:C5"
xaxis="R1:C2..R1:C5"
legend="R2:C1..R5:C1"
width="250"
height="200" }%
```

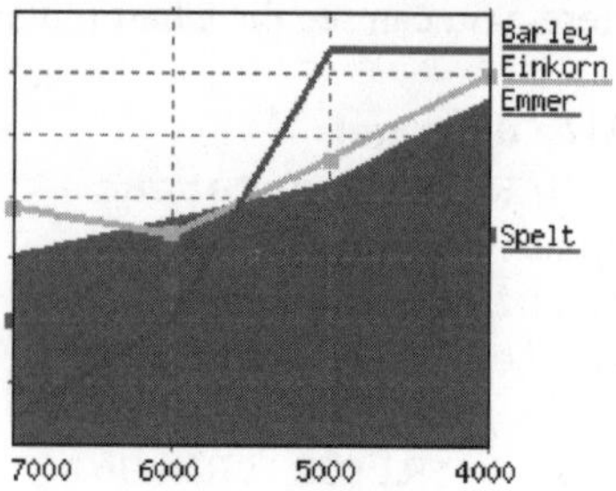

Combo diagram II:

```
%CHART{ type="combo"
sub-
type="bar,pline,point,
line"
name="Grain_cultivation
_combo_two"
R5:C5"
xaxis="R1:C2..R1:C5"
legend="R2:C1..R5:C1"
width="250"
height="200" }
```

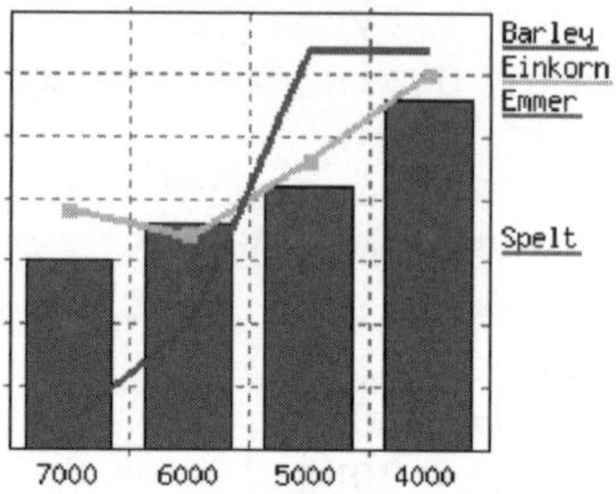

In the event that the necessary parameters are not defined, an error message is displayed instead of the diagram.

Default settings

Many of the variables that you can use to design a standard diagram in the default settings (Plugin page) should be familiar to you from the parameters of the `%CHART%` variables: `TYPE`, `WIDTH`, `HEIGHT`, `AREA_COLORS`, `LINE_COLORS`, `BGCOLOR`, `GRIDCOLOR`, `NUMYGRIDS`, `DEFAULTDATA`, `SCALE`, `LINEWIDTH`, `POINTSIZE`. In addition, you will also find specific options here for the bar graph:

Tab.23.5

Variable	Significance
`%BARLEADING SPACE%`	Number of pixels before the first bar. Example: `Set BARLEADINGSPACE = 6`
`%BARTRAILING SPACE%`	Number of pixels after the last bar. Example: `Set BARTRAILINGSPACE = 6`
`%BARSPACE%`	Number of pixels between the bars. Example: `Set BARSPACE = 5`

23.5 Final Steps: Feedback and Documentation

Feedback

The post-processing of projects is often neglected. However, it is very important with regard to future projects to pool experiences. The aspects that went well and those that could have gone better should be documented. Positive feedback and an honest inventory provide motivation for new tasks. Unexpressed and unresolved conflicts, on the other hand, have a debilitating effect. If a round of feedback is missing, the project is not complete.

For the group itself, the evaluation of the project has a significant function. Especially in the final, stressful phases, misunderstandings can crop up, or tension may build between participants that was never able to be addressed.

It is once again important that insights can be gleaned from the consequences and earnest improvement for future projects can be expected. It is not uncommon for final reports of projects to land, unread, in the binder, which is a source of further frustration.

Evaluation

Set up a separate page for feedback on which both positive and negative feedback can be collected. This can be done on an anonymous basis in a separate evaluation meeting. The discussion should clarify the following questions: Were the goals reached? Why or why not? What should be done differently next time, and what proved to be successful?

Archiving

Finally, the wiki must be modified for the documentation, if necessary, so that outsiders can also quickly find the information they seek (overview pages). This can, in some circumstances, be very time-consuming. In the ideal case, the wiki will already contain all necessary content. Through the history pages, the wiki documents the development of the project in a detailed manner. However, it is possible that some content still needs to be submitted: Perhaps photographs of the posters, as well as work results and reports need to be worked in. You must decide which areas are to be closed and which are required for continuation of the project.

Note: Be sure to protect sensitive data, such as participant lists and user topics, from unauthorized access.

Photo gallery

A photo gallery that reflects the atmosphere of the project adds a nice as well as popular finishing touch to the project.

V. Go with the Flow: Confluence

24 Installing Confluence

24.1 Atlassian Software Systems

Background

Confluence is a wiki engine currently only available in English whose WYSIWYG editor and integrated user rights administration also make it ideal for use in companies. License owners of this commercial software receive the source code and can develop it further.

The producer of Confluence is the Australian software company Atlassian Software Systems Pty Ltd. Atlassian was founded in 2002 by Scott Farquhar and Mike Cannon-Brookes directly after they finished college with a seed capital of $1,000. In 2006, approximately 100 employees serving around 6,000 customers in 65 countries earned returns amounting to $12.2 million.[1]

In the same year, the two founders won the competition "Australian Entrepreneur of the Year", run by the consulting firm Ernst & Young.[2]

Public Confluence Installations:

A few Confluence installations are publicly accessible, e.g.:

- IBM Wikis for Developers[3]
- Sony Ericsson Wikis for Developers[4]

---

[1] http://confluence.atlassian.com/display/NEWS/Atlassian+History+and+Background

[2] http://www.ey.com/GLOBAL/content.nsf/Australia/EOY_-_2006_Australian_Entrepreneur_Of_The_Year

[3] http://www-03.ibm.com/developerworks/wikis/dashboard.action

[4] http://developer.sonyericsson.com/wiki/display/leftnav/Welcome+to+our+Wiki+community

In focus: companies

- These examples are typical for wikis whose origins lie in software development. Yet Atlassian lays claim to offering "the" enterprise wiki and thus to also serving branches such as banks and insurance companies, biotechnology, telecommunications and consulting.

24.2 Licenses

Anchor in the open source community

Private persons can download Confluence at no charge and try it out with two users. Support is not included.

Beyond that, Atlassian also offers commercial, academic and community licenses. A commercial license for an unlimited number of users costs $8,000, for example. Community licenses offered for open source projects and non-profit organizations are free of charge – if certain conditions are met. In this way, Atlassian supports the open source movement and utilizes it for further developments.[5]

All licenses include the source code and thus enable extensive adaptation to customer-specific demands. In addition, a new hosting service for Confluence is now offered whose costs depend on the number of users, and its configuration options are limited.

A license key is required for installation, which can be generated online and sent per email upon registration.

24.3 Architecture

At the time of this printing, the current version is Confluence 2.5.x.[6] Several application servers and relational databases can be used; for more information, see Chap. 24.5. The standalone bundle offers the following important components, among others:

- Web server and servlet container: Apache Tomcat[7]
- Database: HSQL[8]
- Full-text search engine: Apache Lucene[9]
- Template engine: Velocity[10]

---

[5] http://www.atlassian.com/software/confluence/pricing.jsp
[6] http://confluence.atlassian.com/display/DOC/Release+Notes
[7] http://tomcat.apache.org/
[8] http://hsqldb.org/
[9] http://lucene.apache.org/
[10] http://velocity.apache.org

24.4 System Requirements

Platform independence

Confluence is based on the Java platform Enterprise Edition 5 and is thus available for all conventional operating systems, such as Windows, Linux, Mac OS X and various Unix derivatives.

Tab. 24.1

	< 25 simultaneous users	≥ 25 simultaneous users
Processor	Pentium IV 1 GHz or compatible	Pentium Xeon Dual-Core or compatible
RAM	256 MB	512 MB
Drive space	500 MB	500 MB

The client requires Internet Explorer from Version 6 on, Firefox or another Mozilla-based browser.

Demands to the server hardware especially depend on

- the number of users working simultaneously online
- the number of Spaces – that is, subwikis – and the
- number of pages.

Scalability

Atlassian's recommendations regarding server hardware are summarized in Tab. 24.1. These values can only be considered guidelines, since the configuration options for Confluence – especially with regard to plugins – are very numerous.

Practical experience has shown that quality server hardware is necessary for satisfactory Confluence performance, and that the above equipment represents the minimum. With regard to drive space, especially the attachments, which can quickly take up to 10 times more space than the rest of the data, play a large role. Thus, frequently used attachments should be swapped out to a wiki page wherever possible.

As of Confluence 2.3, a cluster installation is possible. According to the maker, installations with up to 1,700 Spaces, 15,000 users, 100,000 LDAP users and 80,000 wiki pages each are in use.[11] These statistics should be taken with a grain of salt, however, so as not to lead to excessive optimism.

[11] http://confluence.atlassian.com/display/DOC/Server+Hardware+Requirements+Guide

24.5 Installation Options

There are four different options for installing Confluence. They differ in their application contexts.

Note: When installing, make sure that no blank spaces are included in the installation path. Other special characters are also not advisable. Errors of this sort can be difficult to localize later on, since, in the presence of start problems, first the port choice, firewall or virus scanner are checked.

24.5.1 Standalone

The simplest and fastest option to try out Confluence is the standalone installation, which comes in a bundle with a preconfigured HSQL database in a ZIP file of almost 60 MB that is ready to start in just a few minutes. HSQL is a relational database completely programmed in Java, which is also used in OpenOffice.org 2.0.[12]

The bundle Apache Tomcat is integrated as an application server.

24.5.2 EAR-WAR

For serious corporate utilization, an external database should be used, since HSQL does not offer transaction security. The following relational databases are currently fully supported:[13]

- PostgreSQL as of Version 8
- MySQL as of Version 4.1 (not yet 5.0)
- Oracle as of Version 10g
- DB2 as of Version 8.2

"EAR" stands for "Enterprise Application Archive", "WAR" for "Web Application Archive". If Confluence is to be integrated into an

[12] http://hsqldb.org/

[13] http://confluence.atlassian.com/display/DOC/Confluence+Installation+Guide

existing application server, the following are available in addition to Apache Tomcat, mentioned above:

- BEA WebLogic as of Version 8.1 SP3
- Caucho Resin as of Version 2.11.11
- JBoss Application Server
- Ironflare AB Orion as of Version 2.0.2
- IBM WebSphere as of Version 5.1.1.3

Macromedia JRun and Microsoft IIS Server have not yet been tested. Oracle OC4J, Sun Application Server and GlassFish are not compatible.

24.5.3 Cluster Installation

As of Version 2.3, Confluence can be installed in a cluster. This is of great interest to companies in addition to the EAR-WAR installation, to secure the scalability of Confluence. In addition to a special cluster license, an external database and a load balancer are necessary for every node.

24.5.4 Confluence Hosting

Confluence as an ASP solution

Another interesting option for small companies who wish to quickly launch a wiki project is Confluence Hosting via Atlassian.[14] Costs start at $49 for 15 users per month; for 500 users per year, the charge is $4490.

The advantages lie in the clearly limited IT costs, while the disadvantages focus primarily on the fact that no plugins can be installed, LDAP and mail integration are not possible, and the configurations are more rigid in general. Furthermore, the size of the attachments for the hosted version may not exceed a total of 10 GB.

Even those who select another installation variant should nevertheless consider these limitations for their own initial installation, as administration seems to be the least problematic.

[14] http://www.atlassian.com/software/confluence/hosted.jsp

24.6 Standalone Installation

Learn Confluence fast

In this section, we limit ourselves to the installation of the standalone variant with a personal license. On the one hand, it is the quickest possibility to become familiar with Confluence. On the other, the installation options already presented and combinations with various application servers and databases are so multifarious that it would extend the scope of this discussion.

Especially because the standalone installation is so quick and easy, we wish to once again explicitly point out that Confluence integration in the productive IT infrastructure of a company is complex and time-consuming.

24.6.1 Installation under Windows

Windows installation is oriented toward Vista. However, there are hardly any deviations for XP and 2000.

Installing JDK 1.5

The Java Runtime Environment (JRE) will not suffice for Confluence installation; you must install the Java Development Kit (JDK).[15] If you have already done this, you can skip this section.

If you are not sure whether or not JDK has already been installed for other purposes or what version is being used, you can find out by clicking on `Start`, then `Run` and invoking `cmd`. Now enter the following in the command line:

Shell

```
echo %JAVA_HOME%
```

and you will receive something like this:

```
c:\j2sdk1.4.2_10
```

Since Atlassian recommends the faster and more reliable Version 1.5 (1.6 is not yet fully supported) you should download the newer version from the Sun website.[16] The Windows Kit is almost 50 MB in size and can be easily installed in any directory using an installer.

---

15 http://confluence.atlassian.com/display/DOC/Confluence+Installation+Guide

16 http://java.sun.com/j2se/1.5.0/jdk/download.jsp

You should make a note of that directory, e.g. *c:\jdk1.5.0_08*, since you will need this information for the next step.

Now the operating system has to be explicitly told in which path JDK is to be found. To do so, click on **System control**, then **System**, and in the **Extended** tab, click on **Environment variable**. Via the button **New** for the system variables, you can enter the **Variable name** "JAVA_HOME" and as **variable value** "c:\jdk1.5.0_08" and confirm with **OK**. Fig. 24.1 depicts the steps described above.

Confluence Download and Configuration

The license holder must first register as usual,[17] indicating last and first name, email address, password, town and answering the question "Where did you hear about us?" Since this is unfortunately done via an unencrypted connection, you at least should not use the same password as for the corresponding email account.

The ZIP file for the download is just under 60 MB in size and can be unpacked with WinZip or a similar tool to any directory, such as:

```
c:\confluence-2.5.4-std
```

Now you have to create another directory in which Confluence will keep its data, e.g.

```
c:\confluence\data
```

For a standalone installation, usually only one manual modification needs to be made to a configuration file. In the directory

```
c:\confluence-2.5.4-std\confluence\WEB-
INF\classes\
```

the Confluence Home directory just created must be indicated in the file

```
confluence-init.properties
```

For instance:

```
confluence.home=c:\confluence\data
```

CFG

Only the comment symbol ("#") needs to be deleted and the Unix slashes ("/") changed to backslashes ("\").

[17] http://my.atlassian.com

Fig. 24.1

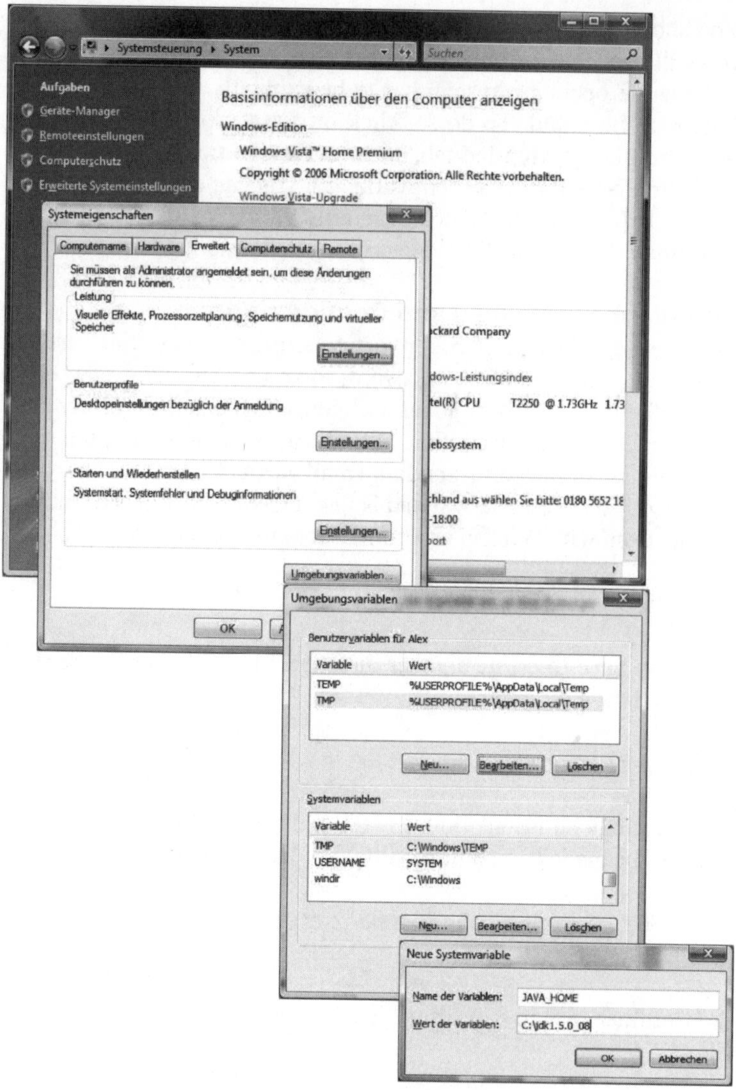

If Port 8080 is already occupied, the Confluence start described in the next chapter will not work, and an alternative port must be entered in the file `server.xml` in the directory

```
c:\confluence-2.5.4-std\conf
```

in place of "8080:"

CFG

```
<ConnectorclasName="org.apache.coyote.
tomcat4.CoyoteConnector" port="8080"
```

First Confluence Start

After completing the configuration described above, you can start Confluence for the first time. To do this, the batch file `startup.bat` in the directory

```
c:\confluence-2.5.4-std\bin
```

must be opened with a double click. It may take several minutes for the final line to appear in the DOS window after a series of status messages. This line will read something like this:

```
INFO: Server startup in 60220 ms
```

Now the Confluence server can be opened in the browser as "localhost" at Port "8080:"

```
http://localhost:8080
```

URL

After a few seconds, the start page of the "Confluence Setup Wizard" appears. Now the license key mentioned above will be required, which you must copy into the text box. For standalone variants, you must then select **Standard Installation** (see Fig. 24.2).

Fig. 24.2

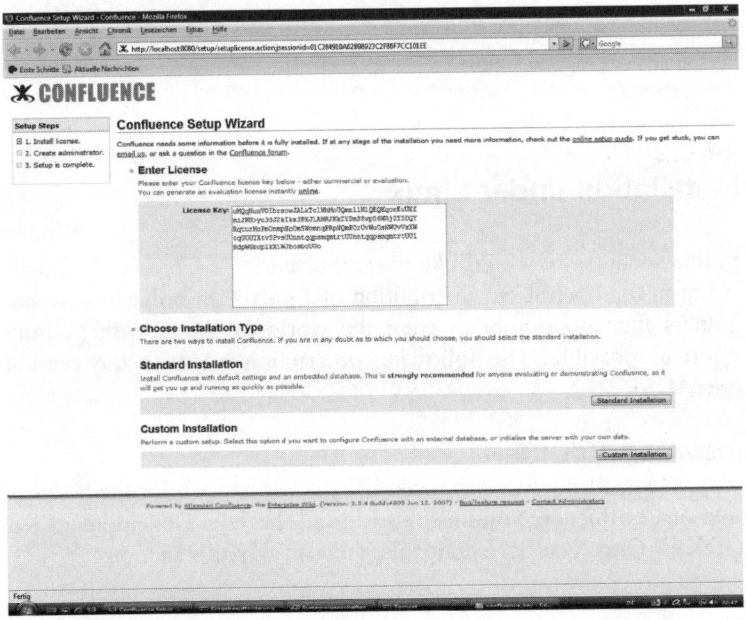

To end Confluence, you must invoke

Shell

```
shutdown.bat
```

in the same directory.

In the next step, the administrator account with user, password, name and email address is generated (see Fig. 24.3). This completes the setup, and Confluence can be started for the first time. The user will see the start page (Dashboard) described in Chap. 25.2 (see Fig. 25.1).

Fig. 24.3

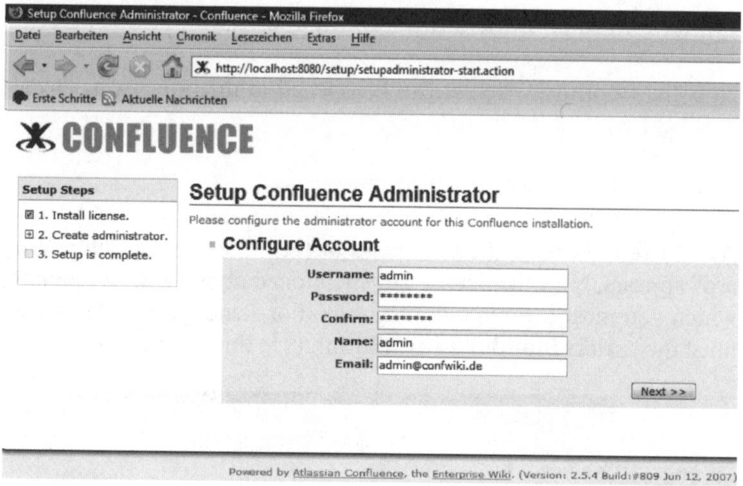

24.6.2 Installation under Linux

In this section, we would like to only discuss the Confluence installation in the openSUSE distribution of Linux,[18] in order to give beginners the opportunity to enter the world of Linux with as little effort as possible. The following description refers to the version openSUSE 10.2.

Installing JDK 1.5

The Java Runtime Environment (JRE) is not enough for the installation of Confluence; you must also install the Java Development Kit (JDK).[19] Once you have done this, you can skip this section.

---

[18] http://www.opensuse.org/

[19] http://confluence.atlassian.com/display/DOC/Confluence+Installation+Guide

You can download JDK for Linux from Sun. In our example, it is called

```
jdk-1_5_0_08-linux-i586-rpm.bin
```

It is best to save it as a root in the directory `/temp`.

Using the following command, you can run the script in the terminal in this directory and unpack JDK.

```
sh jdk-1_5_0_08-linux-i586-rpm.bin
```

During this procedure, you need to click through Sun's license agreement with the "enter" or "space" button and finally confirm it with `yes`.

Now the unpacked rpm file can be installed using the command

```
rpm -i jdk-1_5_0_08-linux-i586.rpm
```

JDK will be installed in the following directory:

```
/usr/java/jdk1.5.0_08
```

Confluence Download and Configuration

The license holder must first register as usual,[20] indicating last and first name, email address, password, town and answering the question "Where did you hear about us?" Since this is unfortunately done via an unencrypted connection, you at least should not use the same password as for the corresponding email account.

The Tar.gz file for the download is just under 60 MB in size. Using the terminal command

```
tar xzfv confluence-2.5.4-std.tar.gz -C /opt
```

Confluence is unpacked to the directory `/opt`.

Now another directory must be generated – e.g. with the aid of `mkdir` – where Confluence will keep its data, e.g.

```
/var/confluence/data
```

For a standalone installation, usually only one manual modification needs to be made to a configuration file. In the directory

```
/opt/confluence-2.5.4-std/confluence/WEB-
INF/classes/
```

[20] http://my.atlassian.com

the Confluence Home directory just created must be indicated in the file

```
confluence-init.properties
```

For instance:

CFG

```
confluence.home=/var/confluence/data
```

Only the comment symbol ("#") needs to be deleted in the last line and the path altered accordingly.

If Port 8080 is already occupied, an alternative port must be entered in the file `server.xml` in the directory

```
/opt/confluence-2.5.4-std/conf/
```

in place of 8080:

CFG

```
<ConnectorclasName="org.apache.coyote.
tomcat4.CoyoteConnector" port="8080"
```

First Confluence Start

After completing the configuration described above, you can start Confluence for the first time. To do this, in the directory

```
/opt/confluence-2.5.4-std/bin/
```

the following terminal command must be invoked:

Shell

```
sh startup.sh
```

A series of status messages then immediately appears, until the final line, which looks something like this:

```
Using JRE_HOME: /usr/lib/jvm/jre
```

appears.

Now the Confluence server can be opened in the browser as "localhost" at Port "8080:"

URL

```
http://localhost:8080
```

After a few seconds, the start page of the "Confluence Setup Wizard" appears. Now the license key mentioned above will be required, which you must copy into the text box. For standalone variants, you must then select **Standard Installation**. Fig. 24.4 shows the corresponding screenshot.

To end Confluence, you must invoke

Shell

```
sh shutdown.sh
```

in the same directory.

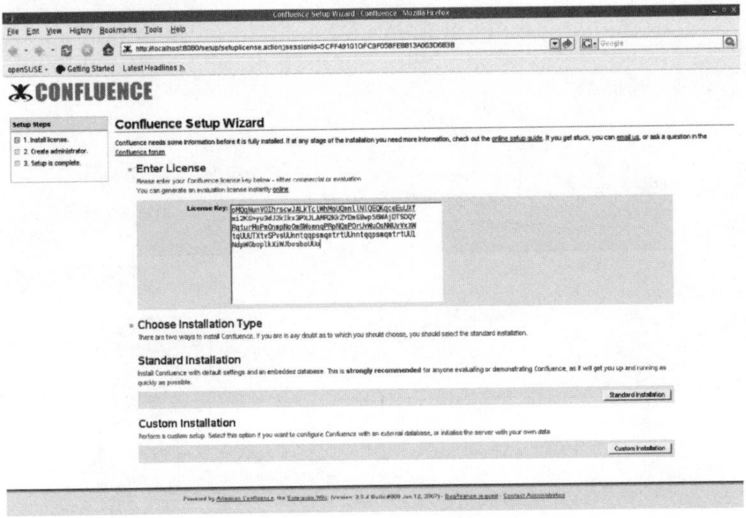

Fig. 24.4

In the next step, the administrator account with user, password, name and email address is generated (see Fig. 24.5). This completes the setup, and Confluence can be started for the first time. The user will see the start page (Dashboard) described in Chap. 25.2 (see Fig. 25.1).

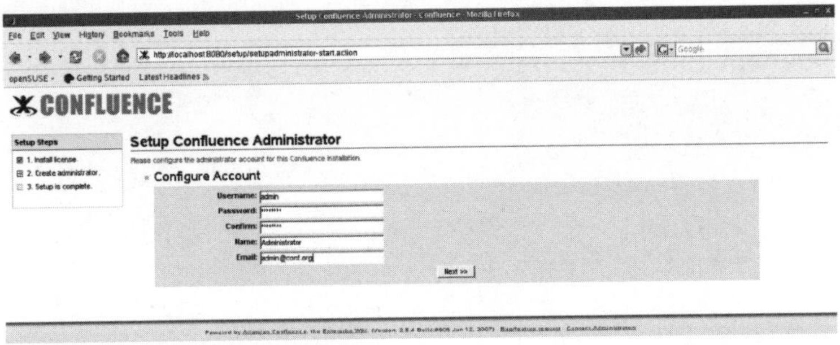

Fig. 24.5

25 Overview

25.1 What are Spaces?

The "Wiki Space" concept

Wiki Spaces are subwikis that are used by companies for individual departments or projects. In addition, there are also "Personal Spaces", sort of like a homepage for individual users which are always accessible via the editing entries linked to the author. There is a smooth transition here to social networking tools such as Facebook.

Spaces can be linked to each other at will:

Wiki

```
[SpaceKey:PageTitle]
```

Since they can possess various degrees of authorization, not every user may be able to follow every link. In addition to a thematic limit, there is also always an authorization limit between the spaces.

25.2 Dashboard

The "Dashboard" as a starting point

The start page of the Confluence installation is the "Dashboard". The display can be divided into 5 areas:

- **Spaces (1):** On the left, the wiki "Spaces" (subwikis) are listed for which the registered user possesses at least reading rights. Via the globe symbol, users can then directly browse the Spaces. A colored article symbol indicates that a user also has writing rights. If a star symbol is yellow instead of gray, the space has been marked as a favorite and, for a better overview, appears in the tab **My**.

Fig. 25.1

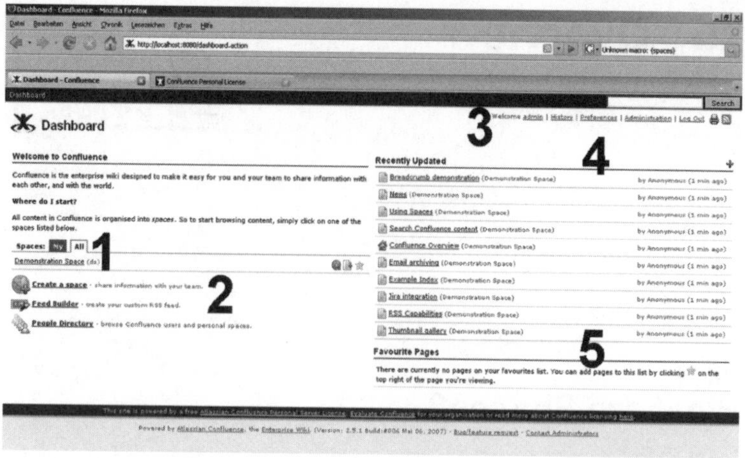

- **Quick Links (2):** Under the Spaces, there are three links. With **Create Space**, you can easily generate another Space. **Feed Builder** creates a link for a personally configured RSS feed. **People Directory** leads to a page in which you can browse other Confluence users. By the way, these users can also create their own “Personal Spaces” and fill them with content.
- **Tools and Search (3):** At the very upper right, there is a search box for full-text searches (see also Chap. 25.2), and underneath are links to the personal profile and/or Personal Space (here, **admin**), to a list of recently visited articles (**History**), to personal settings (**Preferences** – see also Chap. 25.3.2), in this case to the administrator realm (**Administration**) of the Confluence installation, and finally to log out (**Log Out**).
- **Recently Updated (4):** Here, recently generated or modified articles are listed in chronological order. New spaces and altered user profiles also appear here – with their own symbols. The list can be extended using the green “+” sign. However, you can never see more than the last 20 updates.
- **Favorites (5):** At the bottom right, there is a list of the user’s favorite pages, which can be selected by clicking the star symbol at the page level (just as with the Space favorites). A further click on the star, which is then yellow, will then remove Spaces or articles from that particular Favorites list.

25.3 Page Overview

Page-structure

This chapter will explain in more detail the typical areas of the pages:

- **(1) Orientation and Search** (Chap. 25.3.1)
- **(2) User area** (Chap. 25.3.2)
- **(3) Work area** (Chap. 25.3.3)
- **(4) Edit page** (Chap. 25.3.4)

The above areas are numbered correspondingly in Fig. 25.2.

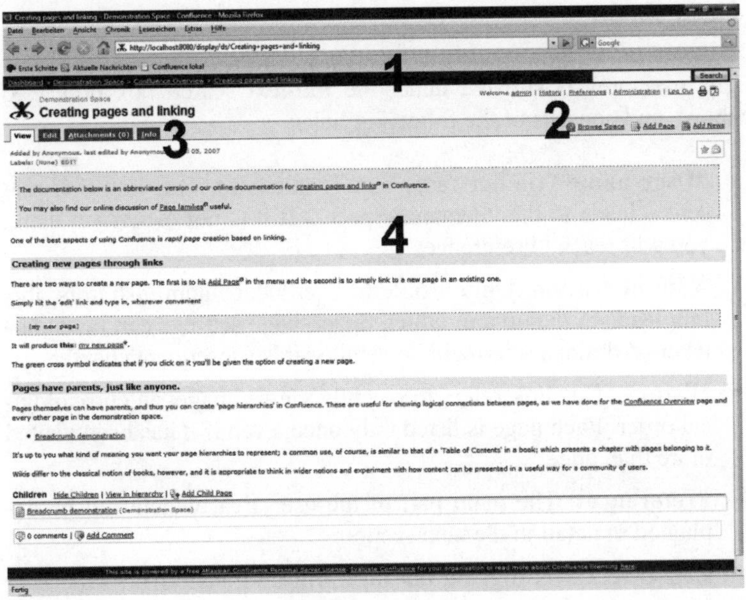

Fig. 25.2

25.3.1 Orientation and Search

Standard Breadcrumbs Navigation

In the upper left browser window, you can always see the so-called “Location breadcrumbs”. Just as in the fairy tale “Hansel and Gretel”, the user can leave a trail of “breadcrumbs” for orientation. From right to left, the respective parent pages of the previous page can be seen. Thus, in Fig. 25.3, **Confluence Overview** is the parent page of **RSS Capabilities**, and so on.

Fig. 25.3

In the upper right browser window, there is a text box for a full-text search. Terms are linked by "AND" by default, but can also be linked by "OR". An advanced search can only be performed after the initial search has produced a results list – more on this later. In contrast to MediaWiki, for example, Confluence does not lead directly to the corresponding article, but rather always shows a list of the search results.

Fig. 25.4

25.3.2 User Area

User-related settings and displays

The user area is situated under the full-text search box described above, and consists of the following links:

- **"User name"** (in our case, Tim Troglodyte). This link – if present – leads to the "Personal Space". If it is not or not yet there, you will reach "Preferences".
- **Administration.** Only visible to Confluence administrators, this link leads to the area in which Space-wide settings can be undertaken. Administration will be detailed in a subsequent chapter.
- **History.** This link refers to recently viewed pages in chronological order. Each page is listed only once, even if it has been visited more than once.
- **Preferences.** The main part of the user area, which will be explained in detail in the next section.
- **Log Out.** Users logging out here will be transferred to the **Log In** page.

User settings in five areas

The personal user settings – **Preferences** – are divided into five areas, assigned to the following tabs:

- **View Profile:** This is where the user name, full name and email address are stored. This information is accessible to anyone who clicks somewhere on an author link. Under **Profile Summary** the user sees to which groups he or she is allocated and which time zone he or she has selected within the wiki. In addition, the user is asked if he would like to receive a daily email informing him of current edits, whether this information is also to be sent in the event that the user himself makes changes, and which email format is preferred (e.g. HTML). Other available statistical data include the registration date of the Confluence user, the date of the last login and the number of authored pages. From this tab, users can also create a **Personal Space** offering the user a sort of personal homepage within the wiki and linked to all of the places where the user has contributed authoring efforts.

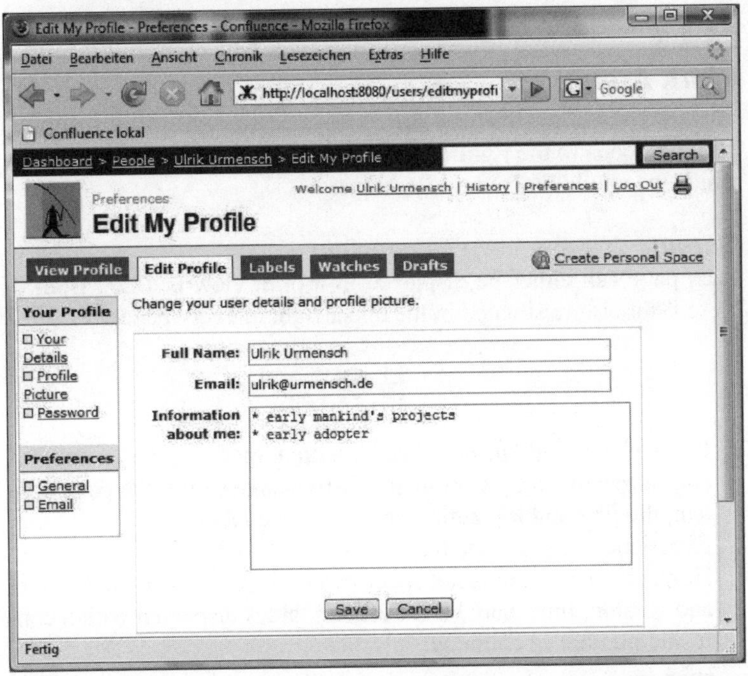

Fig. 25.5

- **Edit Profile:** In this tab, the information mentioned, such as name, email address and other information in a text box can be edited. A picture can be uploaded, which appears on this author page and is also visible if you would like to browse the **People Directory**, to which we referred above. In addition, users can change their passwords here, as well as make or edit settings concerning email messages, time zones, etc.
- **Labels:** The last labels used are listed here. If the word "my" appears in front of these labels, they are only visible to the respective user. Further information on labels can be found in Chap. 25.1.2.
- **Watches:** Here, the user sees what content (pages, news items, Spaces) he or she is currently watching. If changes are made there, the user receives an email containing the edits and a link to the

respective content. Further information on this topic can be found in Chap. 25.4.

- **Drafts:** This tab contains drafts, that is, non-saved, edited pages. From here, you have the opportunity to delete these edits or click them to continue editing them. The number of days since that version of the draft was generated is also indicated. In Chap. 25.5, drafts will be discussed more specifically.

25.3.3 Work Area

The two icons to the right of the User area belong to the Work area, which we would like to briefly discuss:

Output

Two output options

Each page can either be displayed as a print view or PDF. Both of these symbols are situated in the upper right of every page.

Fig. 25.6

- **Print view**: Underneath a header with a Space log and name, the output generated by Confluence here displays only the page content, the first and last author and the issued labels.
  Experience has shown that users like to print out wiki pages. However, the layout is not spectacular: Depending on the browser and version, lines may be cut off and tables displayed with a confusing number of columns.
- **PDF Export**: The PDF Export function has also not yet been perfected. In the meanwhile, at least embedded images are shown, most links function and images that are too wide are scaled to size.
  However, the Export function cannot always handle macros, such as “Gallery”. Certain formats, such as subscript indices, cannot as of yet be processed.

The header of every page indicates the Space name and logo as well as the page name. Underneath this, four tabs appear whose contents will be briefly mentioned and later explained in detail.

Page Editing and Information

Each page has four tabs. This is where the majority of work in the wiki takes place.

Fig. 25.7

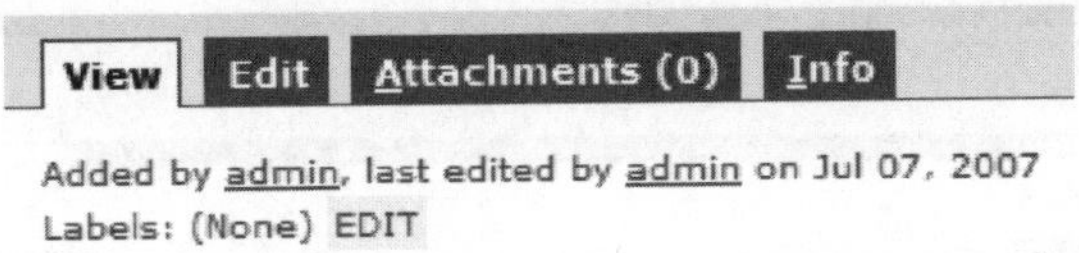

- **View**: When you go to a page, View mode is set by default. You see the first and last author as well as the date of the last edit. A confusing and, from a usability standpoint, questionable limitation: Labels can only be *edited*, that is, added or deleted, in View mode.
  Users can view or hide child pages – even in the hierarchy – and add child pages.
  In addition, users can leave a comment at the foot of the page.
- **Edit**: This is the center of wiki work. The page can be edited in several ways and formatted with two different editors.
- **Attachments**: In this area, the user can upload, comment, edit and delete attachments from the hard drive or any drive. Images that are to be integrated directly into the text appear here automatically.
  The list of attachments can be sorted according to file name, size, author (the person who uploaded the file) and date (of upload). The editing options of the individual attachments are relatively new: File name, comment and file type can be modified. In addition, the attachment can be moved to another page and the user can decide whether the links to this attachment are to be updated in the entire confluence installation – that is, beyond just the Space.
  While attachments to a page can be downloaded as a Zip file (**Download All**), uploading can only be done individually by default. This is made somewhat easier by the fact that the upload dialogue is offered several times in a row (**Attach more files**), thus saving a few clicks.
  The attachments are versioned if they are uploaded more than once under the same name. A small triangle to the left of the file name indicates that several versions are available. The respectively newest attachments are linked and, in the case of images, displayed.

Attachments

Fig. 25.8

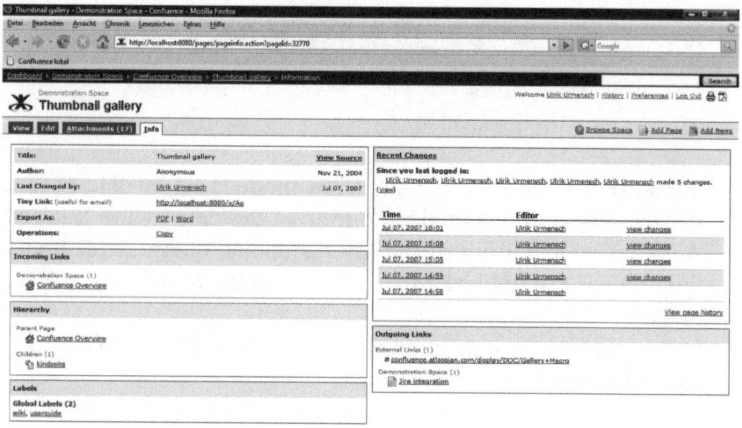

Metafiles on the wiki page

- **Info**: In addition to general information on the page, the Info tab offers a series of other interesting options.
  In addition to the title, the first author (whereby **Author** is perhaps not the most fitting description) as well as the last – each with the date of the edit – are displayed in the upper left.
  Links to and from the page are listed. For the latter, the **External Links** leading to destinations outside the wiki are listed separately.
  Finally, the page lists its respective **Global Labels** and **Recent Changes**. Recent changes to the page include author and time stamp, and any two versions can be compared with one another. Newly added content appears highlighted in green, and deleted content in red. Underneath the time stamp, any comments made by the author regarding his or her edit procedure are displayed.

Browsing

A decisive link for navigation in Confluence is **Browse Space**. In a normal Space, or so-called "Personal Space" (see Chap. 25.1), a magnifying glass is depicted in front of the drawing of the globe, as in Fig. 25.9.

Fig. 25.9

Browsing on eight levels

When you click on **Browse Space**, you can see the following tabs (see Fig. 25.10):

- **Pages:** This tab offers the orientation and navigation aids **Recently Updated, Alphabetical** and **Tree**, which are described in Chap. 27.1.1.
- **Labels:** Labels, which can be assigned to individual pages, are summarized here in an overview. There is a detailed description of this tab in 27.1.2.
- **Attachments:** All attachments of the Space are displayed in an overview under this tab. More information can be found in Chap. 27.1.3.
- **Mail:** If configured to do so, emails – e.g. as a CC – can be sent to Confluence. The mailbox can be viewed using this tab. Details on the topic of "Mail to Confluence" can be found in Chap. 27.1.4.
- **News:** This tab basically represents a blog. News entries and their respective dates appear in chronological order. There is more on this function in Chap. 27.1.5.
- **Activity:** This relatively new function provides information on reading and writing right within a Space or – for Confluence admins – also beyond Space limits (see Chap. 27.1.6).
- **Advanced:** A virtual smorgasbord of informational and organizational options for the user can be found here. In Chap. 27.1.7, you will find additional information.
- **Space Admin:** This tab is only available to the Space admin, who can perform certain settings here (see Chap. 27.1.8).

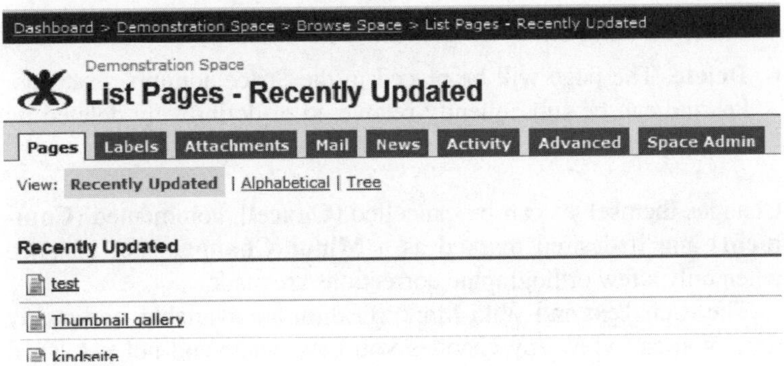

Fig. 25.10

Adding Content

Parent/child relationship between pages

Add Page adds a new (child) page to the current one. Confluence is organized in a hierarchical manner. Its tree structure facilitates browsing and is also the basis of the authorization structure for individual pages.

Add News adds a new news message to the page. The current date is automatically included in the entry.

25.3.4 Editing a Page

Editing and assigning pages

The following actions can be performed for every page:

- **Rename.** Changing the name in the text box ("child page" in our example) does not affect the link leading to that page. The page has a specific, internal ID that it retains throughout its entire life cycle and thus is not connected to the page name.
- **Reassign.** The wiki pages in Confluence are hierarchically arranged. You can reassign pages in this hierarchy at any time – including their child pages. Reassigning also does not affect the internal wiki link: they are retained.
- **Edit.** A Rich Text Editor – similar to Word – as well as a Wiki Markup Editor that requires knowledge of Confluence wiki syntax, are available.
  Edits are cached by default every thirty seconds. If you leave the editing page without having saved it, it will appear under "Drafts", mentioned above, and can be edited further at any time. Other users cannot see whether a draft of another version of the page exists. The advantage is that revisions can be purposefully generated by clicking **Save**. The disadvantage is that it is difficult to synchronize several drafts.
- **Save**. Clicking **Save** will generate a new version.
- **Delete.** The page will be placed in the Space admin's wastebasket and can be subsequently recovered or definitively deleted by the Space admin.

Changes themselves can be cancelled (**Cancel**), commented (**Comment**) and if desired marked as a **Minor Change** – for instance when only a few orthographic corrections are made.

The Rich Text and Wiki Markup Editor are available, and at any time, you can view any changes you have made and not yet saved with **Preview**.

Reading and writing restrictions can also be set here (**View / Edit Restrictions**). Finally, labels can also be assigned (**Labels**).

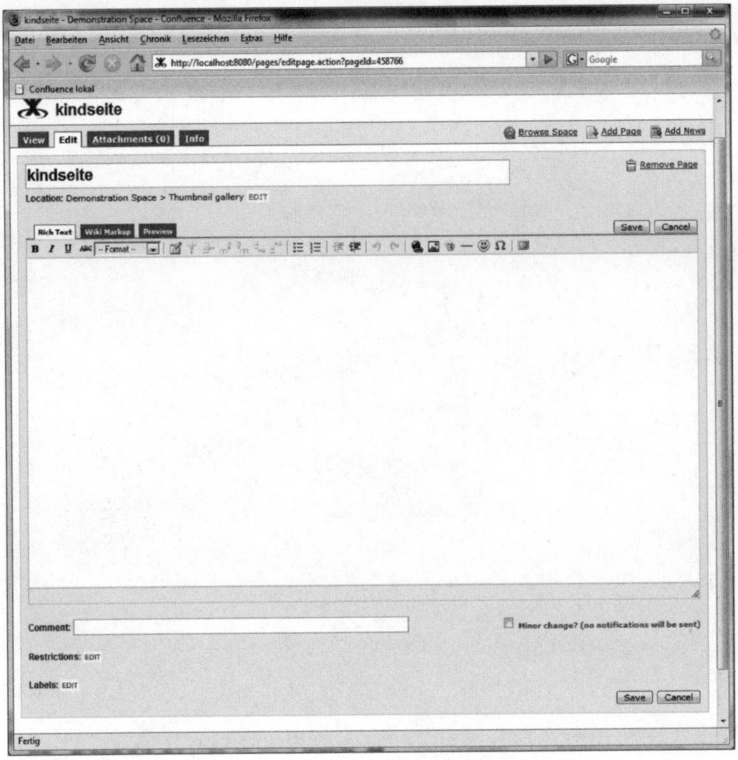
kindseite - Demonstration Space - Confluence - Mozilla Firefox
Datei Bearbeiten Ansicht Chronik Lesezeichen Extras Hilfe
http://localhost:8080/pages/editpage.action?pageId=458766
Google
Confluence lokal
kindseite
View
Edit
Attachments (0)
Info
Browse Space
Add Page
Add News
kindseite
Remove Page
Location: Demonstration Space > Thumbnail gallery EDIT
Rich Text
Wiki Markup
Preview
Save
Cancel
Comment:
Minor change? (no notifications will be sent)
Restrictions: EDIT
Labels: EDIT
Save
Cancel
Fertig

Fig. 25.11

26 Formatting

26.1 The Difference between Wiki Markup and Rich Text

Two editing options

Two editors are available with which to write wiki articles (see Fig. 26.1):

- Wiki Markup Editor
- Rich Text Editor

The Rich Text Editor is a so-called "What You See Is What You Get" (WYSIWYG) Editor that allows the majority of formats familiar from word processing programs. However, you can switch back and forth between editors at any time, and the preferred editor can be set as the default with a click of the mouse (e.g. on **Make Rich Text Default**).

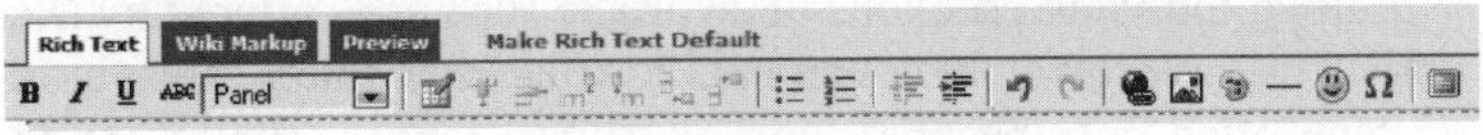

Fig. 26.1

26.1.1 Wiki Markup Editor

Using this editor, you can directly enter Confluence syntax. Macros can only really be reasonably edited here. Even if the most important formats can be learned quickly, experience has shown that the "normal" end user without an IT background prefers the Rich Text Editor.

26.1.2
Rich Text Editor (WYSIWYG)

As of Version 2.0, Confluence contains a WYSIWYG Editor that makes using it even more significantly easier. This so-called "Rich Text Editor" is comparable to the toolbox in MediaWiki, but possesses additional functions that are listed and explained in the table below.

The icons recognizable from Microsoft Word are used in this editor. Highlighted text is formatted via icons. The extent of formatting options is considerably more limited than in the Wiki Markup Editor.

Use not problem-free

There are certain bugs that are problematic:

- Text that is copied and pasted from programs such as Microsoft Word or PowerPoint is often displayed in an anomalous format.
- Frequent switching between the two editors can lead to unwanted fill characters (" ") and distorted formatting, and
- The Preview view often deviates from the Rich Text Editor view.

On the whole, the Rich Text Editor makes a more undeveloped impression. Do not underestimate this with regard to the introduction of wikis: Demands of most end users on usability are very high.

That is why it can be useful to initially teach users the most important Markup commands of the more reliable Wiki Markup Editor. This also shifts the focus to the core of wiki work: the writing and illustration of comprehensible texts that stimulate readers to comment on and further develop them.

Editing individual sections of an article such as is offered by MediaWiki is unfortunately not an option with either editor. This disadvantage often only becomes apparent when longer articles are edited: Scrolling up and down with the scroll bar within the article as well as in the browser window is cumbersome and not very ergonomic.

Advanced users wish for at least a simple syntax highlighting function in the Wiki Markup Editor that will allow formatting commands to be set apart more clearly from text and macros – especially in longer articles. The boundaries between it and HTML editors in such a case become blurred.

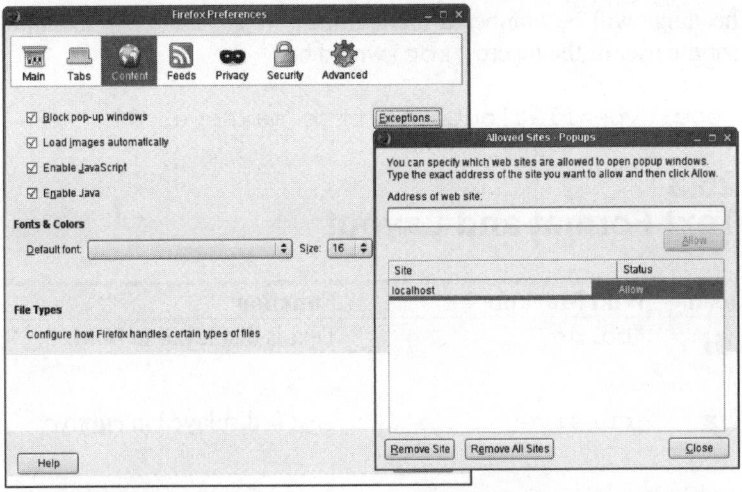

Fig. 26.2

In our example, the following exception may have to be defined in the browser for the pop-up blocker, since the Rich Text Editor works with pop-up windows. :

```
http://localhost:8080
```

URL

26.2 Headings

Confluence also conforms to the headings scheme of HTML:

Tab. 26.1

Icon	Wiki Markup	Function

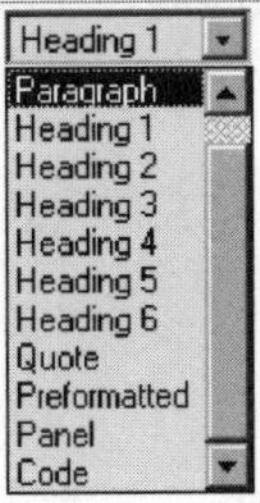	`h1. Largest heading`
	…
	`h6. Smallest heading`
	…
		Text is displayed in headings of the sizes 1 through 6.

Closely linked to the heading sizes is the macro `{toc}` ("Table of contents"), which automatically generates a table of contents. The headings are linked, and various layouts are possible: in list form or flat on a single line. If the parameter "outline" is set to "true", the headings will be numbered hierarchically (e.g. "2.1"). An example for the user of the macro {toc} would be:

Wiki
```
{toc:type=flat|outline=true|maxLevel=3}
```

26.3 Text Format and Layout

Tab. 26.2

Icon	Wiki Markup	Function
B	`*bold*`	Text is displayed in **bold**.
I	`_cursive_`	Text is displayed in *cursive*.
	`??quotation??`	Text is displayed as a *quotation*.
ABC	`-strikethrough-`	Text is crossed out.
U	`+underlined+`	Text is underlined.
	`^superscript^`	Text is displayed in ^{superscript}.
	`~subscribed~`	Text is displayed in $_{\text{subscript}}$.
	`{{Code}}`	Text as `Code`
	`bq. blockquote`	| Text as a block quote

	`{quote}`
	`Block quote of more than one paragraph`
	`{quote}`	

	`{color:red}`
	`Red text`
	`{color}`
		Determines the color of a text block.

	`(blank line)`	Starts a new paragraph.
	`\\`	Inserts a manual line break.

Tab. 26.2 (continued)

Icon	Wiki Markup	Function
—	----	Inserts a horizontal line over the entire width of the page.
	---	Inserts a dash ("–").
	--	Inserts a hyphen ("-").

As in HTML, the text color can also be entered in hexadecimal form, that is for example:

```
{color:#ff0000}
```

26.4 Links

Confluence wiki links have the following structure:

```
[linkalias|spacekey:pagetitle#anchn|linktip]
```

or

```
[linkalias|spacekey:pagetitle^att.ex|linktip
]
```

The "linkalias" is optional. It gives the link a name if desired. It can be omitted, along with the following pipe "|", which shows the link in plain text. The Spacekey is a clear shortcut within a Confluence installation. On the Dashboard, this shortcut is displayed in parentheses behind every Space name. The Spacekey can be omitted along with the colon ":" if the link leads to a wiki page within the same Space.

The "pagetitle", too, may be omitted if there is a link within a page to an anchor ("anchn") or an attachment ("att.ex"). Finally, "linktip" can also be left out. It displays a text as soon as the mouse is rolled over the link.

Before links can lead to them, anchors within a text must be marked in the desired spot in the text in the following way:

```
{anchor:anchorname}
```

Attachments, in turn, before they can be linked, must be uploaded. In links to attachments, the complete file name must be included.

The link components described can be used in all reasonable combinations – in the order stated.

For links to news messages or blog posts, the notation is as follows:

Wiki
```
[/2007/08/09/News1]
```

If "/News1" is omitted, all news messages of that day will be displayed.
You can also link directly to database IDs. These IDs are somewhat hidden for wiki pages: The links to attachments that are displayed when you roll over the corresponding document under the **Attachments** tab with the mouse always contain the ID or the corresponding page, e.g. "32787":

Wiki
```
[$32787]
```

Currently, you cannot avoid this type of link when linking to emails that are sent to a Space.

A further type of link is used for links to Confluence users:

Wiki
```
[~ttroglodyte]
```

A person symbol is placed in front of such links. The first and last names of the user are also displayed. If present, the link leads to the "Personal Space" of the user or otherwise to his or her profile page. How do you obtain the ID of a desired user? The easiest way is performing a search via the Dashboard in the **People Directory** and rolling over the corresponding name. The ID is part of the link displayed in the lower part of the browser. The same procedure can be used in those spots in which the user name is displayed: on the Dashboard, in the page history, etc.

Shortcut links can be defined at will by the Confluence administrator. Default definitions include:

URL
```
http://www.google.com/search?q=
```

with the shortcut `[@google]`. Any search terminology can be inserted in front of the "@" which is to be included when invoking a Google search.

Links to the WWW are also simply placed in square brackets, e.g.:

Wiki
```
[http://de.wikipedia.org]
```

Email links are preceded by a “mailto:”, as in, for instance:

```
[mailto:tim@troglodyte.org]
```

Wiki

This type of link is indicated in the display with the symbol of an envelope preceding it.

Finally – according to Atlassian – links can be established to local files or fileshares, albeit only via Internet Explorer:

```
[file://c:/temp/foo.txt]
```

Wiki

However, this does not as yet work with Internet Explorer 7 on Windows Vista.

All link types described can be combined with “linkalias”, “spacekey”, and “linktip”. Tab. 26.3 provides an overview of the link types mentioned.

Tab. 26.3

Icon	Wiki Markup	Function
	`[pagetitle]`	Link to a wiki page within the same Space.
	`[spacekey:]`	Link to the homepage of a Space.
	`[#anchor]`	Link to an anchor within the same wiki page
	`[^attachment.ext]`	Link to an attachment within the same wiki page.
	`[/2007/08/09]`	Link to all news messages of the day for 09 August 2007.
	`[$12345]`	Link to an internal database ID. Required for email links.
	`[~username]`	Link to the “Personal Space” or profile page of the respective user.
	`[searchterm@google]`	Link to a shortcut defined by the Confluence Administrator.
	`[http://web.de]`	Link to the WWW

Tab. 26.3 (continued)

Icon	Wiki Markup	Function
	`[mailto: tim @troglodyte.org]`	Link to an email address – leads to the starting of the mail program
	`[file://c:/foo.txt]`	Link to local files or fileshares. Does not work with all operating systems or browser versions.

26.5 Lists

Numbered or bulleted lists are possible. Indentation is done according to the number of times the symbols are used in sequence (e.g. "#", "##", "###"). Bullets and numbers can also be combined, such that, for instance, under "2." there is a bulleted list and no more numbers (e.g. "#*").

The main complaint users have about this function is that it is not possible to generate a blank line between the individual points or subpoints, nor is it possible to achieve nested numbers (e.g. "2.1"). Such output can only be generated using the `{toc}` macro (see Chap. 26.2).

Tab. 26.4

Icon	Wiki Markup	Function
	`* Point A`	Bullet point (hash mark)
	`- Point B`	Bullet point (square)
	`# Point 1`	Numbered point

26.6 Inserting Images

Images, or more precisely, GIF, PNG and JPG files, can be embedded from any website. You can upload them as attachments and integrate them from any wiki page, including into news entries.

One popular option is the embedding of an image as a thumbnail[21]. Especially in the case of large images, the text is thus not torn

[21] A thumbnail is a miniaturized display of an image. It is linked to the image in its original size.

apart too much, and clicking on a thumbnail leads to the display of the image in its original size.

Alignment and vertical and horizontal spacing can also be included as parameters.

One useful macro in this regard is called `{gallery}`.

This macro enables all attached images to be displayed in a defined number of columns, and you can also click through them in their original sizes as a slideshow, e.g.:

```
{gallery:columns=3|title=Gallery}
```

Wiki

Tab. 26.5 shows an overview of the options described for integrating images.

Tab. 26.5

Icon	Wiki Markup	Function
	`!http://www.server.com/image.gif!`	Embeds an image from the WWW.
	`!image.png!`	Embeds an image that had previously been uploaded as an attachment to the current wiki page.
	`!space-key:pagetitle^image.jpg!`	Embeds an image from any wiki page.
	`!/2007/08/09/News1^image.gif!`	Embeds an image from a news article.
	`!image.gif | thumbnail!`	Embeds an image as a thumbnail.
	`!bild.gif|align=right, vspace=4!`	Embeds an image, aligns it and provides spacing.
	`{gallery}`	Embeds the images attached to the current wiki page in gallery form.

26.7 Inserting Tables

Tables can only be inserted in a very rudimentary form. For instance, it is not possible to combine cells, insert vertical text, or do any sorting, to name a few. On the other hand, the notation is very easy. The header, whose cell beginnings and ends are each marked with "||", is automatically displayed in bold and given a light gray background. The column width adjusts to the longest text line, and line breaks ("\ \") are possible.

Lines and columns can easily be inserted or deleted in the Rich Text Editor using a series of icons.

We should briefly explain how a wiki page is divided into various columns. Columns can be defined for individual so-called "sections" independently of one another. The column widths are indicated in percents. The content is not automatically distributed among the columns, but explicitly allocated to columns. If necessary, boundary lines can be displayed. Here is a simple example:

Wiki

```
{section}

{column:width=30%}
Text for Column1
{column}

{column:width=70%}
Text for Column2
{column}

{section}
```

The primary difference from normal tables is that the column width is explicitly predefined, and there are no lines per se.

Tab. 26.6 lists a summary of the notation for tables including the corresponding Rich Text symbols.

Tab. 26.6

Icon	Wiki Markup	Function
	`||Co1||Co2||` `|Cell11|Cell12|`	Insert a table with highlighted header, content line and two columns
		Delete column
		Delete line
		Insert column after
		Insert column before

Tab. 26.6 (continued)

Icon	Wiki Markup	Function
		Insert line after
		Insert line before

26.8 Miscellaneous

There are several other formatting options, especially the simple insertion of text boxes, e.g.

Wiki

```
{warning:title=Warning}
Warning
{warning}
```

or the display of certain content, e.g.

Wiki

```
{userlister:online=true}
```

The use of these formatting options is comparable to the others mentioned with regard to ease of use, and is also described in the "Notation Guide" linked in the Wiki Markup Editor. Finally, Tab. 26.7 lists the remaining icons of the Rich Text Editor.

Tab. 26.7

Icon	Wiki Markup	Function
		Indentation
		Cancel indentation
		Undo last step
		Restore last step
	:)	Inserts one of 21 possible symbols; here, for instance, a smiley

Tab. 26.7 (continued)

Icon	Wiki Markup	Function
	∑	Inserts one of 198 possible special symbols, here, for instance, "∑"
		Switches between normal and full-screen mode

26.9 HTML Input

Avoid direct HTML input when possible

Using the `{html}`macro, the HTML Code can be "locked in" within wiki articles and displayed accordingly. Thus, for example, small calculations spanning more than one input field can be achieved with JavaScript.

You should carefully consider whether or not you really want to offer this macro. The boundary to a Content Management System for the intranet, which we assume is also present, would be further weakened: Those who are already used to HTML might primarily enter HTML instead of utilizing the Confluence options; the display of tables, for instance, can vary greatly.

However, on the other hand, it is advisable to define which stable and "official" content and which content that is complex in layout will still be used with the existing intranet and the corresponding editors – and what dynamic content could migrate to wiki pages and be accordingly linked to the intranet.

27 Organization

27.1 Browse Space – Navigation

The link **Browse Space** leads to the central Confluence navigation, which takes place on the following eight levels:

- **Pages**
- **Labels**
- **Attachments**
- **Mail**
- **News**
- **Activity**
- **Advanced** and
- **Space Admin**

and which will be explained in more detail in the following sub-chapters.

27.1.1 Pages

Experience has shown that the navigation system, especially in commercial wikis like Confluence, is of extreme significance. Therefore, Confluence has three standard navigation options:

- List of recent updates (**Recently Updated**) for the corresponding Space. Up to 30 versions are listed here along with author, date and content type (e.g. page, comment, attachment, etc.) in chronological order – similar to the Dashboard across all Spaces.

Fig. 27.1

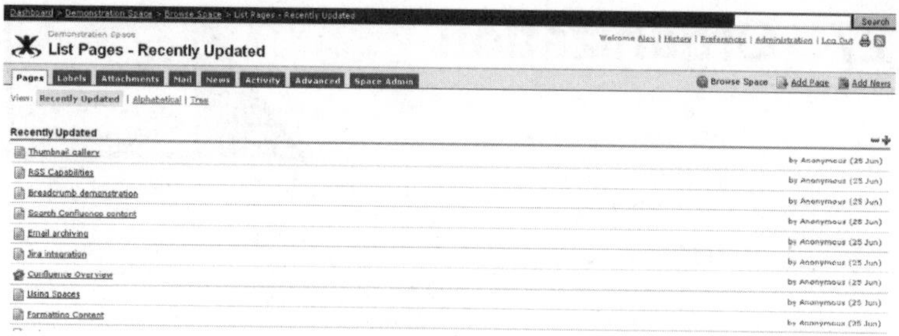

- Alphabetical sorting according to page names (**Alphabetical**). You can click any letter of the alphabet, appearing in a long row, and access the corresponding page. This type of navigation has two shortcomings. Firstly, pages beginning with numbers or foreign diacritical marks do not appear in the list – and especially numbers are important to the sorting of child pages. Secondly, it is simply not apparent which letters harbor pages behind them and which do not (e.g. by shading them gray).

Fig. 27.2

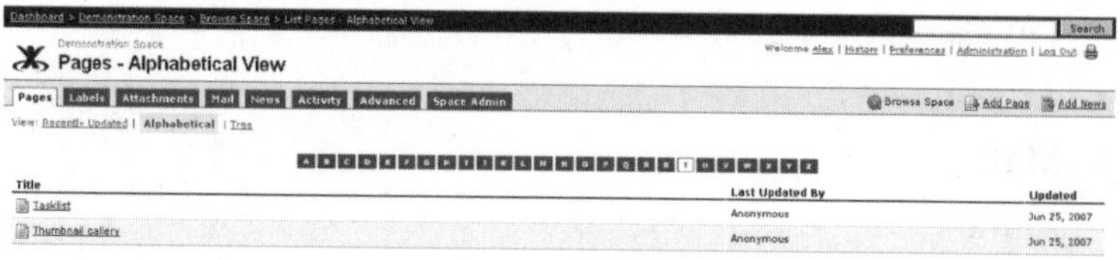

- Tree (**Tree**). Confluence places the pages in a hierarchical structure. Each page has one parent and any number of child pages. However, pages can also be saved on the root level (**Home**), (so-called "orphaned pages").
  This type of structuring and navigation is generally well received. Pages can be reassigned – along with their child pages – at will. This does not affect the linking within the wiki (see Chap. 27.6).
  This poses the disadvantage that the navigation becomes more complicated if there are very many pages and levels of hierarchy. Unfortunately, an open tree is not buffered when you click on a page. If you go back using the corresponding browser button, the tree is closed again. The only way to get around this is to open a new window with the right mouse button.

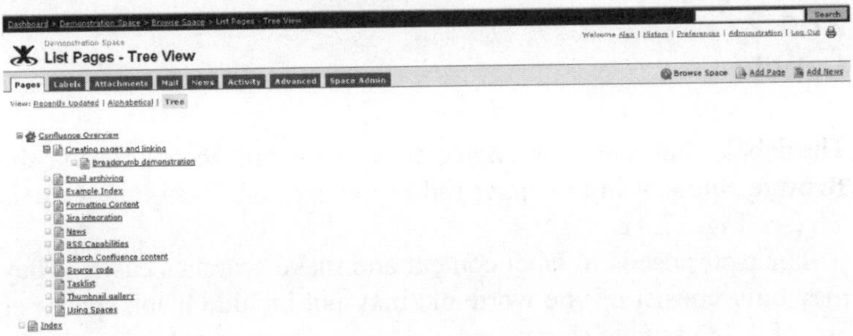

Fig. 27.3

In addition – in the broader sense – the following navigational tasks can be performed:

- Marking **Favorites** for quick access
- **Full-text search** that can be configured according to various criteria
- Via a macro (**Scrollbar**), a scrollbar can be integrated into the display. It accesses the current tree structure and establishes links to the previous and subsequent sibling pages and the parent page. In this case, the page sorting is decisive in the tree view: If you do not wish to navigate alphabetically, you must work with preceding numbers (starting with "01" if there are more than 10 pages, etc.). The integration of this popular macro, however, has not been without its problems with regard to performance and stability.
- Labels (**Labels**) can be assigned to any page (see also Chap. 27.1.2), with which you can navigate through the Space. The efficiency of this method of navigation depends, of course, on a consistent employment of the labels.

Atlassian has come up with a few good ideas for navigation. Yet many end users still feel disoriented, perhaps because there are too many options.

Navigation as a fundamental problem

The navigation and orientation problem – especially in such dynamic hypertext bases as in a wiki – is a general one, and can currently only be solved through a number of links and overview pages. Each author should be aware that various readers' interests will be guided by diverse perspectives and that links should be placed along these assorted paths.

27.1.2 Labels

Labels as a starting point for a "Semantic Wiki"

The labels that can be assigned to a space are accessible via the **Browse Space** – in the upper right of every page – and the **Labels** tab (see Fig. 27.4).

Their purpose is to label content and make searches easier. They may only consist of one word and may not include blank spaces or any of the following characters:

```
: ; , .  ? & [ ] ( ) # ^ * @ !
```

Labels can be assigned on the personal, group and Space levels. The administrator can assign or remove these Space labels to all pages in an overview or assign the attribute "sticky". Sticky labels are then handed down to all child pages.

As you can see in Fig. 27.4, you can display the labels in alphabetical order or as a so-called "tag cloud". In a tag cloud, too, labels are ordered alphabetically in lines. However, the size of the font varies according to the frequency of the corresponding term: The more often a term is used as a label, the larger the word is written. In Fig. 27.4, "wiki" was used the most frequently; the **popularity** of that word is thus the highest in that Space. To the right, this popularity ranking appears again in the form of a list, and above it, a list of recently used labels.

The labels have active links in the lists and the tag cloud. If they are clicked, the user sees a list of pages that use the corresponding label. Furthermore, **related labels**, or labels assigned along with the searched label, are also displayed.

Fig. 27.4

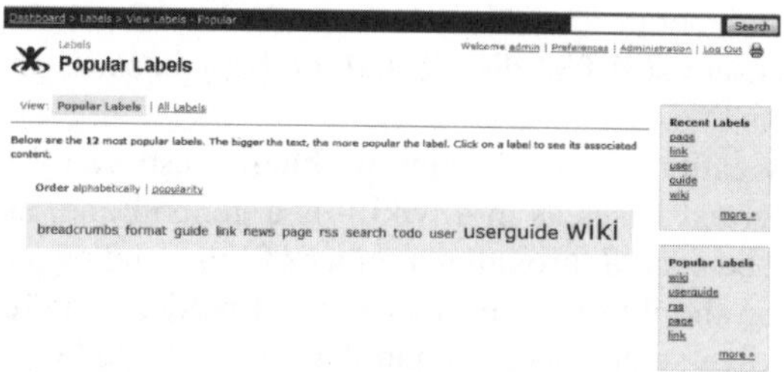

One problem with regard to labels is certainly their consistency, especially in relation to synonyms and abbreviations and the like – and particularly for multilingual users. Nevertheless, labels are an initial step toward a "Semantic Wiki".

Problematic: the consistent assignment of labels

27.1.3 Attachments

All attachments of a Space can be displayed via **Browse Space** and the **Attachments** tab. Filtering according to file extension is possible, and sorting can be done according to name, size, author, or **Creator** (in this case the person who has added the attachment), date and respective page (see Fig. 27.5).

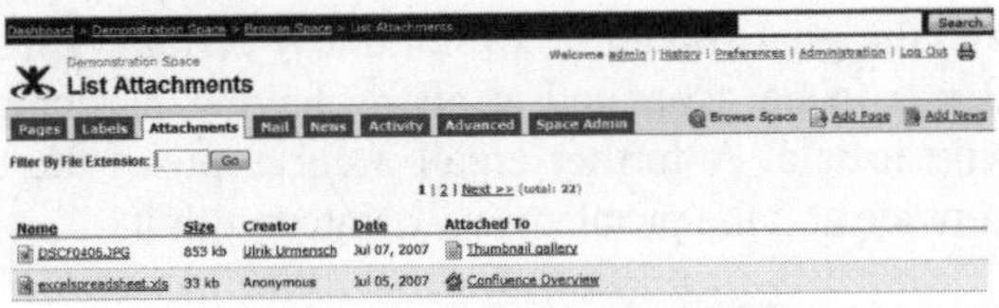

Fig. 27.5

Frequently used attachments should only be uploaded once whenever possible, and the pages using the attachment or image should link to that image. Unfortunately, this only works directly in Wiki Markup with the following sample command for images:

Use storage space sparingly

```
!ImageCollectionPage^favoritepicture.jpg!
```

And for links to existing attachments:

```
[AttachmentCollection-
Page^favattachment.pdf!]
```

Of course, you must keep in mind that the corresponding attachments can only be maintained centrally from a single page. Updates immediately affect all pages linking to the corresponding attachment.

So in what sort of scenarios would such a procedure – albeit complicated and one on which all authors must agree – be useful? Well, for starters, it could be employed for documentation that uses the same icon for reasons of consistency, such as a small light bulb that marks a tip. In addition, it could be used in connection with

Consistency, administration, data volume

templates, to identify various page types – e.g. documentation, glossaries, and the like – having a uniform set of various symbols.

27.1.4 Email

Interface to the email medium

Even if it sounds tempting to use this route to quickly shovel content into Confluence: You should use the email function wisely, if only for organizational reasons. The actual wiki work lies in the preparation of content, e.g. as in a summary of a lengthy email exchange. If all mail lands in the wiki on a 1:1 ratio, you will have to deal with the same problems there as with a mail client.

Media selection and migration

The problem of media selection – in this case: When do I use email and when do use a wiki article – surfaces here as well. When this happens, the goal should be to not allow certain types of email correspondence to be generated at all by having participants work within a wiki article. A further email archive poses the danger of saving data twice and the problems associated with it.

Fig. 27.6

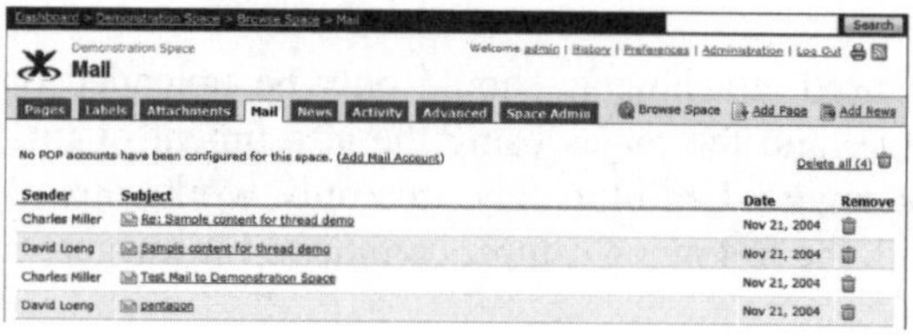

27.1.5 News

Blog as a wiki component

In Confluence, **News** designates a sort of blog. You can click on **Add News** from any page. News basically refers to full-fledged wiki articles, whose authors and date of creation are highlighted in the first or last lines. Comments are also possible. The entries are sorted in reverse chronological order, and a calendar is offered for searches through which users can page.

Thus, the location where the news is stored is predefined and cannot be changed. Also, restrictions cannot be set: Individual users or groups can either generate or delete news – or not. The actual news can then be edited by any participant.

This function is ideal for separating organizational from content-based information – in the form of a regular wiki article. Here, you have the chance of diverting a certain volume of pure email traffic that serves only informational purposes. Still, you should not fool yourself about the powerful position of the established medium of email: Email systems rule with regard to disseminating asynchronous information – and getting used to blogs or News functions instead is a long-term process.

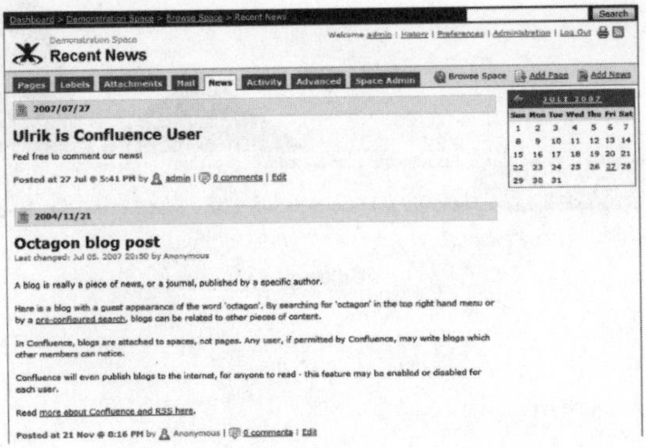

Fig. 27.7

The News example illustrates quite well the degree of complexity – from the standpoint of the user – that can be generated through the "simple" medium of the "wiki". Previously, users could disseminate information via email (CC list), telephone (conferences), the intranet homepage or meetings or conversations.

Now they also have the option of writing a wiki article and/or additionally sending that email to Confluence and/or publishing a News piece. The question as to whether every member of the target group expects the corresponding information along a particular route is of vital importance.

27.1.6 Activity

The tab **Activity**, which is accessible from any page via **Browse Space**, provides information in the form of a bar chart regarding writing and reading access within a Space or – for admins – beyond the boundaries of a Space (see Fig. 27.8).

Fig. 27.8

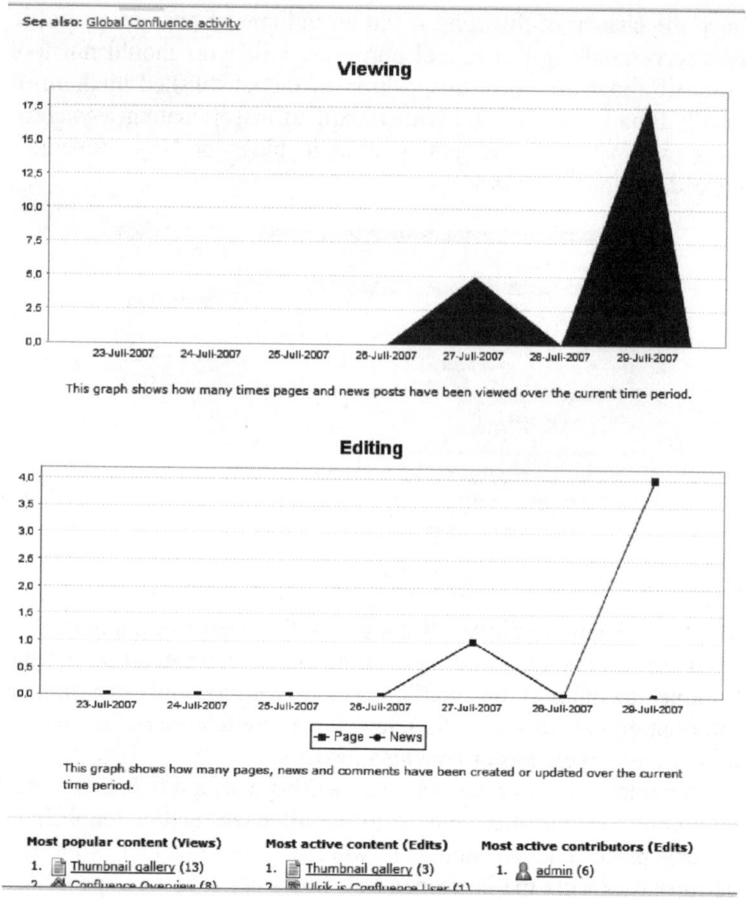

Wiki monitoring, privacy and acceptance

Additionally, three rankings are displayed: the most popular content (views), the most active content (edits) and the most active participants (number of edits).

These ranking displays can be generated in daily, weekly or monthly views. To date, export functions or extended, freely configurable statistics functions are not available. The interpretation is certainly difficult; nevertheless, it represents an initial step toward wiki monitoring or controlling. Whether or not a list of the most active participants serves to motivate or demotivate employees most likely depends on the company and its culture – and perhaps also on the benevolence of the workers' council.

Despite all of the positive transparency a wiki can bring to cooperative work, data protection is always viewed with a critical eye. In moderation, employed publicly, wiki monitoring may well stimulate motivation for working with a wiki and thus its acceptance (like a "Wiki Employee of the Month"); but in an environment steeped in

Orwellian antipathy toward privacy, motivation is no longer a buzzword.

27.1.7 Advanced

The **Advanced** tab can be accessed from any page via **Browse Space**. The informational and organizational options offered to users – depending on their respective authorization profiles – are divided into the following areas:

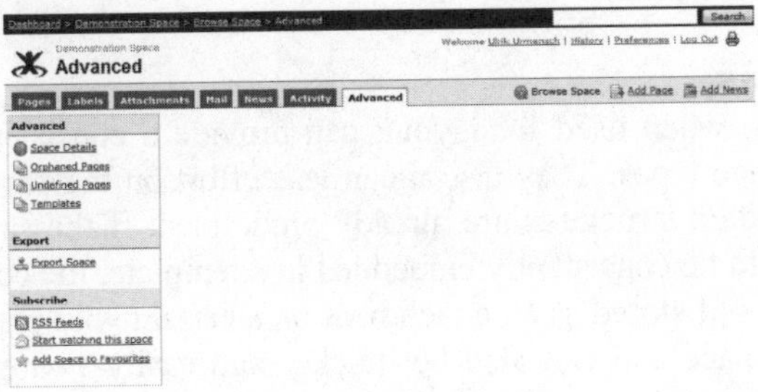

Fig. 27.9

Multi-space organization options

- Under the rather inappropriate term "Advanced" – the same name given to the tab – details on the current Space are listed:
- **Space Details**: name, (explicit) shortcut ("key"), the Homepage set up, creator with date, Space and Team labels, as well as a description.
  This refers to **Orphaned Pages**, meaning pages that have no parent page. They appear on the same level as the Homepage and have not yet been ordered according to theme. A page can become orphaned if the parent page is deleted in the edit area under **Edit Location** or if a page having children receives a new **Location** – thus moved in the **Tree** with the checkbox **move children** not having been marked.
- **Undefined Pages** – as is conventional in other wiki engines – has been planned but not yet realized. If, in Wiki Markup, you enter a link to a page in square brackets that does not yet exist, the corresponding link (alias) appears in red by default and marked with a small, superscript green cross at the end. The reader immediately sees that further work can be done here. In the list of Undefined Pages, the respective parent pages are also noted.

- **Templates** are prestructured pages designed to help with layout for authors entering routine elements, thus achieving a uniform look of various page types.
- **Export**: Each Space can be exported in different data formats, either completely or partially (see below). Thus, you can generate an offline version or swap Wiki Spaces between various Confluence installations.
- **Subscribe:** Here, users can subscribe to RSS feeds, watch the entire Space (i.e. receive emails announcing page edits or comments) or enter it as a favorite: the Space then appears on the Dashboard under the **My** tab.

Templates

Templates, when used for layout, can provide a consistent look in various page types. They also mean less effort on the part of users, since standard structures are already predefined. If the same image or icon is to be consistently embedded in a template, the corresponding image – if stored as an attachment on a certain wiki page – saves memory space and can also be quickly and easily swapped on all relevant pages.

Templates in Confluence terminology are thus completely different from those in, say, MediaWiki. Templates in Confluence are aids, but they cannot force input. Users can either partially or completely delete or alter the prescribed structure in a template – thus they have a certain amount of flexibility which, however, can also lead to inconsistencies.

Whenever users generate a new page using **Add Page**, they have the opportunity to select a template for that new page via the link **Select a page template** beneath the page title and location.

Fig. 27.10

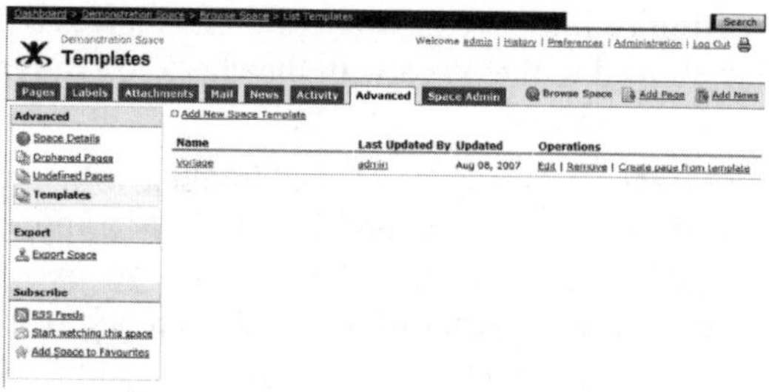

Export Space

A Space can be completely or partially exported in the formats HTML, PDF and XML. For this, you have the option of individually selecting a page to be exported and adding comments and attachments if desired. Attachments can only be honored in an XML export. So what purpose do the various export formats have?

- **HTML**: Ideal when you must or want to present your wiki Space offline. The links are present, but not all macros and plugins used can be emulated.
- **PDF**: This format is advisable if the space is to be printed, as in book form. As we have mentioned, this type of output still has a few drawbacks: Not all formats are converted, and if there are large images or tables, there may be display problems.
- **XML**: The only format that allows the loss-free export of a Space, including all attachments. It is used to migrate a wiki Space to another Confluence installation or version – with the additional help of the **Import** function.

HTML and XML exports are prepared as Zip files. Depending on the size of the Space, the generation of the export file may take a while.

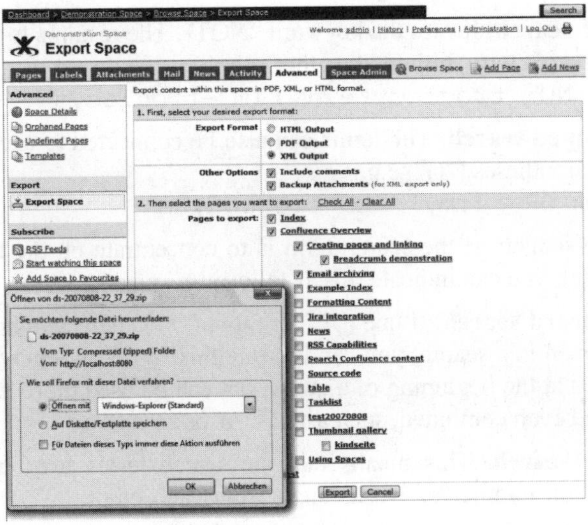

Fig. 27.11

27.1.8 Space Admin

The Space admin can undertake certain settings in this tab. Details on these tasks are described in Chap. 26.1.

27.2 Full-text Search

Confluence search terms

The full-text search using the text box in the upper right (Search) offers a variety of options after the initial search query has been sent. Let us first have a detailed look at the search syntax:

- **Exact search**. In this search, text is contained in quotation marks, e.g.: `"tim is a troglodyte"`
- **OR search**. This search uses the keyword "OR". The search result should include one of the two terms queried, e.g.:
  `tim OR troglodyte`
- **AND search**. It uses the keyword "AND". The result is to include both terms, e.g.:
  `tim AND troglodyte`
- **NOT search**. It uses the keyword "NOT". The result is to include one search term, but not the other, e.g.:
  `tim NOT troglodyte` or `tim -troglodyte`
- **Grouped search**. The terms can also be connected to each other via parentheses ("()"),e.g.:
  `(tim OR tammy) AND troglodyte`
- **Title search**. If the search term is to concentrate on the title (of a page), you can indicate this as follows: `title:tim`
- **Wildcard search**. If one ("?") or more ("*") characters are to be left open in a search, you can indicate this. Wildcards may not be placed at the beginning of a query, but can be used more than once and even combined, such as in: `t?m` or `troglo*`
- **Near search**. This means that the search terms may only be a certain number of words apart from each other. "0" as a distance indication is not possible. For instance:
  `"tim troglodyte"~2` may return:
  `"tim is a troglodyte"`

- **Range search**. Searches for terms falling alphabetically between the two named terms, such as: `[tim to troglodyte] would find "torchlight"`, for instance
- **Fuzzy search**. This search finds similarly written words, e.g.: `"troglodite~"` would also return `"troglodyte"`
- **Combined search**. All named searches can also be combined with one another, such as in: `ti* AND troglodyte~ AND ("wiki" AND "confluence")`

The search results can be limited even further, according to:

- the Space in which it is to appear (**Location**)
- the type it should be:
  - **All Content**
  - **All Content (No Mail)**
  - **Pages**
  - **News Items**
  - **Mail**
  - **Comments**
  - **Attachments**
  - **Profiles**
  - **Space Descriptions**
- the time period in which it was modified
  - **Today**
  - **Yesterday**
  - **Last Week**
  - **Last Month**

Finally, it is also possible to group the search results according to **Type** or **Space**. Even if, for example, the search for **Profiles** has not as of yet functioned flawlessly, the search function as a whole is quite powerful. Fig. Abb. 27.12 illustrates the search function.

Labels are taken into consideration for searches. Pages labeled accordingly appear further up in the result list, and links to labels related to the search term are offered. After these links are accessed, all correspondingly labeled pages are shown.

Fig. 27.12

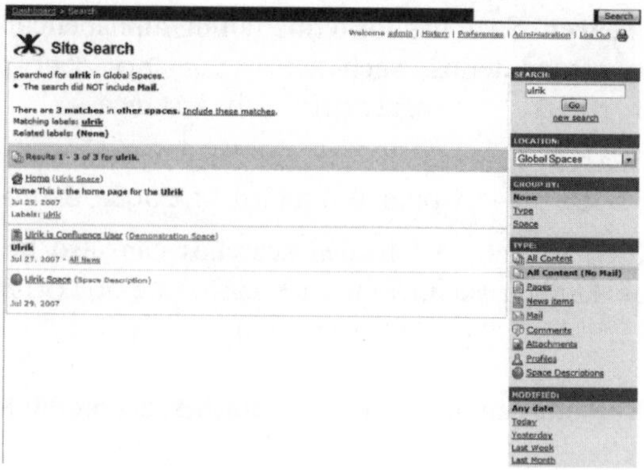

27.3 Permissions Concept

The permissions concept used by Confluence consists of three levels:

- **Confluence Admin (Global Permissions)**: In this role, tasks may be performed that affect the entire Confluence installation. This includes the areas **Configuration**, **Look and Feel**, **Administration** and **Security**. You can find details on these in Chap. 28.2. Here, permissions for the standard groups Confluence users and Confluence administrators are regulated. This part of Confluence can be invoked via **Administration** in the user area.
- **Space Admin (Space Permissions)**: This level – set by default as a member of the Confluence administrators group – controls the following task areas related to a space: **Space Operations**, **Security**, **Mail**, **Look and Feel** and **Import**. They are described in detail in Chap. 28.1. On this level, the basic Edit and View Restrictions are assigned for the corresponding Space (see Chap. 28.1.2). This part of Confluence can be opened via **Browse Space** and the tab **Space Admin**.
- **Space User (Page Restrictions)**: In this role, access rights for individual pages can be limited even further. However, it is not possible to expand the dominating Space permissions (see Chap. 27.3.2).

27.3.1 Global Permissions

On this level, users and groups are set up whom the Space admin – one level lower – can grant permissions for his Space. If you would like a task to be decentralized, you must use the "Custom Space User Management Plugin".[22] To the right of the **Space Admin** tab, the **Manage Users** tab then appears, and the Space admin can set up new users and allocate groups.

There are five permissions that can be granted to groups:

- **Can use**: necessary in order to be able to register in Confluence.
- **Attach Files to User Profiles**: This permission in Confluence 2.5.1 is a relict from a time when there were not yet any personal spaces. It is still present, but has no function.
- **Personal Space**: When this option is activated, every group member has the possibility to set up his or her own Space – sort of like a homepage within Confluence. The start page of the personal space is accessible via the links with the user names that are automatically "left behind" due to edits. Especially companies will find it useful to give users the opportunity to post the current profiles of the firm's expertise.
- **Create Space(s)**: Members of these groups can set up wiki Spaces and thus automatically become the Space admin for those Spaces.
- **Administrate Confluence**: This permission provides access to the administrator console of the Confluence installation, described in Chap. 28.2.

You should generally try to administer users in groups, but there is also the option of giving individual users permissions, and anonymous access can also be granted. Especially the last point is very interesting for companies: Should an employee be given the right to also write and comment on articles anonymously as well? Experience has shown that, when evaluating an article, it helps to know the name of the authors.

Another point that is important for user and group management is that – for historical reasons – once users are set up, they can no longer be deleted if they have "immortalized" themselves by serving as an author in any way. Users can only be deactivated by being

[22] http://confluence.atlassian.com/display/CONFEXT/Custom+Space+User+Management+Plugin

Fig. 27.13

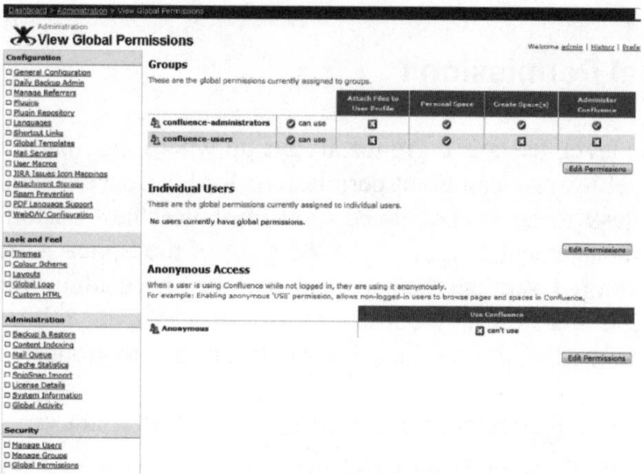

deleted from all groups to which they are allocated and being denied all "can use" rights as individual users as well.

27.3.2 Space Permissions

Conceptual Issues

Permissions administration

A key Confluence function for companies is the possibility of utilizing a permissions administration system. Wiki Spaces can thus exhibit various view and edit rights for individual users or user groups. Especially in larger companies, information is not necessarily accessible to every employee, and it is here where using a wiki is advantageous if not just anyone is to be able to view or edit the wiki pages.

The use of this function is a good indicator of whether or not the wiki has been optimally adapted for the company. A large number of pages with limited viewing or editing access – often in combination with rigid content – is a sign that the wiki is being used for purposes other than those for which it is intended. Such content would be better placed in a Web Content Management System.

Especially in a corporate environment, you should always remember that the success of wikis and the quality of the articles cannot generally be achieved through extensive restrictions, but rather, with a maximum of transparency and contribution.

Only an administrator can set up users and groups for the entire Confluence installation. Cascading groups are not possible. User authentication can be delegated to an LDAP.

Practical Procedure

Via **Browse Space**, the tab **Space Admin** and link **Permissions** in the **Security** area, you can access the following area (see Fig. 27.14):

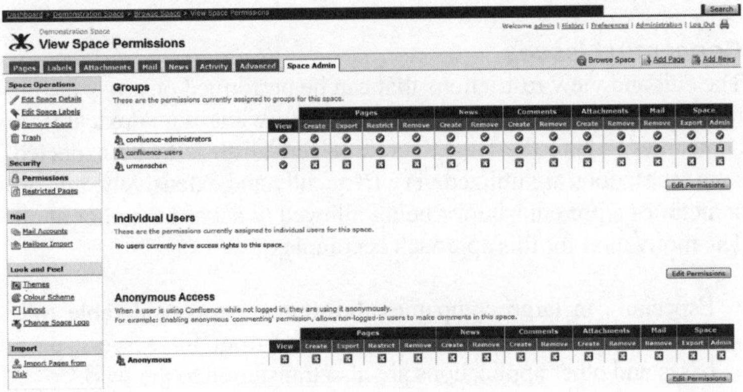

Abb. 27.14

As in the Global Permissions realm, this area is divided into **Groups**, **Individual Users** and **Anonymous Access**. These three groups of users – as long as they were set up at a higher level or granted permission as anonymous users ("can use") – can now be allocated fine-tuned permissions for viewing, editing and restriction rights for Pages, News, Comments, Attachments, Mail and Space:

- **View** refers to reading rights, which, along with
- writing rights (**Create**), can be further restricted at the page level (see Chap. 27.3.3) (**Restrict**).
- **Export** means that the complete Space or individual pages thereof may be exported in the formats HTML, XML or PDF (see Chap. 27.1.7)
- **Remove** means the deletion of content. Here, it is important that the Space admin can currently only undo deleted pages and news. Comments, Attachments, Mails and the Space as a whole are irrevocably deleted when the user clicks on **Remove** – even if users are asked again first whether they really want to perform a delete. This content may still be present in backups, but it cannot be

Deleting can be irrevocable

recovered on an ad-hoc basis like the pages or news in the wastebasket of the Space admin.

- The Space permission **Admin** should only be left to the Space Admin Group (Confluence administrators by default).

27.3.3 Page Restrictions

Conceptual Issues

Use caution in restricting edit and view permissions

The edit and view restrictions that can be performed on any page are both a blessing and a curse for corporate wikis. Paradoxically, in companies, where the least degree of vandalism is to be expected, such restrictions are utilized very frequently and extensively, and are sometimes a prerequisite for being allowed to act as an author at all. The motivation for this approach is complex:

- Especially in large companies, **habit** plays a considerable role, and thus, permission structures familiar from file servers, databases and other applications are also transferred to the wiki.
- **Confidentiality**: a good deal of information is not intended for every employee, especially in larger firms.
- **Verification**. Content intended for the intranet is often closely inspected and approved before it is permitted to be published. You can generally count on that information being valid and, for instance, representing the official standpoint of the company toward customers. This, of course, is not possible in a wiki. However, since a wiki is part of the intranet, it is hard for many to identify the boundaries. In addition, the verified information on the intranet is often more desirable than the consistently tentative data in a wiki.

One possible way to deal with this situation is to initially open wiki Spaces only for individual departments or projects. With time, verified information can then be shifted to the public Spaces.

Nevertheless, especially in companies, for which Confluence was conceived, it is vital to sensitize people to the fact that the high quality of the articles in the wiki cannot be achieved through compartmentalization, but rather through the largest possible degree of contribution and transparency. The more time is spent on administering a complex permissions structure, the slower the actual wiki work becomes.

Practical Procedure

In order to limit restrictions for a page, go to the **Edit** tab and click on the end of the page. Behind **Restrictions**, you will find the link **EDIT**, which opens a display similar to the following:

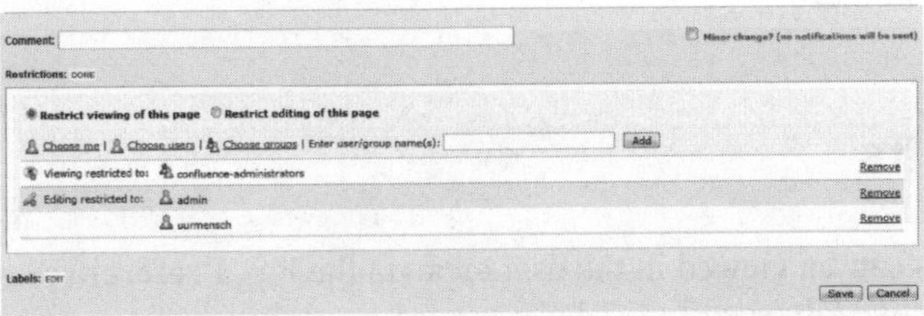

Fig. 27.15

Read permission is handed down, edit permission is not

In the meanwhile, more than a single user or a single group can receive edit and view rights – this was not possible in previous Confluence versions. Especially in cases where small groups work together on the publishing of an article, this is a key feature – particularly in companies.

It is important to note that read permissions are handed down to child pages – but not edit permissions. This is primarily based on the idea that overview pages should only be edited by a limited number of users, in order to ensure a certain degree of stability in the orientation – while the child pages, on the other hand, should be more dynamic and invite participation.

27.4 Notifications

Interface to the email medium

Notifications regarding edits to wiki pages, for instance, via email – already briefly mentioned in Chap. 25.3.2 under "Watches", can easily be switched on and off by clicking the envelope on a page. There is close integration with the medium of email in that realm – otherwise, connections only exist via the "Tiny Link" (Chap. 27.6) and mail links:

Wiki

```
[mailto:user@mail.com]
```

Consciously controlling notification emails

Another benefit of notifications is that sending them can be disabled from case to case by authors. After an edit, an author can check the **Minor Change** box in Edit mode at the end of a page and thus – if only minimal changes were made – prevent an email from being sent to a potentially sizeable number of recipients. Thus, this little

Fig. 27.16

click can have large-scale results, so users should be aware of it right from the start.

27.5 Drafts

Conscious control of versioning

Drafts can be viewed in the user area via the link **Preferences** of the respective tab (see Fig. 27.18).

Drafts are automatically buffered every 30 seconds – an interval that the Confluence Administrator can set. Since this buffering is done for an unlimited time period, the author can consciously control the versioning of his or her page.

However, in practical situations, there is not much trust in this mechanism, possibly due to bad experiences with test systems, and due to the fact that – to put it bluntly – often enough, edits are saved after every altered comma.

This can become a problem if more than one user is working on drafts of a specific page at the same time and they must be synchronized at some point. Of course, this is not problematic for pages that are regularly edited by only one author who has exclusive editing rights.

In addition to the title of a page, its last save date is displayed and links are offered to continue editing (**Resume editing**) or delete the modifications (**Delete**).

Fig. 27.17

A version of this page you were editing at Jul 29, 2007 20:25 was not saved. Do you want to resume editing or discard it?

Fig. 27.18

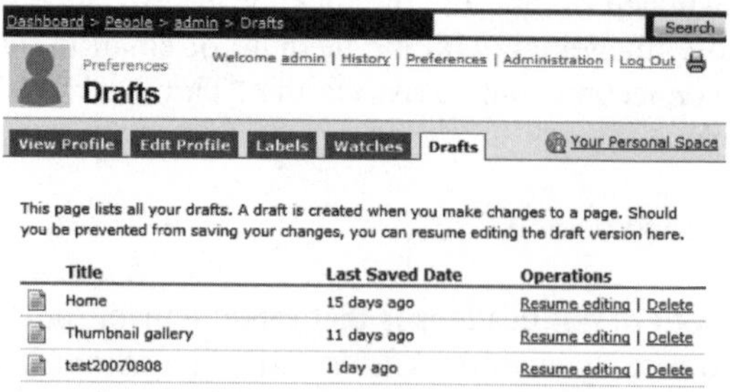

Dashboard > People > admin > Drafts

Your Personal Space
This page lists all your drafts. A draft is created when you make changes to a page. Should you be prevented from saving your changes, you can resume editing the draft version here.

15 days ago

11 days ago

test20070808

The user is also made aware of his draft when he opens the corresponding page in the Edit mode (see Fig. 27.17). Here, too, he has the option of continuing to edit the page (**resume editing**) or discarding modifications that have not yet been saved (**discard**). As mentioned, other users do not even notice drafts from other authors.

27.6 Tiny Links

"Marketing" the wiki in the organization via email

URL

Tiny links are very practical and situated on every page in the **Info** tab. They are automatically generated, and can look something like this:

`http://wiki.intranet/x/Bo`

Interface to the email medium

This type of link conserves link length space and reduces the danger that the link will be broken into parts by mistake during further processing. It also represents the explicit ID of a page that it will retain throughout its life cycle. Even if the article is allocated to another parent page and receives a new name, the link on the wiki page will not die until the corresponding page is actually deleted.

28 Settings

28.1 Space Admin

Space and Confluence Admin

Via **Browse Space** and the tab **Space Admin**, the space admin has the following modification options:

- **Space Operations**: **Edit Space Details** offers the possibility of entering name, description and homepage of a space. It can also convert the space to a Personal Space for any user.
- Under **Edit Space Labels**, labels for the Space or for individual teams can be predefined.
- **Remove Space** deletes the Space irrevocably after the user is asked to confirm the deletion.
- All articles and news entries land in the **Trash** when they are deleted by users (see Chap. 28.1.1).
- **Security**: In this area, the various permissions can be set for the Space level (see Chap. 27.3.2) and the Restricted Pages can be viewed (see Chap. 28.1.2).
- **Mail**: Mail accounts can be set up and mailboxes imported here (see Chap. 27.1.4).
- **Look and Feel**: In this area, you can choose between an initial count of three basic designs: a horizontal navigation (standard), vertical navigation or a simple navigation inspired by Flickr.
- **Import**: This allows you to upload text files from any directory into Confluence. The file name becomes the page's title – if desired, the file extension is cut off – and the file content becomes the page content. You can also choose whether existing pages having the same name can be overwritten. The directory must be entered by hand and, at least in Version 2.5.1, the Import function did not work.

28.1.1 Wastebasket Restore

Only pages and news can be recovered

Only in the wastebasket can pages and news – which are differentiated via the icon – be irrevocably deleted. This unfortunately does not apply to comments, attachments, mails and the Space as a whole. Once they are deleted, not even the Space admin can recover them. That is why you should carefully consider whether or not you want users in the initial stages of Confluence implication to have deleting rights for comments and attachments.

You can completely empty the entire wastebasket irrevocably (**Purge All**) or delete individual pages (**Purge**). Content can be restored using the respective link (**Restore**). If a user follows a link to a deleted page, he or she is informed that the Space admin can restore the page. The Space admin also immediately receives the Restore link.

Fig. 28.1

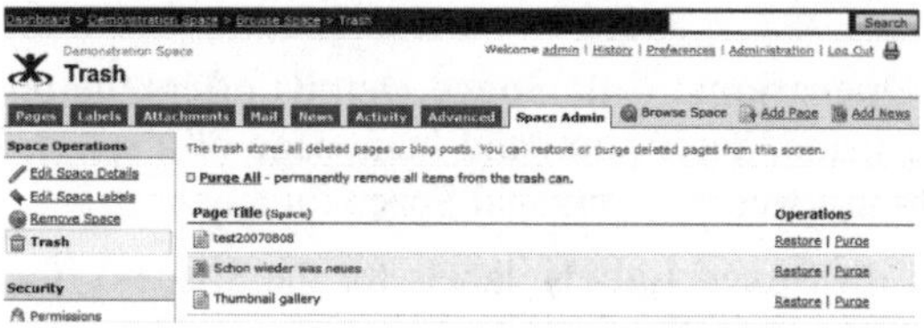

28.1.2 "Restricted Pages" Overview

Here, the Space admin can obtain a list of edit and/or view restrictions. For each page, the list contains the page title and affiliated Space, the type of restriction (**View** or **Edit**), authorized users and/or groups, the person who set the restriction (**Creator**) and the date of the restriction (**Created**). Under **Operations**, icons consisting of open locks are displayed. When such a lock is clicked, the page is completely opened – without further query.

The page itself is linked and can be viewed by the Space admin without his having to cancel any restrictions – he is always authorized to edit and view.

The person who set the restriction is not explicitly informed of the cancellation. The Space admin, however, can restore the restriction (see Chap. 27.3.3).

Restrictions can also be cancelled by Space admins directly on the page – the corresponding lock icons are displayed on the **Info** tab.

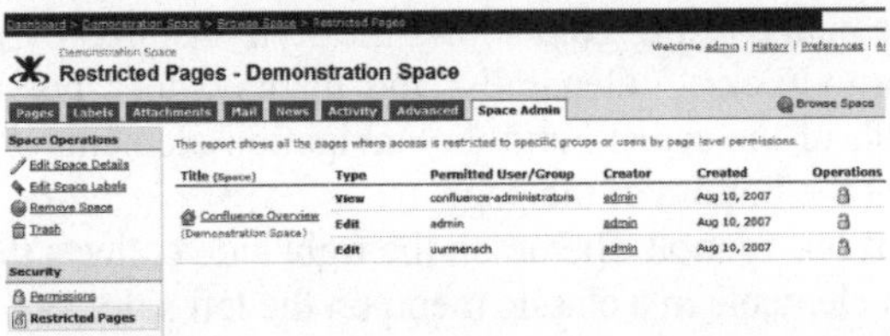

Fig. 28.2

28.1.3 Mail

Under the menu option **Mail**, mail accounts can be set up and mbox files imported. Since email retrieval is done via POP, the emails are deleted on the mail server after retrieval and are only archived in Confluence – and can no longer be exported. A special email account can be set up on a mail server for a particular project, the project-specific mails sent to that email address and the mails accessed via Confluence and linked there. Users must decide for themselves if this is a viable option. It makes sense to at least route certain content directly to the wiki and not through the standard email traffic route.

When first working with Confluence, it is simpler to transfer important emails to Confluence with the “copy & paste” function and process them further there – which is why this topic will not be explored further at this time.

28.1.4 Look and Feel

The Confluence display can be modified to a certain extent via the menu option **Look and Feel**. The various options are detailed in the subchapters to follow.

Themes

There are three themes to choose from: the one shown in the previous screenshots, which is the

- **Default Theme**, the
- **Clickr Theme** and the
- **Left Navigation Theme**.

The center image in Fig 28.3 shows the style inspired by photosharing platform Flickr:[23] Generally, the display does not utilize the entire width of the screen, and the navigation elements are grouped in blocks at the bottom of the page.

The Left Navigation Theme on the right side collects the tabs and navigation elements in a classic menu on the left side.

Fig. 28.3

It is surely difficult to come to a consensus between all users regarding the theme to be applied. Thus it is comforting to know that you can switch back and forth between designs whenever you like – but since people need time to get used to it, you should not indulge in excessive switching.

Color Scheme

The color scheme to be used is easy to change and can be adapted to your respective corporate design.

Fig. 28.4

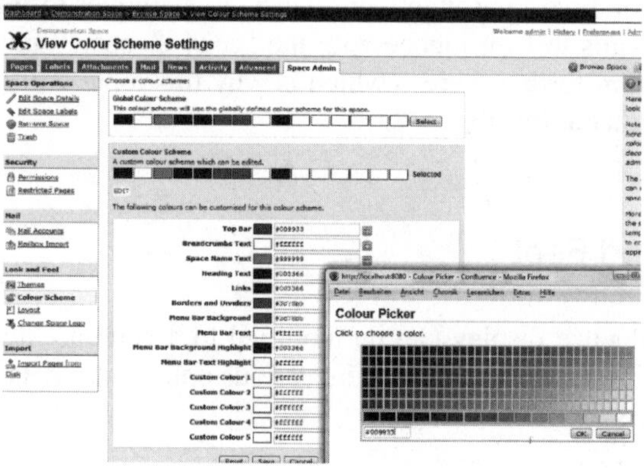

23 http://flickr.com

Layout

Of the previously discussed possibilities of modifying the look of Confluence, the issue of layout is the most detailed. Whereas you have only three options to choose from in the themes, the color schemes enable you to change more than ten colors. Furthermore, with regard to layout, the Space admin has the option of modifying the internal templates used in Confluence for the groups **Site, Content** and **Export Layout**.

Because knowledge of HTML and Velocity is necessary to perform such modifications and as layout questions are not the highest priority when being introduced to Confluence, we will not delve further into this issue.

Change Space Logo

Here, a logo can be uploaded for a Space. The Space logo appears on every wiki page and, accordingly, in the print view. It should be between 30 and 40 pixels high and wide, since it is not scaled.

Fig. 28.5 shows the standard Space logo: the logo used by Atlassian for Confluence. It is easy to replace or switch off. The Confluence administrator can also set a global logo.

Fig. 28.5

28.2 Confluence Admin

The Confluence admin can see a link in his or her user area called **Administration**, which leads to the Administration Console. This is where all settings pertaining to Confluence as a whole are made. The settings are divided into the areas:

- **Configuration**
- **Look and Feel**
- **Administration**
- **Security**

Since a few configurations would extend beyond the scope of this book with regard to an introduction to Confluence, some will only be briefly mentioned. You can see all administration areas in the menu on the left side of the screen in Fig. 28.6.

28.2.1 Configuration

This chapter will discuss a few important general configuration options as well as the Plugin Repository.

General Configuration

Among other points, **General Configuration** includes:

- **Site Configuration:** title and homepage of the Confluence site, welcome message and server URL
- **Feature Settings:** activation, deactivation and defaults for the Rich Text Editor, CamelCase-Links, Threaded Comments, Trackback (incoming/outgoing links), draft save frequency, setting for Breadcrumbs navigation
- **Security and Privacy:** activation and deactivation of the external User Management (e.g. via LDAP), setup of new users via the users ("public signup"), viewability of user email addresses
- **Formatting and International Settings:** Setting the character code (e.g. UTF-8), indexing language (e.g. English, German, etc.) time and date format
- **Attachment Settings:** Maximum attachment size (default: 10 MB), maximum number of attachments per upload (default: 5), maximum width and height of thumbnails

Fig. 28.6

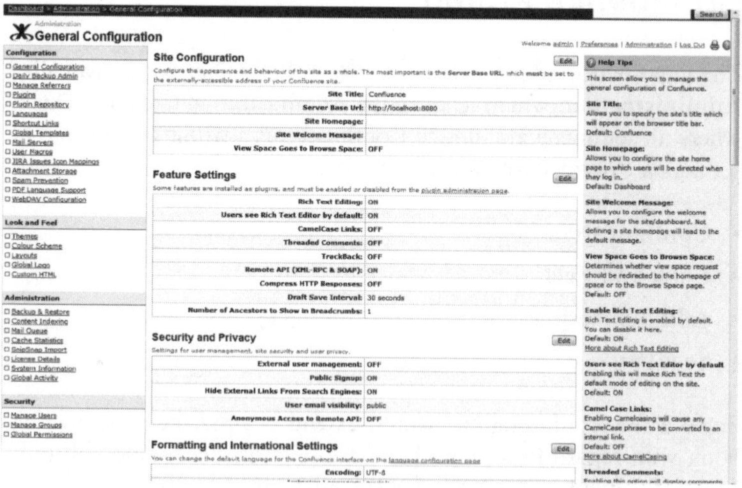

Plugin Repository

The Plugin Repository is a convenient place to look for, install, uninstall and configure most plugins.

At the moment, there are 131 extensions and plugins available. Tab. 28.1 offers an overview of which companies or private persons provide how many plugins. A total of 77 plugins are explicitly free of charge, three come at a cost, and a donation is requested for most of the rest.

Community-driven wiki development

For companies whose core competence does not lie in the realm of software development, their provision of plugins can be somewhat problematic: It is not foreseeable if and within what time period updates will be available for the individual components of Confluence. Further development is thus strongly dependent upon the community of Confluence developers. There are lots of cute little gimmicks, like a Sudoku plugin – yet companies may have other considerations or wishes for improvement.

Tab. 28.1

Developer	**Number of Plugins**
Atlassian Software Systems	60
Adaptavist.com Ltd	17
CustomWare Asia Pacific	15
Bob Swift et al.	11
Pantero Corporation	2
Stepstone Technologies Inc.	2
Others	26

Fig. 28.7 gives you an idea of how one can work with the Plugin Repository.

Another difficulty concerning the use of plugins – especially in corporations – is that they at least partially overlap with existing systems:

Media overlap

- For instance, there is a “Calendar Plugin”, but many corporations have been using Lotus Notes or Microsoft Outlook for ages and do not wish to switch – rightly so – even if it would be attractive from a wiki standpoint
- The same is true for “Form Mail” and the “Dynamic Task List Plugin”. They provide functions that make using Confluence more convenient but that are actually already provided elsewhere.
- The “HTML-Plugin” gives you the opportunity to enter pure HTML code in a wiki article: but why, when Web Content Management Systems are already being used?

Fig. 28.7

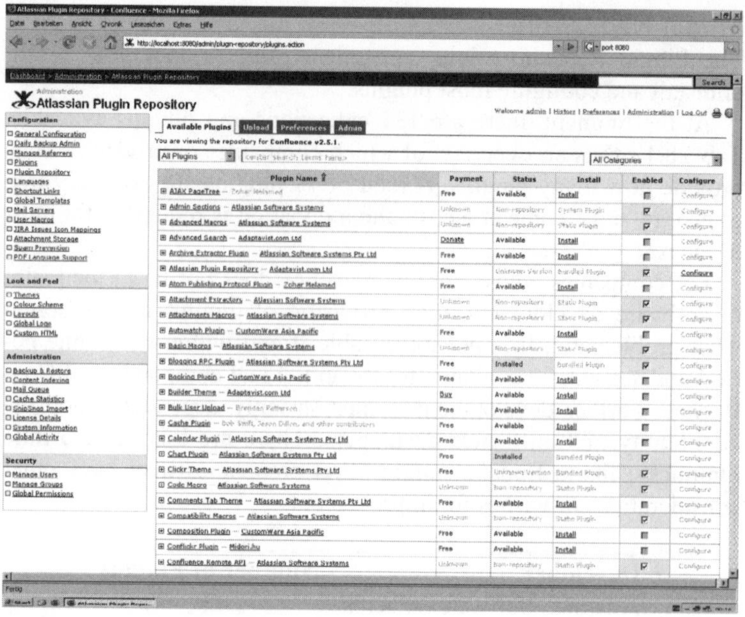

Other Configurations

The other configurations will only be briefly described:

- **Daily Backup Admin**: This allows you to enter a backup path and backup file name convention. If desired, backups can also be made of attachments.
- **Manage Referrers**: Here, you can set whether or not external links – which are found on the **Info** tab of a page – are to be explicitly saved and displayed. In addition, it is also possible to remove individual URLs from the display.
- **Plugins**: All installed plugins are listed – with the Repository mentioned above (see Chap. 28.2.1), they can be administered.
- **Languages**: As we have mentioned, Confluence is currently only available in English. In future, this space will offer a choice of other languages.
- **Shortcut Links**: The Confluence admin can set shortcut links here as described in Chap. 26.4.
- **Global Templates**: Templates that are to be available in all Spaces can be managed here (for more on templates, see also 27.1.7).
- **Mail Servers**: As mentioned in Chap. 28.1.3 for the Space level, an SMTP mail server can also be configured for the entire Confluence installation.

- **User Macros**: These are simple macros that are primarily intended for simple formatting tasks. To write such macros, you should know Velocity.
- **JIRA Issues Icon Mappings**: JIRA is an issue tracker by Atlassian whose interface is configured here.
- **Attachment Storage**: Indication of the path where the attachments are to be saved.
- **Spam Prevention**: Less interesting for internal corporate wikis: Here it is possible to activate a so-called "Captchas". This means users can be asked to enter a number combination displayed on screen before they edit something. Automated spam programs cannot achieve this and thus cannot generate spam.
- **PDF Language Support**: To generate PDF documents from wiki pages, a TTF or TTC file can be uploaded here. Currently, Confluence can only save one font file – which uploads overwrite.
- **WebDAV Configuration**: Using WebDAV, Confluence pages and attachments can be managed as if on a virtual hard drive. A very interesting and important interface – however not necessarily for beginners. You can get a better feel for wiki collaboration if you do without using this option for starters.

28.2.2 Look and Feel

These settings were already described above on the Space level (see Chap. 28.1.4). Here, you can also set up layout options on three levels (**Themes**, **Color Scheme** and **Layouts**) for the Confluence installation as a whole. The respective Space admins can overwrite these settings for their particular Space.

28.2.3 Administration

The most important area in this block is **Backup and Restore**. It generally offers two possibilities to perform manual backups (in contrast to the automated daily backups – see Chap. 28.2.1):

- Backups for the complete Confluence site (in the administration area)
- Individual Space backups as an XML export in the respective Space (see Chap. 27.1.7)

The Site Backups delete all content from the Confluence database while the – incremental – Space backups do not delete everything currently in existence. A database backup for the former case is thus strongly advised as a first step. Currently, backup restores of files greater than 2 GB in size are not supported. Backups are provided as zipped XML files.

Restores are possible via these zipped XML files or via the file system in which daily automated backups can be set (see Chap. 28.2.1). The path via the file system is recommended for large backup files.

Since the backup function integrated in Confluence is quite a memory hog, Atlassian recommends using the backup tools of the database used – especially for large Confluence sites – and additionally generating backups of the Confluence Home Directories.[24]

Further administrative options are briefly cited below:

- **Content Indexing**: The Confluence content is reconstructed every minute by default. Here, an index can be generated – e.g. manually if there are search errors.
- **Mail Queue**: Mails that are to be sent as notifications are stored in a queue and sent every minute. This, too, can be manually controlled.
- **Cache Statistics**: They give an overview of the capacity and efficiency of the internal Confluence cache. For performance tuning on this and other levels, Atlassian provides detailed tips.[25]
- **Snip Snap Import**: Using this function, individual Spaces can be copied from one Confluence site to another as an XML export. Since attachments currently cannot be imported and users can only be identified once, the usefulness of this function has its limits.
- **Licence Details**: This lists details on the license used (type, number of users, support period, etc.). A license update can also be performed here.
- **System Information**: A list of system details: system time, Java version, VM memory statistics, runtime information, etc.
- **Global Activity**: The multi-Space equivalent to Chap. 27.1.6.

---

[24] http://confluence.atlassian.com/display/DOC/Alternative+Backup+Strategy+for+Large+Confluence+Sites
[25] http://confluence.atlassian.com/display/DOC/Performance+Tuning

28.2.4 Security

The User and Group Administration was detailed above within the context of the Confluence permissions concept (see Chap. 27.3.1).

28.2.5 Popular Plugins

Atlassian Plugins

As stated in Chap. 28.2.1 regarding the Plugin Repository, there are several plugins for Confluence that were developed by Atlassian as well as third parties and having various conditions. We would like to briefly present ten of the most popular Atlassian plugins below, to demonstrate their versatility. Our selection is based on evaluations made by Atlassian[26]. Seven interesting third-party plugins are described separately.

You should consider two important points before installing a plugin:

- Every plugin increases the technical complexity of the Confluence installation. Especially with third-party plugins, you run the risk that their further development will at some point no longer be in synch with that of Confluence. The interplay of variously installed plugins should be tested carefully before the system is used productively – the degree of development of the plugins is diverse.
- Every plugin increases the organizational complexity of the dominating media environment in your company. Not every plugin is a good idea for every company. Confluence in itself is a step away from the original wiki concept. Plugins only serve to augment this effect. For newcomers to Confluence, you should stick to the motto: "Think big – start small".

A few of the following plugins are included in the default installation of Confluence. You will find an overview of them in the menu option **Plugins** on the Administration Console.

Calendar

This plugin allows you to display a calendar on any Confluence page – it updates itself without needing to refresh the page. It is also possible to integrate iCal calendars.

[26] http://www.atlassian.com/software/confluence/plugins/

Chart “Chart” generates various diagram types on a Confluence page based on table data. Supporting types include: Pie charts, bar graphs, line graphs, area diagrams and Gantt charts. Diagram size, colors, title and legend can be configured, among other points. Not only a Confluence table but also an SQL query can serve as a database.

WebDAV Using the WebDAV interface, Confluence pages and their attachments can be accessed directly through the operating system (under Windows, e.g. “Web Folders”). Editing and resaving attachments to Confluence can be performed directly in the corresponding application – e.g. Word. Attachments can be moved to a data browser (e.g. Windows Explorer) via drag & drop, and page hierarchies can be reorganized like folders.

For all operations, the permissions structures defined in Confluence apply.

Mark for Review This plugin adds the tab **Review** to the work area of a page. The list of review types can be freely configured. In the **Browse Space** area, the tab **Review Report** appears and lists the feedback that can be further processed by moderators. Review permission can be explicitly granted.

Gallery The option of displaying an image gallery (“Gallery”) on a Confluence page was described above in Chap. 26.6.

Tasklist This – simple – task list can be edited directly on the page in View mode. Once someone has completed a task, he or she can click on the respective line of the list and his or her name is noted there. The degree of completion is reflected with a progress bar.

IM Presence Using the macro “IM Presence”, you can display the online status of users in various Instant Messenger (IM) programs on a Confluence page. It supports AIM, Gtalk, ICQ, MSN, Sametime, Skype, Wildfire and Yahoo.

Blogging RPC After installing the “Blogging RPC”, the Confluence blog posts (**News**) can be posted with every blogging client that supports Blogger API 1.0 or MetaWeblog API. It is possible to enter the blog post in Wiki Markup.

Invite In combination with the **Public Signup**, the “Invite” plugin is designed to speed up the setup of new users in a Confluence Space. Invited users receive a freely formulated email notification and automatically with it, an account, as soon as they click on the link in the mail. The Confluence admin sets whether or not **Invite** is to appear in the **Space Admin** tab or under **Advanced**. In that respective location, there is a list of all invitations. The permissions of the invited users are set by the Confluence admin in the Confluence Repository.

Google Maps With the aid of the “Google Maps” plugin, a map of a defined address can be displayed on a Confluence page. Parameters such as the height and width of the map, zoom level and map type can be indicated.

Third Party Plugins

Third parties also develop attractive plugins. We will briefly present the most popular below.

Gliffy

The "Gliffy" plugin – the name of the company that developed it – enables the generation of simple diagrams, such as flowcharts, UML or network diagrams as well as simple sketches, and their display on a Confluence page. This is done via a link on the page (and not via the **Edit** tab) which opens the Gliffy Editor. The appearance of this editor differs greatly from that of Confluence. The diagrams can be exported as JPG or PGN files.

Metadata

With the "Metadata" plugin, users have a powerful function for working with structured content. Any amount of metadata can be defined for and assigned to any page. Overview tables can automatically be generated on overview pages according to the assigned metadata. Furthermore, for numerical metadata, simple calculations can be performed: sum, average, maximum, and minimum. In combination with the Chart plugin, this numerical data can also be displayed in the form of diagrams.

One example of this would be a multi-language glossary covering a certain topic. The specific entries are individual Confluence pages – made easy for users via the employment of templates. A variety of automatically generated tables is displayed on the overview page which can be organized according to language or subtopics, for instance.

You might thus see something like this on such an overview page:

Wiki

```
{metadata-report:German,definition|
link=German|sort=German asc}
```

On the individual glossary pages, a respective entry might look like this:

Wiki

```
{metadata-list}
|| German | Abrieb ||
|| English | Wear debris ||
|| French | Dechets d'abrasion ||
|| definition | Material scuffed off of a
functional surface due to tribological con-
tact. ||
|| Systematics | Forms of wear ||{metadata-
list}
```

Theme Builder The plugin "Theme Builder" is based on the possibilities that admins have with layout functions (see Chap. 28.1.4). The Confluence navigation can be replaced with a visual editor via a drop-down menu. Logo banners in full page width are also possible, as are fitted footers and menus for special user groups.

SQL With the aid of the SQL plugin, SQL statements can be directly displayed on a Conference page – in table or diagram form. The content is automatically updated with every visit to the site.

Rate The "Rate" plugin allows visitors to evaluate the Confluence site, that is, vote on its quality. The results can then also be displayed graphically in table form or with the Chart plugin. Cookies ensure that each user only votes once.

LaTeX If you work a lot with formulas, you are sure to find the plugin "LaTeX" of interest. Packed in `{latex}`-areas, any LaTeX syntax can be entered in Wiki Markup that is rendered for the **View** mode.

Microsoft Office Add-In One conversion option for Microsoft Word and Excel is the "Microsoft Office Add-In". In both applications, an add-in adds the button **Send to Wiki** and the file is stored completely as a Confluence page – including formatting and images. A preferred Space and parent page can also be selected.

Finally, Tab. 28.2 provides an overview of which plugins described above are included in the default installation of Confluence and which ones come at a cost. "Installed by default" does not necessarily mean that the plugin is ready to use. In some cases, further configuration or the installation of external components may be necessary.

Tab. 28.2

Plugin	Installed by default?	Cost?	Status
	Atlassian		
Calendar	no	no	stable
Chart	yes	no	stable
WebDAV	yes	no	pre-release
Mark for Review	no	no	stable
Gallery	yes	no	stable
Tasklist	yes	no	?
IM Presence	yes	no	pre-release
Blogging RPC	yes	no	stable
Invite	no	no	stable
Google Maps	no	no	stable

Plugin	Installed by default?	Cost?	Status
	Third Party		
Gliffy	no	yes	stable
Metadata	no	no	stable
Theme Builder	no	yes	stable
SQL	no	no	stable
Rate	no	no	stable
LaTeX	no	no	stable
MS AddIn	no	?	production

Tab. 28.2 (continued)

28.2.6 Forecast: Plugin Development

If you are interested in developing your own plugins, you will find a number of resources at Atlassian.[27] The following environment is necessary or recommended for plugin development:

- Java Development Kit 1.5
- Maven 2.0.5, a software project management tool
- application server, e.g. Apache Tomcat (see Chap. 28.5.2)
- optional: a database, such as MySQL (see 28.5.2)
- optional: Subversion, a software system for version administration that is considered a further development of the popular CVS (Concurrent Versions Systems)
- IDE (Integrated Development Environment), e.g. IDEA or Eclipse
- Confluence source code or a distribution

A plugin consists of a JAR file that contains a plugin descriptor – an XML file – and optionally, Java classes and resources such as CSS or Velocity files.

28.2.7 Further Resources for Confluence

On the Atlassian homepage, there are several other resources that can be useful to Confluence users and developers: e.g. documenta-

[27] ttp://confluence.atlassian.com/display/DOC/Confluence+Development+Hub

tion,[28] FAQs,[29] mailing lists,[30] forums,[31] a developer blog[32] and, of course, a number of wikis.[33]
Special attention is paid to the issue tracker JIRA for Confluence.[34] With it, feature requests and bugs can be entered, commented, tracked and evaluated (see Fig. 28.8).

JIRA is a further product by Atlassian, an issue tracker that is utilized for the firm's own Confluence bugs and feature requests.

Fig. 28.8

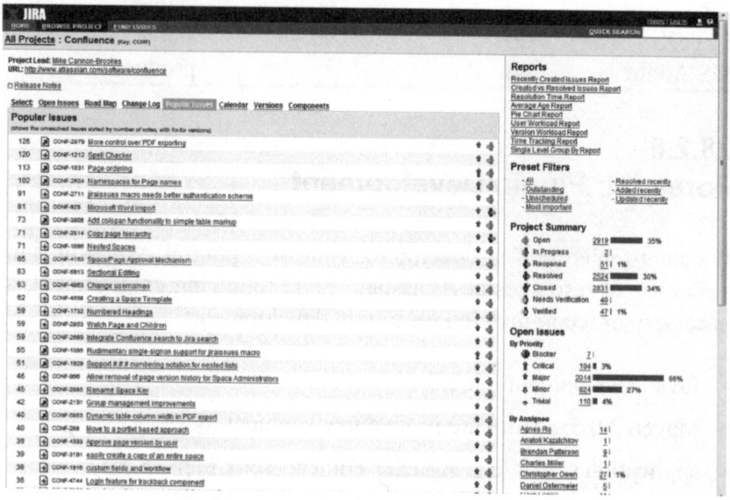

The following chapter offers brief concluding remarks on Confluence.

In conclusion

To conclude this section on Confluence, we wish to encourage as neutral a view as possible on one of the most popular wiki engines for use in corporate environments. Within the context of presenting an introduction to Confluence, it was unfortunately not possible to treat all topics with great detail. However, we hope we have provided you with enough information to give you an initial impression.

Even if the Atlassian homepage seems to suggest it at times: The introduction to Confluence is neither technically nor organization-

---

[28] http://confluence.atlassian.com/display/DOC/Confluence+Documentation+Home
[29] http://confluence.atlassian.com/display/DOC/Confluence+Main+FAQ
[30] http://www.atlassian.com/software/confluence/mailinglist.jsp
[31] http://forums.atlassian.com/index.jspa
[32] http://blogs.atlassian.com/developer/
[33] http://confluence.atlassian.com/dashboard.action
[34] http://jira.atlassian.com

ally trivial – in most cases, it's not even "wikiwiki". To implement Confluence in the workplace, a pioneering spirit is still required today – and especially an affiliation to the wiki philosophy.

Despite its shortcomings, on the whole, Confluence is a fascinating wiki engine that is sure to be able to stimulate a number of evolutions along its path in the workplace.

VI. Tools with a Future

29 Technical Challenges

29.1 Integration, Hybrids and Mashups

Wiki technology has not only prevailed as an autonomous system, but also in combination with other applications. Wikis as an enhancement to other software is often a good idea because many Internet and Intranet solutions cannot be replaced by a wiki alone. In addition, content management systems exist that are already very extensive and whose content it would be extremely complex to transfer to a wiki.

That is why, for instance, the popular content management systems Joomla! and TYPO3 have integrated wiki software.

The widely used eGroupWare also possesses a wiki, for instance to facilitate the documentation and planning of work groups. The online offer Wetpaint is only one further example of the fact that,

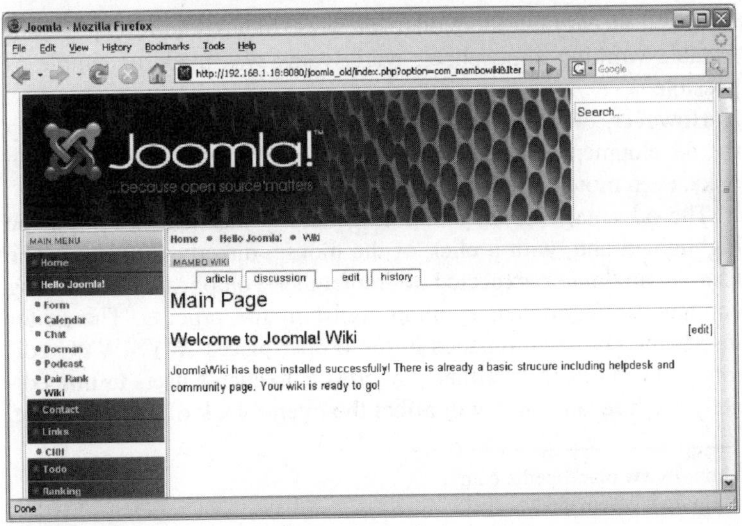

nowadays, one does not run just wikis or blogs or CMS or groupware, but rather a mixture of the software cited (so-called hybrids), which adapt their functionality and are only built up on various base systems. The respective wiki clone is adapted to the other applications upon implementation.

The TikiWiki developer group has gone another path. Here, a wiki was made the centerpiece, and other applications such as an address book, chat, calendar, etc., were grouped around the wiki. Unfortunately, this intriguing approach has not prevailed. In the case of bitweaver, the follow-up to TikiWiki, the wiki has been reduced to just one module among many, albeit an equal one.

Mash-ups

Wikis play a role in mash-ups, as well (a combination of content from various websites). For instance, Placeopedia[1] combines data from Wikipedia and Google Maps. In future, it is possible that wikis will primarily be used as modules in communications packages.

Ubiquitous wikis

At least the connection between the Net and the real world has become closer. Semapedia[2] serves as a role model with the ubiquitous wiki: Directly on site, Wikipedia articles on significant architectural structures can be accessed via cell phone. This works using a sort of 2-D bar code (semacode) attached to a building that includes a URL code. The code can be photographed with the respective cell phone software and subsequently accessed in a WAP browser. This technology is not exclusive to wikis, but it happens to be disseminated by Semapedia in Germany.

29.2 Editors

To enable an easy introduction to the world of wikis and create a comfortable working atmosphere, wiki syntax was made as simple as possible.

However, there has been increasing discussion of late regarding the development of special editors designed to make working with wikis even more convenient.

Mode of operation

The advantage of an editor is generally that text areas can be highlighted and, with a click of the mouse, directly formatted. The user is no longer expected to remember complicated formatting commands. Significant symbols assist in the process. The editor inserts the layout commands in the proper places. WYSIWYG editors go even one step farther. The idea is to enable users to immediately see how a change will affect the overall look of the document,

---

[1] http://www.placeopedia.com

[2] http://www.semapedia.org

as is possible in Microsoft Word, for instance, without requiring the detour through saving the file and viewing the edited version.

Simple editors

In the meantime, simple wiki editors can be found all over the Internet. For example, you have seen one model in *MediaWiki*.

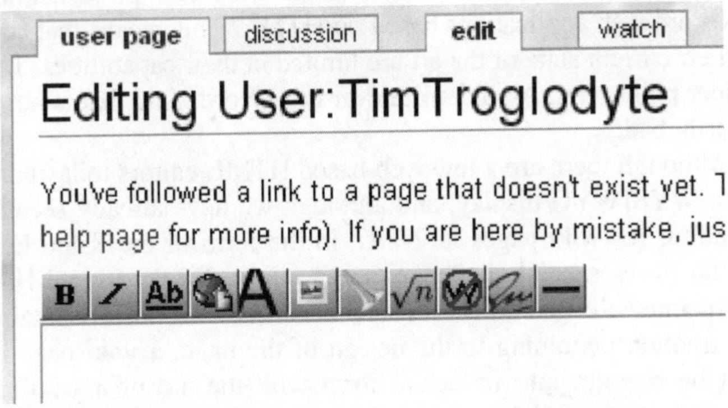

That software helps you design a page with a toolbar with which you can perform common text formats (bold, italics, etc.) using mouse clicks. The introduction of editors was a giant leap in the realm of wiki user friendliness. Even if purist programmers are not enthusiastic, such aids are urgently needed for the average user.

WYSIWYG and browser editors

Eric Möller takes it even farther: "Wikis have […] rekindled interest in efficient browser editors. Browser producers and third-party suppliers have recognized the demand, including with regard to content management systems, very widely popular in the commercial environment, which are not as open as wikis, but offer similar functions."[3] This would mean that the editor is no longer a part of the wiki software, but of the browser, and could thus enable easy editing of wiki or other pages, ideally directly on the WYSIWYG level. However, this is still a vision of the future.

Whatever the case may be, demands for a WYSIWYG editor become louder and louder with every new wiki project. Let us comment on this phenomenon: Of course we are of the opinion that the user-friendliness of wikis is a major contributing factor to their wide acceptance, yet it often receives less attention than it should from developers. A good WYSIWYG editor is certainly a big advantage, but only if it truly works in a stable manner. This should be tested rigorously in advance, because the formation of a community does not necessarily depend on a WYSIWYG editor – even if people often talk as if is the only decisive feature: there are plenty of examples and experience to the contrary. The important question is

[3] Möller 2003.

whether the wiki will serve as a solution to an urgent problem. If so, users will quickly learn to work with it. An editor is surely a great thing to have, but an unstable editor that loses content in the end can thoroughly ruin enthusiasm for the wiki as a tool to such an extent that it may even lead to the failure of the whole project. Finally, wikis are web applications based on HTML. This means that editors in their current state of the art are limited in their capabilities. To put a finer point on it: A wiki will never be a Word. And that is not necessarily bad.

Challenges for wiki editors

Although there are a few web-based HTML editors today that offer a WYSIWYG display, and although we have already seen such an editor for wiki pages in *TWiki*, in the form of the Kupu Editor, a wiki poses special challenges to an editor. While normal HTML documents are generally "independent" because they contain all information pertaining to the design of the page, a wiki page must first be brought into its actual form with the aid of a wiki script (identification of links, replacement of variables, etc.). Since such a script runs on the server, a permanent exchange between server and client would be necessary. This goes beyond the current technical possibilities of the Net. Creative solutions are needed to meet this challenge. Kupu, for instance, directly displays static parts, such as text format, and marks others, such as links or variables, in a certain color to indicate that they are subject to a further processing step. The editor also compares the page to the document structure existing at the start of the editing procedure. Thus, Kupu knows which pages exist in *TWiki*. We have also discussed the *Conference* editor in detail.

With regard to real wiki editors, there is still need for action. An ideal solution would be the development of a common editor for all wikis. However, certain standards are necessary to achieve this.

29.3 In Search of Standards

MediaWiki as a standard?

One great drawback remains the fact that every wiki clone has its own formatting commands that the user has to learn anew every time. That is why efforts are underway to standardize wiki syntax. However, which program should serve as the standard? Jimmy Wales, of course, argues in favor of *MediaWiki*, since it has become the most popular wiki, thanks to Wikipedia. Many people are familiar with its formatting commands and the names of its most important functions. And yet, of course, popularity does not necessarily indicate quality.

Just how difficult it is to achieve consensus on the matter can be seen in the discussion of CamelCase. Some see in it a genuine, typical wiki aspect. The defenders of CamelCase swear by its simplicity with which associations and links can be generated. Others reject it for aesthetic reasons and complain that it continually causes links to be unintentionally set.[4] They have voiced the general insight that the syntax should differ from normal language to the extent that unintentional layout definitions can be avoided. This requires cooperation between several Wikians.

CamelCase

The exchange of data between wikis would also be considerably easier with a standard. At the moment, the transfer of data from one wiki clone to another without data loss is coupled with substantial difficulties. Even if the simplest formatting commands can be easily exchanged between themselves, the devil, as we know, is in the details. It poses a certain risk, since one cannot be sure how long individual wiki clones will be developed further and adapted to the current state of the art. There is also the danger that data will become "trapped" in an obsolete system. If wiki communities would at least agree on a single transfer format for data, some of the insecurities in using wikis could be eliminated. The development of the various wiki clones, however, also means that various approaches and software architectures are being pursued, preventing monocultures.

Interwiki

The initiator of a wiki project is thus placed before a further difficult decision: choosing "the right" wiki software. The following points represent a list of criteria that may help you make that decision:

Which wiki?

- **Programming language.** It is possible that you may have to make an adjustment or two to the scripts. It would thus serve you well if you were familiar with one of wiki's programming languages, such as Perl or PHP.
- **System requirements**. Especially if you do not operate your own server, you must make sure that wiki will run with the software available (operating system).
- **Technical capacity.** If your wiki is very heavily frequented, it is advisable for performance reasons to seek a database solution.
- **Installation effort**. What technical knowledge is required for installation, and to what extent is the set-up automated by routines?

[4] Wales in a personal conversation on Dec. 28, 2004.

- **User administration**. A wiki that is to contain sensitive data must offer the opportunity to block certain areas to general access.
- **Division in areas.** For user administration and the collective work of various groups in a wiki, separable sections can be advantageous.
- **Expansion through plugins**. Plugins usually offer a large variety of additional functions.
- **Interface**. An attractive look invites users to read and work. For one's own pages, being able to design them at will is an important aspect.
- **Intuitive operation.** Can the wiki also be used by inexperienced users without difficulty? At the same time, does it fulfill the expectations of experienced wiki users?
- **Language**. Many wikis only have English interfaces. Can your community live with that?
- **Documentation**. Can one find sufficient information on the operation and maintenance of the wiki on the Net or in technical literature?
- **Further development**. Is it expected that errors in the software will be eliminated and that the software will continue to be adapted to demands in the future? Is the data stored in a format with which, if necessary, it can also be transferred to other systems?

On another level, certain features are decisive for the selection of a suitable wiki clone: for instance, functions such as whether a search can also search in file attachments or whether input can be cached. For organizations and companies, we thus recommend consulting with an expert.

Semantic wiki

A popular topic of wiki development is "structured data" as well as the "semantic wiki". This is due to the fact that wiki pages contain loads of information, but it is situated in free text and only very difficult for computer programs to identify. Thus the challenge is to put the text in a coded, machine-readable format, just as in the case of the links of individual pages to one another, thus rendering it functional for other applications and services.

Social tagging

The situation is different when you combine wikis with social tagging in order to effect a certain degree of categorization (allocation of labels). For this, visitors can assign categories to a page or add to existing categories with a mouse click. In such a case, however, a relatively large community would be required in order to be able to take advantage of the statistical effects of greater numbers.

30 A few Wiki Projects

30.1 Projects of the Wikimedia Group

Wikimedia Foundation

Many Wikians are at work on projects of the Wikimedia Foundation. Thus, in the medium term, that foundation will be an important source for control points for the evaluation, distribution and use of wiki technology. Its content focus lies in the area of public reference works: the construction of a library of free textbooks, study and teaching materials (Wikibooks), a freely accessible dictionary (Wiktionary), a collection of free texts (Wikisource), quotes (Wikiquote) or biological species (Wikispecies). This area is expected to continue to grow considerably.

30.1.1 Free Database: Wikimedia Commons

Images, text, video, music as free downloads

One remarkable project of the Wikimedia Foundation is Wikimedia Commons. It is designed to centrally store images, videos, music and texts for all Wikimedia projects. Images stored there and available for downloading must be in the public domain or be subject to the GNU FDL.

An international communal and multi-language data administration project first of all has the advantage that images no longer need to be individually loaded for each Wikipedia system. Since they are free, they can also be used beyond the boundaries of that system. In addition, we can assume that the data is not subject to copyright laws, which would eliminate the need for extensive research into the holder of that copyright. The Wikimedia Commons project is very strict with regard to the license status of individual images. Information on the license must always be supplied with every image, it source quoted and, if the image stems from a Wikipedia project, the person who originally made the image available to Wikipedia must also be named.

Perspectives

Within only two years, more than one million media files were uploaded to Wikimedia Commons. Thus, this project could become the largest international database with free image and text material. Gallery pages can be generated for images with a particular theme and linked through categories. This makes it easy to find material on a certain topic and utilize the available documents. The wiki principle applies here. A large web catalogue is cooperatively generated and optimized according to the search criteria of users. Results of complex research can be made available to others. This greatly facilities finding relevant data. On the other hand, the opposite could also occur, and users could end up destroying each other's order.

30.1.2
News from "the Bottom up:" Wikinews

News

With Wikinews, the Wikimedia Group has begun a different and challenging project. Only two weeks after the English version was released, a German version also appeared on the Net, in December of 2004. With this project, the wiki community is venturing an attempt to create a daily, updated news overview. Whether or not this project will succeed is a question that is also being closely followed by its initiators. Wikinews has not yet been able to prevail as an alternative news medium, but in the meantime, it exists in 26 languages. And even if the project is growing slowly, it is continuing to develop consistently.

Citizen journalism

Its goal is to establish an international network of "citizen journalists" as they are called, who report on large and small events on site or put together articles from other sources. Especially in countries with limited freedom of the press, Wikinews could thus become an alternative news source. In this regard, the project is certainly comparable with the media network Indymedia. However, while Indymedia considers itself to be a "political" medium, the "Neutral Point of View" (see below) is an important angle at Wikinews: Opinions and assumptions must be identified as such and clearly attributed to those holding that opinion. The entire source material upon which an article is based is to be made available online along with the article itself, so that each reader can form his or her own opinion as to how reliable a news item is.

Problems

The Wiki community initially had to rack its brains over producing its own news. In contrast to Wikipedia, news cannot be corrected in a subsequent communication process; it must be of good quality at

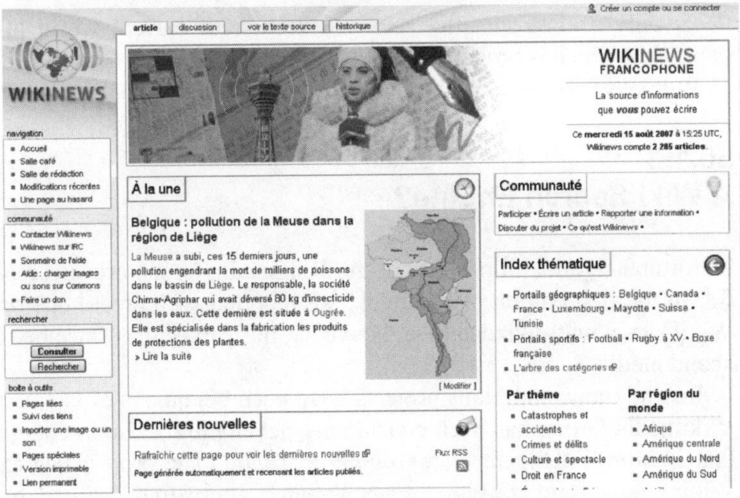

the outset.[5] Thus, a type of editing system was introduced according to which an article must first be confirmed by other users before it is cleared as "published". However, this "clearance" is not a technical process: All articles will continue to be accessible to everyone, except that clearance as published has a status approaching a quality assessment and provides indications as to the seriousness of a news item.

Experiments

The Wikinews concept should be considered an experiment that just may push the wiki principle to its limits. If and under what circumstances "citizen journalists" are really capable of tapping the same or even better sources than the established media remains to be seen. Critics fear that Wikinews could become a rumor mill, because effective editing controls are missing. Yet experience with Wikipedia, which in the beginning was met with suspicion, gives us cause for hope.

Medium of higher network-building bourgeoisie

The demonstrative distinction between it and Indymedia, and its proclaimed self-conception as "citizen's journalism" lead to the suspicion that the conception was in no way as "neutral" as one might like to think. Krüger also has his doubts: "Wikipedia is a project of the Net-educated upper middle class. And Wikinews will also orient itself with regard to theme, content and language more towards the typical *Zeit* than the average *Bildzeitung* reader. The pretense of wanting to report about 'what is happening in the world around us' will likely be reduced to a kind of reporting which re-

[5] Patalong announced skepticism on the side of the established media for 2004.

flects only a class-specific, selective section of current world affairs – but which is probably very well-founded."[6]

Wikinews will also have to face this problem time and again.

30.1.3 A Wiki Search Engine?

Unfortunately, not all projects of the Wikimedia Group are successful. In the first edition of this book, we reported with great hope on WikiData, a wiki-like database. However, this project has since been abandoned.

Communities instead of robots

Instead, new, ambitious projects have been begun. As of late, the Wikimedia Group has been considering developing a search engine that is more intelligent than *Google* or *Yahoo*. The project Search Wikia[7] intends to develop in open-source alternative inspired by wikis. The fundamental concept is not to make search results dependent upon search robots and algorithms, bur rather to integrate users of the Web actively and consciously in the evaluation and categorization of Internet sites in order to improve the search results. With a peer-to-peer search, users would then have the opportunity to not only positively or negatively rate Internet sites, but also themselves participate in the indexing of the Internet. They could make bookmarks and favorite pages available. As freely accessible software, an open and transparent search engine would thus be created. Since the technical complexity for an efficient search engine is enormous, the Wiki Search Project is to be financed via advertising.

However, this project is still in its conception stage, and there are a few hurdles to jump. While it is true that freely published search algorithms allow users to test and optimize the search engine, it is also true that search engine optimizers could deliberately rank Internet sites highly. There is also skepticism regarding the question as to whether enough users will participate in this commercial project. We will let you know in the next edition of this book.

---

[6] Krüger 2004. Regarding the German periodicals mentioned, *Zeit* is a respected national weekly newspaper, and *Bildzeitung* is a national daily tabloid notorious for its sensationalism.

[7] http://search.wikia.com/wiki/Search_Wikia, Feb. 2, 2007.

30.2 Other Wiki Worlds

We will soon turn to further projects of the *Wikimedia Foundation*. However, when focusing on Wikipedia and its sister projects, people overlook the fact that wikis have established themselves along different routes. In several projects beyond the orbit of Wikipedia, experiments are being conducted with wikis and their application possibilities.

30.2.1 Overview

GründerWiki and MeatballWiki

To obtain an overview, you can consult a directory of current wiki projects in the GründerWiki.[8] Here, you can also enter your own project. The German-language GründerWiki and its English cousin MeatballWiki[9] are attractive to everyone wishing to work with, es-

Wiki Tourbus

[8] http://www.wikiservice.at/gruender/wiki.cgi, Feb. 2, 2007.
[9] http://www.usemod.com/cgi-bin/mb.pl?MeatballWiki, Feb. 2, 2007.

tablish or run an online community. A great deal of experiences are shared here, such that you can avoid reinventing the wheel every time you start a new project.

Meatball, a community that has reached cult status and that focuses on virtual communities, network culture and hypermedia, offers the popular Wiki Tourbus.[10] The Wiki Tourbus lines are guided tours through the wiki world. Authors of various wikis have set up and linked "bus stops" here. Thus, you can get on at one wiki and get off at another one to have a closer look at it. The Wiki Tourbus System's name also alludes to the Honolulu airport shuttle bus, called wiki-wiki and evidently eponymous for wiki software.

30.2.2 Subcultures and Communities

With the Wiki Tourbus, the journey to unknown regions of the wiki world can begin. It quickly becomes apparent that people also come together over wikis who share a hobby or special interest.

Wikis have long since become the mainstream for open documentation in the IT realm, such as the *LinuWiki* and *OpenOffice*

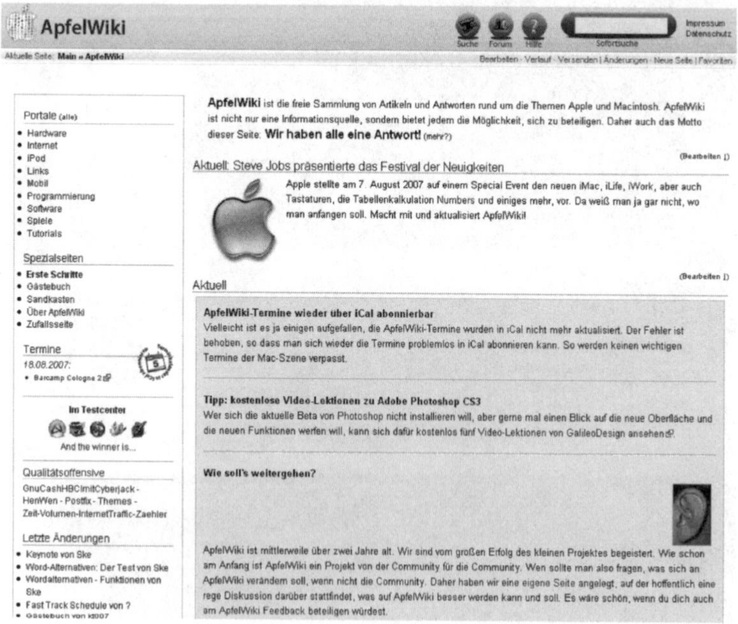

[10] http://www.usemod.com/cgi-bin/mb.pl?TourBus, Feb. 2, 2007.

Wiki, both powered by MoinMoin, or the *ApfelWiki*, a German-based site dedicated to all things Apple and Macintosh and based on pm wiki.[11]

A further familiar example is the very attractively designed *Memory Alpha* site, in which fans of the *Star Trek* television and film series amass interesting information about their favorite show.[12]

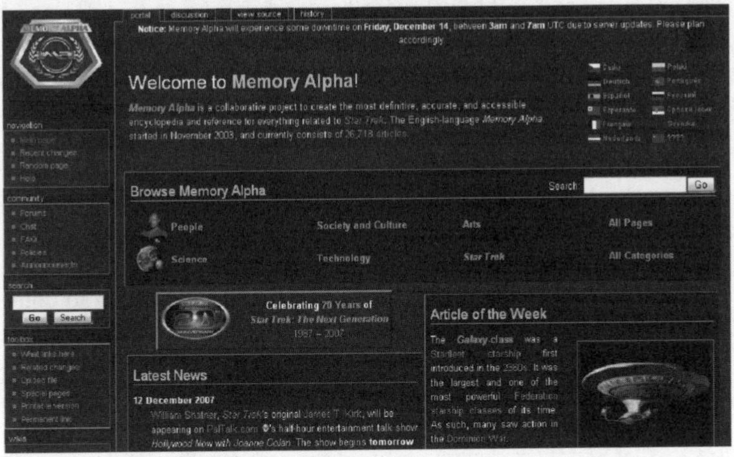

Sites on famous authors, such as the English *TolkienWiki* or the *Digital Christian Morgenstern Archive*, are also popular.[13] Furthermore, wikis have been discovered by self-help groups, although a good deal of development is still required in that realm. Wiki software is ideal for the networking of these groups. For instance, there is a German site called HerzKinderWiki, whose aim to aid children with congenital heart defects, as well as the first wiki projects for the unemployed.[14]

On such sites, topics are discussed that are otherwise only aired on a central online encyclopedia such as Wikipedia in very abbreviated form, if at all. The site *Sub-Bavaria*, for example, tries to very concretely document subcultures and their histories in Bavaria.[15]

From a technical standpoint, the development of wiki communities is made easier by wiki hosting that is offered free of charge by *seedwiki*, *Wetpaint* and other providers.[16] The wiki clones available

---

[11] http://linuxwiki.org; http://www.ooowiki.de; http://www.apfelwiki.de

[12] http://memory-alpha.org

[13] http://www.thetolkienwiki.org; http://www.christian-morgenstern.de

[14] http://www.herzkinderinfo.de/Mediawiki/index.php/Hauptseite; http://arbeitslos.wikia.com/wiki/Hauptseite

[15] http://www.sub-bavaria.de

[16] http://www.seedwiki.com; http://www.wetpaint.com

there are kept extremely simple, yet generally offer all basic wiki functions.

30.2.3 Travel Guides and Local Wikis

City Wikis

The so-called city and travel wikis have achieved a certain degree of popularity. City wikis, like the German Karlsruhe Wiki or the British Open Guide to London[17] are digital travel guides that keep not only visitors and tourists, but also the city's inhabitants themselves, up to date. They offer tips on sights, restaurants, shopping and information on culture and history.

International travel guides

A network of nodes connecting wider geographical expanses is also being developed as a result of the regional offerings. While *OpenGuides* considers bills itself as a network of free wiki travel guides to places around the world, *Wikitravel* is an attempt to compile an all-round travel guide right from outset.[18] A similar goal is being pursued by the new project Wikivoyage, which split from Wikitravel in 2006 for content reasons.[19]

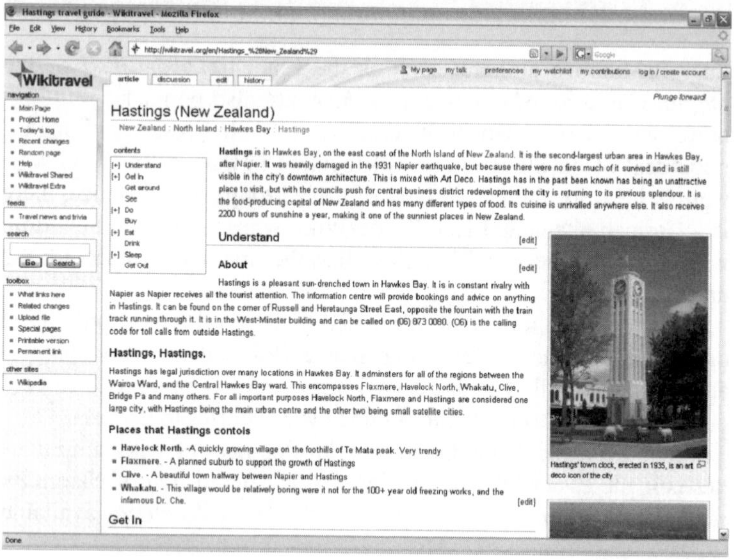

Village Wikis

In view of the city wikis and wiki travel guides, *ProWiki* developer Helmut Leitner refers to the previously largely untapped emancipa-

[17] http://ka.stadtwiki.net; http://london.openguides.org
[18] http://wikitravel.org
[19] http://www.wikivoyage.org

tory potential of wiki software. In his opinion, regional wikis are appealing precisely because of their possibilities regarding community politics: for instance, when renovating a village, formulating local political alternatives or within the context of comprehensive regional development. Local wikis could be very much more than just advertising pages for restaurants. According to Leitner, they could serve as media for an entirely new form of citizen participation; places where ideas for the community are collected and consolidated or where cultural and political life is organized close to the source. However, pioneer work is still necessary.[20] This is the same line of thinking pursued by the Austrian *Dorf-Wiki*,[21] ("Village Wiki"), which is designed to exhibit future perspectives in rural areas and design options for village habitats and microcosms.

30.2.4 Wikis in Education and Science

A large field, which we unfortunately can only briefly mention here, is the use of wikis in schools and universities. In Germany, such institutions are still slow in accepting this new medium, while in its neighboring countries Austria and Switzerland, wikis have been met with great enthusiasm in the area of education. Wikis represent an

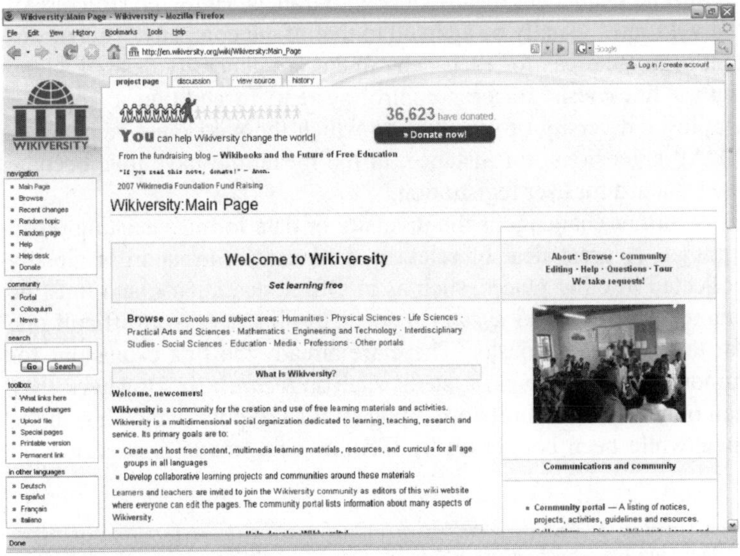

[20] Helmut Leitner in a personal conversation with Anja Ebersbach.
[21] http://www.dorfwiki.org

especially interesting enhancement in schools because they allow experimentation in a miniature version of the WWW, enabling students to discover how the Internet works on a technical and functional level – especially with regard to new developments of Web 2.0.[22]

Countless projects are experimenting with scientific wikis. Here, too, however, development is still in its infancy. That is why we will only refer to one example, the Wikimedia project *Wikiversity*, which launched in mid 2006.[23] Wikiversity is a platform for common processing of scientific projects, the exchange of ideas in technical questions and for the generation of free course materials. The project, as is immediately evident, is a sister project of Wikipedia.

30.3 Wikis in Companies and Organizations

Expansion

Nowadays we cannot discuss wikis without mentioning their use in the networks of companies and organizations. Not much is actually known about those wiki worlds, comparatively speaking, since they are part of protected intranets. However, wikis have long since taken root in private business. For use in corporate environments, a few service providers have entered the market that offer and maintain wiki installations. They frequently possess their own wiki systems that are tailored to the specific needs of companies.

Adaptability in existing software environments

Special challenges await wikis on intranets. Here, the structure of the wiki must usually be adapted to that of the company. This means that separate areas for each department are generally desired, along with a fine-meshed access control system. In addition, companies employ a diversity of software, to which the wiki must be adapted. LDAP extensions, for instance, in the meantime have thus become the standard for user registration.

A further challenge is the diversity of data formats existing on an intranet. A great deal of relevant data and information is already collected in other places, such as in Office documents, and must be entered into the wiki system. Especially this task is a difficult one for the systems to master. There are already the first extensions for importing data into wiki systems such as *MediaWiki*. However, they can only transfer simple formatting. Wiki JotSpot – which has in the meanwhile been bought up by Google – has made great strides in

---

[22] See Anja Ebersbach, Markus Glaser: Das Wiki als Spielwiese für das Internet. in: Johann Stockinger, Helmut Leitner (ed.): Wikis im Social Web. Wikiposium 2005/06, Österreichische Computer Gesellschaft, 2007, 27–39.

[23] http://wikiversity.org

this area, offering spreadsheet, web page or calendar pages types and thus approaching the Office world.

Requirements for the business world

In addition to these technical requirements, particularly the social environment in businesses differs completely from those of public wikis. Wikis in corporate environments must deal with clear command hierarchies and control mechanisms. There are other demands to quality control and assigned responsibilities. Internal wiki projects are often perceived from a "top down" perspective and must compete for acceptance in a completely different way than the free and non-commercial community projects. The "typical" problems are also other ones. For instance, Tim Bartel, who surveyed approximately 200 companies about wikis for his dissertation, found out that the biggest problems in corporate wikis were a lack of participation and disadvantageous structuring. In contrast, vandalism, which is a considerable problem for Wikipedia, does not play a role in wikis of the business world.[24] Furthermore, every situation has its own set of problems. Thus, there is a difference whether a wiki is used as a tool for a small work group or as an internal "Wikipedia" – although that term should not really be used in this context – in a large corporation. The respective organization culture also plays a large role, which, however, could change as a result of wiki implementation.

Future as a project tool

In all, wikis seem to have prevailed in business environments. The advantages of wikis to companies as well as employees are easy to inventory: Whether they are used for concept development, documentation or notification purposes, the number of daily circular emails alone can be reduced. In large corporations, wikis offer a new way of tapping know-how – which is the actual parallel to Wikipedia. In addition, employee search times for current information can be slashed in a well-maintained wiki. This reduces onerous routine work.

---

[24] See http://wikipedistik.de/umfrage, Feb. 10, 2007.

31 The Art of "Sowing" Wikis

31.1 Collaborative Writing

The original hope that wikis would contribute to a new culture of cooperative text production has as of yet only partially come true. It has proven easier in the common generation of technical instructions than for other types of texts. Scientific comments harbor far less potential for conflict than philosophical analyses. Generally, collaborative writing is a great cultural challenge for the simple fact that our society has not developed a culture of free cooperation.

Asynchronous or synchronous?

Möller now rightly sees great potential in the development of tools enabling simultaneous editing of texts in real time.[25] On the other hand, one of the great advantages of wiki technology seems to be the temporal equalization of discussion processes. Basically, both occur in group processes: acceleration and time pressure, as well as the desire for more time to expand certain ideas.[26] It has been observed that many Wikians do not simply start writing, but first do research and organize their thoughts. Kuhlen sees in "asynchronous communication forums" the advantage that a climate of balanced and informationally secure communication can emerge: "Not every question has to be answered immediately. The advantage of greater rationality is to be generally assessed higher than the presumable loss of spontaneity in the synchronous medium with its direct reactive communication styles. However, the success of asynchronous communication processes is largely dependent upon good moderation. This is especially true in learning environments where moderation performance is continually necessary, such as creating incen-

[25] Möller 2005, 200f.

[26] Writings on large group processes repeatedly state that such processes can only be initiated and be capable of working out solutions under enormous time and problem constraints.

tives, generating outlines and summaries, offering orientation aids and providing feedback for knowledge assessment."[27] Kuhlen's reference to asynchronous communication processes and learning environments, however, sees the moderator, who, among other tasks, must create incentives with sophisticated seminar designs, as the central figure. In deviation thereof, we will clarify our assessment of the role of moderator in Chap. 26.2.2. Ideally, that person should not be a jack-of-all-trades, whose perfect seminar design serves an ultimately manipulative function, to which participants only "react", but rather a promoter of productive impulses.

Increase of the degree of reflection

The potential of wikis for a digital writing culture, in our opinion, lies less in the acceleration of processes and more in the increase of the degree of reflection on that which is written. Consolidating, seizing and understanding other thoughts, re-organizing, comprehending and processing are considerable and laborious intellectual achievements. And we can see in several wiki projects that they fail as true wiki projects precisely due to those demands, because for a variety of reasons there is suddenly "not enough time;" because wiki projects are not about posting text underneath other text, but rather enhancing the existing text, editing and consolidating it.

A learning process

The introduction of a wiki is always an exciting process, because thought structures are broken open and collective learning processes set into motion. Wikis can contribute to collaborative and open relationships, but again and again, experience proves that collaborative writing and organizing with wikis must first be learned. "Social web" and "collaborative innovation" are fascinating expressions, but collaborative work skills cannot be assumed. If, for example, group members copy finished text into a wiki, other users usually neither can nor wish to alter that text. Such texts give off the message that they represent something finished and untouchable. In order to develop something collaboratively, it makes more sense to start with an outline and key points and then slowly develop a text, or initially divide sections of texts among members. When a text is then edited, it requires sensitivity, so as not to hurt the feelings of the other authors.

31.2 Collaboration: Wikis as a Project Tool

BarCamps

True collaboration in the generation of texts is difficult and requires special preparation. It is possible that the future of wikis lies more in its characteristic as a project tool, such as in establishing meeting

[27] Kuhlen 2004.

schedules, generating an agenda, prestructuring content or taking minutes.

This is the direction in which BarCamps[28] focus their trials. BarCamp, a conference concept developed in 2005, is referred to as an "unconference". Similar to the open space concept, participants organize their conference themselves. There is no predefined time plan and no lecturers. In the forefront are the principles of self-organization, creativity and spontaneity. The sessions, generally only 30 minutes long, are voted on after a short introductory round in which everyone introduces himself. There is no audience. All participants must contribute actively.

Here, wikis and blogs serve as organizational, documentation and communication tools. All relevant information is found in the wiki. They are maintained, expanded and edited collaboratively by all participants. The participants are encouraged to record the sessions and make them available in blogs or another form of general access. In addition, conference participants communicate with one another during the events. For instance, they let each other know what is going on in other sessions. Thus, BarCamps achieve multi-dimensional environments for very intensive brainstorming sessions.

31.2.1 Advantages and Problems of Wikis in Projects

Wiki: a fundamental decision

Yet wikis can also be tools for considerably more comprehensive projects. If and to what extent the planning and execution of a project is based on wikis is also always a fundamental decision about the character and work form of a project. Of course, one can also design traditional project management with wikis, but if the project is not open for real changes "from the bottom up", the question remains as to why one should employ wikis at all, which are tailored to dynamic and open processes. Congruent to its state of development, wikis are not always simple to use – although it is remarkable what we can already do today with a single wiki. Thus, each individual case should be examined before deciding whether or not using a wiki corresponds to the issues and to the group executing a project.

Advantages

Before implementing wiki technology as a central communicative and planning medium, one must weigh the pros and cons. Arguments in favor of using wikis include the following:

---

[28] http://barcamp.org

- Wikis are generally cost-free, open-source programs.
- A wiki should motivate the team or other participants to define structures and responsibilities in a cooperative manner. This results in the development of a strong integration effect, and participants will identify more deeply with the project.
- Through their openness, wikis promote transparency and provide an overview. Problems or faulty developments can be identified and discussed at an early stage.
- Wikis offer a simple, uniform system in which ideas can be collected. This can counteract a strict isolation of work groups and promote networked thinking.
- While several versions of a single document can circulate in a project, with wiki technology, it is possible to offer participants central access to the current version of a document.
- Wikis adapt themselves very rapidly to a project and mirror its project dynamics.
- The versatility of a single piece of software offers the opportunity to use it as a central publication and organizational system. The wiki system serves as a uniform administrative and reporting system, among other uses, in which decision processes or progress reports may be documented immediately.
- At the same time, the wiki enables a decentralized organizational structure which can cut down channels and work times. Editing, publishing and documentation concur in a single work step. For instance, content must not first be approved by an Internet editor before going online.

Problems

If you decide to work with a wiki, you will have to accept the following peculiarities:

- Based on the current state of development, wiki technology is not comparable to specially tailored, expensive project software. It offers no finished project templates, automation in process control, human resources planning or financial administration. It still lacks sufficient tools for scheduling and appointment planning.
- The decentralized hypertext structure can lead to initial coordination and acceptance problems. In the case of larger projects, complexities frequently arise that must be minimized. This means that

navigation bars and overview pages must be conceived and maintained.

Since a wiki offers so much freedom, it requires more attention and self-discipline from its participants. For example, they must adhere to stipulated conventions so that others can also quickly find the right information within the wiki. In addition, it is necessary to think beyond one's own work area with a view to coordination ("What is everyone else up to?"). Otherwise, chaos, edit conflicts and redundant work are only a matter of time. Yet, as larger wiki projects have demonstrated, structured, successful work is possible under certain conditions, even in very large groups.

31.2.2 Flat Hierarchies: Relationship between Moderator and Team

Conflicts

"Project", "cooperation", and "self-organization" all sound great. Yet what on paper looks like an easy and unproblematic strategy is suddenly plagued with a number of difficulties. As in any cooperative project, the same problems crop up again and again. Agreements are not met or adhered to. Personal differences and misunderstandings occur. You find out too late that individual participants are more preoccupied with other obligations than you had expected, to the extent they do not treat the current project with priority, or that they are overburdened. There are differences in opinion with regard to the procedure. Personnel fluctuations and changes to the project goal present additional problems. There are insufficient if any guidelines or procedures with which to solve problems. Conflicts are seen by many as disturbing. They cost time and nerves. However, conflicts can also be a source of dynamics and further development.[29]

Team = group of individual personalities

Whether you have an open wiki or are putting together a team for a larger project, you need to keep in mind that some participants have never worked together and will not be able to cooperate with each other ad hoc. In addition, there are lone wolves who wish to maintain as much autonomy as possible. A variety of work styles and communication methods will converge. The opportunities of co-determination and the margin for creation may make some people initially feel insecure and thus wish to receive clear-cut assignments.

---

[29] Dealing with conflicts is a question of experience, among other things. In any case, managing significant "disturbances" has priority over continuation of a project.

Respect and mutual trust must first be established through cooperation and continually updated.

Thus, it is advisable to make sure that the participants have the opportunity to get to know each other personally, insofar as possible. The assignments, requirements and work pressure limitations must be clarified in as early a stage as possible. The project requires simple but clear rules that are acceptable to all.

Broad involvement

We began by mentioning the significance of flat hierarchies for successful self-organized group processes. In the preliminary stages, the individuals in charge of implementing the project or whose participation is necessary should be included in the processes of determining goals and structure. Such individuals include project team members and, in organizations, the respective superiors. However, it is also advisable to include external individuals who are directly affected by the project or have marginal roles in it, a step which frequently supplies new perspectives.

Conviction

For the dynamics of self-organized group processes, it remains decisive that the individuals be truly convinced of the sense of the project's goal and see the result as a type of personal gain.[30] The participants must be familiar with the goal, ideally having worked it out together. This cannot be forced or demanded. Regarding the development of a project culture in open software projects, Stefan Meretz explains: "Whether or not a project truly results in a community cannot be manipulated. In contrast to prescribed projects in private enterprise, open projects are based on a strong degree of participant interest, specifically in that of good, usable software."[31]

Hierarchy?

The more people that are involved in a project, the more urgent is the question of coordination, supervision, but also the division of power, authority and hierarchy. This is not only related to the project itself; existential dependency relationships are often inhibitory, such as when superiors are integrated into projects as "watchdogs".

The extent to which hierarchies are functionally necessary was also contentious in the history of the emancipation movement. Ultimately, it depends on how the respective roles are filled and what real intervention options exist for the participants, in order to counteract any tendencies toward bureaucratization.

Moderation: Accompany, don't direct

If the group is responsible for the goal and the result of the project, someone will need to take on the role of moderator. The moderator serves as a sort of midwife, so to speak. That is to say, he or she provides assistance in maintaining the organizational environment and the communicative process. At the same time, he or she

[30] This is where non-democratic economic orders reach insurmountable limits. That, however, is a subject all its own.
[31] Meretz 2003, 106.

must make sure that stipulated conventions and discussion rules are observed. However, it is the group that stands in the foreground, not the moderator. Rather, the latter allows the course of the project, with regard to content, to be determined by the group. His or her motto should be: "Accompany, don't direct", refraining from over-zealous regimentation in order to preserve important group processes. The wiki philosophy, the conception of open software development and the notion of moderators in open-space conferences all rest on the same principle: that of leaving control of the process to the group.[32] It is the group that possesses the professional competence and responsibility.

Double duty

In web logs, Internet forums or wikis, moderators often also take on technical tasks, such as serving as wiki admins. They aid in user administration, text maintenance, etc.[33] Furthermore, within the debates and in the wiki system, there is an ongoing need for tidying up. Interim results must be collected and content supplemented or demanded; also, several tasks might crop up all at once. The immediacy of wikis, in which, contrary to moderated mailing lists, texts are published right away, brings stimulation into the discussion. Suitable "starting points" are required at central nodes in the system, especially on the start page, that aid in quickly bringing users to their desired content. In larger systems, a work plan is necessary here as well.

To moderate and be moderated

In wiki projects, participants frequently take on moderation duties or act as maintainers who take on additional tasks to maintain the functionality of the overall project, receiving wiki administrator privileges in the process. It is not unusual for moderators and admins to be elected and, following their "term", subsequently pass the job on to others.

The best bet is to continually be prepared for a *mutual* learning process in which you may also be dependent on other moderators. Moderation alone is fast becoming its own work area, and should be taken on by people who are not obligated to provide content to the project, so that they can maintain a clear head for their job. Of course, your group can also agree that moderators be changed on a regular basis. Just as in the case of admins, it is advisable to have at least two moderators.

Superiors should not moderate

Superiors are less suited to be moderators for the simple fact that they are heavily involved in the content or legal aspects of a project, and conflicts of interest may quickly arise. It is better to either opt for external moderation, or for people from the same organization

[32] See Meretz 2003, 103ff.

[33] See re: duties of moderation e.g. Dauscher 1998, 29ff.

but a different department. The latter have a good idea of the subject matter, yet they are not mired in content issues. Of utmost importance is that the group trust the moderators.

31.2.3 A few more General Tips

"Sowing" wikis is actually a skill, and today we know much better than a few years ago that the desired "wiki effect" does not happen by itself. It takes a "green thumb" and a suitable environment. Helmut Leitner also complains of low participation in several public wikis. He sees a certain asymmetry in some users: They feel only the others should reveal themselves and be transparent; the step needed to bring oneself into the process and say, "Here I am" is still a very big one for many participants. Even if, as a lone wiki fan, you only have limited influence on group processes, there are still a few elementary rules we have learned from experience and would like to point out:

Access

- If you are eager to start, don't hesitate to ask the mundane question as to what equipment the target group possesses: Often, people who are to participate in working on a wiki lack the necessary Internet access, both at work and at home.

Involve key persons

- While it is true that wiki projects thrive on spontaneity, we still want to be well prepared and have spoken to key persons in organizations. For instance, the introduction of a wiki could meet with resistance if the workers' council feels you have gone over their heads. That is why you should really take time to clarify the function and content of the wiki. After all, a collaborative work atmosphere is prerequisite to the "wiki effect" – as we have intimated, it is a very delicate plant. Generally, environments in which knowledge is a weapon are not ideal for wikis. Often in companies, the question is raised as to if and who can and may evaluate the log file. What does participation or non-participation in the wiki mean for my professional future? Will I make myself superfluous if I offer my knowledge publicly? Such questions regarding data protection are inevitable in such a radically open system as a wiki, and it is worth taking these questions seriously and discussing them.

Patience

- While you should not become discouraged too quickly, experience has shown that euphoric illusions and false expectations can also lead to the failure of a wiki project. An overload of expectations can rapidly cause even its advocates to become disappointed. Patience is a virtue in this case.

- Don't plan a Wikipedia at the outset: Be realistic in estimating the probable size of your wiki project. There is a big difference between using the wiki as a medium for a team or small group and for a large group with over 30 members or so. In the latter case, direct communication between all participants is no longer possible. Smaller groups will crystallize, similar to that café where you sit by yourselves but can still be seen by other groups. In the wiki, this means that the control of the overall project can no longer be carried out by a singe person. It also means, though, that smaller groups, for instance, can do without editing typing errors or that moderators are needed.

Estimate the size of the wiki

- An empty wiki will stay empty: Even if a system of complete freedom is permitted, a new wiki should still posses a certain prestructuring of content. You can make it much easier for future authors if the structure of the page and the articles can be seen in one or two examples. "Sowing" wikis means providing "pictures" of how text could be written and setting up an initial system of organization from where work can progress. Introductory workshops can speed up at least the clarification processes important to a wiki.

Don't put up an empty wiki

- There is no such thing as "my" wiki: Some wiki systems differ greatly in their configurations and expandability. The best answer is to tailor a suitable open-source wiki to one's own needs and work out the basic content structure with people experienced in wikis. Nevertheless, do not despair, because the golden rule is still …

Retrofit your wiki technology

- Keep it simple. Too many technical features, regulations and categorizations can squelch the creativity needed to enable the wiki to unfold. Optimal usability is elementary for wiki software.

… and don't overload it

- Let it grow: In the "social web", trust is important. In a wiki, it is essential. If you try to keep control of the process, you just might succeed in suffocating it. The responsibility for the process is in the hands of the participants. Wikis give you room to organize work processes yourself in a meaningful way, beyond rigid regulations. They enable group processes that demand more from their participants because they are to take over conceptual work, but they will only do so if they have a clear perspective on implementing it, and if they are truly involved and in control of the process.

Delegate responsibility

32 Social Perspectives

32.1 Clash of the Wikis

32.1.1 Wikis as an Engine for Social Change?

Media revolution?

What do all of these technical developments really mean? Are we witnessing a "secret media revolution"? Are web logs, wikis and free software changing the world from behind? These are some of the questions Erik Möller asks in a book of the same name. It indicates that we are faced with difficult problems: What is the relationship between technology and social progress? Something seems to be getting out of hand with wikis. Defenders of free software and Wikipedians see great benefit in it. Others fear these uncontrollable developments.

Fundamental question of social principles

It seems to be impossible to speak of wikis without being immediately confronted with fundamental problems: objectivity and partiality, intrinsic and extrinsic motivation, central and decentralized control mechanisms, hierarchical and antiauthoritarian order structures. And, last but not least: the question of other lifestyles and other property relationships. The debate about wikis gains energy because it is taking place right in the middle of a phase of accelerated social change. It is true that, in the case of wikis, as in that of free software, we are talking superficially about the use of the new information and communication technologies; yet the discussion can neither be understood nor conducted without the fundamental question of social principles thus raised by it.

Collective intelligence

At this point in the first edition of this book, we turned to the topic of technical determinism using the example of research into artificial intelligence. We pointed out that technology and software cannot change anything on their own; technical developments remain neutral towards society. It is ultimately people who plan and change. Today, however, we have to adjust this standpoint a bit: Because while the development of artificial intelligence is still a theme in science and research, this debate has shifted somewhat especially under the influence of the mass phenomena on the Internet. Today, the dominant discussion revolves around "collective intelligence".

Information as an agent?

Since the 1990s, the "information society" has been propagated in the mass media. The significance of "communication" and "information" for the structuring of a society was overemphasized. "Information" was even stylized by some scientists into being an agent itself, while every historical and social relationship and the individual himself were relegated to the background. Other scientists began investigating so-called "emergent" phenomena. The idea was to develop resilient models for intelligent behaviors of "superorganisms". "The whole is more than the sum of its parts:" Emergence theory is focused on processes that cannot be explained based on their subsystems.

Swarm intelligence

This concerns wikis and wiki projects to the extent that the central question of wiki discussions is whether or not self-organized collectives, even if they are unconscious, can deliver more precise results than individuals. If so, how do they do it? What role does "information" play in it? Are people exposed to mechanisms on the Internet that they themselves can hardly control? Are they controlled by their instincts and drives? In other words: If there is a media revolution, it would be nice to know who is driving it and with what goals and whether or not the result would be a kind of "progress" or what possible actions would emerge in the upshot.

When the buzzword "swarm intelligence" hit the scene, we were suddenly able to put our finger on it. The term "swarm intelligence" comes from the research field of artificial intelligence. Yet here, the attempt is to use insects living in colonies – such as ants, bees or termites – as models for the development of networked software agent systems serving to shape social processes. And here is precisely where the danger lies of networks, swarms or the masses being declared independent subjects. However, it becomes evident that, in contrast to technology discussions of the 1970s, today fewer inventions of *humans* serve as archetypes for determinist world explanation models; instead *nature* is serving this purpose.

Are we currently experiencing a shift from technological determinism to a sort of biological determinism? At least *Telepolis* author Ralf Grötker can refer to several trend researchers who have identified a new model in "swarming organizations", who talk of a "new age of networked intelligence", in which "connections are more important than the parts".[34] This bio-determinist is primarily searching for flexibility and adaptability, for the recovery of a stable whole.

Digital Maoism?

We cannot pursue these very intriguing questions with the necessary depth of attention, but rather simply stimulate more precise scrutiny of the debate on this medium and the communities surrounding it – because reductional views such as the transfer of the agent model of "swarm intelligence" to the complex human social reality have met with harsh criticism in the free software scene, for example. The most well known critique is without doubt an essay by Jaron Lanier, who, not long ago, spoke of a "digital Maoism" and rejected any overemphasis of the collective in wiki projects.[35] Lanier's essay launched a widely noticed debate.[36]

In general, no one disputes the fact that large groups are commonly capable of making statements on current (!) circumstances that will draw a consensus. There are also certainly statistical effects with which current processes can be effectively exhibited. Reductionist interpretation patterns, on the other hand, pursue the goal of denying any level of reflection on the part of other people and legitimizing sovereignty and non-democratic social systems. Yet reality in wiki projects is often quite different than what some geeks might piece together from books. Wiki technology and wiki communities, when examined closely, and this is our point, *especially cannot* be used for determinist philosophies.

32.1.2 Wikis and Ideology

Ideologically critical approach

Let us dwell a moment on wikis and their significance in the discussion of social developments. Wikis are "hip" for a great variety of reasons. We can approach this fact in an ideologically critical manner and inquire about the historical and social circumstances that enable it. Even the classic Marx referred to the circumstance that the bourgeoisie cannot exist under the rule of competition "without continually revolutionizing the instruments of production (…)".[37] Technical innovations are supposed to conquer and secure markets or lower production costs. Research and development become part

---

[34] "Willkommen im Schwarm", telepolis 9.11.2006, (http://www.heise.de/tp/r4/artikel/23/23822/1.html).
[35] http://www.edge.org/3rd_culture/lanier06/lanier06_index.html, Aug. 16, 2007.
[36] See the end of Lanier's essay.
[37] MEW 4, 465.

of a political and economical overall strategy. For instance, the "information society" has already been criticized often with regard to a technical integration ideology in which the focus is on the securing of definition rulers, the organization of approval and the mobilization of resources. Thus, there is an attempt to integrate every technical and social invention, including wikis, into the existing circumstances in order to revamp these circumstances. There are several examples in which the user of wikis is solely designed to demonstrate that one has reached the technological state of the art.

Furthermore, there is the practical approach of experimenting with wikis to simplify or restructure work processes. The motivation behind this, regardless of the person, is the individual wish to have to work less or have more time for more meaningful work. Himanen warns of the danger of making social progress dependent upon technological progress: "We are quickly falling for the illusion that technical progress will automatically structure our lives in a less work-focused way. The network society does not question the Protestant work ethic. Fending for oneself continues to dominate the spirit of capitalism aimed at work."[38]

That brings us to those wiki users that try to mobilize the as yet unrealized emancipation potential of society. Here, it is wiki technology and successful communities that exert a special fascination – a fascination that primarily affects the users of successful wiki projects themselves. Because as a rule, tools create latitude because they overcome natural limitations. They open perspectives: Relationships become evident and the future thus becomes plannable. There is no doubt that the history of humans is closely related to technical innovations, tools and machines. According to Rauter, "People exist because they make tools. The tools that man develops not only decide whether man lives, but also how he lives. The experiences he has when he manufactures and uses tools change him. His changes flow into the tools. The tools affect how people deal with each other."[39]

Reactions

This shows that tools have an effect on humans in their capacity to interpret. According to our experiences, this effect is all too often ignored in the discussion of wikis: because in wiki projects, these reactions can be especially intense, since interaction with the social environment is generally deeper than in chats or other applications. This may also lead to a strong polarization between wiki enthusiasts and wiki pessimists.

[38] Himanen 2001, 31.
[39] Rauter 1977.

As the authors of this book, we are naturally also exposed to these effects. In the book, we show several great features of wikis and refer to encouraging wiki projects. In doing so, we are also always "ideologists", if you will. No matter how, the success of individual projects as well as negative developments do not enable us to draw general conclusions regarding a society or people. We can really only illustrate possibilities and list experiences under whose conditions wiki projects do not work or which social opportunities are linked to this technology.

This brings us to the last fascinating point in this chapter: the question as to how far wiki technology itself contributes to contemplation of alternative socializing models. Are wikis an especially democratic medium?

32.1.3 Wiki, a Democratic Medium?

First of all, we know that human planning fundamentally predates the construction and utilization of tools such as wikis. For example, the Internet is the result of planning on the part of the U.S. military. And that, in turn, demonstrates the close relationship between the development of tools and the goals, experiences and assumptions of their "creators". Tools are embedded in people's culture and society with their specific decision structures and power relationships. The completion of an object marks the end of a labor and planning process that has taken on material form. The new tool can now be further developed and used. Often it also becomes valuable for a completely different realm or is even used for the absolute opposite of its original intention. A tool, or more precisely, the development of tools, is thus in no way socially "neutral". Unfortunately, it is an illusion to think that inventions are made completely free of purpose and that society takes up these inventions. Society must at least provide the material prerequisites for scientific freedom.

The Internet is an example of a technology that was initially developed for military purposes but has become a large system that now fulfills completely different and public purposes. This is what is known as the "dual use" of a technology. You can use it one way or the other. Nevertheless, there are still differences. For instance, developments such as the atom bomb have hindered social progress more than promoted it. After all, a bomb can only either be detonated or not.

Democratic use of a medium

What about wiki technology? Is it "inherently democratic" (Cunningham)? Have irreversible developments been put into motion by wikis?

In the early 1970s, Enzensberger, with regard to the mass media of television and radio, argued that not the media itself but the utilization of that media makes a difference.[40] In his *Baukasten zu einer Theorie der Medien (Constituents of a Theory of the Media),* he offers further suggestions for an emancipatory use of the media that can also be translated to the interactive use of the Internet: decentralized programs, every recipient a potential sender, mobilization of the masses, interaction of participants, feedback, political learning processes, collective production, and social control through self-organization. Similarly, Rilling believes: "The Internet offers no room for decisions, but places for political debates, communication and the forming of opinions."[41]

The wiki invention

What Brecht said about radio applies to wikis: "It was not the public that had been waiting for radio, but radio that had been waiting for the public."[42] Cunningham's invention was initially intended to solve a practical problem. It was all about creating simple software documentation and, as far as we know, nothing more. His notion that uncomplicated and non-hierarchical cooperation is part of successful software development was included in the development. If he had thought that software development would not be possible without authoritarian, central control, the program code would have developed differently. The result is a program whose further use would only become apparent with time. We can say that in the development of the first wikis, ideas came into play that were "inherently democratic". And the developers of a technology or software do not even have to necessarily be aware of these ideas. However, a democratic effect through wikis is not automatically a done deed, even if they have opened new possibilities in that direction. On the contrary, today wikis are employed in private companies and organizations without being the cause of any fundamental changes.

Research policy

Given the above, we can ask how research and development will be organized in the future. Who decides what will be built and promoted? It is the question as to whether or not we wish to continue making technological development dependent upon military and private application interests in the hope that something civilly useful will come out of it.

---

[40] See Enzensberger 1970, 173.
[41] Rilling 2004.
[42] Brecht 1930/1967, 128.

Decisive in the assessment of whether tools were and are able to bring about any socially beneficial effects depends, *firstly*, on the question of which goals its creation was based upon and *secondly*, with which goals it is used; this must be seen before the backdrop of the extent to which social circumstances have been cemented or accordingly changed.

Goals and structuring process

32.2 Ownership

Wiki: free software

A hot topic, not only for the wiki community, is the significance of licenses and free software. Generally, digitalization and the world wide web as a world wide copy machine have rekindled the fundamental debate on the role and function of ownership, primarily that of intellectual property (copyright, patents, trademark protection). The wiki communities also needed to face this issue, for the simple fact that, with the publication of wiki software and every further wiki clone, a fundamental decision regarding their conditions for use had to be made. Does a legal entity have the right to appropriate the software or parts of the software, and for what purposes? Many wikis today are subject to GNU-GPL regulations, meaning they are free software programs that may not be sold.[43] Thus, wiki programmers are among the defenders of free software.

Free content

However, we are confronted with exploitation rights not only with regard to software, but also to the content of wiki pages.[44] To whom do the texts and images belong? When is a text a text? Who is legally responsible? Research into whether image material is part of the public domain is a very time-consuming effort at Wikipedia. After all, the site strives to guarantee that Wikipedia truly remains a "free content" encyclopedia. This means that it supports a copyright which allows anyone to copy, alter or otherwise use text for any purpose.[45] The original or altered version may be freely distributed. The opposite also applies: If you contribute content to Wikipe-

[43] We already discussed licensing in Sect. I.1.5.2. The best introduction to the history and issues of free software is provided by Grassmuck 2002.
[44] See Möller 2005, 171f.
[45] The GNU Free Documentation License (GFDL), which governs Wikipedia articles, is the most common license for "free" content. The FreeBSD Documentation License, on the other hand, is not a copyleft license. Furthermore, Creative Commons releases licenses which however do not ensure "free content" for all.

dia, that text is automatically subject to that license, and you cannot retroactively assert copyright claims.[46]

Wave of privatization

Making available freely-accessible knowledge stands in deliberate contrast to the current trend toward the privatization of public goods, a trend that spares no area of society: from the hollowing out of the public character of companies to the privatization of water supply or education. The debate on the ability to patent gene sequences or software is also part of the issue.

Academies and monestaries

Partisanship for the reclamation of commons (Allmende) and public goods from the culture of the private are the order of the day. With regard to open source codes, Himanen speaks metaphorically of the "academy" in which scientists make their work available to others so that it can be utilized, tested and further developed.[47] In contrast, he metaphorically refers to closed models that withhold information and demonstrate authoritarian relationships as "monasteries". However, critical social theorists question whether a simply ethical critique is perhaps insufficient. The bone of contention is whether a call to "social responsibility" paired with "competitive ability" is trying to bring together two diametrically opposed principles.

Property Rights Regime

Once again, valid social control models – and not the morals of individuals such as Bill Gates – need to be investigated. The privatization of commons is the prerequisite to be able to market these goods: in this case, software. To make information products commercially utilizable, a shortage must be created. In the case of software, this means withholding the source text and limiting it through licensing and patents. Software is subject to a property rights regime. This results in an uneven fight, with attempts of infiltration, criminalization and rejection and the development of new strategies and counter-strategies.[48] There is doubt as to whether this can be traced back to a basic anthropological constant ("That's just the way people are") or to seemingly "objective" necessities that result from an economic constitution that eliminates or controls existential fundamentals of competitors.

High hopes in free software

The free software community represents a counterdraft to the commercialization of information products – especially as an alternative to Unix. Free software functions here as an alternative model that generates the hope that the expansion of the information tech-

---

[46] As a private individual or firm, you can subject your texts to a free content license (copyleft). You can find the GFDL on the Internet at: http://www.gnu.org/copyleft/fdl.html. Links to further licenses such as Open-Content License or the GPL can be found at: http://www.ifross.de/ifross_html/lizenzcenter.html

[47] Himanen 2001, 91ff.

[48] For an introduction to the discussion, see e.g. Meretz 2003 and Nuss 2003.

nology-based leading sector can be able to be seriously blocked by making available stable and free software. These hopes have only been partially realized. The property rights regime was in no way questioned by the demand for freedom of information. Several forms of ownership can coexist. Free goods can be utilized very well as a component of an overall product; for instance, in the case of free software, through support and books.

Wikimedia Projects

In the attempt to transform digital goods into commodities through copyright, patents and trademarks, the music industry is leading the way, in its fight against "bootleg" copies with their motto: "downloading is theft". On the opposite side, with the Wikimedia group, a significant player is growing that is turning against the marketing of software patents, image, film and text rights with its free content by pursuing the goal of building up enclaves of digital commons.[49] The Wiki Commons project has already been mentioned, as has Wikibooks, whose focus is the provision of cost-free textbooks whose commercial alternatives must be obtained at great cost. This is done in the hope of expanding access even to social classes with less disposable income.

A nerve struck?

To what extent the nerve of an emerging high-tech capitalism has been struck with the blockade of privatization tendencies in information technology is debatable. In his book *The Age of Access: The New Culture of Hypercapitalism, Where All Life is a Paid-For Experience* (2000), Jeremy Rifkin sees the question of "access" as the successor to the ownership question. In contrast, others have raised the objection that the "old economy" and its accompanying ownership relationships, over which the new technologies are simply superimposed, are thus being masked.[50] Furthermore, in various instances, the argument has been voiced that a greater danger is growing from the property rights regime through the direct contact between producers and consumers than through the provision of cost-free services.

Legal political initiatives

The "key legal political invention" (Rilling) of the free software culture is the GPL license. It serves as the basis of further free content licenses, such as FDL or Creative Commons. Using such licenses, and based on the respective national legal systems, an attempt is being made to utilize the legal framework to secure open goods and commons. In this regard, however, the discussion cannot stop at the topic of digital and intellectual property. The question will be posed with regard to the overall concept of civil ownership. When attempting to answer the question, it could help to remember

---

[49] In addition to others, such as the *Free Software Foundation*, *Creative Commons* or the hacker culture.
[50] e.g. Haug 2003, 67f.

that the issue of ownership does not focus on the relationship between a person and a thing, but rather the relationship between people with reference to a thing.

32.3 Forms of Work

Alternative organization models

It has been hinted on various occasions that the wiki philosophy inspires one to rethink the future organization of work. Centrally planned, controlled and regulated organizational models are countered with those that are decentralized and self-organized. One motive for this is that the tendency to subject work processes to bureaucratic controls (for instance in the course of quality or issue management) limits room for design and suffocates any intrinsic motivation. As early as the introduction of Linux, the free software movement not only confronted Windows with a new operating system, but also with a decentralized and democratic organizational philosophy. Alternatives are being sought to heteronymous and estranged work relationships, which ultimately also affect one's entire lifestyle, private life and the organization of one's free time. Some of the defenders of free software see here the budding of a new, non-capitalistic social order and hope that the production methods of programmers can be carried over to other social realms.

In this regard, wikis are one in a series of free software success stories. It is being proven that, as in the case of other software projects, free work forms can be employed to surmount even complex problems. In the long run, their products and services will even demonstrate a high degree of permanence, because more people are involved in the development process right from the start.

Counter-concepts?

The extent to which Linux and the wiki philosophy are already examples of true counter-concepts thus remains to be seen. The Net world is currently an anarchistic one, yet it also reproduces existing control models. During the Linux debate, Nuss already argued that the decentralized work form could also assist less free production paradigms:

"Their [free software's, R.H.] production method is based on public knowledge, cooperation, flat hierarchy, flexibility, international networking, and largely unpaid work, usually without contractual obligations. The production model of open source and free software has been serving as a role model for industry for quite some time now."[51]

[51] Nuss 2003, 154. Candeias develops the thought farther (2004, 179ff.).

Large private companies are also searching for solutions to their structural crises and for ways to be more flexible on the market. However, centrally regulated control models prove too rigid at an early stage. Employees have been independently compensating for the resulting problems for ages. They have been counteracting errors, faulty planning and malfunctions. "Without the targeted deviation from plans and instructions, company specifications cannot be fulfilled."[52] This means that companies, too, have been dependent upon the autonomous actions of their employees all along. Some see the solution to all problems in the promotion of employee self-organization. The goal is to make work enjoyable again, motivate volunteerism or include customers in development processes. However, this is coupled with unsecured jobs and a consolidation of working hours through – computer-assisted – optimization. Corporate planning security is shifted to the detriment of personnel planning security. Yet the ability to plan is a prerequisite of human self-actualization.

Self-responsible control processes in companies

The wiki communities are propagating their idea that work organization "from the bottom up" can work by trying it out, and with a good measure of success. Their work organization model differs from the conventional pattern through a certain openness for results: The responsibility for planning and execution of the work process is completely transferred to the producers. The wiki communities, with their actions, promote social ingenuity. Their attempts at initiating large wiki projects not only have an external effect, but are also a form of self-enlightenment in such experiments.

Social ingenuity

32.4 Objectivity

Open systems are often met with mistrust. Forgoing an intermediate (quality) control causes many to doubt the credibility of the information, which is less a product of the philosophical dimension discussed above. Mistrust is directed at the question as to whether or not the masses even have enough knowledge to produce something trustworthy. In addition, it is difficult to verify from whom the information originates. Are some postmodern theorists correct when they speak of a disappearance of the author? On the Internet, it is easy to take on another identity – one need only think of the "sock puppets" mentioned at the start of this book. Furthermore, in cooperatively written texts, individual authors often can no longer be discerned. Also, after the previous discussion on the political dimen-

Credibility problem

[52] Candeias 2004, 179.

sion of the wiki phenomenon: Is this not in fact a process of manipulation and counter-manipulation? We need to take this question seriously. How can objectivity and quality be achieved?[53]

Motivations

Let us begin with the motivations of wiki authors. The problem of vandalism has already been described. Destructive practices of anonymous users are a lasting problem of open systems. However, it is interesting to examine the other reasons why authors refrain from wanting to be named.

Appreciation and work forms

Similar processes can be observed in wikis as have been discussed with regard to the free software community and critical information technology. In open processes, authors do not disappear – quite the opposite is true. Within the communities, many discover an appreciation and work forms that they seldom find in professional life. The Wikimedia projects, as the free software initiatives before them, enable self-determined work in a sensible project directed at the good of the community. Recognition and the fact that one's own contributions are noticed and discussed, motivate participants in a project to continue working. However, this also means that most Wikipedia texts in fact are not created anonymously. On the contrary – as we will see when observing the statistics – a group of people forms that know each other and establish trust in each other. This is generally applicable: In the evaluation of open systems, one must not forget the concrete social relationships behind them.

Quality system

Good will alone is not enough. That is why wiki systems must develop assessment possibilities and conventions that promote verification and trackability. Once again, Wikipedia, for which a package of such measures has been developed, serves as a positive example. Initially, many people look at the articles in the encyclopedia. Ideally, they would immediately edit any discrepancies. Then admins check the edits of articles. The recent changes function offers a quick overview. In addition, frequently vandalized pages are placed under special supervision. This permanent effort is the price of an open system. Furthermore, conventions regarding language, methodology and balance of content have been stipulated, for example, with regard to the extent to which every opinion should be cited in an article.

NPOV

This is the point where the Wikipedia community conducts its debate on the relationship between objectivity and partiality, which equally applies when dealing with every other medium. We are talking about the debate on the neutral point of view (NPVO). Basically, it states that articles in Wikipedia are to take a neutral view-

[53] To what extent the traditional mass media in their current form are "objective" would extend beyond the scope of this book.

point into account.[54] This initially means a minimum of quality measures and the adherence to certain conventions: objective language, a reporting perspective and indirect speech. For instance, the observation "Picasso was the greatest painter of the 20th century" becomes "In the art world, Picasso is considered to be one of the greatest painters of the 20th century."

A variety of positions

Then there is the representation of a variety of positions. An article "should fairly represent all sides of a dispute".[55] The English version of Wikipedia stresses that an objective standpoint is not possible, thus exhibiting a greater awareness of the problem. One motivation for this phenomenon is the desire not to simply declare truths. Readers are encouraged to make their own decisions and form their own opinions. However, this point of view can often unintentionally lead to relativizations, such as the following:

"**Holocaust denial** is the claim that the mainstream historical version of the Holocaust is either highly exaggerated or completely falsified. Experts, witnesses, and historians almost universally regard Holocaust denial as untrue. Holocaust deniers prefer to be called Holocaust revisionists. Most people contend that the latter term is misleading."[56]

Absolute neutrality impossible

Among Wikipedia authors, there are various opinions in this regard. A few consider neutral, objective portrayals to be possible. For others, neutral points of view, even in an encyclopedia, are impossible: "We can only seek a type of writing that is agreeable to essentially rational people who may differ on particular points" (Jimmy Wales).

If science used to claim to be objective, a new perception has taken hold in the last century in which every statement is initially selective.[57] A view is already present in the selection of a topic, the terminology, explanatory patterns and models. We know that, his-

---

[54] e.g. it has been stated: "To whatever extent possible, encyclopedic writing should steer clear of taking any particular stance other than the stance of the neutral point of view. The neutral point of view attempts to present ideas and facts in such a fashion that both supporters and opponents can agree. Of course, 100% agreement is not possible; there are ideologues in the world who will not concede to any presentation other than a forceful statement of their own point of view."
http://en.wikipedia.org/wiki/Wikipedia:Neutral_point_of_view,
10 Jun 2005. For the current version, see ibid.

[55] http://en.wikipedia.org/wiki/NPOV, 15. Jan 2005.

[56] http://en.wikipedia.org/wiki/Holocaust_denial, 15. Jan 2005.

[57] Extreme postmodernists take this notion as far as relativism, or find that everything is constructed.

torically, dictionaries have always been an expression of the knowledge of a certain time and class (as a rule, the educated bourgeoisie).

Critical theory

Critical theory has tried to handle this dilemma, among other ways, by indicating that the subjective person creates objective relationships. The theory considers objective perceptions to be identifiable among the contradictions of the circumstances. To put it very simply, the difference between what is and what could be results in a standard with which individual practices and ideas can be "measured" – a viewpoint that can also be employed within the context of publications in wikis. The discussion on objectivity could benefit from considering critical theory.

So what do we do to obtain as much objectivity as possible?

Partiality

1. Whether we like it or not, subjectivity is prerequisite to objective consciousness. Objectivity is not a freedom from values. Those wanting to be objective must have a point of view and be able to say where they want to go. Only then can statements be discussed. The important factors are verifiability, logical argumentation, and measuring arguments with proclaimed goals and their observance.

Sociographics

2. Striving toward objectivity is always also a form of self-education. For instance, this means asking who uses a piece of wiki software; because even if the new media tend toward bursting traditional social classes, use of the Internet, up to now, has been characterized by considerable social inequality.[58] This is no different in wikis, at least not as of yet. According to Wales, 10% of the users of Wikipedia perform 80% of the edits, and 5% perform 66% of the edits. Thus, despite the openness of the system, core groups of authors have crystallized. Research into this phenomenon is still in its initial stages, and has yet to be intensified. Under consideration of these circumstances, it is better to estimate which projects are operated by which social groups and which attitudes they represent in the process. What is their social and historical position from which their actions originate? Using this requirement, we must clarify to what extent partial or total interest can be represented. This requires additional knowledge of the sociology of group processes.

Power gradients in wikis

3. As we have already demonstrated in our model of levels in the first section of this book, wikis, too, are internally not authority-free zones. There are various power relationships that are related to access rights, for instance. In addition, real power relationships

[58] Regarding the inequality of the social user profile and power relationships on the Net, see e.g. Rilling 2004.

(ownership, employment relationships, capitalistic order structures, etc.) intersect with the functions within the wiki community. This fact, too, must also be taken into account.

32.4.1 Progress?

Problematic progress

In the 20th century at the latest, progress has transformed into a problematic term. For example, Walter Benjamin writes: "Marx says the revolutions are the locomotives of world history. But perhaps they are something different altogether. Perhaps revolutions are the hand of humankind riding in the train grabbing for the emergency brake."[59] His criticism is directed at estranged lifestyles that bank on historical change taking place with or without the intervention of humans. His utopia is very similar to that of many free software developers. It is about the crystallization of a truly self-determining lifestyle. This means that the idea of what progress is must continually be revised and agreed upon. In the process, the emphases of social labor shift.

Initial steps

In the example of the wiki communities, we see that the first step is a very small one. Enzensberger remarks that every socialist strategy of the media must aspire to eliminate the isolation of individual participants in social learning and production processes. "This is not possible without self-organization of the participants. This is the political core of the media issue."[60] The Wikipedia project appears to be re-figuring the conditions of change. One important point is the mutual acceptance of one's counterparts as reasonable – and we would like to add non-competitive – entities. The enormous difficulties coupled with this process cannot be ignored. One could perhaps speak of progress when wikis become a truly collaborative and integrative medium extending beyond certain social groups. But if there is to be collaboration, then with what goal?

Beginning

Wikis are fascinating tools, but not cure-alls. They must continually be filled with new ideas in order to be able to advance toward the distant goal of free development of the individual as a condition for the free development of the collective. In the wiki world, this has already been realized today in several small areas.

[59] Benjamin GS, I, 1231.
[60] Enzensberger 1970, 169.

Appendix

A Installations in TWiki

Perl

Unfortunately, some Perl installation lack modules required by TWiki or its plugins for smooth operation. Thus, they must be subsequently installed. The program CPAN will help you do so, which must be configured after you have opened it for the first time.

Caution: CPAN requires an Internet connection for the installation of the new modules!

Under Cygwin, you must first enter the following lines:

Shell
```
export TEMP=/c/temp
```

Now you can start CPAN in Cygwin, as in Linux, with

Shell
```
cpan
```

When you first open CPAN, it must be configured. That means, you will need to answer a host of questions that can all be confirmed with <ENTER>, until you are asked to indicate your area of the world. Enter the number of your continent, e.g. for "North America", and in the next question, your country, e.g. "USA". Now you will see a list of servers that you can select by entering one or more numbers separated by a space. Now you should see the `cpan>` prompt.

The program is ready, and you can set up the missing modules using the `install` command. TWiki, for example, requires the following three packages:

Shell

```
install Net::SMTP
install Digest::SHA1
install MIME::Base64
```

Perl is then equipped for all eventualities of TWiki operation. You can leave CPAN with the command `exit`.

Shebang

The Perl script files must be adapted so that they refer to the Perl interpreter. This allows the web server to "know" what to do with the file. Under UNIX, it is possible to indicate the type of file or program with which the script is to be executed at the beginning of a document, in the so-called shebang line. In our case, it must refer to the Perl interpreter. The TWiki scripts are set up by default such that they refer to the standard Perl path under Linux. Thus, under Windows, you will most likely have to adjust this. You can use the Cygwin shell to do so. The method shown is also valid for Linux.

First, switch to the *bin* directory and create a backup for the event that something does not function properly:

Shell

```
cd /twiki/bin
mkdir .backup
cp * .backup
```

With the command

Shell

```
head -1 view
```

you can display the current shebang line of the *view* scripts. The following Perl command changes the lines of all files in the directory. The Perl path is the entire path in Unix notation, including the name of the program, i.e. "perl". In our example, it is *c:/cygwin/bin/perl*.

Shell

```
perl -pi~ -e        ↵
 's;#!/usr/bin/perl;#!perlpfad;' *[a-z]
```

If you now display the first line again, you should see the new path. Otherwise, delete the files and retrieve your backup from *.backup* to try again:

```
rm *
cp .backup/* .
```

If the changes have been successful, you can delete the backup files and directory again:

```
rm .backup/*
rmdir .backup
```

Changing *RCS* Owners

To manually adapt the RCS locks in the Cygwin or bash shell, first switch to the data directory and make a backup of the files:

```
cd /twiki/data
tar czvf alles.tar.gz */*
```

Now change the entry for the owner using the following Perl command (put it all on one line):

```
perl -pi~~~ -e 'NR <= 10 && ↵
  s/nobody:/username:/ ' */*,v
```

To be on the safe side, let us check to make sure everything has been changed. If you do not receive a message at this point, the operation was a success. In that case, you can delete the old files.

```
grep 'strict;$ ' */*,v | grep -v username
rm */*~~~
```

Should something have gone wrong, you can restore the former status by copying the backup back over. This is done using

```
tar xzvf alles.tar.gz
```

Otherwise, delete the backup file with

```
rm alles.tar.gz
```

When we open *testenv* again, we will still receive a warning, but this time we can happily ignore it.

B Comparison Chart

	bitweaver	Confluence	DokuWiki	HalloWiki	MediaWiki
Current version	1.3.1	2.5.4	2006-11-06	Sunrise	1.11
Homepage	www.bitweaver.org	www.atlassian.com	wiki.splitbrain.org/ wiki:dokuwiki	www.hallo-wiki.biz	www.mediawiki.org
Audience	systems with heavy user traffic	mainly for enterprise intranets	private users, small and medium-sized businesses	all	all
System requirements					
Webserver	Apache, IIS	Apache and others	Apache and others	Apache, IIS	Apache, IIS
Language	PHP	Java	PHP	PHP	PHP
Datea storage	MySQL, PostgreSQL, Oracle, Sybase	MySQL, PostgreSQL, Oracle, Sybase	file based	MySQL, PostgreSQL	MySQL, PostgreSQL
Security					
Access control per page	plugin	yes	ACL	yes	no
Special features					
Subsections	no	yes	no	no	no
Structured data	no	no	no	no	no
Internationalization: Available languages	30	no	39	>100	>100
PDF-Export	yes	yes	no	yes	plugin
Workflow	no	no	no	yes	no
Comments	threaded	threaded	discussion page (plugin)	discussion page	discussion page
Usability					
Administration surface	no	yes	no	yes	no
Section editing	no	no	yes	yes	yes
WYSIWYG editor	optional	yes	no	yes	no
File attachements	yes	yes	yes	yes	yes
Extensions	yes	yes	yes	yes	yes
Special features	wiki is ultimately a module within a comprehensive content management package.	has to be licensed.	light weight, easy to use.	based on MediaWiki; with many extras.	system of Wikipedia. discussion page combined with articles.

	MoinMoin	PmWiki	ProWiki	TWiki	Wetpaint
Current version	1.5.8	2.1.27	2.0.045	4.1.2	--
Homepage	moinmoin.wikiwiki web.de	www.pmwiki.org	www.prowiki.org	www.twiki.org	www.wetpaint.com
Audience	WikiFarms, less than 100.000 pages	all	small and medium-sized Wiki projects, mainly wiki farms	medium and large-sized businesses, communities	all
System requirements					
Webserver	Apache, IIS, and others	Apache, IIS, and others	every webserver with perl support	Apache and others	--
Language	Python	PHP	Perl	Perl	--
Datea storage	file based	file based	file based	file based	--
Security					
Access control per page	ACL	plugin	yes	yes	yes (only control of edit rights)
Special features					
Subsections	no	yes, groups	yes, complete wiki	yes, 1 level	no
Structured data	no	no	yes, variables	Forms	no
Internationalization: Available languages	approx. 25	26	7	13	English
PDF-Export	plugin	plugin	no	plugin	no
Workflow	no	no	no	no	no
Comments	no	discussion page (plugin)	no	threaded	threaded
Usability					
Administration surface	no	no	no	no	no
Section editing	no	plugin	yes	plugin	no
WYSIWYG editor	yes	plugin	no	yes	yes
File attachements	yes	optional	yes	yes	yes
Extensions	yes	yes	no	yes	no
Special features	optimized for use in wiki farms	well arranged, robust, equipped with (almost) any feature	fractal wiki: Individual wikis within a wiki can be created	optimized for use as intranet in businesses	commercial AJAX-based; hosted wiki, no installation necessary

Glossary

Add-on. An independent program that performs additional services for a certain piece of software. → Plugin.

Administrator (Admin). Software user with special rights. Has the task of installing, maintaining and updating the software and of establishing the conditions that normal users need to perform their daily business with the software.

ASCII. Refers to a standard of code for characters on a computer. ASCII text often stands for simple, non-formatted text. ASCII art is the depiction of drawings using simple text. Requires that the text be rendered in a non-proportional font.

Authoring tool. An application with which various data, such as text, graphics, sound or animation, can be assembled to create multimedia content.

Back end. Refers to that portion of a software application that runs on the server and administers the data. In comparison, the program that displays the data to the client is known as the front end. The back end area is only accessible to administrators.

Backlink. A link on another page that leads to the current page.

Blog. ("Weblog"). A type of web-based diary in which a "blogger" can quickly publish articles. These entries are displayed in a list, beginning with the newest entry. Other users can usually comment on but not alter entries.

Browse space. The central navigation link in Confluence that enables browsing according to content type (page, attachment, label, etc.).

CamelCase. Special practice of writing words together to form a link in wikis. A word begins with a capital letter and has at least one other capital letter in the middle. Usually, several words are simply joined together, e.g. "WikiWord" or "WhatIsCamelCase".

Clone. In wiki terminology, the not exactly precise designation for all programs that are based on Cunningham's ***WikiWikiWeb***.

Community. The group of people who work and interact together in a wiki.

Content Management System (CMS). Software for the storage, administration and search for documents or content. Web-based CMSs are often used to jointly create a homepage.

Copyleft. License model that guarantees the possibility of freely copying, distributing and editing a work provided that the free license is distributed along with the work.

Creative Commons. Free license that regulates the use of a document at various levels. The author has the option of stipulating that his name be cited, as well as of permitting commercial use and prohibiting, allowing or generally permitting alteration if the license is observed ("share alike"). Creative Commons is thus not necessarily the same as copyleft. The license text is available in three versions: a short version for the layperson, the legally accurate long version and a machine-readable version (e.g. for search engines). This text has been translated into several languages.

CSS. Cascading Style Sheet. A formalism that describes the way in which an HTML file looks. With CSS, layout and formats of a website can be centrally administered with little effort.

Dashboard. Default start page in Confluence with an overview of all Spaces, recent changes in all Spaces and personal favorites.

Draft. All edits are cached every 30 seconds by default. Only the author can see drafts. Only after they are saved are they visible to others. There is a personal overview of drafts, and if applicable, when a page is reloaded the user is asked if he or she wishes to continue working on or discard the draft.

Diff. A function in wiki that displays the differences between two → Versions of a page.

Edit War. Two or more users repeatedly delete each other's articles from the wiki.

Escape character. A character that "masks" a subsequent character. It is used to make a character that normally has a specific significance to the computer be treated as a normal character.

Extreme Programming. ("XP"). Programming technique in which two people always work on the same computer and the program parts are integrated into a running test system at very short intervals. This enables closely customer-oriented programming. The wiki was originally developed to meet the demands of XP.

FDL. ("Free Documentation License"). A license for documents emanating from the software license → GPL. It guarantees that the use of the document adheres to → Copyleft. The user is obligated to name everyone involved in the generation of the document and to distribute the document exclusively in connection with the FDL. The license text must be displayed or printed along with the document, which is problematic especially for smaller documents. In addition, the FDL is only available in the English language. An alternative is the → Creative Commons license.

Flame War. Two or more users engage in the exchange of senseless and insulting name-calling in a forum such as a wiki, or others.

Front end. That part of a web-based piece of software that is accessible to all users. The opposite of → Back end.

GNU GPL. ("General Public License"). Software license that established the → Copyleft principle. Guarantees that programs subject to this license may be copied, distributed and passed on under the condition that the license is not altered. For documents, the → FDL was developed as an offshoot.

Groupware. Software that supports collaboration in a group. This includes such tasks as setting appointments, producing collective notes and having collective access to documents, task management, and of course communication possibilities as well.

Hash. The symbol "#".

History. List of all → Versions of a page. Using it, the history of edits to that page can be tracked.

Hypertext. Instead of a single long text, several text parts are connected via links.

Implementation. Concrete execution of a program in a programming language.

Label. Labels can be assigned to every Confluence page. It is also possible to predefine labels. They support the search function.

License. The granting and regulation of user rights to a work or document by the author. The licensing of documents is a very new phenomenon that is closely linked to the digital existence of documents and their ability to be copied. Innovations are expected in this area in the coming years. → Copyleft, Creative Commons, FDL

Maintainer. Wiki user with special technical access rights. Makes sure that wiki content is maintained, conventions are followed and the climate in the → Community is and remains pleasant.

Macro. Sometimes used as a synonym for a plugin. As a rule, functional Confluence extension for editing that must be entered in the Wiki Markup Editor in curly brackets and that can often be transferred to parameters.

Mind map. Associative depiction of ideas. Various keywords are ordered around a central theme and connected with lines. These keywords can, in turn, serve as starting points for further associations.

News. Basically a blog in Confluence. The same formatting options are available as for Pages. Date and author are highlighted.

Newsfeed. Computer-readable summary of a website that is queried at regular intervals by a reading program and prepared for the user. The reader is thus kept abreast of any changes. → RSS.

Open edit. A text that anyone can alter such that the alterations appear in the original text.

Open source. The source text of a program is freely accessible and may be altered and distributed by anyone.

Open space. Model of a group workshop in which the management of participants is kept to a minimum, and great trust is placed in the powers of self-control of the group itself.

Open text. An existing text that can be used freely by anyone. The original, however, remains unaltered.

Page. A page in Confluence. Generally consists of a parent page and can also have several child pages.

Parent page. In TWiki, the page from which another page is generated. It can also be edited manually in order to establish a hierarchy.

Pipe. The symbol "|".

Plugin. A program component which can be coupled to an existing piece of software in order to provide it with supplementary functions. → Add-on.

Production mode. Refers to the use of software "in real life". The opposite of this is the test mode.

RecentChanges. A wiki page that lists the most recent changes to a page.

Revision. TWiki term for → Version.

Rollback. (also "revert"). Restoration of a previous → Version of a page.

Root directory. Starting point (root) of a directory structure.

RSS. Standard for → Newsfeeds. Is supported by several → RecentChanges pages in wikis.

SandBox. Test page in a wiki on which anyone can learn how to use the software.

Script. A small program that is usually in source text and can be executed with the aid of an "interpretation program" (interpreter).

Shebang line. The first line of → Scripts that indicates in Unix the language in which the script is written and/or what program is required to execute it.

Space. Confluence consists of one or more subwikis – the Spaces. They can have various "permissions", that is, edit and viewing rights for the Space and be linked with each other.

Syntax. Notation type or convention, in this case, for computer files. It must be observed exactly so that the computer can "understand" what is meant.

Sysop. → Administrator.

Tag. A type of label with which information is indicated about a certain area of a document. In HTML, tags are used to indicate formats.

Template. Layout prototype into which further content is integrated by the software (e.g. by a wiki).

Tiny links. Intended for sending Confluence Pages links via email. They are active throughout the life of a page, and independent from the page name and parent page.

Topic. TWiki term for a wiki page.

Troll. A troublemaker in a wiki who tries to gain attention by posting senseless or provocative articles.

Vandal. Deletes or destroys pages in a wiki with a destructive intent. → Troll.

Version. The status of a page at a particular time. With every edit, a new version is generated; however, old versions still remain accessible (usually via a version number).

Web. In TWiki, an enclosed area in which the → Topics are located. Otherwise, it is an abbreviation for the World Wide Web (WWW).

Web host. The service provider who makes storage space and the address for your homepage available.

Workflow. Precisely defined flow of work steps to execute a certain task. Serves to coordinate cooperative work.

WYSIWYG editor. "What you see is what you get." Refers to editors with which text can be edited directly in its correctly formatted form. Thus, while you are entering text, you can already see what the text will look like in print or on the display.

Bibliography

Aronsson, Lars (2002): *Operation of a Large Scale. General Purpose Wiki Website. Experience from susning.nu's first nine months in service.* http://aronsson.se/wikipaper.html, Sep. 18, 2007.

Benjamin, Walter (1972–1989): Gesammelte Schriften, 7 vol., Suhrkamp, Frankfurt a. M. (GS)

Brecht, Bertolt (1930/1967): *Der Rundfunk als Kommunikationsapparat*, in: Gesammelte Werke, vol. 18, Frankfurt a. M., 127–134.

Candeias, Mario (2004): *Neoliberalismus – Hochtechnologie – Hegemonie. Grundrisse einer transnationalen kapitalistischen Produktions- und Lebensweise. Eine Kritik*, Argument, Hamburg.

Dauscher, Ulrich (1998): *Moderationsmethode und Zukunftswerkstatt*, 2nd edition, Luchterhand, Neuwied/Kriftel/Berlin.

Degele, Nina (2002): *Einführung in die Techniksoziologie* (=UTB Vol. 2288), Fink, Munich.

Ebersbach, Anja and Glaser, Markus (2004): *Towards Emancipatory Use of a Medium: The Wiki*, in: International Journal of Information Ethics 2/2004,
http://container.zkm.de/ijie/ijie/no002/ijie_002_09_ebersbach.pdf

Ebersbach Anja and Glaser, Markus: *Das Wiki als Spielwiese für das Internet.* in: Johann Stockinger, Helmut Leitner (ed.): Wikis im Social Web. Wikiposium 2005/06, Österreichische Computer Gesellschaft, 2007, 27–39.

Enzensberger, Hans-Magnus (1970): *Baukasten zu einer Theorie der Medien*, in: Kursbuch 20, 159–186.

Ferber, Reginald (2003): *Information Retrieval*, Dpunkt, Heidelberg

Grassmuck, Volker (2002): *Freie Software. Zwischen Privat- und Gemeineigentum*, Bundeszentrale für politische Bildung, Bonn.

Haug, Wolfgang Fritz (2003): *High-Tech-Kapitalismus. Analyse zu Produktionsweise, Arbeit, Sexualität, Krieg und Hegemonie*, Argument, Hamburg.

Himanen, Pekka (2001): *Die Hacker-Ethik und der Geist des Informationszeitalters*, Riemann, Munich.

IBM (2003): *History Flow. Visualizing Dynamic, Evolving Documents and the Interactions of Multiple Collaborating Authors: a Preliminary Report*, http://www.research.ibm.com/history, Sep. 18, 2007.

Kluge, Friedrich (2002): *Etymologisches Wörterbuch der deutschen Sprache*, bearb. v. Elmar Sebold, 24. Aufl., Berlin/New York.

Krüger, Alfred (2004): *Wikinews geht an den Start*, telepolis vom 01.12.2004, http://www.heise.de/tp/r4/artikel/18/18928/1.htm, Sep. 18, 2007.

Kuhlen, Rainer (1991): *Hypertext*, Springer, Berlin u.a.

Kuhlen, Rainer (2004): *Wenn Autoren und ihre Werke Kollaborateure werden – was ändert sich dann? Oder: wenn Kommunikation ein Recht, gar ein Menschenrecht wird – was ändert sich dann?*, in: C. Bieber; C. Leggewie (ed.): Interaktivität – ein transdisziplinärer Schlüsselbegriff, Campus, Frankfurt. As a PDF on the Internet at: http://www.inf-wiss.uni-konstanz.de/People/RK/publikationen.html, Sep. 18, 2007.

Leuf, Bo and Cunningham, Ward (2001): *The Wiki Way. Quick Collaboration on the Web*, Addison Wesley, Boston.

Maleh, Carol (2000): *Open Space: Effektiv arbeiten mit großen Gruppen*, Beltz, Weinheim/Basel.

Marx-Engels-Werke, Berlin/DDR, 1957ff. (MEW)

Möller, Erik (2003): *Bearbeiten Sie diesen Text. Tanz der Gehirne*, http://www.humanist.de/erik/tdg, Sep. 18, 2007.

Möller, Erik (2005): *Die heimliche Medienrevolution. Wie Weblogs, Wikis und freie Software die Welt verändern*, Heise, Hannover.

Meretz, Stefan (2003): *Freie Software – Ideen für eine andere Gesellschaft*, in: Anja Ebersbach, Richard Heigl, Thomas Schnakenberg (Ed.): Missing Link. Fragen an die Informationsgesellschaft, Universitätsverlag Regensburg, Regensburg, 99–134.

Nielson, Jakob (1995): *Multimedia and Hypertext*, AP Professional, Boston.

Nuss, Sabine (2003): *Download ist Diebstahl? Eigentum in einer digitalen Welt*, in: Anja Ebersbach, Richard Heigl, Thomas Schnakenberg (ed.): Missing Link. Fragen an die Informationsgesellschaft, Universitätsverlag Regensburg, Regensburg, 135–158.

Patalong, Frank: *Wiki-News. Und noch ein Blog …*, Spiegel online, http://www.spiegel.de/netzwelt/web/0,1518,331152,00.html, Dec. 6, 2004.

Petri, Katrina (2000): *Open Space Technology*, in: Roswitha Königswiese and Marion Keil (ed.): Das Feuer großer Gruppen. Konzepte, Designs, Praxisbeispiele für Großveranstaltungen, Klett-Cotta, Stuttgart, 146–163.

Portny, Stanley E. (2001): *Projektmanagement für Dummies*, mitp-Verlag, Bonn.

Rauter, E. A. (1977): *Vom Fauskeil zur Fabrik. Warum die Werkzeuge den Menschen und die Menschen die Werkzeuge verändern*, Weismann, Munich.

Raymond, Eric (1999): *Das Erfolgsgeheimnis von Linux. Die Kathedrale und der Basar*, translated from American English by Reinhard Gantar, http://catb.org/~esr/writings/cathedral-bazaar/, Sep. 18, 2007.

Rilling, Rainer (2004): *Internet* (=Stichwort für das HKWM, vol. 6/II), http://www.rainer-rilling.de/texte/inkrit-internet.html, Sep. 18, 2007.

Schwall, Johannes (2003): *The Wiki Phenomenon*, http://www.schwall.de/dl/20030828_the_wiki_way.pdf, Sep. 18, 2007.

Weizenbaum, Joseph (1977): *Die Macht der Computer und die Ohnmacht der Vernunft*, Suhrkamp, Frankfurt.

Index

S

T

U

V

W

X

Printing: Krips bv, Meppel, The Netherlands
Binding: Stürtz, Würzburg, Germany